Hopped Up

HOPPED UP

*How Travel, Trade, and Taste Made
Beer a Global Commodity*

JEFFREY M. PILCHER

OXFORD
UNIVERSITY PRESS

Oxford University Press is a department of the University of Oxford. It furthers the University's objective of excellence in research, scholarship, and education by publishing worldwide. Oxford is a registered trade mark of Oxford University Press in the UK and certain other countries.

Published in the United States of America by Oxford University Press
198 Madison Avenue, New York, NY 10016, United States of America.

© Oxford University Press 2024

All rights reserved. No part of this publication may be reproduced, stored in a retrieval system, or transmitted, in any form or by any means, without the prior permission in writing of Oxford University Press, or as expressly permitted by law, by license, or under terms agreed with the appropriate reproduction rights organization. Inquiries concerning reproduction outside the scope of the above should be sent to the Rights Department, Oxford University Press, at the address above.

You must not circulate this work in any other form
and you must impose this same condition on any acquirer.

Library of Congress Cataloging-in-Publication Data
Names: Pilcher, Jeffrey M., 1965– author.
Title: Hopped up : how travel, trade, and taste made beer a global
commodity / Jeffrey M. Pilcher.
Description: New York, NY : Oxford University Press, [2024] |
Includes bibliographical references and index.
Identifiers: LCCN 2024020133 (print) | LCCN 2024020134 (ebook) |
ISBN 9780197676042 (hb) | ISBN 9780197676059 (epub) | ISBN 9780197676073
Subjects: LCSH: Lager beer—History. | Brewing industry—History. |
Globalization.
Classification: LCC TP577 .P475 2024 (print) | LCC TP577 (ebook) |
DDC 663/.4209—dc23/eng/20240605
LC record available at https://lccn.loc.gov/2024020133
LC ebook record available at https://lccn.loc.gov/2024020134

DOI: 10.1093/oso/9780197676042.001.0001

Printed by Sheridan Books, Inc., United States of America

Contents

Preface	vii
Introduction	1
1. Before Hops	17
2. Brewing Capitalism	42
3. Inventing Pilsner	74
4. Imperial Hops	108
5. National Beers	140
6. Global Lager	173
7. Peak Hops	205
Conclusion	240
Acknowledgments	251
Notes	255
Select Bibliography	305
Index	323

Preface

I CAME OF age at a world historical moment for beer, not that I noticed it at the time. Turning twenty-one in 1986, as a senior at the University of Illinois, I went with my friends to Treno's, a tavern in Champaign that featured Molson on tap. The Canadian beer seemed cosmopolitan compared to the Busch we had been drinking at the Thunderbird, a dive bar that served underage students in Urbana. Looking back, the two brands of pale lager were not so terribly different, at least not when compared to the rich taste of Samuel Smith's Taddy Porter and Nut Brown Ale, occasional splurges at a specialty liquor store in town.

The following year, I left the Midwest for graduate school in New Mexico and Texas, at what turned out to be the tail end of the Corona boom. For a time, I happily submerged lime slices in longneck bottles, but while researching the history of Mexican food, I switched from what my Mexican friends considered to be a brick-layer's beer to the more refined Bohemia and Negra Modelo. Then in 1994, I made another abrupt change when I started teaching at The Citadel in Charleston, South Carolina, where my local was an Irish pub called Dunleavy's. Although the cluttered interior made it look as if the owners had been pulling drafts of Guinness there for decades, they had arrived from New England only two years ahead of me.

By this time, the craft beer movement, seeking to revive and reinvent more flavorful styles such as India Pale Ale and London porter, was already in full swing. But my only encounter had been on a weekend visit with a friend studying microbiology at the University of Wisconsin, a department where tenure decisions reputedly depended on the quality of a professor's homebrew. I was still oblivious in 2005, when I moved to another craft beer hub, the University of Minnesota. Years later in Canada, someone asked me if I had ever been to the Town Hall Brewery, which happened to be the closest bar to the history department offices on the West Bank of the Mississippi

River. I knew Town Hall's beer was good, but I never dreamed it had an international following.

Nor had I pondered how my changing taste in beer reflected upheavals in the wider world. Over the course of a decade, I had gone from drinking beer made in nearby St. Louis to imports from Canada, Mexico, England, and Ireland, to name only the most prominent sources. Another decade later, in 2008, Anheuser Busch, formerly the world's largest brewer, had been subjected to a hostile takeover by InBev, a company headquartered in Belgium and managed by Brazilians educated at Harvard and Stanford.

I'm not suggesting that my own beer choices or those of an entire generation of yuppy consumers brought down that venerable St. Louis brewer. To the contrary, the availability of beer in pubs and bottle shops, the disposable incomes of young urban professionals like myself, and the travails of Anheuser Busch were all shaped by the wider forces of capitalism. *Hopped Up* takes the beer mug as a lens for viewing the history of that world system and the lives of people caught up in it.

The spread of pale lager as a global commodity over the past two hundred years has been decried as an example of industrial capitalism obliterating local brewing styles, but those styles were themselves industrial products, and the craft beer revolution has become simply another expression of commodity brewing. All of these modern beers arose through transformations in technology, society, and taste centered around three critical moments of innovation: the medieval introduction of hopped beer, nineteenth-century mass production, and mid-twentieth-century improvements in efficiency and brewing processes. These new technologies were driven in turn by larger societal changes, medieval commercialization and urbanization, nineteenth-century industrialization and imperialism, and twentieth-century nationalization and globalization. Although social and technological factors influenced beer styles, taste also shaped consumer preferences, from the clean, pure drinkability of pale lager in the age of industry to the strong, distinctive flavors of craft beer in a postindustrial age.

Craft aficionados often look with disdain on consumers of pale lager, but I have gained a renewed appreciation for both tastes on holiday visits with my mother's family on a Kansas farm, where some cousins drink Bud Light while others post craft beer tasting notes on an internet forum. Whatever your personal preference, knowing the long history of beer can inspire self-reflection about the meaning we attach to this quintessential beverage.

Hopped Up

Introduction

You can't be a real country unless you have a beer and an airline.

—FRANK ZAPPA, *The Real Frank Zappa Book* (1989)

IN 2009, THE PureTravel website imagined a United Nations of brewing on a map titled "Around the World in 80 Beers."[1] Each country appeared with its best-selling or most iconic brand, from Budweiser in the United States to Tsingtao in China. But this global diversity went only as deep as the label, for virtually every brand was a pale lager—clear, light, sparkling, and interchangeable. The exception that proved the rule was Guinness Stout, representing Ireland. Even Muslim-majority countries without a local brewery appeared on the map under Beck's non-alcoholic lager, known in the Middle East as "Mullah lite."[2] What accounts for the ubiquity of pale lager?

The spread of a particular variety of beer as a standardized commodity would seem to reveal the power of global capitalism to obliterate local traditions and tastes, which had flourished through the nineteenth century. Supposed victims included Britain's regional ales, fermented with variegated yeasts that differed from town to town. In 1896, brewing professional J. E. Browly observed that "in the city of Birmingham a full-bodied, luscious beer, full of beady condition and a permanent closed head, with a fair amount of colour, is the most popular article, whilst half an hour's journey outside the city, to the Bromsgrove district of Worcestershire, the people like a pale, dry, thin article, much more quiescent."[3] Even as he spoke, giant brewers were already extending their reach into the countryside, and the dark, coffee- and caramel-flavored London porter, forerunner of Arthur Guinness's Dublin stout, was disappearing. Regional diversity had likewise existed among Central European lager beers, made with a unique strain of cold-loving yeast that sank to the bottom of the tank when it finished the work of fermentation. German Chancellor Otto von Bismarck reportedly favored the full-bodied,

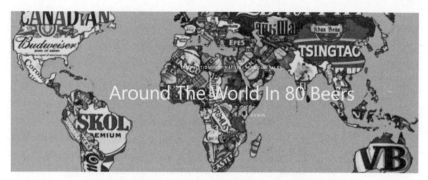

FIGURE 1.1 PureTravel website map representing each nation with its bestselling or iconic brand—all pale lagers, except for Ireland's Guinness Stout. Screen capture. https://www.puretravel.com/blog/2009/09/08/around-the-world-in-80-beers/.

dark Munich lager, while at the Universal Exposition of 1867, Paris experienced an "overwhelming fashion" for the aromatic, amber-colored Vienna lager.[4] In Belgium, more than 2,600 breweries produced all manner of beers, including bottom-fermented lagers, both a blonde called Bock and a dark *petite Bavière*; top-fermented ales whose "predominating taste is a bitter one except in the Flemish district where the beers are a little acid"; and, in the area around Brussels, "beer is made without any additions of yeast at all. The wort [brewing liquid] when cooled is run directly into casks where it ferments by itself."[5]

Outside of Europe, a thirsty traveler could have sampled an even greater variety of beers, if the term is defined broadly to include alcoholic drinks fermented from grains and other starches. Andean brewers made a maize beer called chicha, which was "strong and thick, like porridge," according to sixteenth-century Spanish conquistadors. Sometimes it had "an oily layer on top," which turned different colors to form an "arc like a rainbow on its surface."[6] The Bemba people of southern Africa served a millet beer in giant calabashes and drank it "through a hollow reed two or three gulps at a time." It appeared to anthropologist Audrey Richards as "a cloudy fluid, often full of gritty particles, with a clear, sharp taste not unlike the bitter flavour of English beer."[7] In Mexico, women fermented a beer-like beverage called pulque from the sap of the agave (century plant). "The odor of the freshly extracted sap is herbaceous, by no means unpleasant, and the taste is sweet, so that even the uninitiated generally find the drink agreeable," observed geographer Henry Bruman.[8] Nevertheless, the brew quickly went sour, as nineteenth-century traveler Fanny Calderón de la Barca discovered. "The taste and smell combined took me so completely by surprise that I am afraid my look of

Introduction 3

horror must have given mortal offense to the worthy alcalde [mayor], who considers it the most delicious beverage in the world."[9] While outsiders struggled to appreciate unfamiliar drinks, for insiders the tastes could evoke beauty, passion, and humor. Seventeenth-century Japanese poet Ikeda Sōtan was so fond of sake that he took up residence in the renowned brewing town of Itami. Inspired by the fermented rice beverage, aged in fragrant cedar casks, he mused:

fumarekeri hana	*trodden blossoms*
guchi oshika	*open your drunken mouths and*
ima ichi-do sake	*bloom just once more*

In a play on words, the concluding line also meant "more sake please!"[10] By the mid-twentieth century, all of these indigenous drinks had been displaced by European beer as the leading alcoholic beverage in their home country.

Even the globalized pale lager of today traces its lineage to one of the most renowned local beers of the nineteenth century, Pilsner. Its origins have become the stuff of legend, beginning around 1840, when the citizens of Pilsen (Plzeň in Czech), the principal town of western Bohemia, became disgusted with the poor quality of the local beer and pooled their funds to build a modern brewery. They hired a Bavarian brewmaster, Josef Groll, to reproduce the fashionable lager beer, which had previously been imported from Munich. Using a state-of-the-art English kiln, Groll gently toasted Moravian barley malt to a golden color. On October 5, 1842, he brewed the first batch, mashing in the malt with soft, local water and adding aromatic Saaz hops. At a ceremonial tasting, the citizens cheered their new beer. With the expansion of railroad lines in subsequent decades, the Citizen's Brewery (Bürgerliches Brauhaus) built export markets, first in neighboring Germany and Austria and eventually around the world. But rival brewers imitated the fashionable beer, and over time the term "Pilsner" lost its association with the town of Pilsen and came to mean simply a golden lager beer.

The transformation of unique local products into standardized global commodities characterized the wider industrial economy, from the interchangeable parts of the assembly line to the measured circle of ketchup on McDonald's hamburgers. Even before the rise of modern factories, commodification was well underway in fifteenth-century Bavaria, where town governments decreed that beer could be brewed only with malted barley, hops, and water; at the time, yeast was poorly understood, and wheat beers were monopolized by the nobility. These municipal regulations have come to be known as the Reinheitsgebot, supposedly Europe's first food purity law. But as historian Karin Hackel-Stehr has shown, the rules were intended to control grain markets and their burden fell most heavily on female brewers, who added diverse grains and botanicals to their beers.[11]

By the nineteenth century, giant brewing factories exported their beers on newly built railroads and steamships, enabling them to outsell less efficient competitors. Industrial technology also served to standardize beer by reducing biological variation, particularly through the use of pure yeast cultures, which were introduced in 1883 by Danish brewing scientist Emil Christian Hansen. Regional differences persisted, as the *Deutsche Brauer-Nachrichten* (German Brewer's News) noted in 1928: "Every brewer knows that even if one transports water and all the raw materials to a research station (*Versuchsbrauerei*) and works in the same manner as in the original brewery, the beer will still taste different."[12] Nevertheless, within a few decades, improvements in biological control allowed firms such as Anheuser Busch and Heineken to brew the same brand in factories across continents and around the world. No longer the unique products of St. Louis, Missouri, or Amsterdam, Holland, Budweiser and Heineken had become pure commodities, reproducible anywhere.

By the mid-twentieth century, pale lager beers had become so standardized that most consumers could not identify the difference between them in blind tests. Brewers had to compete on qualities other than taste, and price wars drove countless small- and medium-sized breweries into bankruptcy. Even industry leaders found these struggles to be prohibitively expensive and settled into oligopolistic markets in which a few large firms competed through the invented characteristics of promotional campaigns. Heineken adopted its iconic green bottle to make its beer stand out in bars and liquor stores, while also hiring advertising agencies to compose such memorable slogans as "Heineken refreshes the parts other beers cannot reach."[13] Beer labels often appealed to nationalist imagery, such as the Molson Canadian maple leaf or the Budweiser eagle. Such patriotic claims belied the continued consolidation of the brewing industry, as global giants bought up local brands in the final decades of the twentieth century. Even the American industry titan, Anheuser Busch, fell to the Belgian-based conglomerate InBev in 2008. Reversing Frank Zappa's observation about beer and nationhood, brands that had once carried the flag around the world became vehicles for multinational corporations to sell commodity beers in local markets.[14]

The fall of Anheuser Busch shocked many Americans as a loss not only of industrial competitiveness but also of geopolitical power, for pale lager had long been associated with imperial domination. Scorning native brews

Introduction

as primitive and unsanitary, European merchants and settlers around the globe had imported beer from the metropolis at great expense. When the late nineteenth-century advent of refrigerated technology allowed controlled fermentation in tropical climates, Europeans established lager breweries in the colonies. Massive brick factories resembling Central European castles were built from St. Louis, Missouri, and Orizaba, Mexico, to Istanbul, Turkey, and Qingdao (the modern spelling of Tsingtao), China. Lager beer, with its clean, fresh taste, became a symbol of hygiene and civilization that continued to attract consumers even after decolonization in the mid-twentieth century. Local elites demonstrated their modernity and sophistication by guzzling chilled lagers and shunning traditional beverages. This persistence of European habits and consumer goods, long after the end of formal empires, has been described as cultural imperialism, with soft power consolidated in the hands of multinational corporations.

The global concentration of the brewing industry has in turn spawned a reaction over the past fifty years by those seeking to return brewing to the local, artisanal, and communitarian roots of the premodern alehouse. Dissatisfied with commodified lagers distinguishable only by brand names, craft enthusiasts prefer beer styles with recognizable origins and distinctive flavor profiles: the bitterly hoppy citrus of India Pale Ale (IPA), the full-bodied richness of Munich lager, and—the Holy Grail of beer seekers—the barnyard funk of Belgian sour ales.

Yet the craft movement's focus on style begs the historical question of what exactly beer styles are and how they came into being. "Although we tend to imagine that the modern concept of beer style is itself ancient, it is not. In fact, it is not even old," observed brewing professional Garrett Oliver in *The Oxford Companion to Beer*. The categories that distinguish beers in the marketplace are themselves products of industrial capitalism. Their names evoke particular places, like Pilsner and Munich lagers, London porter, and India Pale Ale, but they generally do not come from those places, unlike the wines of Burgundy and Champagne, which can only be made within legally defined districts. Although brewers in the cities of Pilsen and Munich sought similar protection for their geographical designations beginning in the late nineteenth century, their claims received scant attention in the imperial capitals of Vienna and Berlin. Meanwhile, the idiosyncrasies of Belgian ales were largely ignored in an industrial era that prized mass production and marketing. When such beers finally gained notice from aficionados in the postindustrial era, a taxonomy of local styles was, as Oliver explained, "essentially invented out of whole cloth by the late beer writer Michael Jackson in his seminal 1977 book *The World Guide to Beer.*[15] Whether mass-produced lagers or artisanal ales, the attributes of beer styles—standardized characteristics, imagined geographies, and commercialized consumption—conformed to the demands of industrial capitalism.

Even the seemingly primordial Belgian lambic was a product of modernity, despite the patina of antiquity cultivated in present-day Brussels. Lambic brewers carefully preserve the microclimate of airborne yeasts that carry out fermentation by maintaining dense thickets of spider webs, while folkloric taverns serve the beer in ceramic jars modeled on those appearing in sixteenth-century paintings by Pieter Bruegel the Elder. Nevertheless, in 1899, brewing professional J.-Th. De Raadt wrote: "As far as the modern beers *faro* and *lambic* are concerned, their names have been around only since around 1820."[16] The commercialization of lambic occurred as a byproduct of another nineteenth-century industry that invented an ancient lineage to market itself, champagne. Around 1840, Belgian brewers began to reuse the sturdy, dome-bottomed, and non-returnable bottles of sparkling wine that savvy marketers such as Barbe-Nicole Ponsardin, known as the "widow" or Veuve Clicquot, placed in royal courts and fancy restaurants across Europe. Employing the techniques of secondary fermentation, which added a fresh dose of grape juice and sugar to put the sparkle in champagne, these brewers invented *gueuze*, a sherry-like mixture of aged and young lambics; *kriek*, a lambic refermented with sour cherries; and *faro*, a mild lambic sweetened by candied sugar. Demand for these beers took off in the 1890s, particularly in the cabarets of Brussels. An early advertisement for Arthur Buyssens' Brasserie de Lembecq depicted their intended audience: sharply dressed bourgeois consumers out for a night on the town.[17]

The evolution of beer styles in turn reflected the changing nature of commodities and the new meanings products gained first through industrial standardization and later through a backlash against it. Discussions of commodities often refer to agricultural staples, and indeed organic diversity came to be standardized through nineteenth-century technologies such as grain elevators, cylindrical towers that transferred products from train to barge to ship. For the elevator chutes to function, wheat, rice, maize, and barley had to be removed from the farmer's sack and mixed with the harvest from neighboring farms, or indeed with crops from around the world. As a result, grains could no longer be judged by their unique characteristics and instead were graded into the standard categories that define bulk commodities. Meanwhile, tea and coffee merchants used a similar process of mixing and grading to establish mass-market brands such as Lipton and Folgers.[18] The standardization of beers came about through the invention of

FIGURE I.2 *Fin-de-siècle* lambic drinker, not Bruegel's peasants but a sharply dressed bourgeois out for a night on the town. "La réclame de la Brasserie de Lembecq," *Le Petite Journal du Brasseur* 18, no. 825 (July 8, 1910): 789. Courtesy of Bibliothèque Royale de Belgique.

styles, which were intended to assure product differentiation but were quickly copied around the world. In the twentieth century, the so-called food from nowhere produced by commodity agriculture inspired a demand for goods that could be traced to a unique location, as all goods had been a century earlier. Connoisseurship in bread and beer, like wine and tea, created a nostalgic commodity value defined by scarcity rather than abundance.

The global spread and commodification of beer can best be understood as part of the history of capitalism. In precapitalist, agrarian societies, grain-based fermented beverages were the cheapest form of alcohol and therefore an essential lubricant for festive occasions and everyday socializing. Nevertheless, anthropologists have found that beer was often an indicator of status within kinship-oriented, subsistence-level societies, if only by differentiating those who had regular access to it. In her observations of the Bemba in what is present-day Zambia, Audrey Richards related: "The Paramount Chief told me that a great ruler should drink beer every day without exception." By contrast, "tribal drinking customs make it impossible for any one except a chief to become a regular drunkard."[19] Within tributary states such as medieval Europe and imperial China, hierarchies of status came to depend on differences in quality as well as quantity. Fancy beers were brewed for the elite using more and better ingredients, thereby achieving a distinctive taste and higher alcohol content.

Nevertheless, even these societies were not completely immune to the effects of capitalism. The Bemba people observed by Richards had already begun to engage in wage labor for British colonial enterprises. Likewise, some tributary states, such as Babylon in the first millennium BCE, had economic patterns prefiguring capitalism, including long-distance trade, private property, and wage labor, at least until the conquests of Alexander the Great. Beer, the drink of choice in ancient Mesopotamia, was homebrewed with barley by the masses, while a stronger variety made with dates could be purchased for cash. These differences foreshadowed the development of beer styles, although unlike modern commodities, the choice of beer in ancient Babylon likely indicated group status—elites and commoners—rather than expressions of individual taste and identity.[20]

With the early modern rise of capitalism, hierarchies of beer proliferated through the growth of market relations and social mobility. In Europe, the commercialization of beer depended on the preservative qualities of hops, the cone of a flowering bine that was present in wild form around the world. A relative of cannabis that was believed to contain narcotic properties, hops were eaten as a vegetable in diverse ancient societies from Rome to China. The value of hops for brewers lay in the bitter resins within the cone, which were used for medicinal purposes in medieval monasteries. Around the year 1200, brewers in Bremen, Hamburg, and other northern German towns learned to tame the bitterness of hops while keeping the preservative values of the resins. This more shelf-stable beer became an article of maritime trade for the Hanseatic League, an alliance of free merchant cities that was best known for its commerce in salted herring. Brewing reached a golden age in the sixteenth century, as export markets for beer expanded throughout the North and Baltic Sea basins, allowing successful brewers to adopt new technologies and increase the scale of production. At the same time, the early modern intensification of commerce contributed to the growth of global networks of trade and empire. Europeans provided alcohol to help ensure the compliance of workers, whether enslaved, indentured, or waged. Even in areas that remained free from European imperial power such as China and Japan, the early modern era often brought a thriving growth of commerce as well as the

Introduction 9

pursuit of new forms of social distinction. Consumers with the means to do so began to demand higher quality beers to differentiate themselves from ordinary folks. Brewers meanwhile sought to claim exclusivity by associating their products with particular locations, such as the hopped beers of Hamburg and the fragrant sake of Itami.

Modern beer styles became a means of standardizing production and commoditizing consumption during the industrial era, beginning in late eighteenth-century Britain and in the nineteenth century in continental Europe and settler colonies. Unlike technological developments that spurred the textile and railroad industries, the first mass-produced beer, London porter, was brewed using traditional methods. Thermometers and other new instruments were adopted later to prevent the financial losses that would result from the contamination of enormous vats of beer. Social arrangements of production likewise began to change, as traditional guild training was replaced by scientific education. Innovation often came by bringing together technologies that had been developed in multiple locations. The lager beer industry emerged from the confluence of British mass production with Bavarian bottom fermentation. Networks of brewing scientists, technical schools, and research stations introduced these innovations to breweries throughout Europe and its settler colonies. Lager beer continued to evolve as it traveled globally; North American brewers found that the addition of rice and maize improved the brightness and stability of beers. By the end of the century, corporate giants dominated the industry, although many small firms continued to survive on the margins of the market by appealing to local tastes. Thus, even as Pilsner came to be viewed as a uniquely modern beer, alternatives like Munich lager and Guinness stout retained their value in niche markets, demonstrating the importance of consumer choice to capitalist modernity long before the craft beer revolution.

Indeed, commodification also transformed patterns of marketing and consumption in the nineteenth century. Brewers appealed to consumers with new forms of advertising such as bottle labels and beer coasters. Practices of drinking during leisure time took on the rhythms of industrial labor, as groups of workers shared "rounds" of beer. Each member had to buy a round of drinks for the entire group, encouraging solidarity; failure to pay and drink meant social exclusion. Workers also began to drink standing up at bars, an item of furniture that first appeared in English pubs about 1800 and spread across large parts of Europe and its settler colonies. Historian Wolfgang Schivelbusch has proposed "one of the ways to gauge the extent to which commercialism has saturated a given culture is by the length of its bars."[21]

European beer styles, particularly pale lager, were carried around the world at the vanguard of imperial expansion in the nineteenth century. India Pale Ale, the fabled beer of empire, was marketed not only as a taste of home to British merchants and soldiers in India but also to indigenous elites thirsty for European modernity from the Yucatán to Yokohama. By the 1880s, exports of British ale faced competition from German lager breweries in the old Hanseatic port towns of Bremen and Hamburg. In the long run, both British and German exporters lost out as lager breweries established factories in settler colonies. British investors financed countless lager breweries, iron-ically ensuring the triumph of Central European beer styles over traditional British ales. Some of the most ardent adopters of lager beer were the Japanese, who embraced many elements of European technology and culture to avoid the fate of colonized societies around them. Eventually, Japanese brewers contributed to the development of their own empire, sourcing ingredients and building factories in Korea, China, Taiwan, the Philippines, and the Dutch East Indies. The reception of beer was more complicated in colonized societies, where European rulers often banned native subjects from pur-chasing alcohol for fear of drunkenness and disorder. When workers insisted on drink as a prerequisite for labor in South Africa and elsewhere, municipal governments established beer halls to sell native brews to workers and used the profits to finance segregated townships. In the process, traditional women brewers lost a source of status within their communities. The transformation of drinking relationships did much to upset traditional social patterns, at times undermining communal solidarity and introducing capitalist market re-lations into the countryside. Nevertheless, the process of localization created new versions of pale lager adapted to diverse drinking cultures.

The first half of the twentieth century brought a growing nationalization of beer markets. Cross-border commerce in beer and other goods that had flourished during the nineteenth-century age of globalization declined as world wars and the Great Depression led to restrictions on trade and mi-gration. At the same time, technological changes encouraged the growth and consolidation of breweries within a handful of oligopolistic firms and, in some markets, complete monopolies. Improvements in efficiency increased the production of beer from existing factories at the same time that packaging and transport technologies made it easier for brewers to sell their brands directly through supermarkets rather than pubs and taverns. Technological improvement also enabled brewers to produce ever lighter beers, not only in Europe and North America but also in other parts of the world. Japanese brewing scientists, for example, used new forms of

Introduction   11

fermentation and filtering to eliminate rough flavors. Demand for these lighter beers formed part of a larger shift in tastes as the food-processing industry continued to develop in the post–World War II era. Beer became enshrined as the national drink in many former colonies of Africa and Asia, as elites educated in European capitals pursued the modernity and hygiene of industrial production. Even in socialist countries such as Maoist China, beer appealed to consumers, despite the lack of free markets and capitalist advertising. Whether under capitalism, communism, or the "third path" of non-aligned nations, beer's associations with modernity made it an ideal focus for national development.

The concentration of national markets set the stage for a renewed burst of cross-border mergers around the turn of the twenty-first century. Global capital markets facilitated this consolidation, as managers clawed back the hard-won wages of union activism, while free trade encouraged the growth of beer exports. Advertising became ever more important as the standardization of pale lager made it necessary to find new ways of differentiating and selling products that were increasingly indistinguishable. Shifts in the brewing industry did not always benefit long-established firms such as Anheuser Busch and Bass Ale. Instead, there was a fundamental move away from the traditional brewing centers of Europe and North America toward firms based in Africa, Asia, and Latin America, where youthful populations offered potential for market growth. While some European brands from small countries such as the Dutch Heineken and the Irish Guinness have become global icons, firms that had grown complacent within large national markets often failed to adapt to cutthroat international competition. These challenges were heightened by successive transitions in management, from brewing professionals to advertising executives and finally to investment bankers—a trend that did not augur well for the quality of beer.

Indeed, customer dissatisfaction with pale lager inspired the supposed revolution of craft beer beginning in the 1970s, although in retrospect these changes hardly seem revolutionary. From a production level, the craft beer industry remained dependent on skills and commodity chains developed by giant firms, and the craft movement became globalized through the same professional networks as mass-market beers. Likewise for consumers, craft was far from the proletarian revolution predicted by Karl Marx. As if to emphasize the consumerism behind this supposed uprising, the Chicago-based Revolution Brewery repurposed Communist-era imagery to sell craft beer to local hipsters, replacing the hammer and sickle with an ear of barley and subverting the yellow star of the Soviet flag with the six points of the medieval

FIGURE 1.3 Revolution Brewery in Chicago's Logan Square, with Soviet-era imagery repurposed to sell bourbon-barrel-aged ales. Photo by the author, 2014.

brewer's guild. Thus, craft-brewing companies deployed small-scale advertising that was not so different from media promotions for the supposed refreshing power of Heineken. At the same time, craft brewers invented a language of beer connoisseurship modeled on wine appreciation, while also using moral judgments to differentiate their offerings from mass-market beers by arguing for the anti-modernism of local, artisanal production, making claims for environmental sustainability, and fostering a communal culture of consumption. Sociologist J. Jackson-Beckham summarized the contradictions within the craft movement: "Though the microbrew revolution is frequently heralded as anticorporate, it did (and continues, through retelling, to do) much to reinforce the logics of the dominant capitalist regime by asserting that the most estimable form of leisure activity is that which generates a profit—that

Introduction   13

rebelliousness does not resist the corporate imperative, but rather extends it by making money at play."[22]

In narrating the history of beer's commodification and the triumph of pale lager, *Hopped Up* takes a global perspective, unlike the regional or national focus of much previous scholarship.[23] Although beer is an inherently local product, generally uneconomical to ship long distances, the industry developed through intertwined forms of mobility—including the trade in beer as a commodity, the migrations of brewers and consumers, and the transfer of production knowledge and taste preferences. Mobility was particularly important during three key moments of transformation: the late medieval introduction of hopped beer, the nineteenth-century industrialization and spread of lager, and the twenty-first-century consolidation of global firms. Hopped beer spread out from northern Germany through seaborne trade as a premium good at first but became an everyday item of consumption across large parts of Europe through the migration of skilled brewers and the transfer of technical knowledge. A similar pattern took place in the nineteenth century, as railroads and steamships transported new varieties of ale and lager, which then came to be manufactured locally by migrants and settlers. The twenty-first-century concentration of brewing firms began with a growing trade in premium brands such as Heineken and Guinness, but it was consolidated by capital transfers and the purchase of breweries, most notably Anheuser Busch. Even craft beer was globalized through the same circuits of trade, migration, and knowledge that had carried pale lager a century earlier.

Although the spread of pale lager may seem to illustrate the forces of globalization, in fact, this style has been successively reinvented around the world, from North American adjunct grains to Japanese microfiltration. Rather than simply a force for globalization, Pilsner was also a product of globalization. Indeed, brewers from the Global South learned the art so well that they have come to dominate the industry in the last few decades.

In looking at the history of beer within the framework of capitalism, there may be a tendency to overemphasize material factors at the expense of social and cultural meanings. Such thinking motivates the common notion that people brewed in the past because they did not have access to pure drinking water. It is true that water supplies were often contaminated in premodern cities, and alcohol does have antibacterial properties. But to purify water, boiling works fine, without the trouble of fermentation. Although beer does provide vitamins and minerals not otherwise available from grains, it is, at best, an inefficient dietary staple. One expert has calculated that, even in the relatively efficient brewing industry of sixteenth-century Europe, the "nutritional loss in making beer instead of bread out of grain was something over 75 percent."[24] Societies that drank beer as a significant part of commoners' daily diets were either relatively well fed to begin with, such as medieval England, or were ones that fermented substances other than staple grains, as in the case of Mexican pulque. Authorities often forbade brewing during times of famine, and societies at the margin of subsistence reserved alcohol for festive occasions or to mobilize labor. Simply put, reducing diverse social and psychoactive properties to the functionalist level of sanitation misses the point of beer.

Hopped Up also explores the social patterns of gender, race, and class that shaped the commodification of beer. Many kinship-based societies considered brewing to be a form of feminine domestic labor, while tributary empires often drafted women brewers to mobilize male laborers and support imperial ideologies. As commercialization made brewing profitable in the early modern era, male-dominated guilds began to marginalize women and monopolize the lucrative trade. Already in the sixteenth century, the municipal brewing regulations now called the Reinheitsgebot functionally excluded women from the brewing profession. Nevertheless, family businesses ensured a place for women in the brewery until the nineteenth-century spread of corporate organization and scientific brewing. The craft beer movement has not brought much of an improvement, as women are often unwelcome in its masculine culture. Beer also contributed to social distinctions of lineage, known in modern times as race and ethnicity. From ancient times on, fermented beverages have been markers of social difference, distinguishing insiders from outsiders. Racialized fears of violence inspired prohibitionist regimes in European colonies as well as in former slaveholding societies of the Americas. Segregation of drinking spaces remained after the repeal of prohibition in North America and South Africa, while craft beer continues to preserve these long-standing ties to whiteness. Finally, drink became a means of class differentiation, most clearly established in the drinking cultures of the English pub of the nineteenth century, where shared rounds of beer reinforced the social solidarity of the proletariat. By contrast, the craft movement has individualized drinking cultures through the proliferation of taps serving esoteric styles rather than the communal pitcher.

Finally, the book examines taste as an agent in shaping the commodification of beer, both as an independent sensory experience and as an instrument of social distinction. A focus on taste highlights one of the enduring interpretations of the history of beer in the United States, where Prohibition (1920–33) was blamed for the replacement of local, artisanal beers with a "watery swill brewed from cheap corn and rice." Historian Maureen Ogle, in her book *Ambitious Brew*, showed that "almost every aspect of that oft-told tale of skullduggery, greed, and woe was false."[25] The narrative persists nevertheless, in part because it diverts attention from the vagaries of public taste to the actions of supposed villains, in this case overbearing government officials and corporate malefactors. And yet a similar debate had already begun more than two decades before Prohibition with the rising popularity of Pilsner. The American fashion for pale lager dismayed a Munich-trained brewer, Carl Rach, who pined nostalgically for the dark beers of his youth. "We want to ferment large volumes of wort in a short time and are no longer faithful to the good, old principles of bottom fermentation."[26] A colleague, Francis Wyatt, inquired whether consumers were "unreasoning and unsophisticated . . . or do they drink our light and pale American beers because they like them?"[27] Rach replied emphatically: "We have it in our power to form and develop the tendency of the public taste." He elucidated his point within the logic of capitalism: "The large brewers early made the discovery that the light-colored, vinous, well-hopped beers were best adapted for their manufacturing processes, and business requirements and influenced by the success of these few, the bulk of the brewers have followed their example."[28] Thus, the idea that industrialists shaped consumer taste to heighten profits, one of the basic tenets of the Frankfurt School's critique of mass culture, articulated in the mid-twentieth century by philosophers Walter Benjamin and Theodor Adorno, was anticipated fifty years earlier by a Munich brewer.

Ultimately, it was not greedy brewers alone but the broader forces of modernization that drove shifts in the quantity and quality of production as well as the spaces and practices of consumption, fundamentally transforming beer from homebrewed subsistence to industrial commodity. Pilsner exemplified commodity beer, and its light clean taste appealed to nineteenth-century consumers with the industrial promise of pure food. In the late twentieth century, the ubiquity of pale lager spawned the craft beer movement as a form of postindustrial social distinction through the "safe danger" of strong flavors.[29] Nevertheless, *Hopped Up* shows that craft styles such as India Pale Ale, London porter, and even Belgian sours were likewise products of industrial modernity. Although microbrewers have imagined themselves as countercultural and anti-capitalist, the quest for profit and expansion has often supplanted the original communitarian focus on local pubs and homebrewing. The resulting synthesis of commodity and craft provided a capitalist beer for the twenty-first century.

Pale lager, as the purest form of commodity brewing, demonstrates how the interplay between production and consumption transforms the nature of goods under capitalism. In seeking to explain the system's success in binding workers to the tyranny of the wage, Marx and his followers attributed mystical powers to commodities, comparing them to the primitive fetishes described by colonial ethnologists. Anthropologist Sidney Mintz carried the argument further, suggesting that the opiate of the masses was not religion but sugar and other "drug foods."[30] The drawn-out shift from homebrew to commodity has indeed enticed the workers of the world, like a cold beer on a hot day. And yet claims of false consciousness are themselves expressions of religious belief, pitting the workers' paradise of socialism against the bourgeois gospel of wealth. A similar doctrinal dispute played out among brewing professionals a hundred years earlier during the golden age of Pilsner, as Munich traditionalists and American modernists debated whether it was profit-seeking brewers or flavor-minded consumers who determined the preference for lighter beers. In blurring the lines between craft and mass production, twenty-first-century capitalism has resolved this dilemma, at least for the moment, by marketing traditional beer as a modern commodity.

I

Before Hops

THE FINNISH POEM the *Kalevala* recounted the invention of beer as an epic encounter with supernatural forces in which Osmotar, the original brewer, enlisted the help of magical maidens and small but heroic animals in her quest for the secrets of fermentation. To prepare for the wedding of the blacksmith magician Ilmarinen and the Rainbow Maiden of the North, Osmotar boiled together barley, hops, and water, but she could not give it life. "What will bring the effervescence," she pleaded, "who will add the needed factor, that the beer will foam and sparkle, may ferment and be delightful?"

Osmotar turned first to a snow-white squirrel, who scurried through the forest, evading the eagle's talons, to pluck the tender cones and shoots of pine and fir trees, but they "brought no effervescence." For her second attempt, a gold-breasted marten flew over the mountains to the "grottoes of the growler" to gather foam dripping from bears' lips and tongues, "the froth of anger." Bear drool may have looked like fermenting beer, but it "did not make the liquor sparkle." On the third try, a honeybee gathered the sweetened juices of fragrant flowers growing on water-cliffs beside a sleeping maiden. When Osmotar added the honey, "the wedding-beer fermented; rose the live beer upward, upward . . . foaming higher, higher, higher . . . overflowing all the cauldrons."[1]

This tale of primordial fermentation illustrates the difficulty of interpreting documentary sources on early brewing. The *Kalevala* was patched together from scattered folk poetry and lyric songs in the 1830s and 1840s by Elias Lönnrot, who slighted foreign women such as Osmotar and the Northern Maiden when crafting a masculine, nationalist epic in the style of Homer and Virgil. In contrast to Lönnrot's telling, another version of Osmotar's brewing, with just the squirrel and pinecones, was recited to folklorists in 1872 by a Karelian woman named Nasto, who used the scene of female domestic labor as a prologue to male drinking and violence. Despite the fragmentary nature of the sources, it is still possible to glimpse the vernacular knowledge of brewing before the rise of industrial capitalism.[2]

A literal reading of the *Kalevala* might suggest that ancient Finns basically followed sixteenth-century Bavarian regulations that restricted brewers to barley, hops, and water, but Osmotar's three magical ingredients also had a place in the history of beer. Part of the confusion arose from Lönnrot's strategy of distancing folksongs from their pious Lutheran singers to give the epic a pre-Christian aura of authenticity more appealing to nineteenth-century romanticism. In pagan times, beer was unlikely to include hops, whose first use was recorded in medieval monasteries, although that has not stopped some modern authors from anachronistically citing the nineteenth-century text as evidence that hopped beer originated in Finland. A more traditional choice for an early Finnish beer was *sahti*, brewed with rye and flavored with juniper, an evergreen whose seed cones may have been the secret ingredient that saved the day in Nasto's tale but was rejected as worthless by Lönnrot. Outside of Europe, brewers employed all manner of grains as well as diverse technologies for malting, a process for converting starch into fermentable sugars. That crucial step was also seemingly overlooked by the *Kalevala*, but is belied by the mention of saliva. Brewers in many societies masticated grains, using enzymes from human—if not bear—saliva to create a fermentable malt. Although Lönnrot acknowledged only the honey, a common source of yeast, all of Osmotar's mystical mix-ins were potentially valuable in brewing.[3]

If not very helpful as a technical manual, the epic at least situated beer accurately within the social contexts of brewing and feasting. Throughout history, fermented beverages have been associated with celebratory ritual and female labor, but that did not mean that the stories ended well for the women involved. The Northern Maiden was murdered soon after her wedding, either by Ilmarinen's goatherd, according to Lönnrot's sanitized version, or by the blacksmith magician himself, who then abducted and raped her younger sister in the folksongs performed in many villages. Nevertheless, brewing was a source of income and independence for many women around the world. Even when they labored under the control of male kin or tributary states, female brewers were essential for reproducing family lineages, mobilizing communal labor, and, in societies such as the Inka, legitimizing imperial ideologies.[4]

The most difficult quality of premodern beer to recover historically is taste. The *Kalevala* described Osmotar's brewing kit in great detail, from oaken casks to silver pitchers and copper-banded mugs but mentioned only its "honeyed flavor." Many societies around the world prized sweetness in fermented beverages, but sourness was a common characteristic of beer because of the complexity of fermentation, the threat of bacterial contamination, and the perishability of low-alcohol drinks. If flavor is considered as a holistic sensory experience, reaching beyond just the taste buds, one of beer's most important characteristics was its tactile liveliness, "fermenting, sparkling."

The *Kalevala* depicted beer as an animate being with the ability to speak "in merry accents, through the tongues of the magicians, through the tongue of many a hero, through the tongue of Wainamoinen, famed to be the sweetest singer, of the Northlands bards and minstrels."[5] Although women were indispensable for economic production and social reproduction in kinship-oriented societies and tributary states alike, they could often speak only through the capricious medium of beer. Surveying the drinking cultures of precapitalist societies, whether organized around egalitarian kinship or tributary empires, reveals the ways that people made meaning around beer. The global diversity of early brewing traditions in turn has provided the nostalgic raw materials for industrial brewers to market modern beer styles.

Brewing Technologies

Since the 1950s, archaeologists have debated the proposition that beer instead of bread inspired the Neolithic Revolution. Proponents of this view suggested that the initial cultivation of wild grains in the Near East by Natufian foragers around the end of the last ice age, 11,000 years ago, was intended to make alcohol for feasting rather than bread to relieve hunger. This "Natufian beer hypothesis" ran contrary to accepted theories about the origins of agriculture, which held that humans first began actively producing food in response to an increasingly arid climate that threatened the food sources available to hunters and gatherers. Few scholars accepted the hypothesis because of both the lack of physical evidence and the technological demands of brewing. Therefore, it came as a great surprise to many in 2018 when a Paleolithic brewery from a Natufian site occupied 13,000 years ago was unearthed by archaeologist Li Liu and her colleagues. Even this dramatic finding did not end the beer-bread debate, as another team of archaeologists published evidence of an even more ancient bakery. Together, the two discoveries opened a new chapter in understandings of human culinary invention. From these ancient origins, people around the world have devised endless variations on the recipe for beer.[6]

Quite simply, alcohol occurs in nature when the omnipresent single-celled fungi called yeast encounter sugars, whether fructose and glucose from honey and fruit or sucrose from maple syrup and cane sugar. Indirect evidence of ancient, fermented beverages includes a depiction of a hunter using smoke to drive bees from their hive from as early as 8000 BCE in the Matopo Hills of Zimbabwe. Although the honey could have been consumed immediately, it ferments naturally into mead when diluted in water. Archaeologists have found physical remains of alcohol in pottery residues at the Neolithic village of Jiahu in China from c. 7000 BCE; chemical analysis revealed a cocktail of rice, honey, and grape or hawthorn fruit. No single ferment will work on all natural sugars. Lactose, the sugar in dairy products, is indigestible to beer yeast. Nomadic peoples of Central Asia, who had domesticated horses by 4500 BCE, used a complex culture of lactic acid bacteria to break down the lactose in mare's milk and yeast to transform it into an alcoholic beverage known today as *koumiss*. The inhabitants of Mesoamerica employed a similar bacterial ferment to transform the sap of the agave (century plant) into *pulque* by the beginning of the Common Era.[7]

The uniqueness of beer lies in the technological requirements of brewing with grains like barley, wheat, rice, and maize, because yeast cannot ferment the tightly wound strands of carbohydrates, which plants use to protect their seeds from predators. When the seeds alight in a favorable environment, enzymes go to work unpacking the carbohydrates into simple sugars to feed the emerging sprouts. Humans learned to hijack this stage of plant development through the process of malting, which involved first soaking the grains to jumpstart the conversion of sugar, then roasting the tender shoots before they could grow. The fire had to be carefully regulated to provide just enough heat to kill the plant while preserving the enzymes, because malt still contains more carbohydrates than sugars, limiting the strength of the final beer. A second step called mashing, or simmering the malt in water, allowed the enzymes to complete their work of extracting fermentable sugars. Modern industrial brewers seek to optimize the diverse enzymatic reactions by cooking the mash at a precise sequence of temperatures around 60° Celsius, then finishing with a boil to gelatinize the starches. But such accuracy is not strictly necessary. A few hours on a gentle fire will produce a sweet liquor known as wort. After straining to remove the spent grains, a process known as sparging, the wort is boiled for another hour or so with flavorings, diverse herbs and spices in premodern times before the adoption of hops. When cooled to room temperature, the wort can either be inoculated with yeast from a previous brewing or simply left in an open container for yeast to settle from out of the air to begin the fermentation. After bubbling for a day or two, the liquid becomes beer.

The practical knowledge of biology needed to malt grain and ferment beer was accessible to observant hunters and gatherers. Paleolithic-era foragers at the Near Eastern site of Ohalo II were gathering and grinding wild cereals to provide a significant portion of their diet some 21,000 years ago. The Natufian brewery at Raqefet Cave discovered by Liu and her colleagues comprised just a pair of funnel-shaped mortars carved into boulders about the size of beachballs with additional bowl-like mortars in the bedrock. Residue from the interiors of these utensils came from at least seven different plants, including barley or wheat, oats, legumes, and flax. Microscopic analysis of starch samples revealed the enzymatic action of malting, which creates distinctive pitted surfaces and hollowed-out interiors. Meanwhile, the fiber remains were twisted and tangled, suggesting that they had been spun or woven into baskets. The brewers likely used heated stones to mash the brew in the bedrock mortar, completing the process of saccharification, then left it to ferment with ambient yeast from the cave. To test their interpretations, the archaeologists brewed a beer using replicas of these ancient utensils. The cloudy brew offered a fitting toast to the stone carving, basket weaving, malting, and brewing skills of the Natufians.[8]

Before the recent discovery of Raqefet Cave, the oldest known Middle Eastern brewery was Hierakonpolis in Egypt. Dating to around 3500 BCE, it contained parallel rows of ceramic vats, with an estimated total capacity of at least 100 gallons. Black residue on the interiors of the surviving vats contained acidic byproducts of cooking a sugar-rich mash. Archaeologist Jeremy Geller described Hierakonpolis as a "predynastic St. Louis or Milwaukee, insofar as it was a thriving regional center in which the brewing of beer was one of a number of industries that helped to support an industrial and political elite."[9] A Fifth Dynasty relief at Saqqara portrays the brewers at work, grinding and sifting flour, straining liquid into a vat, and preparing and sealing beer jars. Tomb paintings and accompanying statues situated breweries adjacent to bakeries, where figures performed similar tasks of grinding, kneading, and baking bread, illustrating the close relationship between the two forms of production.[10]

Some scholars have drawn an even closer association between these two staple foods by suggesting that bread was used as an ingredient in ancient Near Eastern beer. Such an interpretation fit with ethnographic descriptions of *bouza*, a yeasty, yellow, mildly alcoholic beverage made from a combination of lightly baked loaves of bread and malt, which remained popular in rural societies of the eastern Mediterranean well into the twentieth century. Nevertheless, ethnographic comparisons are always suspect, and Egyptian tomb painters did not aim to provide accurate instructions to ghostly brewers

FIGURE 1.1 Painted limestone statuette of a woman making beer. From Giza. Egyptian civilization, Old Kingdom, Dynasty IV. Cairo, Egyptian Museum. G. Dagli Orti / © NPL—DeA Picture Library / Bridgeman Images.

in the afterlife. Archaeologist Delwen Samuel found little evidence that bappir referred to bread in her study of beer at Luxor. Using microscopic analysis of brewing residues, she showed that barley and emmer wheat had been malted directly. Husks were also absent from the residue, suggesting that the beer had been filtered during the brewing process. These findings indicate considerable technological changes from the predynastic brewery excavated by Geller to Samuel's New Kingdom sites, occupied 2,000 years later.[11]

Mesopotamian physical remains and textual sources complement the brewery sites found in ancient Egypt. Residues of "beerstone," calcium oxylate, a by-product of the brewing process, have been found in wide-mouthed jugs dating to around 3500 BCE at Godin Tepe, a town in the Zagros Mountains. The beer jugs appeared alongside wine amphorae, suggesting trade between the beer-brewing Mesopotamian lowlands and the wine country of the high Iranian plateau. Moreover, the jugs at Godin Tepe were marked with the proto-Sumerian pictograph *kaş*, meaning "beer," one of the first words written by human hands. The "Hymn to Ninkasi," from around 1800 BCE, lyrically celebrated the Babylonian beer goddess "who bakes the *bappir* in the big oven . . . who waters the malt set on the ground . . . who holds in both hands the great sweet wort."[12] Like the *Kalevala*, the hymn concluded with a gushing metaphor comparing the goddess's beer with the Tigris and Euphrates rivers.

Early Sumerian reliefs depicted groups of people drinking communally through straws from wide-mouthed jugs similar to the one found at Godin Tepe. The straws, which were apparently used to filter out husks of grain floating on the surface, appeared throughout the Near East. Particularly luxurious versions made of gold, silver, and lapis lazuli were buried in the tomb of Queen Puabi of Ur around 2500 BCE, thereby ensuring that her beer was free of impurities in the afterlife. By the Middle Babylonian Period (c. 1500–1150 BCE), contemporaneous with the Egyptian New Kingdom, brewing vats with perforated bottoms made it possible to filter the beer and serve it in small individual cups instead of the communal serving jars and drinking straws.[13]

Despite regional differences in brewing methods, there seems to have been considerable exchange in technologies and drinking cultures across the Near East, although the evidence is too scattered to draw definitive conclusions about the directions of influence. Certainly there was a long-distance trade in beer, despite its perishable nature. Wine, with its higher alcohol content and greater potential for aging, became a mark of elite distinction among beer-drinking lowland regions of Mesopotamia and Egypt, which were too hot and dry for largescale grape production. Nevertheless, the presence of beer at the trading post of Godin Tepe suggests that early Sumerian merchants carried this along as their everyday drink, even on visits to the wine country. Egyptian brewers applied a thin layer of clay to prepare jars for storing or transporting beer. The ancients no doubt understood that stronger beers would keep and travel better than those with a lower alcohol content. One of the most sought-after beers of the Mediterranean world was brewed in Qode, a coastal region of northern Syria. Hieroglyphs distinguished genuine Qode beer from imitations made in Egypt by foreign slaves, just as today the Pilsen brewery in the Czech Republic claims the title "Urquell" (the source) in contrast to Pilsner-style beers made around the world.[14]

Sub-Saharan Africa provides further evidence of technological innovation and transfer, although the continent's archaeological record is even more fragmentary than that of the Fertile Crescent. Mead from honey was replaced on an everyday basis with the invention of grain-based beers, which could be produced in greater quantities and without the risk of bee stings.

Sorghum, domesticated in Sudan around 6000 BCE, spread across the Sahel grasslands, below the Sahara, from Egypt to the Atlantic. While the grain is still used widely for brewing, the oldest direct evidence for beer in Africa dates to around 3000 BCE in the form of a cliff painting in the Tassili n'Ajjer Mountains of Algeria. Executed in rich red pigments across the ochre rock face, the painting portrays the ceremonial consumption of beer through straws from round, decorated jars. The scene resembles contemporary Near Eastern drinking cultures, but it is unknown whether the brewing technology was imported from Egypt or developed independently. Later hieroglyphic texts, which distinguished Nubian beers from Egyptian varieties, could well refer to beers made of sorghum. The Kushite kingdoms of present-day Sudan produced abundant pottery known to archaeologists as "beer jugs."[15]

In China, although physical evidence of alcohol dates back to the Neolithic era, the earliest known breweries were founded in the village of Mijiaya, on the northern plains, around 3000 BCE. Two separate facilities were each equipped with similar kit of wide-mouthed pots for mashing and fermentation, pottery stoves to heat the mash, funnels for filtering, and amphorae for storage. As in other ancient brewing sites, the barley and millet had been pitted and channeled by malting and mashing. The site provides some of the earliest evidence of barley in China, suggesting that the grain was introduced for its superior malting and brewing characteristics. By the Shang Dynasty (1600–1046 BCE) brewers had developed a more sophisticated range of equipment, made of bronze instead of pottery, including an upside-down bell-shaped vat (dubbed the "general's helmet"), jars and urns of various sizes, and a funnel. The remains of carbonized millet, peach, plum, and jujube pits, and hemp and jasmine seeds at one site suggest fruity, aromatic brews.[16]

Chinese brewing made another major step forward with the development of microbial ferments capable of transforming rice and other grains directly into alcohol in one continuous process, thereby combining the separate stages of malting, mashing, and fermentation. Originally discovered in the late Zhou Dynasty (1046–221 BCE), qu (known as koji in Japan) comprised various molds, fungi, and yeasts that simultaneously broke down starches and carried out fermentation. The process gained acceptance during the Han Dynasty (206 BCE–220 CE), and around 300 CE, scholar Jiang Tong explained: "Legend says it was through the effort of Princess Yi Di or Prince Du Kang. But most likely, left-over cooked grain was left in the open. Soon it was covered with a verdant (microbial) growth, and upon further storage a fragrant liquor ensued."[17] Two centuries later, Jia Sixie described the process of producing qu in sealed huts to ensure proper humidity. Manufacturers combined steamed, roasted, and raw wheat to make high-quality ferment, while using only roasted grain for ordinary varieties. Expensive ferments were pressed into round cakes to distinguish them from lower-quality bricks.

Although qu was produced commercially, brewing remained largely a domestic activity. A home cook simply cleaned the outer surfaces of the cake, crumbled it in water for a week or ten days until it began to bubble, then added more or less cooked rice or millet, depending on the quality of the qu and the desired flavor. Fermentation generally took a couple of weeks to complete. Qu had the advantage of converting more starch into fermentable sugars, yielding a final alcohol content of up to 15 percent, compared to 4 or 5 percent common among European and African malt-based beers. Chinese fermented beverages had enough alcohol to allow their export as far as Java by the Yuan Dynasty (1279–1368 CE). The technique also spread to Korea and Japan, while in India, grain-based alcoholic beverages, known as *surā*, were made from a similar ferment (*kiṇva*) and flavored with spice mixtures (*saṃbhāra*) beginning around the turn of the Common Era.[18]

Yet another approach to the saccharification of starch employs human saliva, which contains the enzyme amylase. Societies ranging from Japan to West Africa have chewed grain to produce a fermentable mash, but the technique reached its greatest productivity in the Andes Mountains of South America under the Inka Empire (1438–1533 CE).[19] Early Spanish chronicles and modern archaeologists have described two characteristic vessels of the Inka brewery for making chicha: a round, wide-mouthed pot (*olla*) used for fermenting masticated maize and a tall, high-shouldered jar (*aríbalo*) with handles for storage or transport. These containers were often too heavy to lift when full, but with rounded bases, they could be tipped for pouring. The Spaniards, perhaps disgusted by the thought of mastication, glossed over the production process, but ethnographers Hugh Cutler and Martin Cardenas described a mid-twentieth-century practice: "The flour is moistened very slightly with water, rolled into a ball of convenient size and popped into the mouth. It is thoroughly worked with the tongue until well mixed with saliva, after which it is pressed against the roof of the mouth to form a single mass." The resulting wedges "resemble sets of false upper teeth."[20] Fortunately, women brewers did not have to chew their way through the entire pile of maize flour; a relatively small starter was enough to inoculate a larger batch with enzymes. Saccharification and fermentation took several weeks to complete.

In Mesoamerica, where maize was domesticated, some people consumed a chicha-like beverage called *tesgüino*, but more often they saved the staple grain for eating and instead drank pulque. Archaeological evidence of agave fermentation dates to the classical city of Teotihuacán (100 BCE–700 CE), and the drink had spread widely throughout Mexico's central plateau by the postclassical era that followed. Once the agave had reached maturity, after about eight years, a skilled tapper cut open the plant's central heart and harvested the sweet sap intended to nourish the plant's flowering stalk. Agaves could yield as much as 1,000 liters over several months before the leaves shriveled and collapsed. The brewer, often the tapper's wife, started the fermentation with a yeast and bacteria cocktail called "mother of pulque." Because the beverage soured quickly, considerable skill was needed to keep the starter fresh. Each brewer also maintained her own personal recipe for "pulque medicine," a mix of roots, herbs, and bark used as flavoring and preservative.[21]

European beer has often been traced to Near Eastern origins, but classicist Max Nelson has argued for its independent invention in northern Europe. Physical evidence of brewing in the form of cereal and other plant residue on pottery has been found on remote Scottish islands from as early as 3000 BCE. In the following millennium, a common set of drinking wares, bell-shaped beakers named after the town of Baden, Germany, spread widely across Europe. Early brews likely started as mead, extending the precious honey with various cereals, while also flavoring and preserving it with herbs, spices, meadowsweet, heather, cranberry, and even the poisonous henbane. Little physical evidence remains, suggesting that brewers used perishable wooden vessels and mashed their malt with heated stones. By the first millennium BCE, bronze cauldrons had become common, and evidence of malted barley has been found in Denmark and Sweden from as early as the first century CE. Celtic peoples made perhaps their greatest contribution to brewing technology with the invention of wooden barrels, which were first described by Strabo in 21 CE, although archaeological evidence dates back a century or more before the Common Era. Beer production was quite sophisticated in Roman Gaul, as can be seen from the ruins of a fourth-century brewery with separate rooms for malting, brewing, and fermenting discovered near Namur, Belgium.[22]

In the Middle Ages, brewing was a household activity, utilizing simple equipment available in most rural cottages: a vat or trough for malting, a shovel or pitchfork to stir the grains, a kettle for mashing and brewing, ladles to pour out the wort, and barrels or other containers for fermentation and storage. Domestic brewers typically used a single vessel for mashing the malt and boiling the wort, combining all the ingredients in a single step. After ladling out the wort into a barrel for fermentation, they added water to the brew kettle to reuse the grains, producing multiple batches of progressively weaker beer. Some well-to-do women malted or brewed commercially for their neighbors and invested in more specialized items such as malting kilns and hand mills as well as multiple kettles, but their output paled in comparison to the production in monasteries, noble courts, and, by the eleventh century, many towns as well. Plans for the St. Gall Monastery, designed around 820 as a model for the Holy Roman Empire, called for three separate breweries, one each to serve noble guests, monastic consumption, and pilgrims and the poor. The quality of medieval beer corresponded to the social hierarchy; aristocrats savored the finest wheat and barley beers, while commoners made do with inferior grains such as oats. The religious presumably consumed beers according to the strictness of their rule. Whereas the famously austere order of the Cistercians may have shared the beers of the poor, more indulgent Benedictines may have enjoyed finer brews.[23]

Human societies have been endlessly inventive in overcoming material limitations to produce alcoholic beverages. Although going by diverse names, these beverages shared a common goal of transforming productive agricultural staples into fermentable sugars, thereby maximizing the brewing potential of a particular environment. Technologies changed over time as brewers discovered new means of extracting alcohol from raw materials, and this knowledge in turn was distributed widely through the migrations of brewers as well as through trade in beer, despite the relatively short shelf life of premodern brews.

Social Drinking

Capitalism has reduced beer to a rather frivolous commodity, guzzled at bars, sporting events, and fraternity parties, but in earlier times, the drink held greater significance. Tribal societies producing for their own subsistence saved up grain to brew for weddings, funerals, and harvest festivals. Rulers of complex societies extracted grain as tribute from peasants and either consumed it themselves to demonstrate their privileged status or used it to pay workers constructing pyramids and temples. Women generally performed the labor of brewing, although in more commercialized societies, men often profited from the sale of beer. Whether organized by kinship or tribute, societies had differing rules for consumption; some drank beer moderately with meals that dulled the effects of alcohol, while others took it as a drug, imbibing large quantities on an empty stomach to heighten the narcotic effects. Even those who drank socially viewed alcohol with ambivalence, welcoming conviviality and fearing debauchery.

Kinship-oriented societies drank to celebrate the lifecycle, from marriage and reproduction to funerary rites and the afterlife. Fertility symbols abounded in the wedding beer of the *Kalevala*, from the magical maidens and sleeping virgins to the foamy beer cascading out of the barrels. Likewise, the cliff painting at Tassili n'Ajjer has been interpreted as a wedding feast uniting two nomadic clans, whose elders presided over the ceremony. At the entrance to each tent sat a senior woman with elaborately coiffed hair and ruffled skirts and shawls, while in the center, a fully bearded man assisted the young groom in drinking beer through a straw. The bride held a similar vessel, separated from the groom's clan by a small herd of animals, perhaps the dowry, completing a scene that recalled ethnographic accounts of beer ceremonies among Iteso pastoralists of East Africa. At the end of life, beer provided both immediate solace for the mourners and the prospect of a comfortable afterlife for the dead. Elite burials in northern Europe included the material culture of brewing and drinking, such as the bronze cauldron and gold inlaid drinking horns found at a site in Hochdorf, Germany. Warriors could thus get an early start on the passage to Valhalla, where they were believed to fight all day and drink all night. Elite women were often buried in a similarly ornate fashion, although perhaps without anticipating such a violent afterlife.[24]

Brewing beer, whether daily or for special occasions, contributed to domestic labor in many kin-oriented societies. Direct sources from such societies are limited because written languages usually contribute to the rise of social hierarchies and tributary states. Peasants laboring under kings and emperors also considered brewing a female contribution to household reproduction. For example, moralists in Egypt and Mesopotamia warned a good wife not to neglect brewing as part of her domestic duty. Across medieval Europe, large parts of Asia, and the Americas, homebrewing contributed to peasant households. Oral traditions and ethnographies from African societies likewise demonstrate the importance of brewing for the maintenance of society. For instance, the Kofyar of Nigeria revered a cultural hero who founded communities by brewing beer, thus attracting migrants from other lands. Yet beer could also stimulate social change and the breakdown of communal solidarity, as prominent individuals enhanced their own status by exploiting the labor of neighboring farmers and brewers.[25]

Certainly with the rise of the archaic state, drinking rituals were used to justify social distinctions. Ancient Egyptian tomb paintings portrayed the labor needed to maintain an elite lifestyle—not just the brewery workers at Saqqara and elsewhere but also servants ministering to drunken ghosts. One slave was shown holding a basket for her vomiting mistress, while

FIGURE 1.2 Nomadic pastoralist wedding, cliff painting, Tassili n'Ajjer, present-day Chad, c. 3000 BCE. The young groom drinks beer through a straw, surrounded by elders, both bearded patriarchs and elaborately coifed matriarchs. In the top right is a second vessel of beer, perhaps carried by the bride, along with a herd of livestock, which may represent a dowry. This Neolithic Rembrandt has portrayed the animals with as much individual personality as the humans. Redrawn by the author after Patrick McGovern, *Uncorking the Past: The Quest for Wine, Beer, and Other Alcoholic Beverages* (Berkeley: University of California Press, 2009), after 128.

others carried away passed-out drinkers. Meanwhile Babylonian reliefs from the time of Hammurabi depicted temple prostitutes drinking beer through straws while copulating. In China, archaeologist Sarah Nelson found evidence of state formation in changing drinking rituals. At early burial sites, drinking vessels tended to be left in disorder, tipped over and shattered, presumably evidence of the lamentations of the living. Beginning with the late Shang Dynasty, Nelson observed a more orderly arrangement of funerary bronzes—offerings to the dead rather than leftovers from mourners—which she interpreted as evidence of new respect for the ancestors as guardians of the living. Over time, the emperor came to derive political legitimacy by offering sacrifices to these spirits and ancestors.[26]

Drinking cultures also defined civilizational boundaries, for example, in the Mesopotamian epic of Gilgamesh. Displeased by King Gilgamesh, the gods created a rival named Enkidu, who lived among animals and ravaged the land. According to the Old Babylonian version of the epic, he was tamed by offerings of beer, bread, and sex with a temple prostitute named Shamhat. In a reversal of the usual course of events, after a wild night drinking seven jugs of beer, Enkidu became human. The moral of the story was not so much about alcohol in general but rather the superiority of grain-based food and drink over the fermented milk consumed by Enkidu's real-life counterparts, nomadic raiders from the plains of Central Asia who later became known as Scythians and Cimmerians.[27]

Although Shamhat likely brewed the beer that seduced Enkidu, the production of alcohol became increasingly masculinized in many complex societies. Some evidence indicates that men had entered the Mesopotamian brewing trades as they became commercialized in the second millennium BCE, while wine making was always a high-status male profession in ancient Egypt. King Charlemagne, a hearty beer drinker, encouraged brewing in monasteries, among the few medieval institutions with large amounts of surplus grain. An early Indian text used masculine terminology for "a strong brewery worker, placing a great brewer's basket into a deep pond of water," although women brewed and drank surā at home and for weddings and other celebrations.[28] In China, homebrewing likewise remained a female task, but male brewers such as Liu Baiduo had gained renown by the sixth century for ales that could be shipped to distant markets without spoiling. The commercial production of microbial ferments (qu) was also a male occupation, although hints of female origins remained in the ritual employment of young boys. "Before sunrise on the first day of the seventh moon (usually August), a boy in dark clothing is sent to draw twenty *hu* of water while facing west," Jia Sixie recorded. "The ground grain and water are mixed to a firm consistency by workers who face west. For the caking of the *ferment*, only young boys are employed and they too must work facing west."[29]

Ancient texts also revealed the dangers inherent in alcohol and the regulation of drinking by authorities. Both the Mesopotamian beer deity Ninkasi and her Egyptian counterpart, Hathor, were goddesses, and capricious ones at that. In one Egyptian myth, the ruling god, Re, became angry with humans and sent Hathor to take revenge, which she did with brutal abandon. Shocked by her fury, Re called for a giant vat of blood-red beer to be poured out on the field to lure Hathor away from her hapless victims. She got drunk, and as a result human lives were spared. The Code of Hammurabi imposed harsh penalties on women tavern keepers in Babylon who failed to maintain strict order, suggesting that their establishments were also houses of prostitution. Egyptian officials likewise associated taverns with illicit sex and kept close watch over them, although a Fifth Dynasty text suggests that women may have been able to sell beer in public places without harming their reputation. As patriarchal authorities asserted their power over female sexuality, alcohol became a source of great concern.[30]

Ancient Mesoamericans likewise feared the power of alcohol and sought to constrain it with social regulations. Textual accounts of the origins of pulque varied, but all shared elements of embarrassment and exile. According to one version, the trickster god Tezcatlipoca used it to defeat his rival, Quetzalcoatl, who became drunk, committed incest, and fled from the Toltec capital of Tula. In another tale, a Huaxtec chief was banished after drinking five cups, stripping naked, and dancing wildly. Despite its associated dangers, pulque offered Mesoamericans a valuable medium to communicate with the divine. Tapping the maguey plant by cutting open its heart resembled the human sacrifices offered to the gods. The *Florentine Codex* recorded an Aztec decree that only the elderly and sick could drink pulque, but many peasants likely continued to drink it, at least when the rulers were not watching.[31]

Asian societies also attached great importance to alcohol, while fearing its threat to proper governance. In a foundational act of Chinese statecraft, the Zhou overthrew the Shang Dynasty, about 1046 BCE, based on its supposed failure to maintain good order. According to an early Zhou text, "people flocked together in drunkenness, their stench was smelled on high." By contrast, later generations praised the strict order imposed by the Zhou: "As to those serving in his administration, in serving wine they would not dare to get drunk, when assisting at the *chai* and *zheng* sacrifices, they would not dare to make merry."[32] Scholars have questioned the Zhou's claims of moral superiority—the late Shang was a time of carefully ordered funeral rituals—but moderation remained a cardinal virtue for the Chinese. In India, Vedic texts call for a Superintendent of Surā, assisted by male and female secret agents, to maintain order and collect taxes in drinking houses. Brahmins were prohibited from drinking alcohol, which was believed to defile their purity, but this restriction did not apply to other castes. Nevertheless, Surā was portrayed as a demon or a goddess with drinks in each of her many arms. Origin stories emphasized the chaos that followed from the introduction of alcohol, with even cats getting drunk and allowing mice to nibble on their ears, whiskers, and tails.[33]

The Greeks and Romans preferred wine, and their disdain for beer carried over to Catholicism. The classical prejudice against beer appeared as early as the fifth-century Athenian dramatist Aeschylus, who used the grain-based beverage as an indicator of both barbarism and effeminacy. In Platonic philosophy, beer-guzzling barbarians served as a foil for the moderate wine drinking of the elite symposium. Aristotle classified intoxicants directionally: wine might cause a person to tip any which way, but beer drinkers invariably fell backwards. Theophrastus proposed a biological explanation for beer's negative effects: the act of malting killed the grain so fermentation was therefore decay. Greek historian Dionysius of Halicarnassus wrote in the first century CE that the Celts "used wine of barley rotted in water, a foul-smelling juice."[34] Diodorus of Sicily illustrated the barbarism of the Gauls with claims that they drank beer through their bushy moustaches to filter out floaters. The Catholic Church inherited this preference for wine and sacralized it in the Eucharist. On various occasions, saints reenacted the miracle at the wedding of Cana by turning beer into wine.[35]

Although the Church eventually accepted beer, and monasteries offered it to visitors, brewing remained primarily a female task in medieval Europe. St. Brigit of Ireland exemplified this female ideal in the fifth century. When her wetnurse became ill, the infant transformed water into beer, simultaneously nourishing herself and curing the nurse. On another occasion, she brewed an Easter beer for an entire diocese of eighteen churches using only a small quantity of grain; the celebrants continued to tap the barrel for an entire week. Historian Judith Bennett observed that in medieval England beer was often shared communally because the typical batch was larger than a family could consume before it went sour. In other situations, women marketed the surplus to neighbors, placing a branch or bush outside the door as a sign to customers and expecting them to take the beer home in their own pails. Just as a modern brewpub emphasizes sociability, medieval commerce in beer was often wrapped in webs of social exchange. To raise money for a good cause, individuals could brew a bride-ale, church-ale, or help-ale. Customers willingly paid more than the market price to help a young married couple get started, to endow church works, or to assist a neighbor who had fallen on hard times.[36]

Medieval authorities carefully regulated the brewing and sale of beer, both as a lucrative source of revenue and to avoid social disorder. Continental authorities maintained a monopoly on the beer additive gruit, which often included bog myrtle growing on uncultivated lands that belonged to the emperor. Charlemagne and his successors granted the income from the *gruitrecht* to nobles, bishops, and some towns. By contrast, English municipal governments regulated brewing and collected taxes through the Assize of Bread and Ale. Given the heavy regulation and widespread homebrewing, male guilds formed only slowly. But even without guilds, Bennett emphasized

Before Hops 33

the unequal burden of the Assize on "brewsters, who were more likely than their male counterparts to have no part in the enforcement of the rules of their trade . . . and to suffer frightening and humiliating punishment [of dunking in water] on cucking-stools."[37]

Tributary empires often maintained state breweries for mobilizing labor and justifying their rule. The warlike Assyrians equipped their garrisons with breweries to ensure strategic supplies of beer for the troops. The Pharaohs meanwhile ordered the founding of breweries at construction sites for the pyramids. Hierakonpolis alone produced an estimated 100 gallons at a time, or more if beer was brewed and fermented in separate containers. This volume of beer could have supplied about 500 workers with daily rations of about 2.5 liters. A gang of laborers at the great pyramids of Giza immortalized themselves in graffiti as the "drunkards of Menkaure."[38] But ancient empires of Andean South America ascended the highest summit of state-sponsored drunkenness.

The Tiwanaku Empire, founded about 500 CE in the Lake Titicaca region of present-day Peru and Bolivia, had a "mania for maize beer," in the words of archaeologist Paul Goldstein. They were not the first in South America to ferment corn, and evidence suggests that new brewing methods introduced in the first millennium BCE may have encouraged a form of competitive feasting that contributed to Andean state formation. Such feasting continued as a central element of Tiwanaku policy, which according to Goldstein was founded not on imperial conquest but rather on a shared "chicha economy." Like other early societies in the Americas, the Tiwanaku built pyramids and plazas, but they also left behind vast numbers of pear-shaped fermentation vessels (*tinajas*) and flared drinking goblets (*keros*). The Tiwanaku expanded out from the Andean highlands, where the staple crop was potatoes, to colonize valleys more favorable for growing maize, but they likely did so in a peaceful fashion. Rather than impose uniform ceramic patterns across the empire, the Tiwanaku allowed local potters to incorporate their own stylistic innovations. Moreover, keros generally appeared not in temples and public sites that might associate chicha with imperial ideology but rather in domestic spaces where people could celebrate by drinking with family and friends. Goldstein described Tiwanaku influence as a "'soft' variety of state expansion" linked to trade in an innovative beverage with wide appeal throughout the south-central Andes.[39]

The Wari, northern rivals of the Tiwanaku, likewise used alcohol as a tool for imperial expansion but in a more militaristic fashion. They brewed a distinctive form of chicha with the fruit of the Peruvian pepper tree (*Schinus molle*), perhaps to differentiate themselves from the Tiwanaku. Evidence also points to social inequality in consumption, with the largest keros holding nearly two liters and decorated with the sun-rayed head of the paramount deity. The Wari painted wild designs on their fermentation vessels, hinting at the celebrations to follow. Smashing empty drinking cups is common in many societies, but the Wari destroyed entire breweries. A facility at the imperial outpost of Cerro Baúl comprised separate chambers for grinding grain and for cooking the mash, which were connected by a central patio with twelve fermentation vats, each capable of holding 150 liters. The brewery was ceremonially burned to the ground and the settlement abandoned when the empire declined around 800 CE. In some cases, the Wari dumped the bodies of young women on top of shattered pots, suggesting that the brewsters were sacrificed for religious reasons rather than as a judgment on their beer.[40]

The Inka united the former lands and drinking cultures of both Tiwanaku and Wari in a postclassical empire that spanned the Andes Mountains from modern-day Ecuador to northern Chile. Subject communities were required to provide male laborers for both agriculture and public works such as palaces, granaries, and roads. To justify their rule, the Inka imposed a second labor draft of *aclla* (chosen women), who cooked and brewed chicha for male workers. Unlike the Tiwanaku, who expanded peacefully into maize-growing regions, the Inka relocated entire highland communities to maize fields in the valleys below to satisfy their voracious thirst for chicha. They also imposed uniform ceramic styles for cooking, storing, and serving vessels as a symbol of the Inka state. In contrast to the utilitarian cups of commoners, Inka nobility drank chicha from elaborate keros modeled on those of the Tiwanaku, thereby claiming the mantle of that ancient civilization. As historian Peter Gose observed, "when the Inka state presented itself as a benevolent proprietor toward its conquered subjects, offering them food and drink in return for tributary labor, it exercised power in a specifically female form."[41]

In kinship-oriented societies and tributary empires alike, women's brewing contributed to dietary needs while also supporting the ideologies that bound societies together. At times men took over the activity of brewing when it might prove profitable, but generally it remained a female activity. Although historical and archaeological sources can tell us a great deal about brewing in the past, the question remains of how the actual taste of ancient beers contributed to social differentiation.

FIGURE 1.3 Tiwanaku *kero* earthenware chicha drinking vessel, a design imitated centuries later by Inka lords as a nostalgic link to an earlier civilization. Heritage Image Partnership Ltd / Alamy Stock Photo.

Tasting Beer

The flavor of fermented beverages varied widely in the premodern world, but that does not guarantee the cultural recognition of stylistic differences beyond the basic social division between "our beer" and "foreign beer." Ancient Egyptians not only distinguished the "Nubian beers" of people living on the Upper Nile, but also they acclaimed "Pelusian beers" made on the eastern edge of the Nile Delta and Qode imported from Syria. The Chinese recorded the most elaborate geographical distinctions, such as the chauvinistic claim of Hangzhou brewer Zhu Yizhong that northerners "only use wash water and call it *xin shui* (trusty water)."[42] In the seventeenth century, Gu Qiyuan catalogued specialties from every notable city, including the yellow millet brew of Peking, the pearl barley favored in Jizhou, a lychee beverage of Guangdong, a honeyed crabapple drink in Yangzhou, and the "three whites" of Suzhou. The latter, brewed with white flour, white rice, and clear water, had a "piquant taste and makes people thirsty and giddy."[43]

The choice of grains provided both basic flavors and practical grounds for categorizing beers. Modern brewers can choose from a global basket of grains, ranging from Mediterranean barley and American maize to African sorghum and Asian rice, but early societies each relied on their own local staples. Ancient Egyptians differentiated between beers made of white, black, and red barley, as well as spelt. Chinese brewers fermented all of the "five grains," even while differing over exactly what that classical phrase meant. Two native millets had their own categories, *chi* and *shu*, as did rice (*dao*), while the imported grains wheat and barley were grouped under the rubric *mai*. Legumes (also *shu*) rounded out the collection, although they were generally fermented into condiments such as soy sauce rather than beverages. In medieval England, women preferred barley for its malting capacity but also brewed with wheat, rye, and oats—whatever they could buy cheaply on the market. Father Cobo wrote that "in addition to making *chicha* from maize, [Andean women] also make it from *quinoa* seeds and *oca* roots, from the berries of the *molle* tree, as well as from other things."[44] Malting imparted a basic sweetness to grains, but its flavor could be adjusted in many ways; for example, European roasting often left a smoky taste still present in some Bavarian beers.[45]

In addition to basic grains, brewers have used endless additives as flavorings, preservatives, and at times narcotics. The bitterness of hops is a common denominator of most modern beers, but many early societies preferred sweetness. Historian Jackson Guo observed: "Ancient and medieval Chinese scholars widely characterized the flavors of alcoholic drinks as *gan* (sweet), *chun* (mellow), *xiang* (scented), *ku* (bitter), *lie* (refreshing), *bo* (light) and *hou* (heavy). It seems that sweetness was the most prized flavor among all these qualities." Over time, however, the literati elite came to prefer more complex flavors. As eleventh-century connoisseur Zhu Yizhong wrote: "Sweetness is easy to brew, but piquancy is hard to ferment!"[46] The British also had a longstanding preference for sweet beer and began to complain about the bitterness of continental brews as early as the eighth century. Sedulius Scottus, a ninth-century Irish cleric who spent time at Liège, longed for a blond, clear, sweet beer. The widespread use of gruit on the continent may have contributed to these negative reactions. Although the exact recipe is unknown, it likely included bog myrtle, an astringent herb with a peppery, pine-like aroma. Yet even on the continent, many expressed negative early reactions to the bitterness of hops. As late as 1610, residents of Antwerp felt strongly enough to record in the town archive that "this community finds the taste of strongly hopped beers unpleasant."[47]

Alcohol obviously contributed to the physical experience of drinking beer, although it does not fit easily within traditional conceptions of taste. Participants in one study uniformly described a 10 percent solution of ethyl alcohol as bitter; some also considered it sweet, while others called it sour. Pure ethanol is experienced mostly through touch, a burning sensation in the mouth and nose that can be particularly intense with distilled spirits. While there is little historical evidence about the flavor of alcohol, people certainly recognized and valued its psychoactive effects as well as the antibacterial properties, which allowed beverages to keep longer. The Babylonians brewed a "one-year-old beer," which may well have been hyperbole. Anglo-Saxons made a "double beer" by mashing grain in ale instead of water, although they may have been wasting their grain, since the presence of alcohol can inhibit the work of enzymes converting starch to sugar. During the Zhou dynasty, before the advent of microbial ferments, Chinese court brewers added successive batches of freshly cooked grain in the hopes of producing a more potent beverage for the ruler and his ministers. All of these strategies ran up against the limited alcohol tolerance of yeast, which generally cannot survive at concentrations above 5 percent. The category of strong beer was therefore always compared to weaker ones, those made with smaller proportions of malt or with leftover grain from previous batches.[48]

Drinkers today usually encounter yeast only as a bit of sediment at the bottom of bottle-conditioned or unfiltered beers, but in premodern times it had a more direct presence. Because it floats on the surface during fermentation, it can be skimmed off or avoided by drinking from a straw. Even if they took these measures, consumers likely got more than a few mouthfuls of yeast, which has been described as bready, nutty, and cheesy. More consequential for the flavor of beer are the byproducts of fermentation, particularly esters, chemical compounds that "are formed by the reactions of organic acids and alcohols created during fermentation," in the words of George Philliskirk. To modern tastebuds, these esters have their own unique notes: "isoamyl acetate (banana, peardrop), ethyl acetate (light fruity, solvent-like), ethyl caprylate (apple-like), ethyl caproate (apple-like with a note of aniseed), and phenylethyl acetate (roses, honey)."[49] Unlike modern beers made with pure yeast, ancient fermentation passed through multiple stages, unless consumed immediately, allowing different varieties of yeast to work successively through the batch, rather like aged British and Belgian ales.

Sourness was the bane of premodern brewers, although they occasionally found it useful. During the Middle Ages, the English added spices to prevent beer from going sour. The worst sour beers were called "foxed," a term that also meant drunk. In the *London and Country Brewer*, William Ellis described fox as "the tenacious Thickness and Ropyness of the Drink, and the evil stinking scent that arises therefrom."[50] He listed a number of possible causes, including dirty utensils, filthy water, musty malts, thick worts, and overheated fermentations. Yet some bacteria could actually be beneficial in the brewery. *Lactobacillus*, which is commonly found in malt and is used in dairies to make sour cultures like yogurt, inhibits the growth of more dangerous bacteria. Still common in Belgian and German sour beers, it may have been known already in ancient Egypt; Samuel found traces of the distinctive rod-shaped bacteria in her samples. Perhaps the most extreme transformation in the brewing world appears in Mesoamerican pulque, which although sweet and herbaceous when fresh, "quickly undergoes a putrescent decomposition and acquires a most objectionable stench," according to anthropologist Weston La Barre.[51]

Mouthfeel also contributed to the sensory experience of ancient beers, far more so than in the highly filtered products of modern times. Even though straws were widely used across the Mediterranean basin and sub-Saharan Africa, a certain amount of particulate matter and yeast may have been unavoidable. Filtering the beer through colanders, beginning in the Near East about 2000 BCE, allowed the shift from communal pots to individual cups, but could not have removed all extraneous matter. European brewers learned to grind their malts rather coarsely to avoid clogging the filters when pouring off the wort before fermentation. Maize beers of the Americas were often quite gritty and almost gruel-like in consistency but still an improvement over the maggots in the bottom of beer pots described in Finnish folklore. Tang dynasty poets reveled in their unfiltered brews as a Chinese version of bohemian authenticity: "my house is poor—only muddy brew," wrote one author. Another compared the residues of fermentation to "pearly floating logs."[52] Although floaters were an acquired taste, the dance of carbonation in the mouth has been widely appreciated. Modern bartenders often take great pride in pouring beers with just the right amount of foam, another highly specific cultural preference. Mesoamerican people believed that foam animated the living, breathing spirits of the gods. The Codex Magliabechiano indicated foam with dots above communal pots and individual bowls of pulque. A drunken woman, sprawled out and vomiting beside the pulque goddess's pot, provided an object lesson to revelers about the dangers of overindulgence.[53]

The methods of consumption also shaped the taste of these beverages. Asian consumers often took their beverages warm, and Shang dynasty bronzes stood on legs so that the brews could be heated over a fire. Drinking from a straw could agitate liquids, providing an effervescence to otherwise flat beers. Perhaps the most unusual method of drinking was the Mesoamerican pulque enema, which not only ensured rapid absorption into the bloodstream but also activated chemical receptors that are located at the far end of the digestive tract. In the days before Heineken, pulque refreshed the parts that other beers could not reach.[54]

In societies organized around privilege, beer styles provided a means of claiming status. The brothers at St. Gall may have brewed a different beer for each of the three orders—clergy, nobility, and commoners. Inka rulers drank from distinctive keros, although without written recipes it is impossible to say how the taste of noble chicha may have differed from commoners' drinks. It is also hard to interpret the social connotations of ancient Egyptian "iron beer," "garnished beer," and "sweet beer," although clearly one gained status by drinking the genuine Qode. Once again, the Chinese excelled in brewing cultural hierarchies. Ninth-century poet Huangfu Song ranked alcoholic beverages according to Confucian virtues: "those having rich but refreshing flavors and a sweet aftertaste can be compared to the sages; mellow but bitter

FIGURE 1.4 Aztec portrayal of pulque from the Codex Magliabechiano. Dots on the top of communal pots and individual bowls indicated foam. A drunken woman, top left, sprawled out and vomiting beside the pulque goddess's pot, provided an object lesson to revelers about the dangers of overindulgence. Codex Magliabechiano, folio_85r. Internet Archive.

with a golden color can be compared to the worthies; sour and light with dark color can be compared to simpletons." Suspicious of the merchant class, the literati preferred homebrews to commercial products: "the hosts who intoxicate guests with glutinous rice-based homemade drinks are gentlemen; with millet-based homemade drinks are middlemen; and with unclean ashed drinks bought from the market are villains." By the sixteenth century, Guo notes, many scholars had embraced commerce and opened the Ming Dynasty equivalent of craft breweries, selling drinks with "elegant names and superior qualities in terms of their colors, smells, and flavors, such as jade light (*yuhua*), immortal apricot (*xianxing*), jade water (*yuye*), pearl dew (*zhenzhu lu*), or green tide (*cuitao*)."[55]

Kinship-based societies may have constructed their own beer styles, but there is a lack of documentary evidence either way. Anthropologist Jack Goody used African women's brewing as the basis for a grand civilizational typology separating the haute cuisines prepared by male chefs in literate, hierarchical societies from the undifferentiated, domestic porridges and beers made by women in more egalitarian, tribal societies. Yet critics have warned that outsider anthropologists may simply have failed to recognize signs of luxury that were obvious to cultural insiders. Whatever the case, tributary empires certainly expressed social distinctions through the beers that they produced, and with the growth of commerce those styles became increasingly oriented toward the market.[56]

Although the history of brewing is often told as a linear narrative that begins with the discovery of beer in ancient Sumer and runs by way of medieval Europe to the modern industrial era, this history is better seen as a maze of different routes toward the common goal of making affordable and enjoyable alcoholic beverages. Technologies of production changed over time, as brewers became ever more efficient in extracting alcohol from available raw materials. In Africa and Europe, brewers generally followed a three-step process of malting, mashing, and fermenting grains, preferably barley because of its high enzyme content, although other ingredients were widely used to stretch the brew. The discovery of microbial ferments allowed Asian brewers to combine these stages and ferment alcohol from highly productive rice. In the Americas, mastication allowed brewers to malt the staple maize. The material culture of brewing in ancient societies displayed endless variety, which was later sacrificed by industrial capitalism on the altar of efficiency.

Before Hops 41

Despite their diverse local forms and meanings, these brews served the common purposes of lubricating sociality and mobilizing labor. Patrick McGovern concluded his magisterial survey of alcohol in the ancient world by observing: "The great monuments of the human civilization—for example, the Egyptian pyramids and the Incan royal centers and irrigation works—were built by rewarding the workers with vast quantities of alcoholic refreshment."[57] In kinship-based societies, as in tributary empires, fermented beverages played an important role in communal feasting and work parties. The widespread presence of alcohol in mythological tales, from the Finnish *Kalevala* and Mesopotamian Gilgamesh to Mesoamerica's Tezcatlipoca and China's Princess Yi Di, pays tribute to its social importance, while also warning of the dangers of consuming to excess. These stories serve as a reminder of the prevalence of patriarchy in the production and consumption of alcohol. Although women typically brewed beer as a form of household labor, men took over when they could profit from its sale.

The fragmentary nature of sources makes it difficult to determine the meaning of beer styles in the premodern world. Regional differences and ingredients distinguished fermented beverages from one society to the next. At times, particular cities like Qode and Suzhou gained a reputation for high-quality brews. Stylistic differentiation seems to have reached a peak during the commercial booms of Chinese Song and Ming dynasties. Yet even with the growth of commercialization, what united these styles is that they all contributed to group identities. With the transition to capitalism, beer styles became a source of individual identity.

2

Brewing Capitalism

HILDEGARD VON BINGEN, the twelfth-century abbess, composer, scholar, mystic, gardener, and brewer, took a dim view of hops. In her medical treatise *Physica*, she declared it "a rather useless plant, which causes melancholy and weighs down the innards." She even worried that it could cause insanity, although she did concede that "in its bitterness it prevents spoilage in those drinks to which it is added, so that they can last much longer."[1] The physicians of Salerno, Italy, prescribed heavily hopped beer as a diuretic, and monasteries raised hop gardens along with other therapeutic plants by the eighth century. But the harsh bitterness of hops seems to have limited these ancestral IPAs to medicinal purposes. Recreational hops took off around the year 1220, when brewers in the port town of Bremen learned to make a more palatable beer while maintaining the plant's preservative qualities. With this shelf-stable product, northern German brewers increased their scale of production and built markets for beer across large parts of Europe over the next three centuries.[2] In doing so, they displaced female homebrewers such as Hildegard and contributed to a wider shift from local subsistence to a capitalist economy.

Just as there were endless regional versions of fermented grain beverages, there was no single source for the origins of capitalism. Whereas Marx imagined progressive stages leading inexorably toward the industrial system he observed in nineteenth-century Germany, capital accumulation and wage labor took diverse institutional and social patterns in Europe and around the world. Imperial conflict and global trade in silver, spices, and sugar contributed to the rise of capitalist enterprises, but so too did everyday commodities such as textiles, pottery, and beer, which helped to draw ordinary people into new patterns of production and consumption.[3] Old timers in any given society might have resisted the allure of novelties, but those with aspirations saw the market and the tavern as appealing spaces for adopting new identities. Replacing local ale with imported, hopped beer or, in Mexico, ordinary pulque with cured varieties, offered new opportunities for consumption, leisure, and status.

Taste played a critical role in the early modern transformation of beer, although commercial products were not always immediately appealing to the senses. Sweetness had long been a desirable quality in ale, and the introduction of bitter hops met with considerable reluctance. The ability to consume exclusive and fashionable products represented a second form of taste—signaling to others one's good taste—which satisfied the ego rather than thirst and helped to overcome existing preferences. Brewers sought to market their products with status associations and invented traditions from the earliest days of commercialization. Nevertheless, the physical experience of taste was still important for determining value in the marketplace. Brewers in many societies experimented with new technologies and sought to discover how ingredients from particular locations affected the taste of the beers they made, thus anticipating the modern concern with geographical origins of particular products. Beer styles were not simply the premodern legacy of regional differences; early modern brewers around the world actively pursued urban consumers by inventing distinctive recipes for German hopped beer, Mexican pulque, Japanese sake, London porter, and Bavarian lager.

Hops Take Command

Enterprising European merchants ensured that locally produced hopped beer spread from northern German port towns of the Hanseatic League to destinations throughout the continent. Although medieval ship captains traded in luxury goods such as spices and lace, they balanced their cargoes with staple foods—grains, salted fish, and beer, once hops had been added as a preservative. To map this early trade in beer, economic historian Richard Unger pored over municipal tax records in Germany, the Low Countries, Scandinavia, the Eastern Baltic, and Britain. He found that the transformation of medieval brewing anticipated later patterns of industrial development, from technological innovations around the year 1200, through a growing scale of production and trade, before reaching a level of maturity in the sixteenth century.[4] The tax records did not document how these early hopped beers tasted, but they did show that the status associated with imports was already tempting consumers in medieval Europe.

The revival of trade and towns in the High Middle Ages required new approaches to brewing. The earliest urban brewers were generally migrants from the countryside who brought with them their skills and equipment but found a hostile environment for homebrewing in crowded and polluted towns. Although fire hazards, water shortages, and tax collectors all burdened this incipient industry, potential customers packed the streets, and unlike peasants, artisans and merchants paid cash. To meet the growing demand, brewers adopted new equipment, replacing ceramic, wooden, and iron vessels with copper kettles, which could safely and efficiently heat larger volumes of ale. By the twelfth century, the professionalization of brewing had given rise to a new vocabulary with words such as the Middle English *breuhus* for brewery and the Latin *panadoxator*, for a male brewer, and *panadoxatrix*, his female counterpart. The Black Death in the fourteenth century further spurred the commercialization of brewing. Workers who survived the plague earned higher wages, and they spent it on consumer goods like textiles, meat, and beer.[5]

The market towns of northern Germany were the birthplace of large-scale commercial brewing, although hops had been used for centuries on a limited basis. Bremen established a reputation for exporting high-quality hopped beer early in the thirteenth century, and brewers from Hamburg, Rostock, and Wismar had learned the new technology by midcentury. Hamburg ultimately surpassed its rivals following a fire in 1284, which allowed for the rebuilding of breweries especially designed for making hopped beers. Although the institutional structures of the Hanseatic League were founded on herring, beer was an equally vital commodity in this formative era of trade.[6]

To produce a drinkable hopped beer, medieval brewers had to experiment with precisely when to add the hops, in what quantities, and how long to boil them. Overcooking evaporated the antibacterial resins that preserved the beer, while too short a boil left a harsh bitter taste. Because hops float vigorously on the surface of the wort, boiling time alone proved an unreliable guide to estimating the dosage in any batch. For greater control over the extraction of resins, brewers often immersed the hop cones in straw hampers in order to tame the strong medicinal flavors of their brews. This was not simply a matter of taste; when used properly, hops allowed brewers to extract more beer from the same amount of malt. But these advantages were balanced against the added costs of labor, fuel, and equipment in making hopped beer. Although beer kept longer than ale before going sour, it had to be aged to achieve the desired taste, which tied up capital. Economies of scale therefore made it difficult for domestic alewives to compete with commercial beer breweries.[7]

FIGURE 2.1 Botanical depiction of the hop plant with its fragrant cones in the top right. From Otto Wilhelm Thomé, *Flora von Deutschland, Österreich und der Schweiz* (Gera: Eugen Köhler, 1886), after 34. Wikimedia Commons.

The technological challenges of brewing with hops gave early German beer exporters a competitive advantage over rivals. Beer kegs were transported by water far more easily than by land, and commercial breweries generally shipped their product to neighboring markets. The North Sea brewing towns of Bremen and Hamburg built a profitable trade to the Low Countries, while brewers in Danzig, Lübeck, and Rostock specialized in the Eastern Baltic, and Wismar merchants looked north to Scandinavia. But not everyone shared this fashionable new taste for foreign beer. In the 1320s, Count William III of Holland banned imports of German beer and local brewing with hops to protect traditional gruit beers, a major source of tax revenues. Protests by beer lovers led him to reverse the ban and tax hops instead, which proved highly lucrative. Brewers in Amsterdam soon began adding hops to their own brew, but it took them a full century to match the quality of German imports and regain control of local markets.[8]

The spread of beer from coastal to inland regions followed a pattern that has been called "trickle trade"—breweries that had begun using hops to replace imports in local markets became exporters in their own right, searching out new customers for hopped beer.[9] In some cases, the migrations of skilled craftsmen sped up the development of regional brewing industries. For example, a Bremen brewer who settled in Riga in the thirteenth century gained a local following. Dutch migrants had likewise introduced beer to England as an item of trade by 1400, although local beer brewing took off slowly there. By the sixteenth century, widespread knowledge of brewing with hops had caused the former leading export cities of Danzig, Lübeck, and even Hamburg to experience a brewing "involution" of declining production and to focus on local markets. Meanwhile, innovative brewers in the Rhineland and the Low Countries began to transport their beer overland to reach new customers. The town of Einbeck, whose merchants had shipped beer in the fifteenth century upriver through Hamburg to the Baltic, looked south in the sixteenth century to Bavaria, where brewing with hops got off to a late start. By way of this trickle trade, beer displaced wine as the preferred beverage across large parts of central and western Europe.[10]

In addition to being a major commodity, beer and the public houses that served it became critical infrastructure for the growth of European capitalism. Demand for ingredients in large urban areas contributed to the commercialization of agriculture. Already in the thirteenth century, Hamburg brewers purchased grain from Elbe River Valley farmers, who in turn purchased beer and other urban manufactures. The growth of London alehouses likewise led to a restructuring of the English agrarian economy, giving rise to a dedicated group of "maltmen" who carted barley to the city from Hertfordshire and Bedfordshire. Commercial hop growers marketed their products in specialized trade fairs along Germany's northern coast and at Nuremberg to the south. To serve all of this beer, public houses, known variously as cabarets and inns, *Schenken* and *Wirtshäuser*, arose to offer food and lodging, though bar tabs were the innkeeper's biggest source of revenue. Moralists denounced taverns as "mainly for scoundrels" and "haunts of evil people."[11] Nevertheless, they served as important hubs of early modern commerce, attracting businessmen to meet clients, display merchandise, and make deals. Innkeepers also acted as local currency exchanges, post offices, coach services, and money lenders, offering credit to customers at the bar as well as farmers and merchants.

By the sixteenth century, the beer brewing industry had reached a level of maturity in both technology and organization. Working with larger kettles, brewers not only increased the scale of production but also achieved efficiencies, extracting more beer from the same amount of malt. The vertical design of brewhouses employed gravity to do most of the work in moving water through a network of pipes, valves, and false bottoms. Brewers improved the quality of their product, for example, by installing closed chimneys on their furnaces to avoid smoke contamination. Although the nature of yeast remained a mystery until the nineteenth century, progressive brewers attained a practical mastery of fermentation. In parts of the Low Countries, they cultured yeast and pitched it into each batch rather than trusting the vagaries of spontaneous fermentation. Brewers in Flanders encouraged *Lactobacillus* to produce a more acidic beer that resisted spoiling. To brighten their beers, brewers used straw filters to remove debris that remained after sparging, or draining the liquid wort from the malt. Later they began to import Russian isinglass, the dried swimming bladders of sturgeon, to clarify the beer still further.[12]

With changing technology and industrial organization in the sixteenth century, brewing privileges came to depend on access to capital. The freedom to brew, enshrined in early town charters for all citizens who paid the gruit tax, had become obsolete. Municipal authorities supervised the beer trade closely to ensure collection of taxes, especially in Hamburg, which was eager to protect its unofficial reputation as the "Brauhaus der Hansa" (Brewhouse of the Hansa). Inspectors kept careful watch on beer destined for export and regulated the local sale of hops and grain to prevent speculation in these essential commodities. Official surveillance slowed the emergence of brewing guilds, which acted less to police the trade than to represent the interests of masters in dealing with civic authorities. Small brewers, who lacked the capital to invest in new technologies, often petitioned governments for limits on the industry's volume of production, but they were generally ignored. Adding to their troubles, municipal brewers in central and eastern Europe often had to compete with nobles, who maintained breweries on their estates, tax free, and sold the surplus in nearby towns.[13]

The growing scale of production also affected relations between workers and masters. Because breweries could operate with as few as three employees and rarely had more than ten, the transition from kinship-based, medieval craft production toward capitalist wage labor proceeded more slowly than

FIGURE 2.2 The growing scale of production among brewing guilds in early modern Germany depended on capital investment, new technologies, and division of labor. From Jost Amman and Hans Saches, *Eygentliche Beschreibung aller Stände auff Erden, hoher und nidriger, geistlicher und weltlicher, aller Künsten, Handwercken und Händeln* (Frankfurt am Main: G. Raben, 1568). Beinecke Rare Book and Manuscript Library.

in labor-intensive industries. Richard Unger calculated that wages accounted for only about 10 percent of the total cost of production, and firms with more employees generally expanded into related trades such as malting, barrel-making, transport, and marketing. Brewery work was demanding but, compared to other industries, not particularly dangerous. Accidents did happen, such as when an English apprentice fell into a brewing kettle and drowned. Nevertheless, the growing scale of production in larger towns increased the distance between brewery owners, who often had no formal training and employed managers to oversee production, and workers, who were increasingly unable to afford the capital needed to open their own shops.[14]

The demand for capital increasingly excluded women as well as itinerant guild workers known as journeymen from owning breweries in early modern

Europe. Family firms remained the norm, and wives and daughters often assisted in the brewery work and could inherit businesses. Many tasks continued to be considered female ones, including mixing the malt with water and boiling the wort. As late as the fifteenth century, women composed a full third of London's brewing guild. Nevertheless, they faced significant disadvantages in keeping up with the growing scale of production. They were less able than men to borrow money, form partnerships, or maintain business relationships necessary for marketing beer, especially in long-distance trade. Most brewing guilds did not formally exclude women, as Amsterdam brewers did in 1632, but neither did they actively accommodate women within their ranks. Women were not restricted from owning or visiting inns and taverns but those who did put their reputations at risk.[15]

The commercialization of brewing also led to the recognition and valuation of stylistic differences in beers, although this commodification did not happen automatically.[16] In the Middle Ages, names attached to beers generally indicated their town of origin, although these denominations could be misleading. When Hamburg first challenged Bremen in foreign markets, its products were sometimes sold under the label "Bremen beer." Export beers generally used more grain to produce a higher alcohol content, which helped to preserve the product for travel. But reputation also mattered, and many consumers were willing to pay more for genuine German beers than for hopped beers made locally. The allure of the foreign may have contributed to the success of a fifteenth-century Hamburg drinking hall called the *Eimbecksche Haus*, which served beers from Einbeck. By the late sixteenth century, Heinrich Knaust listed 150 different beers in Germany alone; he ranked the barley beers of Gdansk and the wheat beers of Hamburg as the finest.[17]

The proliferation of distinct names for beer resulted from both consumer demand for high-quality products as well as the desire of municipal authorities to standardize, classify, and, most importantly, tax goods. The Danzig specialty, *Joopenbier*, perhaps originally just the local dialect's term for "hopped beer," acquired a reputation as a premium export and was widely imitated throughout the Low Countries. Brewers devised new names as inferior copies undermined the status of the originals. According to legend, a popular beer called *Mumme* was created in 1492 by a Braunschweig brewer named Christian Mumme, but references to the term date back to 1425, suggesting that this tradition may have been invented for marketing purposes, like the fabled abbot of Champagne, Dom Perignon. Likewise, a sixteenth-century Hannover brewer named Cord Broihan supposedly applied the

Flemish method of lactic fermentation to Hamburg's renowned wheat beers. His name came to be associated with a sour, white beer that spread across Germany, although contemporary documents refer more to his position in the guild than to his innovations in the brewhouse.[18]

In late medieval and early modern Europe, taste preferences for beer reflected not only social distinctions of fashion and exclusivity but also the physical perceptions of flavor. Although consumers appreciated the status and masculine associations of their high alcoholic content, strong beer also conveyed a sense of fullness in the mouth and warmth throughout the body. Elite beers like Joopen or Mumme were valued for their sweetness as well as strength and spiciness. Surviving recipes for Mumme, perhaps not the original version, included such ingredients as fir bark, pimpernel, birch, marjoram, and eggs. Fermentation also influenced the taste of beer. Early modern authors positioned these flavors on a scale that ran from mild all the way up to the sourness of vinegar. Eighteenth-century German economist Johann von Justi summarized "the art of wheat beer (Weißbiere) and in particular Breyhane (sic)" as raising the fermentation to "a very sharp and wine-like (weinichten) flavor of the highest grade, just below the point of sourness"—a description that evokes the lactobacillic tang of a modern-day Berliner Weisse. By contrast, brewers fermented barley beers to a much lower level, "except for Braunschweig's Mumme and a few others that have almost a wine flavor"[19]— perhaps similar to Flemish red ales.

The introduction of hopped beer among the Hanseatic towns of northern Germany enabled long-distance trade and the growth of scale among brewers. Unlike the primal allure of sweetness, the bitterness of hops alone did not drive the transition from ale to beer; economic efficiency was far more important.[20] The golden age of export breweries came to an end during the general crisis of the seventeenth century. A period of extreme climate change, known as the "Little Ice Age," caused harvest failures, raising the price of brewing grains and decreasing consumer incomes, while the Thirty Years' War (1618–48) and the Dutch Revolt (1566–1648) compounded hardships by devastating the beer heartlands of Germany and the Low Countries. New competition for beer arose. Distilled liquors, such as gin, brandy, schnapps, vodka, and rum, provided a cheap drink for hard times. Coffee and tea appealed to many social drinkers. Beer remained the favorite drink across northern and western Europe, but consumers increasingly turned to local products, which undercut the revenues of exporters from Hamburg to Haarlem. As with many declining industries, concentration ensued; small and inefficient brewers folded, while surviving firms purchased ever larger kettles.[21] The boom-and-bust cycles and the subsequent consolidation also characterized brewing industries beyond Europe.

From Indigenous Homebrew to Pulque Plantations

Even as European commerce achieved a global reach in the early modern era, the profits of imperial merchants depended on indigenous communities, which were fed in turn by local farmers, cooks, and brewers. Consider the silver mines of New Spain, as colonial Mexico was known, a vital link in global trade from American mines to the Spanish Crown, and then by way of German bankers and Portuguese merchants to Asian entrepots in return for Indian cotton and Chinese porcelain. Mexican miners were predominantly free native workers from villages that preserved their autonomy through control of maize and maguey fields. Spaniards demanded tribute in labor and kind but otherwise left matters to indigenous rulers; even the silver miners guarded their workplace independence and sold contraband ore on the black market. Nevertheless, the agrarian economy became increasingly commercialized in the eighteenth century, as millionaires with noble titles dominated not only silver mines and textile workshops but also the production of maize and pulque.[22] Even after Mexico gained independence in 1821, consumption of the native brew remained a marker of social distinction. Elites toured estates to sample the freshest pulques while workers consumed lower grades in rough taverns.

Just as the Black Death had allowed European laborers access to greater quantities of beer, the Spanish conquest increased the availability of pulque among those who survived the plagues of the Columbian exchange. In contrast to the Aztec Empire, which had prohibited alcohol consumption, a Spanish survey from the mid-1500s identified eighteen towns that specialized in brewing pulque in the vicinity of Mexico City, including San Juan Teotihuacán, on the ruins of the ancient metropolis. In the provinces, one or two towns in each region made pulque for sale on market days. The greatest quantity of pulque was homebrewed for domestic consumption from wild agaves that dotted the countryside. Spaniards soon came to view natives as drunkards, but according to historian William Taylor, the real objection to indigenous drinking was its ecstatic, religious nature, which contrasted with European ideals of self-control. One colonial official complained: "The Indian uses [pulque] to get drunk and unless he is intoxicated he doesn't believe that he has been drinking."[23] At times, natives snuck into caves to reenact pre-Hispanic rituals, but more often, they drank openly on Catholic saint days. Pulque consumption peaked during the dry season, from November through May, for religious as well as practical reasons. Heavy drinking began in the fall with corn harvest festivals and continued through the Christmas and Easter holidays. Even during the rainy season, many farmers carried jars of pulque with them into the fields each morning. A popular saying held that "pulque is for men, water for mules."[24]

The climate crisis of the seventeenth century acted like a cocktail mixer, blending social groups and drinking cultures with potentially explosive results. The decline of Mexican silver mines, which had financed global trade since the 1540s, exacerbated social conflicts in New Spain. Although the Crown sought to protect native autonomy by segregating colonial society into separate European and indigenous "republics," intermarriage between these populations as well as with enslaved Africans produced a mixed-race underclass of *castas*. Meanwhile in the countryside, commercial estates and native communities competed for land and resources. As in early modern Europe, taverns and inns introduced new drinking practices to rural communities while facilitating colonial trade. Licenses for selling alcohol were supposedly limited to local women, but Europeans and castas, many of them widows, opened public houses along the highways of New Spain. In 1672, Mexico City licensed a total of thirty-six *pulquerías*, two-thirds for men, the rest for women, although authorities had little success enforcing gender segregation and soon gave up trying. Social mixing provoked still greater anxiety just two decades later, in 1692, when Spaniards blamed a food riot in the capital on drunken natives and castas. Officials condemned not the pure, white pre-Hispanic beverage but instead nefarious mixtures of pulque with rum, mezcal, brown sugar, fruit, chile, and peyote, alcoholic counterparts of racial mixing.[25]

As the global silver trade surged again in the eighteenth century, Spaniards' greed overcame their fears of drunken workers, and pulque became an essential commodity within a revitalized colonial economy. Jesuit priests first recognized the commercial potential of pulque plantations in the 1730s and began cultivating orderly fields of maguey at the Hacienda of Santa Lucia, a former sheep ranch near the silver mines of Real del Monte. Following their example, a Spanish merchant named Manuel Rodríguez de Pedroso built his own pulque estates at nearby Zempoala and used the revenue to purchase the title Count of Jala. By midcentury, the Jesuits and Jala each supplied a fifth of all the pulque consumed in Mexico City. Low labor costs contributed to the profitability of the trade, because after

Brewing Capitalism

the initial planting, the sturdy maguey required little care. Skilled tappers (*tlachiqueros*) recruited from nearby Otomí villages earned more than many Hispanic workers, but just a few could manage an entire rancho, collecting enough sap to supply a busy Mexico City pulquería. Although women had traditionally fermented pulque, Spanish overseers hired men for these tasks as well. Commercialization thus heightened inequalities within indigenous communities between a few well-paid, male workers and their impoverished neighbors and wives. Social stratification also increased in the provinces, where a few men, such as wealthy, native pulque hacienda owner Juan Luis Sánchez in Oaxaca, controlled the industry. Around Mexico City, the wholesale pulque trade was dominated by the merchant nobility, who intermarried to preserve their wealth and privilege. Jala's daughters received doweries of pulque estates and Mexico City taverns on their marriages to the heirs of the Count of Regla, who had made his fortune in mining. For his part, Regla had purchased Santa Lucia after the expulsion of the Jesuits in 1767, thereby allowing him to recoup the wages paid to miners at Real del Monte by selling them pulque at inflated prices.[26]

Concentration and exploitation also characterized the marketing of pulque in late colonial Mexico City. Rapid fermentation meant that pulque had to be consumed within twenty-four hours before it soured. Packtrains carried the pulque to market in leather hides on the backs of mules. Muleteers notoriously drank the pulque en route or sold it to passing travelers and then topped up the containers with brackish water. By the 1780s, the city had forty-five licensed pulquerías. Most were in the suburbs, where natives and castas lived, but some operated in the city center, just steps from the Viceregal palace. Municipal ordinances limited these establishments to simple storerooms, fronted by a small tent, with no furniture and open on three sides to allow for police surveillance. In defiance of these rules, many shops were completely enclosed, with ample seating and dancing space for 500 people or more. Such pulque palaces opened at six in the morning for workers, who were enticed to skip their shifts at the Royal Tobacco factory to spend whole days drinking, eating, gambling, and dancing. Heedless of municipal officials, the noble owners rented the shops on long-term leases on the condition that managers serve only pulque from their estates. In addition to licensed houses, Mexico City had a vast contraband trade with as many as 850 illicit pulque and tepache bars. Officials did not even try to count the number of petty vendors, women from nearby villages who wandered the streets and plazas selling pulque from small jugs.[27]

FIGURE 2.3 Maguey tapper extracting sap from the heart of the plant. Having removed the leaves with an axe, he siphons the liquid into a gourd, and transfers it to a pig skin bladder. Brantz Mayer, *Mexico: Aztec, Spanish, and Republican* (Hartford: S. Drake, 1852), pg. 58. Internet Archive.

The Mexican elite associated the smell of pulque with common laborers, but they nevertheless consumed more refined versions of the native beverage. Scientist Alexander von Humboldt, who passed through Mexico City in 1804, compared the drink to cider with "a smell of rotting meat," while noting that American-born Spaniards "who have conquered the disgust caused by the fetid odor prefer pulque to all other beverages."[28] After Mexican Independence in 1821, liberal intellectuals gathered in pulque shops to debate the political issues of the day. Manuel Payno listed the types available—"fine pulque, sweet pulque, strong pulque, ordinary pulque, *tlachique*"—recommending that consumers seek out the fine.[29] The lowest grade, tlachique, the dregs left behind for the tappers, was described by Manuel Orozco y Berra as "bad tasting, slimy, and thick."[30] The Spanish colonial aversion to mixed pulques was replaced by a fashion for *pulque curado* (cured), made with diverse fruit flavorings such as pineapple, almond, lime, peanut, and cactus fruit. A folklorist later declared that "curados were a taste of the casual customers (*parroquianos*, literally, the parish goers), but the good drinkers, connoisseurs of pulque, only drink white pulque, *a natural.*"[31] To ensure freshness and purity, elite connoisseurs visited particular haciendas known for the quality of their pulque in an early form of culinary tourism. Otherwise unfavorable lands were believed to produce the finest pulques; Humboldt singled out the agaves grown on the volcanic slopes of Ocotitlan, while the geographer Manuel Rivera Cambas praised the pulques from the cold, dry plains of Apan. Fanny Calderón de la Barca, who had choked on the native drink when she first arrived in Mexico in 1840, left tasting notes of the "particularly good" pulque at San Bartolo and the "superior excellence" of the beverage at the Hacienda of Ometusco.[32]

While the Mexican elite denigrated pulque as a mark of backwardness, or at best a form of patriotic nostalgia harkening back to the Aztec emperors, pulquerías came to represent a space of urban modernity for workers. Politicians campaigned in these taverns during the freewheeling elections of the early republic, and the midcentury capitalist development program called the Reforma brought improvements to pulque's commodity chain. The first stage of the railroad connecting Mexico City to the port of Veracruz ran through the agave districts of Apan, and by the late 1860s, entire carloads of pulque were offloaded daily in the capital. Ignacio Torres Adalid, the so-called King of Pulque, controlled 100 of the more than 850 licensed shops in Mexico City in 1909, and his company maintained a laboratory to ensure hygiene. Customers came largely from the ranks of rural migrants, who sought out pulque and its accompanying socialization as a respite from long hours working in factories and peddling.[33]

Pulque had been sold in marketplaces since the fall of the Aztecs, but the expansion of the pulque trade came about in periods of rapid and unequal economic growth. During the eighteenth-century silver boom, aristocratic and Jesuit entrepreneurs consolidated the production and marketing of pulque to Mexico City. They centralized and dominated a formerly female trade, although women continued to make and sell the beverage as unlicensed street vendors. As commercial haciendas encroached on formerly autonomous village lands, desperate farmers from the arid pulque zone joined insurgent armies after 1810, helping to topple the Spanish colonial government. Within fifty years, the arrival of railroads sparked a new wave of industrial development in the Mexican capital and the pulque trade that supplied it. Cycles of boom and bust as well as hierarchies of status and taste played out in a similar fashion across the Pacific Ocean.

"Double White" and "Four Coppers"

Many Japanese today consider sake an old-fashioned drink, in contrast to the modern beers of Asahi and Kirin, but by the early modern era sake brewing was already a highly mechanized, capital-intensive industry that helped to drive economic growth. Although Japan fits uneasily within western models of capitalist development, the history of sake offers striking parallels with that of European beer. Homebrewed since ancient times, sake had entered courtly culture by the Nara Period (710–84), around the time Charlemagne came to the throne, and it was marketed widely to commoners in the thirteenth century, when Hanseatic brewers first shipped hopped beer across northern Europe. With the expansion of commercial agriculture under the Tokugawa Shogunate (1603–1868), the sake market became increasingly segmented between refined "double white," crafted for demanding connoisseurs, and rotgut, sold to urban workers for the price of just "four coppers" a shot. The scale of production increased rapidly at the turn of the nineteenth century. An industrial survey taken in 1874, shortly after the fall of the shogunate, found that sake brewing accounted for a fifth of the nation's entire manufacturing output, surpassing even woven textiles.[34] Although sake brewing remained largely a rural undertaking, disconnected from the capitalist industries that followed in the twentieth century, it nevertheless had a vital role in the social and economic history of Japan.

As in other parts of the world, sake brewing was long a female domestic activity that later became commercialized and masculinized, although women's early brewing has been hopelessly romanticized. Historian Eric C. Rath has observed that popular accounts of virgin girls chewing grains to ferment beverages in Jōmon villages of the second to first millennia BCE are based on a misreading of a single historical document. The origins of *koji*, a microbial ferment used to brew with rice, similar to the Chinese *qu*, is likewise the subject of debate. Some believe the starter was imported from the Asian mainland, while others argue that it was indigenous to Japan. In any event, the fermented rice beverage attained a ceremonial role in the ritual sharing of sake between a new emperor and the sun goddess. The modern word for a sake master, *tōji*, derives from a female clan leader, and women were certainly prominent in medieval sake guilds. By the fifteenth century, the imperial capital Kyoto supported more than 350 commercial sake breweries, often using rice that was paid as land taxes, although a rough, homebrewed rice beer called *doburoku* remained a common article of consumption, especially in rural areas. Toward the end of the sixteenth century, Portuguese Jesuit João

Rodrigues estimated that the Japanese brewed a third of their rice harvest into sake.³⁵

Tokugawa policies of urbanization and commercial agriculture, intended to ensure peace after centuries of civil war, made rice and sake more affordable than ever. The Shogun broke the power of samurai warriors by ordering them out of their rural strongholds to work as bureaucrats under the supervision of *daimyō* lords in "castle towns," which grew into administrative centers with up to 10,000 inhabitants. The daimyō, in turn, were required to spend alternate years in the warrior capital of Edo, modern-day Tokyo, and their retinues and laborers helped to swell the population to more than a million by 1700. To support the ranks of sake-swilling samurai, the government undertook massive public works of irrigation and land reclamation,

FIGURE 2.4 "Hey try my sake, I have usunigori (clarified) too." "Sake Seller" from *Poetry Contest by Various Artisans* (*Shokunin zukushi uta'awase*), a woodblock print copy published in 1744 of *Poetry Competition of Seventy-One Artisans*. Metropolitan Museum of Art, Howard Mansfield Collection, Gift of Howard Mansfield, 1936. My thanks to Eric Rath.

expanding rice production beyond narrow valleys into broad lowland plains. Ordinary peasants also contributed to rising productivity through innovative farming practices, intensive use of fertilizer, and the adaptation of seeds to new environments, allowing for multiple harvests. Some prescient samurai even chose to abandon their sword-bearing privileges and the accompanying stipends to invest in land and join an emerging class of wealthy farmers. Inequality pervaded both town and country, as urban elites and large landholders acquired a taste for polished rice and refined sake, while poor artisans and farmworkers subsisted on buckwheat and barley.[36]

With the growing commercialization of the economy, rice merchants began to take up sake brewing, especially in the agricultural heartland of the Kinai. Farmers in the fertile plains stretching from Kyoto south to Nara and west to Kobe delivered their taxes in rice to Osaka merchants, who sold a portion of the harvest locally and shipped the balance to Edo. Sake proved a natural sideline for these grain traders, allowing them to manage demand in volatile commodity markets by converting surpluses that might otherwise depress prices into a valuable and shelf-stable product. Merchants in non-rice-growing provinces likewise brewed as a way of ensuring regular demand for a costly import. Nevertheless, most castle towns relied on local guilds for sake and other consumer goods, at least through the seventeenth century. Guild members were required to obtain licenses and pay hefty taxes in return for monopoly rights on sales within the town. The government also limited the amount of rice that each brewer could use in a year, although these restrictions were largely ignored, except during periodic famines. A survey taken at the end of the seventeenth century counted 27,000 sake brewers in Japan, including many small establishments in hamlets and villages outside of castle towns.[37]

The culture of sake consumption shifted during the Edo period from restrained samurai ritual to more boisterous drinking by commoners. For hundreds of years, sake had lubricated elite society, as the Jesuit missionary Rodrigues observed: "the first and chief courtesy and token of interior love and friendship is the [sake cup] *sakazuki*; this is to entertain with wine, and two or more persons drink alternatively from the same cup as a sign of uniting their hearts into one or their two souls into one."[38] When fifteenth-century Shogun Ashikaga Yoshinori hosted the Emperor GoKamatsu, he served an astonishing seventy rounds of sake, although admittedly the cups were small. Edo-era inflation steadily eroded the purchasing power of samurai stipends, while merchants and manufacturers flaunted their newfound fortunes in defiance of sumptuary laws. Sake brewers, in particular, were stock figures of the

Brewing Capitalism 59

nouveau riche in Tokugawa literature. Elites sought to assert their social distinction by showing off their knowledge about food and drink, creating new standards of sake connoisseurship. Meanwhile, drinking moved into popular venues, including teahouses, sumo matches, kabuki theater, and the so-called floating world of the Yoshiwara pleasure district, where elegant prostitutes plied their suitors with fine sakes. At the bottom of the social pyramid, legions of migrant laborers could buy a cup of rough sake for "four coppers," a low-denomination coin, to accompany their meals of soba noodles, tempura, or grilled eel at street stalls and izakaya taverns.[39]

Sake brewers responded to growing demand by crafting more refined products. Technological innovations had begun in the sixteenth century among Buddhist monks in the temples of Nara, who created a new variety of sake called *morohaku* (double white), in which polished rice was used both for the koji starter and for the grains used in brewing. Grinding away the dark outer husk removed lipids and proteins that imparted harsh flavors. Today, the most refined sakes are made from rice that has been polished down to a third of its original weight, leaving only pure starch. The monks of Nara inoculated the rice with koji, then added water and yeast on elaborate brewing schedules to increase the alcohol content. After several weeks, they filtered the sake through silken cloth and heated the sealed bottles to provide an early form of pasteurization. These temple secrets were soon disclosed to commercial brewers in Kyoto and Osaka, who added improvements of their own. Lacking the unpaid labor of temple initiates to polish the rice by hand, businessmen automated production using rice mills powered by foot pedals, which had come into use by 1650. Despite the resulting savings in labor from mechanization, leading firms hired dozens of brewery workers in addition to specialized carpenters and coopers to supply vats and shipping casks.[40]

Competition was based not only on price but also on quality, as brewers developed regional styles with unique tastes. Within the Kinai district, connoisseurs had come to prize the sakes of Kyoto, Nada, Itami, Ikeda, and Tonda by the end of the seventeenth century. Brewers in the town of Nada, on the coast near Kobe, seized the top end of the market in the eighteenth century by giving rigorous attention to all stages of production. They used only the highest quality rice and water and extended the fermentation time to ensure a smoother taste. Nada soon became a hub in the coastal sake trade from the Kinai to Edo, employing more than 300 ships by the early nineteenth century. Products from other towns were soon dismissed as "country sake." Nada merchant Yamamura Tazaemon was so fanatical in his attention to detail that he systematically exchanged the various inputs of raw materials and labor between two of his breweries to determine why one made better sake than the other. In the end, he discovered that hard mineral water from a particular well produced the distinctively dry Nada taste known as *miyamizu*. By contrast, the soft waters of Kyoto gave the local sakes a sweeter flavor profile. Inspired by Nada brewers, Nagasaki merchant Miura Senzaburō performed his own experimentation, creating a style with a fruity bouquet.[41]

The sake industry became increasingly competitive in the eighteenth century, when the military government sought to expand the tax base by encouraging rural economic activities. The Tokugawa regime mandated winter brewing, which greatly improved the taste and shelf-life of sake. Winter brewing also allowed farmers to supplement their income with wage labor, while freedom from guild and municipal restrictions further benefited rural brewers. Osaka merchants happily sold equipment to rural competitors, without a thought for the city's guild. As elsewhere around the world, brewmasters traveled widely looking for promotion or better pay, and the inland Tanba region west of Kyoto became a recruiting ground for skilled tōji. Lords created monopolies within their domains, which increased their own revenues while also serving as marketing groups for local producers, helping them to compete with the big wholesalers from Osaka and improving the quality of their brands. The shift to rural producers accelerated in the second half of the eighteenth century, devastating artisan guilds in provincial castle towns. At least 300 Osaka breweries went out of business. Restrictions on brewing during periodic famines drove many marginal producers into bankruptcy, and new producers took advantage of the instability to gain market share. Nada firms continued to cut costs and increase scale, installing larger mills, brewing vats, and storage tanks, and streamlining brewery design for heightened efficiency. Nevertheless, by the early nineteenth century, Nada brewers had begun to lose market share to new competitors in the distant regions of Nagasaki and Owari as well as in the nearby towns of Nishinomiya and Imazu.[42]

The spread of sake and other forms of craft production to the countryside enabled a late Edo boom in rural consumption. Refined goods such as tea, tofu, and professionally made *mochi* (rice cakes), which were once affordable only to an urban elite, became objects of rural consumption, at least on special occasions. Teahouses, among other sites, introduced urban tastes to the countryside. Originally catering to pilgrims near remote religious shrines, they spread and gentrified along the Tokugawa road network to supply travelers, including daimyō, samurai, and their retinues, as well as merchants and migrant workers. In addition to tea, they sold sake and mochi alongside umbrellas, sandals, and other goods to assist in travel. Rural schoolteachers also helped to introduce elite, urban culture to the children of wealthy farmers. During the late eighteenth century, for example, former students in the village of Ono bought rounds of sake to honor a beloved but profligate old schoolteacher named Shisan.[43]

Commercialization of sake began in medieval Japan and accelerated with the early modern prosperity of the Edo period. Technological improvements, including the mechanization of rice milling and improved fermentation, enabled relatively efficient production, even in small rural breweries. The growth of rice agriculture and interregional trade stimulated production for urban markets, which in turn led to product differentiation. The finest sakes came to be associated with particular towns, where brewers took care to ensure high quality, while bulk-produced rough sake became available to manual laborers.

London Porter and the Triumph of Scale

Unlike the small-scale production in rural Japan, large-scale brewing took off in the great cities of Britain. There, beer brewing took a secondary role in the rise of industrial capitalism, following the demand created by other sectors of the economy.[44] Mass production began with the brewing of London porter for the working classes, followed by the pale ale brewers of Burton-on-Trent, who crafted the finest malts into a sparkling beverage for the gentry and, later, the rising middle classes. The industry was so profitable that leading brewers could purchase seats in Parliament and even noble titles. Contrary to the classic image of an industrial revolution led by entrepreneur-inventors, beer production grew to a massive scale using traditional methods and only later adopted new technologies of temperature control and mechanization. Whatever their origins and timing, these new methods ultimately transformed the production of beer and set the stage for global growth.

Initially, the English were slow to adopt hopped beer, the commercial brew of the late Middle Ages, and the beverage bore the stigma of its foreign origins among Dutch immigrants. Hops grew wild in the British Isles and had been used in monastic brewing before the Norman Conquest of 1066, but ale remained the preferred drink for centuries thereafter. Dutch immigrants had founded the first commercial beer breweries in London before 1400, and King Henry V (r. 1413–22) came to appreciate the economic advantages of beer while provisioning armies abroad during the Hundred Years' War. Returning veterans may have continued to consume the drink as a nostalgic reminder of their service. By 1436, London's ale brewers felt threatened enough to declare that the alien beverage was "poisonous, not fit to drink, and caused drunkenness."[45] That was a risk Englishmen were increasingly willing to take. The supposed introduction of domesticated hops by Flemish Protestants in 1524 inspired the popular but inaccurate ditty, "heresie and beere came hopping into England both in a yeere."[46] Admittedly, the "Dutch" brewing community, as it was known, was far from homogeneous, comprising merchants from Holland, Flemish farmers, and by the 1550s, Rhinelanders fleeing turmoil at home. Nevertheless, these Europeans remained so prominent in the trade that Parliament passed legislation requiring the employment of native workers in order to facilitate the transfer of knowledge of brewing with hops. As the market shifted decisively from ale to beer in the final decades of the sixteenth century, naturalist John Gerard reclaimed hops as a native English plant in his influential herbal manual.[47]

The transition from ale to beer also contributed to the displacement of women from commercial brewing. English brewsters held out longer than their continental sisters, making up a full third of the newly formed London brewers' guild in the 1420s, but they were gradually marginalized from management roles. To explain the masculinization of English brewing, historian Judith Bennett pointed just not to the demands of technology but to the social forces that accompanied it. The greater capital investments required for brewing beer as opposed to ale placed women at a commercial disadvantage, while Dutch control of the industry made it difficult for English women to acquire the particular skills of brewing with hops. Overseeing an unruly male workforce posed yet another challenge, although married women often assisted their husbands in managing breweries and could inherit the businesses from them. Women also continued to homebrew ale, a practice that was encouraged by the ready availability of commercial malt in the seventeenth century.[48]

Amid civil war and the enclosure of village lands, England shared in the global crisis of the seventeenth century, but social upheavals did not slow the concentration of urban brewing. The privatization of smallholdings into commercial estates, which had been underway since the late Middle Ages, accelerated with the growing power of landlords in Parliament. The migration of dispossessed farmers increased London's population from 200,000 in 1600 to more than 500,000 by the 1670s, creating a vast market for commercial beer, which became an affordable luxury for the poor. This market in turn drove a shift from publican brewers, who sold homebrewed beer, to common brewers, who marketed to multiple pubs. The latter had numbered only 26 in 1580 but rose to 194 by 1700, producing an average of 500 barrels a year.

The growth of scale depended on access to capital, both new equipment such as coal-fired furnaces and the ability to extend credit to publican customers. Although foreigners had introduced many of these new technologies, by 1650 they were largely driven from the trade. In addition to domestic markets, common brewers increasingly entered the export trade, making strong beers with plenty of hops to withstand changing weather and rough water. With the expansion of the English maritime empire, shipments of beer reached as far as India by the end of the seventeenth century. In 1683, the Admiralty began opening breweries in major ports to supply navy ships for the wars against Louis XIV.[49]

The scale of industrial production continued to expand in the eighteenth century with the introduction of London porter. According to legend, a Shoreditch brewer named Ralph Harwood invented porter in 1722 by blending beers of different age and strength. Nevertheless, historian Martyn Cornell has suggested a more evolutionary development from ordinary brown beer in the early eighteenth century. As more refined pale ales gained favor among the gentry, London brewers "responded by attempting to produce a brighter, more mellow drink themselves, aging their product for longer to give it more time to clear, and hopping it more, relying on hops' preservative effects to allow the beer to age longer without turning sour."[50] The resulting beer was called "mild" or "butt," after the large storage casks used to hold it. Only in the 1760s did brewers adopt the colloquial term "porter" in honor of their loyal customers, the sturdy laborers who powered London's early industrial economy. Unlike the distinctive black color of modern porters, the eighteenth-century version was a brown ale made from the "high-dried" malts of Hertfordshire. The pronounced smoky taste of the malt covered imperfections in the early industrial brewing process, which allowed a steady growth in the scale of production. Whereas Harwood never brewed more than about 20,000 barrels a year in the 1720s, William and Felix Calvert each produced more than 50,000 barrels in 1748, and Whitbread broke 200,000 barrels in 1796. As the cost of storage casks for aging become a major expense, brewers began to replace their butts with deep vats, which maintained a steady temperature and reduced the threat of surface contamination. The race to build ever larger vats ended only in 1814, when defective hoops on a vat gave way at the Horse Shoe Brewery, flooding Tottenham Court Road and resulting in eight deaths "by drowning, injury, poisoning by the porter fumes or drunkenness."[51]

Technological innovation did not drive the industrialization of British brewing but rather followed from the financial demands of mass production

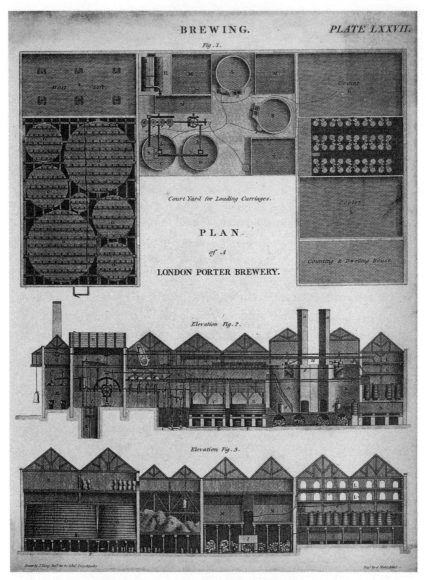

FIGURE 2.5 Already by 1830, London porter breweries had begun to expand the scale of production, as can be seen in the storage vats in the bottom left. These would grow to immense proportions by the end of the nineteenth century. Brewing plan of a London porter brewery, including malt loft cooler, counting and dwelling house, and courtyard for loading carriages. Engraving by J. Moffat, c. 1830, after J. Farey. Wellcome Collection, Wellcome Library, London. Public Domain.

Brewing Capitalism 65

using traditional methods, as business historian Peter Mathias observed. By the end of the eighteenth century, the largest firms held stock worth hundreds of thousands of pounds sterling. To ensure uniform quality and avoid the ruinous loss of a batch or vat, brewers began to employ scientific measurements. Thermometers were used by the 1750s to regulate the mash tun, since overheating killed off the enzymes before they had completed the conversion of starch to sugar. A second instrument, the hydrometer, had been used since the 1720s by tax collectors to determine the strength of alcohol in distilled liquor. Recalibrated for beer in the 1770s, the "saccharometer" allowed brewers to measure the density of sugar within a wort solution and therefore to calculate the level of alcohol that could be expected from fermentation. By 1800, brewers were actively controlling fermentation with attemperators, coiled lengths of submerged copper piping through which cool water was pumped to regulate the heat, thereby making it possible to brew during the summer. Brewhouses had long been designed to use gravity in moving water efficiently, but in the 1770s London porter houses began to use steam engines after James Watt adapted them for milling malt as well as pumping water. Although unwieldy at first, steam power was also used to stir the malts, which left cleaning as the most labor-intensive process in the brewhouse.[52]

The growing scale of production conferred enormous market power on a handful of porter brewers. From the earliest days, porter had undersold ale at a steady price of three pence a quart pot, at least until Parliament raised the beer duty in 1761 to pay for the Seven Years' War. As economies of scale drove down the cost of production, the largest brewers made steadily growing profits. By 1830, twelve brewers accounted for 85 percent of the beer brewed in London. To ensure access to the greatest possible market, brewers purchased properties and leased them out to publicans who sold only their beers. Such tied houses comprised roughly half of the 5,000 pubs in London, according to a report of 1830, which may be a significant undercount. The London porter brewers also maintained a country trade and export markets, but these were small and irregular, often based on personal connections. The tied houses of London, which sold the overwhelming majority of their output, soon came under the same accounting discipline that the brewers used to cut costs in the brewhouse. Yet one efficiency measure that the publicans did welcome was the beer engine, introduced around 1800. Before then, "pot boys" had been employed to run down to the cellars to fill up jugs from the casks. By fitting hydraulic naval pumps to beer casks, the publican could serve his customers directly.[53]

While hearty porter sustained the laboring masses, pale ale graced the tables of the English gentry. The term "ale" had shifted its meaning over the seventeenth century from an old-fashioned, unhopped brew to a bright, clear beer crafted from the finest malt and hops. Unlike the great London porter brewers, ale makers continued to work in small batches and to mature their product in casks instead of vats, for the light malts revealed the smallest flaws in the brewing process. The leading ale brewer, Kirkman, produced only 27,300 barrels in 1800, a tenth of the volume of the giant porter houses. Some of the most prized ales came from the town of Burton-on-Trent, whose mineral-rich waters reputedly preserved ale "for ever and a day."[54] But the town's inland location limited markets until the opening of canal traffic to the ports of Hull and Liverpool in the 1770s. Burton brewers Worthington, Allsop, and Bass soon developed a lucrative trade in the Baltic region, especially among the Russian nobility, who had acquired a taste for English ale under Peter the Great. For more distant markets of India, Southeast Asia, and the Americas, the brewers allowed the beer to go flat before bottling, then induced a secondary fermentation to achieve the desired "briskness," essentially the same technique employed decades later for making sparkling wine in Champagne. Although the Baltic trade collapsed in 1807 when Napoleon closed the continent to English merchants, the construction of railroads in the 1830s opened up a much more substantial market for Burton brewers in London.[55]

In addition to pale ales, another potential competitor for London's porter brewers lay across the Irish Sea. Beginning in the 1730s, Irish politicians encouraged the production of beer in response to a moral panic over the consumption of whisky. British imports captured the bulk of the market at first, but by the end of the eighteenth century, brewers in Cork, Waterford, and Dublin had improved their skills. The rapid growth of the Irish brewing industry during the Napoleonic Wars has often been attributed to favorable tax treatment, but other factors contributed to this shift in production. Wartime restrictions hobbled the London exporters, while increased demand allowed firms such as the one owned by Arthur Guinness of Dublin to increase their scale and efficiency. The depression of 1815–1821 took a toll on Irish brewing, but by the 1840s, Guinness was exporting half of its output of 80,000 barrels per year by steamship to England. Thus, the trickle trade of Dublin porter not only spread across the Irish countryside but even brought porter back to London.[56]

Even before competitors made significant inroads into the home market, London's porter brewers were becoming increasingly concerned about the economics of their industry. Saccharometers revealed that toasting malt to give it the distinctive brown color burned away fermentable sugars. Efficiency-minded brewers began using pale malts instead, adding a small quantity of blackened material for color. These lighter malts also required less aging to mellow out rough flavors, and brewers simply mixed in a portion of stale beer to imitate the desired mature flavor, thereby reducing costly inventories. In 1811, with support from the West Indian sugar lobby, Parliament authorized London brewers to color their porter with caramel. Six years later, Daniel Wheeler patented a new kiln with revolving cylinders borrowed from coffee roasters to produce so-called Patent malts to provide the dark color. But just as the porter houses were essentially brewing pale ale and coloring it brown, ale brewers adopted the technologies of attemperation to produce their beverage on a scale that had been formerly available only to porter. Already by the 1790s, consumer tastes had begun to shift noticeably toward the bright appearance and mellow flavors of mild ale. Fearing the loss of customers, London brewers undertook what historian James Sumner has called the "retrospective invention" of porter, cultivating the creation myth of Harwood along with the now-characteristic black color, made possible by Patent malt, as a form of product differentiation. Nevertheless, their efforts came too late, and the porter market continued to decline.[57]

Eighteenth-century Britain was the first place to brew beer on an industrial scale with the development of London porter. Although attributed to a legendary founder, the brew resulted from a progressive innovation shaped by many brewers as well as by larger structures of industry and government regulation. Workers believed that drinking the thick, brown beverage provided strength for their chores. The gentry meanwhile preferred finely crafted pale ales made in small batches with the finest malts. Over time, the introduction of measurements and controls made it possible for the brewers of Burton-on-Trent to produce pale ale on a scale formerly reserved for aged porter, just in time to appeal to a rising market of middle-class British consumers.

Into the Lager

Even as British porter and ale brewers introduced new chemical and engineering technologies, Bavarians pioneered the biological control of fermentation through the use of lager yeast. There was a certain irony in Munich becoming a brewing capital, for Bavaria had been wine country in the Middle Ages, before the Little Ice Age made grape growing difficult. The preference for wine may have slowed Bavarian adoption of hopped beer, which came only about the turn of the sixteenth century and under the coercion of brewing regulations that later came to be called the *Reinheitsgebot*. Like the English, Bavarians had to import technical expertise from other parts of Europe. Brewers from Einbeck influenced the production of hopped beer in Bavaria, and even the innovation of lager brewing was introduced by Bohemian journeymen.[58] Nevertheless, through a fortuitous confluence of climate, regulation, and entrepreneurship, the brewmasters of early modern Bavaria perfected the art of bottom fermentation.

Unlike the ubiquitous, top-fermenting *Saccharomyces cerevisiae*, which had been used for millennia to ferment ale as well as bread and wine, the bottom-fermenting lager yeast, *Saccharomyces pastorianus*, was first tamed by early modern brewers in Central Europe. Although geneticists believe that *S. pastorianus* resulted from a hybrid between the vigorous *S. cerevisiae* and the cold-hardy *Saccharomyces eubanyus*, the latter's two known strains, indigenous to Patagonia and Tibet, have never been found in Europe.[59] Both bottom- and top-fermenting yeasts float on the brewing liquor while transforming sugar into carbon dioxide and alcohol. Lager yeast produces less froth and sinks to the bottom of the vat after completing its work, yielding a clearer beer. When both strains of yeast are present in the brewery, as was often the case, the type of beer depends on the temperature of fermentation. *S. cerevisiae* works best between 15 and 20° Celsius, becomes uncontrolled at higher temperatures, and goes dormant at lower temperatures. *S. pastorianus* ferments more slowly but remains active at temperatures as low as 5 to 8° Celsius. Early modern brewers thus faced not an ale/lager dichotomy, but rather a continuum defined by temperature. Most often, *S. cerevisiae* reproduced quickly enough to control the reaction, but its sluggish start when cold, such as during a Bavarian winter, could allow *S. pastorianus* to flourish. A change in the weather could even reverse the balance within an individual batch, turning ale into lager or vice versa.[60]

By the turn of the nineteenth century, Bavarians had developed an elaborate system for brewing strong beers during the winter and storing them in deep cellars, where *S. pastorianus* worked its slow magic. The refreshing *sommerbier* or *lagerbier*, served chilled from the lager during the thirsty summer months, won widespread fame. But the components of this *bayerische Arte* (Bavarian style), including bottom fermentation, cellaring, and seasonality, developed gradually, and the archival record is filled with gaps and ambiguities. Karin Hackel-Stehr, who has examined the documents most carefully, explained that a mention of "cold summer beer" in a 1409 ordinance from the town of Landshut referred to a top-fermented ale that had been stored in a cool lager. Bottom-fermented beers were known in the fifteenth century as "Bohemian beers," and journeymen from the region seem to have introduced the practice to Munich.[61] The new beer variety soon proved its value in resisting contamination by wild yeast and bacteria, a common problem with summer beers, and in 1539 Bavarian officials prohibited brewing with barley between St. George's Day (April 23) and St. Michael's Day (September 29). This regulation, reaffirmed in 1553, was not the first such rule, but it did encourage Bavarian brewers to specialize in cold-weather production. By the 1560s, Munich archives began to contain references to *Märzenbier* (March beer), a particularly strong brew made in the spring to keep over the summer.[62] Lager yeasts were also found in the Low Countries, the Rhineland, and England, but mild winters prevented the practice from becoming regular. Jesuit Benno Scharl, author of the magisterial *Description of the Brown-Beer Brewery in the Kingdom of Bavaria* (1814), warned that if cellar temperatures rose above 12 or 13° Celsius, the beer would become "cloudy, thick, and soon go sour."[63] Perhaps as a result of such disasters, the town of Cologne outlawed bottom fermentation entirely in 1603, an early harbinger of the anti-lager sentiment that led in the early twentieth century to the creation of the town's distinctive beer style, Kölsch. Even the Bohemians seem to have largely abandoned bottom fermentation by the eighteenth century.

Another principle of the bayerische Arte, the restriction against additives other than malted barley, hops, and water, has been acclaimed as Europe's first pure food regulation, but far more was at stake than uniform brewing ingredients. The Bavarian edict, proclaimed by Duke William IV in 1516, grew out of Munich market regulations, first passed in 1447 and repeated in 1487, intended to limit the brewing of food grains such as oats, rye, and especially wheat. In addition to holding down the cost of living, this rule ensured the triumph of hopped beer in southern Germany. Hops had been cultivated in the Hallertau region north of Munich since the eighth century, and a hop market was functioning at Nuremberg by the mid-fourteenth century, but a gruit ale known as *Gräwzzing* was still popular a hundred years later. Although these ales might contain potentially poisonous substances such as belladonna and henbane, Bavarian officials were more worried about the potential loss of tax revenue from non-guild brewers.[64] Authorities also feared the socially disruptive presence of *kräuterfrauen* (herbalists) who supported themselves by gathering medicinal plants and brewing them for sale. Munich's brewing ordinance of 1493, intended to professionalize the guild and limit the sale of homebrewed beers, formed part of a wider campaign by communities, guilds, and religious institutions to control social and economic opportunities for women.[65]

Despite these standardizing regulations, Bavarian beer retained considerable variety in the early modern era. Limits on brewing ingredients exempted *Weissbier* (wheat beer), which like bottom fermentation had been introduced from Bohemia in the fifteenth century. In 1548, Duke William IV granted Hans von Degenberg the privilege of brewing Weissbier at Schwarzach for sale northeast of the Danube River, and nine municipal breweries produced it elsewhere in Bavaria. At Nuremberg, a Dutch brewmaster made a Hamburg-style Weissbier (white beer), and in Bavaria the terms "wheat beer" and "white beer" became synonymous, in contrast to "brown beer" made with just barley. In 1602, with the extinction of the Degenberg line, Duke Maximilian I declared a monopoly on Weissbier, requiring municipal breweries to pay licensing fees and relocating the staff from Schwarzach to Munich. The ban on summer brewing with barley made the Weissbier monopoly all the more lucrative, as towns typically set the price of barley summer beer at twice that of winter beer. Despite the fixed prices, regional variations existed, including sweet beer, bitter beer, *Jungherren* (young man's beer), *Doppelbier* (double-strength beer), and *Bokbier* (made in the style of Einbeck). In his 1826 book, Benno Scharl observed that many people preferred the winter to summer beer because it did not contain as much hop bitterness, an early expression of the later stylistic difference between Bohemian Pilsner hoppiness and Bavarian lager maltiness.[66]

Bavarian officials strictly controlled consumption as well as production to ensure steady revenues. Although innkeepers were allowed to sell beer as an essential service to travelers, a municipal regulation called the *Bierzwang* (literally, "beer coercion") dictated a sort of tied house system that restricted the breweries from which they could purchase beer. This rule served to limit competition for the *Hofbräuhaus*, a Munich drinking hall established in 1589 as an outlet for the personal brewery of Duke Maximilan I. Nevertheless, many people chose instead to purchase beer from independent *Zäpfler* (tapsters), who dispensed beer from takeout windows. In 1792, Munich had 60 innkeepers, 67 brewers, and 136 tapsters. Even the fabled Bavarian beer gardens were in part a response to taxation. Urban dwellers had long gone to nearby villages and monasteries to drink with extended family at weddings and other occasions, but as taxes rose in the seventeenth century to pay for the Thirty Years' War, these rural outings became more regular and illicit. Municipal authorities' only means of enforcing ordinances against drinking outside city walls was to catch returning residents when they snuck back into town drunk. Officials tried to recruit spies in village taverns, but "informants were so 'hated and shunned' that no one was willing to serve in this capacity even when offered a share in the collected fines."[67]

By the eighteenth century, a distinctive bayerische Arte had materialized in brewery design with the construction of lagering cellars. As early as 1380, officials in Nuremberg had specified minimum cellar sizes for breweries, but these seem to have been relatively shallow, or even above ground storage, as indicated by a late sixteenth-century manual's advice to place beer barrels in cool, breezy spaces. Cellar flooding was also a concern in many areas. In 1728, a Munich brewery excavated the first stone cellar under the high eastern banks of the Isar River. As the benefits of deep storage became apparent, rivals established their own cellars nearby or to the west of the city under the so-called Hangman's Hill (Galgenberg). By 1760, Johann von Justi considered deep and well-accommodated cellars to be essential for brewing a proper lager beer. For his model brewery, Benno Scharl recommended two separate cellars, one for winter beer and the other for summer beer. The latter should reach almost to the freezing point during winter, although he warned against placing ice directly on the kegs. Even in the heat of summer, lager beer from the best stone cellars will be "so cold that it can hardly be drunk."[68] For shade, brewers planted chestnut trees, whose shallow roots protected the cellar roofs, while also lending a bucolic rural atmosphere to their beer gardens. Nevertheless, the use of natural ice, harvested in the winter from nearby lakes and canals, seems to have begun only around 1830.[69]

Another element of the bayerische Arte was the so-called *dickmaisch* (literally, "thick mash" or decoction). Scharl devoted two full pages to describing this procedure of heating the liquor gradually by drawing off buckets, simmering it gently, and then adding it back to the mashtun. Modern chemistry has revealed the value of this labor-intensive method in providing ideal temperature ranges for various enzymes to work, thereby extracting the greatest possible quantity of fermentable sugars from the malt. Unlike elsewhere in the treatise, the Jesuit scholar did not offer precise temperatures or liquid volumes for the different stages of the mash, instead simply warning against burning the malt. The origins of this Bavarian system are unknown, but one possible source lay in alchemists such as the seventeenth-century Prague-based Pole Michael Sendivogius and his Flemish contemporary Jan Baptist Van Helmont, who used decoction to extract gases from foods that were believed to impede digestion. Theoretically minded English brewers discussed the works of these authors, although they settled instead on the simpler infusion method of heating the mash directly.[70]

The eighteenth-century bayerishe Arte was still distinct from modern lager brewing, but important changes of regulation and entrepreneurship had already begun to set Munich on a path to leadership in the beer industry. By the turn of the nineteenth century, brewers had only just overtaken innkeepers in social position and taxes paid to the city. In 1820, Munich's leading brewer could cellar 40,000 hectoliters, roughly equivalent to 24,000 barrels in the United Kingdom, scarcely a tenth of the volume produced by the largest English firms.[71] Nevertheless, Bavaria had been elevated to an independent kingdom in 1805 through an alliance with Napoleon, and the first monarch, Maximilian Joseph, shook up the insular world of guilds with French-style economic reforms. The abolition of the Bierzwang in 1799 allowed for the proliferation of taverns and beer halls, while the secularization of monasteries in 1802 transferred the medieval breweries of the Augustinian and Franciscan orders into private hands. In 1807, the government began to relax restrictions on businesses, such as limits on the number of employees, and the declaration of free trade in 1825 removed guild control over licensing, training, and production. As the number of breweries declined, their scale of production grew under the leadership of entrepreneurs such as Gabriel Sedlmayr, Sr. The son of a brewer from Maisach, Sedlmayr was appointed brewmaster at the royal brewery in Schleißheim in 1799, at the age of twenty-seven, and was promoted to run the Hofbräuhaus in Munich in 1806. A year later he purchased the antiquated Spatenbrauerei and set about updating and expanding it with a mechanical pump from an Augsburger foundry, a cooling trough from the Tirol, and in 1818, one of the first new Wheeler malt kilns from England.[72]

In describing the essence of Bavarian beer, Benno Scharl said simply, "good malt, good hops, and good lager yeast."[73] But there was nothing simple about the art of bottom fermentation, with its elaborate thick mash, storage chambers, and seasonal rotation. Although structured by the climate and government regulations, the lager beer industry was nevertheless a product of innovative and entrepreneurial brewers, who had built far-reaching markets for their premium beers by the end of the eighteenth century. As in other early modern societies, the increasing commercialization of Bavarian beer marginalized women's domestic brewing.

Beer styles flourished in the early modern world as a form of product differentiation by brewers seeking to compete in growing regional markets. In northern Europe, the addition of hops as a preservative in the thirteenth century made the growth of seaborne trade possible, and by the sixteenth century connoisseurs recognized more than a hundred different varieties of beer in Germany alone. Beer was becoming a market commodity not only in Europe but also in thriving commercial societies from East Asia to the Americas. At first, style referred to beers from a particular place, and over time, brewers experimented to understand the cause of distinctive local flavors, whether the arid climate of Apan's agaves, the waters responsible for Nada's sake, or the lager yeast of Bavarian beer. Nevertheless, marketing also depended on invented traditions attributing particular beers to legendary brewers, such as Mumme of Braunschweig, Broihan in Hannover, and Harwood in London.

The sale of premium beer in turn depended on the growth of disposable income in dynamic early modern economies. Merchants and masters translated their new wealth into social status through the display of elite products such as Burton pale ale and double white sake, while urban workers spent their wages on London porter and four coppers sake. Mobility also contributed to the commercial development of beer by way of technology transfers, itinerant workers, and the trade of products and tastes in expanding urban markets. Social inequalities extended to production, as women were displaced from increasingly profitable markets. Even in Mexico, where women had brewed and sold pulque since pre-Hispanic times, men began to take over the trade in the eighteenth century. Women survived only at the highest and lowest reaches of the market, among them the daughters of the Count of Jala, who inherited pulque haciendas and palaces, and indigenous women who peddled illicit homebrew in the streets of Mexico City. In Japan, medieval women brewers were not only driven out of the trade by the early modern growth of scale, but their earlier contributions were also written out of the historical memory of sake.[74]

The patterns of early modern commercial brewing became magnified with the continued commodification of beer in the nineteenth-century age of industry. Experimentation to define local styles led to the rise of scientific brewing, making it possible to brew ever more standardized products. At the same time, the wages of factory labor allowed greater numbers of consumers to shift from homebrewed subsistence to predictable market goods, including the most famous nineteenth-century beer of all, Pilsner.

3

Inventing Pilsner

ON OCTOBER 5, 1842, a gruff Bavarian brewmaster named Josef Groll created the original Pilsner beer using ingredients from the Bohemian countryside: aromatic Saaz hops from the Žatec basin, golden malt from Moravia, and soft local waters. The one exotic introduction was the bottom-fermenting yeast that he carried with him when hired by the town fathers of Pilsen. But unlike the wine regions of Burgundy, Barolo, Champagne, and Chianti, which took shape around the same time through innovative grape-growing and wine-making practices, Pilsner came to be considered not a geographical designation (*appellation*, in French), unique to its place of origin, but rather a style (*Biertypus*) or a quality designation (*Beschaffenheitsangabe*), reproducible anywhere. These different outcomes resulted in part from the physical nature of the products, since the brewer combined raw materials that shipped more easily and kept longer than the finished beer, while the vintner condensed bulky, perishable grapes into wines that could age for decades. Moreover, the brewers of Pilsen lacked an established reputation and had to struggle for prestige against competitors across Central Europe and around the world. Ultimately, the meaning of Pilsner and other beer styles was a legal construct, determined as much by politicians and judges as by brewers and consumers.

Although named after particular towns such as Pilsen, Budweis, Munich, and Vienna, nineteenth-century beer styles arose from the heightened mobility of a globalizing era. Their development combined new British methods of malting and brewing with Bavarian advances in bottom fermentation. Beers accrued their reputations in continental and global markets, made possible by an extensive network of railroads and steamships. And while brewers in Pilsen and elsewhere had once used relatively local ingredients, industrial production outstripped supplies, forcing them to purchase raw materials from international commodity markets. Finally, the expanding industry depended on the mobility of skilled workers, whether students traveling to learn new methods or brewmasters like Groll taking employment in other lands. As people, goods, and ideas moved back and forth at an accelerating pace, the desire to fix beers to particular locations was both understandable in theory and unachievable in practice.

The nineteenth-century industrialization of lager brewing and the standardization of beer styles also resulted from advances in science and technology. Already in the late eighteenth century, large-scale British brewers had adopted thermometers and saccharometers to avoid costly failures, and those instruments were taken up by progressive brewers on the continent and in the Americas. The microscope was a particularly transformative tool, enabling scientists to uncover the mysteries of fermentation. Major breweries established their own laboratories, and brewing scientists were among the leading theoretical chemists of the nineteenth century. They disseminated this knowledge and institutionalized their profession through brewing schools, research stations, and scientific publications, thereby creating international networks of knowledge. The application of analytical chemistry to industrial quality control, in turn, imposed quantitative standards that helped to ensure more uniform products while also restricting the creativity of practicing brewers.

The increasing mobility of consumers likewise contributed to changing tastes for beer. Industrialization brought migrants from the countryside to the city and from Europe to the Americas. Rising incomes from factory wages in the second half of the nineteenth century allowed workers to eat foods that had once been restricted to elites. The food-processing industry, with its new technologies of preserving and packaging, also held out the possibility of purity and freshness. But as a result, consumers could no longer use their senses to judge quality in the marketplace and instead had to trust brand names. Nevertheless, advertising claims would only go so far if brewers could not ensure consistency from one bottle to the next. Brewers also created new spaces for consumption, transforming traditional taverns into elaborate beer palaces and gardens. Through stylistic conformity, imagined geographies, and commercialized consumption, beer became a modern commodity in the nineteenth century.

A Spectrum of Lagers

The two elegantly dressed young journeymen appeared respectable as they made the rounds of Edinburgh breweries in the fall of 1834, with their lacquered walking sticks and letters of recommendation from distinguished Scottish scientist David Booth. The stocky, blond, Munich brewer, Gabriel Sedlmayr, Jr., and his lanky, dark-haired, Viennese colleague, Anton Dreher, toured the factories with great interest, asking questions and freely sharing their knowledge of Bavarian lager yeast, which was unknown in Britain at the time. As they visited the fermentation room at each brewery, one of the pair distracted their hosts, while the other plunged his walking stick into a bubbling vat of beer. A hidden valve opened to fill the hollow tube with brewing liquor, then closed again as it was withdrawn. Back in their lodging, the Germanic brewers analyzed the stolen samples with a saccharometer that Booth had taught them to use. "It always surprises me that we can get away with these thefts without being beaten up," Sedlmayr wrote to his father.[1] After returning home to the family brewery, Spaten, he applied his illicitly gained knowledge to craft a distinctive Bavarian lager. This novel beer, in turn, was copied by rivals across Central Europe.

In 1867, an Austrian industrial inspector named J. John described the popular *altbayerische Art* (old Bavarian style) as a "brown beer with seemingly stronger concentration brewed from dark malt and with an unusually long cooking of the hopped wort."[2] Although often attributed to sixteenth-century brewing regulations, crucial elements of the style were scarcely thirty years old at the time. Bavarian lager had not been, as a rule, *dunkel*, the dark-brown color that John and others had come to expect. In 1829, as the young Sedlmayr set out on his journeyman tour of Central Europe and the British Isles, the *Wöchentlicher Anzeiger für Biertrinker* (Weekly Beer Drinker's Gazette) reported a sample of Munich beers comprising twenty-eight *weingelb* (wine yellow, perhaps wheat beers), twenty-two *hellbraun* (light brown), and only one *dunkelbraun* (dark brown). Consistency of color as a marker of style had only recently been pioneered by the makers of London porter, and Sedlmayr helped to introduce this important, although often overlooked, British innovation to continental Europe.[3]

As Sedlmayr sought to synthesize his newly gained brewing knowledge, he began by experimenting with novel malting techniques. In 1835, he brewed a Bavarian lager using English pale ale malt, which he dubbed Märzenbier (March beer). The amber color recalled the strong beers that were stored on ice for consumption through the summer and into early fall, especially at Oktoberfest, a recently invented tradition celebrating the marriage of Bavarian Prince Ludwig and Princess Therese in 1810. For his signature "Munich" beer, Sedlmayr set a more ambitious and technically challenging goal, to brew a full-bodied, dark beer without the British trick of adding

Inventing Pilsner

caramel sugar, which was forbidden in Bavaria. By replacing cantankerous, smoky ovens with the indirect and carefully regulated heat of British flue-kilns, it became possible to toast the malt for about a day "at a gentle, clean heat, without being browned in the slightest degree," and at the very end to "suddenly raise the temperature, which brings out the semi-caramelized substance, believed to explain the peculiar richness and aroma of the beer."[4]

Over the next four decades, Sedlmayr channeled his youthful masculinity—risking violence to steal beer—into building Munich's foremost brewery. In Britain, he had declared, "all is new and entirely different from our ways," and he sought to incorporate industrial methods throughout the brewing process.[5] When Gabriel Jr. and his brother Josef inherited the business from their father in 1839, they brewed just over 24,000 hectoliters of beer. Sibling rivalry quickly divided the firm, and Josef built a successful brand called Leistbräu from their father's original brewery. Meanwhile, Gabriel Jr. renovated Spaten, excavating a new lager cellar in 1842 and installing a steam engine four years later. By 1851, with a production of about 43,000 hectoliters, he had outgrown the old space and began constructing a new factory with dedicated steam engines for each of three brewing houses. The company's expanding export business also benefited from a bottling facility, a novelty in Bavaria, where tavernkeepers still held considerable political power and feared competition from bottled beers. By the early 1870s, Spaten's 200 workers brewed almost 300,000 hectoliters of beer annually.[6]

Although justly renowned for modernizing the Bavarian brewing industry, Sedlmayr was not a solitary pioneer. His father Gabriel Sr. had inspired and facilitated his research by establishing a brewing laboratory and purchasing a modern English malt kiln. Like his son, he had a transnational vision, importing hops from Bohemia, Flanders, and even the United States, and exporting beer as far as England. Along with Georg Brey, who purchased the Löwenbräu brewery in 1818, the elder Sedlmayr experimented with Doppelbier and other varieties that had formerly been restricted to the aristocracy and religious cloisters. Brey also expanded ambitiously, competing with Sedlmayr to run the premier Munich brewery. Meanwhile, in 1829, Anton and Therese Wagner began renovating a former Augustinian monastic brewery, and after Anton passed away in 1845, Therese managed the business, installing steam engines and other innovations, until her death three years later. Outside Munich, brewers in Nuremberg, Kulmbach, Erlangen, Augsburg, and other towns likewise built export breweries.[7]

Bavarian dark lagers achieved widespread popularity across Germany in the 1840s and 1850s. In Munich, beer provided a primary source of nutrition for many in the working classes. Single men, no longer bound to a master's household, took their meals in taverns, where they consumed the beverage. Housewives meanwhile lined up with tankards outside of breweries to take home the daily beer to their families. Absorbing as much as half the daily wage, beer largely determined workers' standard of living. When beer prices increased in 1844 and again in 1848, crowds broke into the homes of prominent brewers, tossing the Pschorr family's grand piano out into the street, but scrupulously respecting the brewing equipment. Elsewhere in Germany, Munich beer became gentrified, as brewmaster Ernst Rüffer later recalled sardonically. Taverns, "especially in little country towns, under the name of 'Bavarian Beerhall,' were cheerfully visited by a discriminating clientele, who preferred the 'genuine Bavarian' and so-beloved Doppelbier; many enjoyed it simply because it belonged to 'high society.' "[8] But fashion was not the only appeal. Like many industrial foods of the nineteenth century, lager beer was widely considered to have a fresher taste and more hygienic character than top-fermented ales, which often tasted sour and were believed to harbor cholera. Especially in the 1840s, as the potato blight raged in Ireland and spread across northern Europe, a stomach-filling, double-strength beer offered a satisfying marker of wealth and status.[9]

The growing demand for Bavarian beer offered enormous potential profits for brewers but also inspired new competitors. Even before Munich was connected to the German railroad system in 1840, the industrial city of Leipzig imported 10,000 hectoliters of Bavarian beer annually. By the early 1860s, special beer trains departed twice weekly from Munich for the Rhineland and Paris. To meet the demand for lager, Munich brewers had to purchase ice harvested from the Birnhorn glacier in nearby Austria. In Zurich, the arrival of the first beer train from Munich became enshrined in the historical memory of local brewers, who recalled "from that moment on, the beers of all Swiss breweries increased significantly in body, and the quality became much better."[10] Competition not only raised standards, but also drove brewers to learn the new process. Leipzig cloth merchant Maximilian Speck von Sternburg traveled to Munich in 1836 to obtain the latest lager brewing technology, including plans for the Wagners' reconstructed Augustiner Brewery. Meanwhile in Berlin, Bavarian migrants such as Georg Hopf and Joseph Pfeffer equipped factories with lager storage. Across Germany, as brewmaster Rüffer noted, the fashion for lager "forced brewery owners to abandon top fermentation and make dark, bottom-fermented beers with the same [Bavarian] taste and characteristics."[11]

FIGURE 3.1 As industrial production of Munich lager expanded rapidly in the 1850s, workers harvested ice from the Austrian Birnhorn glacier to meet the demand for cooling beer cellars. Archiv BN21385. Courtesy of Deutsches Museum, Munich, Germany.

The replicability of the lager recipe posed a dilemma for Sedlmayr and other exporters, although the genuine Bavarian article retained a special appeal. By 1870, the southern kingdom produced more than 10 million hectoliters of beer, one-third of Germany's entire output—and not just because the people of Munich drank five times the national average. Secretive guild practices gave way to an open exchange of scientific knowledge, and the "industrial espionage" of Sedlmayr's British mission or, indeed, the contemporary travels of Speck von Sternburg acquired the more neutral term "technology transfer."[12] Perhaps ashamed by the betrayal of his Scottish mentor, Sedlmayr supported aspiring lager brewers throughout his long career. Even his singular triumph of associating the full-bodied, bottom-fermented, Bavarian lager with a distinctive dark color left a mixed legacy. Fashion was fickle, as London's porter brewers had unhappily discovered.

Few visitors in the early nineteenth century might have guessed that the market town of Pilsen, on the road from Prague to Bavaria, would become world renowned for its clear, sparkling beers. Having grown rich from the business of anthracite mining, residents imported Bavarian lagers. In 1840, the town fathers decided to invest some of their mining profits in the construction of a municipal brewery. The first tasting, held on St. Martin's Day, November 11, 1842, brought their home-grown beverage local acclaim. But apart from the basic recipe of Saaz hops, Moravian malt, soft water, and lager yeast, little is known about how Pilsner acquired its legendary status. It was prized, at first, as an exotic "Bavarian" beer, and the malting process relied on British advances in indirect heating, like Sedlmayr's Munich malt, but without the final burst of caramelization. The brewery's capacity of just thirty-six hectoliters, about twenty barrels, meant that the beer was sold primarily in local markets. Brewmaster Groll, a difficult man by all accounts, was sent home when his contract expired.[13]

Pilsner spread slowly in its first decades, through imitation as much as export. According to legend, a teamster named Martin Salzmann first introduced Pilsner beer to Prague about 1845, but rather than expand his carriage trade and profit from growing sales, he settled down in the Bohemian capital and opened a tavern. Although Pilsen's burghers constructed a second brewhouse with larger kettle and mash tun in 1852, it took almost another decade for production to reach 40,000 hectoliters. Sales expanded more rapidly after 1862, with the opening of the Bohemian Western Railroad and the construction of a third brewhouse, followed twelve years later by a fourth. In 1868, a writer for the *Bayerische Bierbrauer* (Bavarian Brewer) attributed the growing popularity of Bohemian beers to their "lightness, carbonation, mild taste and clear golden color." The Pilsner brewery was only one of several regional exporters producing such a beer; others included Egerer and the Prague-based Kreuzherrenbier, Königssaaler, Nussler, and Bubner. Curiously, Budweiser did not make the list; although already renowned for its beers, the town had only adopted bottom fermentation in 1852. The citizens of Pilsen could not even claim exclusive title to their town's name after 1869, when a brewing corporation called Gambrinus opened nearby and started producing a similar clear beer. Thus, the golden Pilsner, like Sedlmayr's dark beers, attracted imitators.[14]

In the mid-nineteenth century, Anton Dreher's Vienna brewery, Klein Schwechat, outshone the reputation of Pilsner. Like his traveling companion, Sedlmayr, he had experimented with combining English pale ale malts and Bavarian lager yeast in the 1830s. Whereas the Munich brewer used the recipe only to produce a seasonal specialty, Märzenbier, Dreher made the amber brew his signature Vienna lager. It became all the rage in the Austrian capital, and Klein Schwechat workers struggled to meet the demand from the rapidly growing population. From an initial output of 16,000 hectoliters in

1836, production rose above 50,000 hectoliters by 1848, then tripled again in the following decade, making "Little Schwechat" the largest brewery in continental Europe at the time. The hyperactive Dreher opened two new breweries to capture regional markets: Michelob in the Saaz district of Bohemia, in 1861, and Steinbruch in the Hungarian capital of Budapest, in 1862, before his death the following year.[15]

The example of Vienna lager illustrates the ongoing refinement of beer styles through an interaction between producers and consumers, ingredients and technology. Frankfurt brewmaster Friedrich Henrich recalled working as a journeyman for Dreher in 1858: "At the time he was famous as a maker of Märzenbier"—as Vienna lager was known in Germany—"and it was his wish that Märzenbier should be more full-bodied than it had been previously, and particularly that it should be different from highly attenuated lager beers."[16] Henrich's listeners understood the reference to drier Bohemian varieties of beer, in which the sugars had been converted more fully to alcohol. The remark clearly indicates Dreher's persistent concern with refining his brewing style—and with his competition.

Already by the 1860s, Central European brewers had created a spectrum of lager beer styles ranging from dark, full-bodied Munich to amber, malty Vienna and golden, dry Pilsner—and that was no accident. Even before the railroads had fully integrated European beer markets, brewers kept a close watch on their rivals and worked to ensure that their own products stood out for consumers. German-speaking migrants carried over this international competition to the Americas as they opened a new world of lager beer.

The Lager Migrations

Although Bavarian migrants such as Valentin Blatz and Christian Moerlein were among the early German brewers in the United States, the knowledge of bottom fermentation traveled through many channels. The Pabst Brewing Company's founder, Philip Best, acquired his original lager yeast from a Milwaukee neighbor who had ordered it from Bavaria. A delay in transit caused the brewer to fear the yeast would not survive, so he sold it sight unseen to Best for the cost of shipping. When the box finally arrived, packed with sawdust and wrapped in hop sacking, Best ran the yeast through a sieve to filter out debris. As brewmaster Max Fueger later recalled: "Neither Philip nor I slept very much while we were trying the new yeast, but it was a success, although we made better lager beer after six months than we did the first time."[17] Through experiments such as this one, immigrants developed original styles of lager beer on the lakeshores of Milwaukee and far beyond.

German immigrants made Chile and the United States the pioneer lager brewers of the Americas, although, unlike elsewhere in the hemisphere, the indigenous peoples of these territories had limited alcoholic beverages of their own. Whereas Spaniards encountered native brewers of pulque and chicha in Mexico and Peru, English and Dutch founded the first breweries in their North American colonies. Even then, most settlers drank rum, gin, whisky, or hard cider. By 1810 only about 150 breweries operated in the United States for a population of 7 million. In the southern states, enslaved and free women of color adapted African brewing traditions to New World ingredients, selling beers made of molasses and sarsaparilla root. Spanish settlers in Chile and California founded vineyards to satisfy their needs for sacramental wine and daily consumption. Chileans also made a version of apple cider called chicha, using the same term as the indigenous fermented corn beverage. British ale became fashionable during the wars of independence in the 1810s, and the inaugural banquet for President Manuel Bulnes in 1841 served Burton ale alongside Bordeaux wine.[18]

Lager beer arrived in the Americas in the 1840s along with German migrants fleeing economic change and political unrest. Early arrivals were often farmers and artisans from Bavaria, Baden, and Württemberg, followed by political refugees from the failed liberal revolutions of 1848. Most settled with their families in the Midwest's so-called German triangle between Cincinnati, Milwaukee, and St. Louis. Much smaller numbers, about 80,000, moved to Chile with official encouragement, founding colonies at Valdivia and Llanquihue, on the indigenous Araucanian frontier. By the 1880s, proletarian migrants from northeastern Germany had largely replaced the earlier agrarian arrivals from the southwest, and the newcomers usually searched for industrial work in cities such as New York and Chicago. Nearly 5 million Germans came to the United States in the century after 1820.[19]

Finding relatively cheap food and high wages, migrants generally improved their standards of living in the Americas, although they were not always welcomed at first. Chicago's Lager Beer riot of 1855 resulted not from a shortage of beer but rather from Nativist attempts to ban the beverage enjoyed by the newcomers. German service in the Union Army during the Civil War created a positive view of the immigrants among northerners, many of whom learned to drink beer while serving alongside German units. Beer gardens became a conspicuous center of German American social life. Likewise in South

America, settlers gathered in social clubs to eat, drink, sing, and play sports, and Chileans soon acquired a taste for "German chicha."[20]

Some notable early brewers, including Valentin Blatz and Christian Moerlein, brought a knowledge of bottom fermentation with them from Bavaria, while many others learned through practice in America, as did Philip Best and Max Fueger. A trade history published by John E. Siebel in 1903, *One Hundred Years of Brewing*, offered a sample of more than 500 profiles of brewers in the United States. Although the book is top heavy, favoring owners over workers, it suggests that prior experience was not a requirement. Of the eighty or so brewers listed as arriving from Germany in the formative decade before 1850, only twenty made lager, and fewer than half of those came from Bavaria. These profiles also show that American apprenticeships were common, even among migrants who had learned the trade in their home country. Historian Perry Duis observed that newcomers usually landed in big cities like New York, Philadelphia, or Cincinnati, where they worked at established firms before setting out for smaller towns or the frontier to become their own bosses. Bavarian connections were likewise useful but not essential in Chile. The most prominent early brewer, a Prussian pharmacist named Carl Andwanter, founded the German settlement in Valdivia after the 1848 revolution and sent two of his sons, Richard and Germán, to study in Bavaria. Of the leading brewery owners in Santiago and Valparaiso in the 1850s, five were German, two Italian, and one Swiss.[21]

Cheap grain and expensive labor shaped a unique approach to brewing in the Americas. Early lager brewers dug cellars from the waterfront bluffs in Milwaukee and St. Louis or in the hills around Cincinnati, but the costs of excavation encouraged a shift to icehouses by the 1860s. Natural ice was expensive, bulky, and messy, limiting the growth of breweries. The arrival of reliable refrigeration in the 1880s allowed for the construction of massive factory complexes with specialized buildings for fermentation, storage, and bottling. Also in the 1880s, brewers began adding so-called adjunct grains, especially corn and rice, to the traditional Bavarian barley-malt recipe. Anton Schwarz, a brewing scientist who had trained in Prague before moving to New York, demonstrated the value of this technique for making bright, clear, and stable Bohemian-style beers. In Chile, the lack of a diversified industrial base limited brewers to machinery imported from Germany. Local farmers raised high-quality barley; hops also grew well, but the cost of labor made it prohibitively expensive to harvest them.[22]

International migration also encouraged eclectic and innovative brewing styles. Dark Bavarian beers held sway until Americans discovered

FIGURE 3.2 The Anheuser Busch Brewery of St. Louis, Missouri, in its day the world's largest brewery. From John E. Siebel, *One Hundred Years of Brewing* (Chicago: H. S. Rich and Company, 1903), 349. Courtesy of the Food and Drink Collection, Shields Library, University of California, Davis. My thanks to Audrey Russek.

Pilsner beer at the Vienna World's Fair in 1873. Within two years, "'Pilsner Beer' mania" had reached Cincinnati, and local brewers were creating their own versions following Schwarz's guidance. To avoid false advertising, they listed the origins of the beer using phrases like "Schlitz (Pilsner) Milwaukie Beer."[23] By 1880, the golden lager had become so popular that Pabst's Chicago sales manager wrote to Milwaukee pleading: "Can't you give us a paler, purer beer?"[24] Meanwhile, after a visit to the town of Budweis, Adolphus Busch recreated a version of the Bohemian beer for a friend, Carl Conrad, to bottle and sell. The beer gained wide acclaim, and a rival soon copied it, right down to the label. When Conrad filed suit in 1880, the defendant replied that a town's name could not be trademarked, and in any event, the beer was not actually made in Budweis. Conrad won the case by arguing that the beer's name referred not to the town but to the Budweis method, although the recipe had in fact been concocted by Busch's brewmaster. Busch later bought the rights and began distributing Budweiser through his own agents.[25] Chilean brewers likewise produced a mix of Pilsner- and Bavarian-style beers, along with a less common Erlanger beer, named after a town near Nuremberg. It is not clear whether this style became popular through visits to the homeland, like Budweiser in North America, as a result of a single migrant from Erlangen who was copied by other Chilean brewers, or perhaps even from a chain migration of Erlanger brewers.[26]

The industrialization of brewing took off in American societies almost simultaneously with the growth of lager beer in Central Europe. Although modeled on beers from the homeland, American brewers adapted their methods to the conditions and tastes of their new countries. Indeed, scientific advances that drove industrialization resulted from knowledge networks that spanned the globe.

The Rise of Scientific Brewing

The nineteenth-century spread of lager beer across Europe and the Americas depended on the exchange of knowledge as well as the migrations of brewing professionals like Anton Schwarz. By adopting scientific methods, progressive brewers sought to promote national economic development, while also differentiating themselves from more traditional rivals. Industry groups fostered this agenda, at times with government support, through the establishment of brewing schools, research stations, and professional journals. Despite the wide applicability of innovations like steam and refrigeration, national differences arose at vital points in the brewing process, especially the selection of grains and fermentation. Scientists also contributed to the standardization of beer styles through the quantitative methods of analytical chemistry.

International collaborations drove the advance of brewing science and technology. The measurement of potential fermentation using saccharometers, developed by Englishmen John Richardson and James Baverstock, was codified in the 1840s by Bohemian chemist Carl Balling. Microscopic observations by three independent French and German researchers, Charles Cagniard-Latour, Theodor Schwann, and Friedrich Kützing, identified yeast as a living organism—*Saccharomyces cerevisiae*, the "sugar-eating fungi of beer," according to its 1838 classification. Louis Pasteur's germ theory in turn provided the theoretical basis for Emil Christian Hansen's isolation of pure yeast in 1883 at the Carlsberg Brewery in Copenhagen. Brewing machinery also bore the imprint of engineers from many lands. The pneumatic malting system invented by Scotsman Patrick Stead was repeatedly updated, by Frenchmen Nicholas Galland and Alphonse Saladin, Bohemian Edvard Hrubý, and American W. H. Prinz. The origins of other technologies were lost in translation, such as French-born, Belgian-trained Jean-Louis Baudelot's nestled cooling pipes, which became known in Germany as the "American cooler."

Refrigerators from Europe, North America, and Australia competed for business until Bavarian Carl von Linde's compressed ammonia system gained widespread acceptance. Germans also pioneered modern filtering systems, while the American Michael Owens's glass machine mechanized the production of bottles.[27]

Operating all this new machinery required skills unavailable through traditional guild training. In the 1830s, renowned chemists Georg von Kaiser of Munich and Carl Balling of Prague began offering brewing courses at polytechnics established on the French model. The Kingdom of Bavaria founded the first dedicated brewing school in 1848 at the summer palace of Schleißheim, which later merged with the School of Agriculture at Weihenstephan. Students came to learn bottom fermentation there from as far away as Chile, in the case of the Andwanter brothers. By 1876, a Czech instructor named Hajek offered lessons in Bohemian malting and brewing alongside the course in Bavarian methods taught by a Herr Pfauth. Schools and programs also flourished in Vienna, Berlin, Zurich, Prague, Leuven, and elsewhere. In the 1880s, American brewing academies were opened by European migrants and native brewers alike, including John Siebel, Robert Wahl, and Max Henius in Chicago and Francis Wyatt and Carl Robitschek in New York City. The establishment of technical schools lagged in the United Kingdom, where companies offered in-house training and consumers equated the phrase "brewing chemistry" with unsavory practices of adulteration. Only the largest Burton-on-Trent factories had laboratories, and the first School of Malting and Brewing, at Birmingham University, was not founded until 1900.[28]

Brewing schools were often attached to scientific research stations, which provided extension services to local industry. Weihenstephan instructor Carl Lintner opened the first such station at Munich in 1876 with the support of Sedlmayr and other southern German brewers, while the imperial government subsidized Max Delbrück's Versuchs und Lehranstalt für Brauerei (Research and Teaching Institute for Brewers, or VLB), founded at Berlin in 1883. As historian of science and technology John Ceccatti observed, these rival institutes took differing approaches: the Bavarians sought to apply science directly to industry, while the northern Germans preferred to adapt new technology to traditional practices. Bavarian rationalism found fertile ground in the United States, where land grant colleges had provided extension services since the 1860s, although many leading American immigrant brewing scientists had not actually trained in the home of bottom fermentation. Düsseldorf-native John Siebel received his doctorate from the University of Berlin; Bohemian

Anton Schwarz worked with Balling in Prague; and Danish-born Max Henius learned pure yeast culture from Hansen at Carlsberg.[29]

Brewing journals provided an important medium for education and extension work. As trade publications, they quoted the latest prices for hops and grains, summarized new scientific research, listed patents and trademarks, answered readers' questions, and editorialized bitterly against the global temperance movement. In 1859, G. E. Habich of Wiesbaden founded the first technical journal, *Der Bierbrauer* (The Beer Brewer), followed in 1866 by Carl Lintner's monthly *Der Bayerische Bierbrauer* (The Bavarian Beer Brewer). In 1868, shortly after his arrival in the United States, Anton Schwarz took over a trade paper, *Der Amerikanische Bierbrauer* (The American Beer Brewer), and transformed it into a respectable scientific publication, setting a high standard for later journals such as John Siebel's *Western Brewer* and Robert Wahl and Max Henius's *American Brewer's Review*. By the first decade of the twentieth century, more than thirty brewers' journals were published in at least eight European countries, the United States, Australia, and Japan. These works facilitated an international dialogue through reprints, translations, correspondence notes, and research abstracts.[30]

Professional societies also fostered international scientific and technological networks. Many of these trade groups formed in response to the threat of taxation, during the Civil War in 1862 in the case of the United States Brewers Association and with German unification in 1871 for the Deutsche Brauerbund (German Brewers Association). Britain likewise had its Country Brewers' Society, but the more scientifically oriented Federated Institute of Brewing grew out of a dining club of Burton chemists called the Bacterium Club, founded in 1876 and later renamed the Laboratory Club. Members included the consulting brewer E. R. Moritz, who had studied in Bonn and Göttingen, as well as Horace T. Brown and Cornelius O'Sullivan, who ran the brewing laboratories at Worthington and Bass, respectively. These professional societies often scheduled their conferences to coincide with world's fairs and trade expositions. The demonstration of American brewing technology at the Chicago Columbian Exposition of 1893 particularly impressed—and at times worried—visiting European brewers.[31]

International students likewise contributed to the exchange of scientific knowledge. British scientists Brown and O'Sullivan, for example, followed their mentor August Wilhelm von Hofmann to the University of Berlin. Many American brewers made pilgrimages to Central Europe to learn the new techniques of lager, although by the end of the century, they generally attended brewing schools in Chicago or New York City. Meanwhile, the return travels of migrant brewers introduced New World techniques to Old World breweries. The VLB became an international center of learning, with more than 100 students each year enrolled in a wide range of beginning and advanced courses. These offerings drew significant numbers of students from the southern German states of Bavaria, Baden, and Württemberg, who numbered 382 out of a sample of 3,777 students attending the school between 1888 and 1913. Two-thirds of the VLB student body came from other parts of Germany, and 20 percent from the rest of Europe, especially the neighboring countries of Sweden and Russia. Small numbers of students traveled even greater distances, 49 from the Americas and 23 from Asia and Africa. The convergence of international students on Berlin reduced the formerly cosmopolitan Weihenstephan to a vocational school for Bavarians, enlivened by the occasional visitor from Scandinavia or the Philippines.[32]

At conferences, schools, and research stations, brewing professionals debated questions such as the use of new brewing materials. The Bavarian decree that beer could be made only with barley, hops, and water, known in the nineteenth century as the *Surrogatsverbot* (ban on substitutes), has become a central tenet of the German brewing industry's identity, but at the time it applied only in the south. By the mid-nineteenth century, brewers across Europe had recognized technical advantages in supplementing malt with raw barley as well as other sources of fermentable sugars. A government committee in the United Kingdom summarized the view that, although the best barley malts might be used alone for some types of beer, "medium or lower qualities of British barley malts are improved by the addition of a moderate proportion of brewing sugars."[33] Robert Wahl attributed the "superiority of American bottled beers, in point of brightness and stability, over those produced some years ago, entirely to the rapidly growing use of maize in American breweries."[34] Brewers in northern Germany and the Austro-Hungarian Empire also used raw barley and adjunct grains, although many remained suspicious of non-traditional ingredients. The ban on grain adjuncts was extended across Germany in 1906 as part of a tax reform intended as much to increase revenues as to improve the quality of beer. The regulations were called the Reinheitsgebot (purity law) for the first time in 1919, when the Free State of Bavaria refused to join the Weimar Republic until the ban on adjunct grains was codified in law.[35]

The biology of the fermentation tank, like the choice of brewing grains, was another focus of scientific inquiry and national pride. Brewers of all nations celebrated Louis Pasteur's *Études sur la bière* (1876), although many rejected pasteurization because they believed it added a disagreeable bready taste to beer. Emil Christian Hansen developed an alternative remedy for contamination in response to an outbreak of spoiled beer in Copenhagen in 1883. Having identified multiple varieties of yeast within each brewery, he isolated the individual strains and propagated them in sterile solutions, thereby creating a pure yeast culture, which he called Carlsberg Number 1. To encourage its widespread adoption, the Danish company initially distributed free samples, although it later earned considerable profits from selling pure yeast. Bavarian brewing scientists quickly embraced the new method, and Hansen's students Wahl and Henius taught it at their Chicago brewing academy. Nevertheless, Max Delbrück considered the system impractical for brewers and called instead for a "natural pure yeast culture," which he "admitted he had borrowed from observations of the practical work in American lager-beer breweries."[36] Hansen's methods were also of little use to British brewers, who relied on the secondary fermentation carried out by multiple strains of yeast to carbonate their ales. G. Harris Morris assigned great importance to the diversity of yeast cultures in defining "the character of English as compared with foreign beers. Foreign beers, as a rule, showed comparatively little distinctive character. There was a great sameness between all low-fermentation beers in any one district."[37]

Even as brewers sought to nationalize beer styles, commodity markets were becoming increasingly globalized. In the case of barley, botanical differences between two- and six-rowed varieties had important consequences for rival brewing methods. British and German brewers traditionally preferred two-rowed barleys, which were high in starch and low in protein; the six-rowed variety, with its greater protein content, was considered better for animal feed. Brewers in the United States, by contrast, employed more six-rowed barleys, whose larger husk provided more enzymatic matter for converting raw and adjunct grains to sugar in the mash tun. By the end of the century, the United Kingdom had come to depend for its food supply on globalized commodity chains, and brewers mixed sugar with six-rowed barley from Egypt and California. American brewers meanwhile improved domestic supplies with high-quality Canadian barley. Even German brewers resorted to cheap, imported, two-rowed barley from the Austro-Hungarian and Russian empires. Scorning American innovations in industrial malting, the Germans coined a term for New World techniques that evoked cowboys of the Wild West: "*Galoppmälzerei.*"[38]

International markets for hops, like those for grain, exhibited distinct flavor profiles that were upended in the second half of the nineteenth century. Many Central European brewers preferred the "bitter, aromatic, herbal"

Bohemian Saaz hops, while ranking those of the Bavarian Spalt, "with their most intense aroma," a close second. Their British counterparts meanwhile prized the "somewhat quince-like aroma" of Golding hops from Kent.[39] Americans planted hops widely in New York State and along the Pacific Coast, but the flavor and aroma from old English cuttings and newly transplanted Bohemian hops were dismissed as "mostly inferior and often bad, according to Continental standards."[40] Although Bavarian hops did not match the prestige of Bohemian varieties, the Nuremberg hop market nevertheless became an international clearing house for the industry, with about thirty major firms, many of them Jewish-owned, and more than 300 other trading houses and commission agents. The international spread of lager brewing, and the widespread insistence on hops from a few favored districts, seemed to offer endless potential growth, but like all commodity markets, boom inevitably turned to bust. A disastrous harvest in 1882 led British brewers to economize on their use of hops, and New World production eventually glutted the market. The adoption of refrigerated storage in the early 1900s freed brewers everywhere from their reliance on the vagaries of the annual crop.[41]

To facilitate communication across national boundaries and between professionals and practitioners, brewers sought to quantify the components of beer through analytical chemistry. Using the methods of Marcellin Berthelot, a longstanding rival of Pasteur, they measured such qualities as the beer's gravity (density compared to pure water), extract (calculated from the degree of fermentation), alcohol content, sugars, proteins, and carbon dioxide. Some researchers insisted on colorimeters for an exact measure of darkness, but few found it worth the effort. Indeed, none of this data really explained the complexity of beer flavors. As a first step to understanding that relationship, Horace Brown and G. Harris Morris cracked open a bottle of Worthington Ale, vintage 1798, and tried to calculate the chemical reactions behind its "extraordinary bouquet, which is exactly like that of aged Madeiras."[42] Although Brown and Morris framed their answer using the later-discredited maltodextrin theory, their work inspired future generations of researchers. Nevertheless, the dangers of quantitative beer analysis had already become apparent in the 1870s, as the publication of data about particular brands raised public concerns about their quality. Angered by a Leipzig laboratory's unfavorable review of Munich beers, Dr. Georg Holzner declared: "Beer analysis, which only serves the purpose of discrediting in a useless and unjustified manner, is not only useless, but causes endless harm."[43] Despite such warnings, scientists continued to publish tables of beer data by city, region, and country, setting exact standards for brewers to follow.[44]

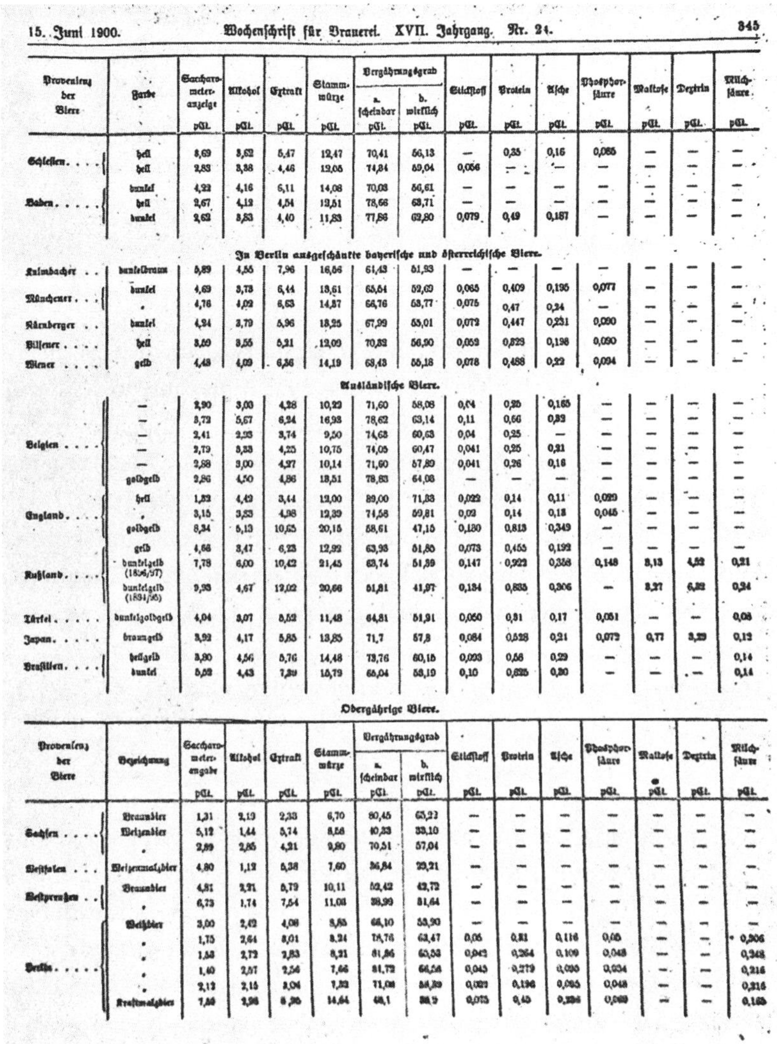

15. Juni 1900. Wochenschrift für Brauerei. XVII. Jahrgang. Nr. 24. 345

Provenienz der Biere	Farbe	Saccharometeranzeige pCt.	Alkohol pCt.	Extrakt pCt.	Stammwürze pCt.	Vergährungsgrad a. scheinbar pCt.	Vergährungsgrad b. wirklich pCt.	Stickstoff pCt.	Protein pCt.	Asche pCt.	Phosphorsäure pCt.	Maltose pCt.	Dextrin pCt.	Milchsäure pCt.
Schlesien	hell	3,69	3,62	5,47	12,47	70,41	56,13	—	0,35	0,16	0,085	—	—	—
	hell	2,83	3,88	4,46	12,06	74,84	59,04	0,056	—	—	—	—	—	—
Baden	dunkel	4,22	4,16	6,11	14,08	70,03	56,61	—	—	—	—	—	—	—
	hell	2,67	4,12	4,54	13,51	78,66	63,71	—	—	—	—	—	—	—
	dunkel	2,62	3,83	4,40	11,83	77,86	62,80	0,079	0,49	0,187	—	—	—	—
In Berlin ausgeschänkte bayerische und österreichische Biere.														
Kulmbacher	dunkelbraun	5,89	4,55	7,96	16,56	61,43	51,93	—	—	—	—	—	—	—
Münchener	dunkel	4,69	3,73	6,44	13,61	65,54	52,69	0,065	0,409	0,195	0,077	—	—	—
	"	4,76	4,02	6,63	14,87	66,76	53,77	0,075	0,47	0,24	—	—	—	—
Nürnberger	dunkel	4,24	3,79	5,96	13,25	67,99	55,01	0,072	0,447	0,231	0,090	—	—	—
Pilsener	hell	3,60	3,55	5,21	12,09	70,82	56,90	0,053	0,323	0,198	0,090	—	—	—
Wiener	gelb	4,48	4,09	6,36	14,19	68,43	55,18	0,078	0,488	0,22	0,094	—	—	—
Ausländische Biere.														
Belgien	—	2,90	3,00	4,28	10,22	71,60	58,08	0,04	0,25	0,165	—	—	—	—
	—	3,72	5,67	6,24	16,93	78,62	63,14	0,11	0,66	0,32	—	—	—	—
	—	2,41	2,93	3,74	9,50	74,63	60,63	0,04	0,25	—	—	—	—	—
	—	2,79	3,33	4,25	10,75	74,05	60,47	0,041	0,25	0,21	—	—	—	—
	—	2,88	3,00	4,27	10,14	71,60	57,89	0,041	0,26	0,16	—	—	—	—
	goldgelb	2,86	4,50	4,86	13,51	78,83	64,08	—	—	—	—	—	—	—
England	hell	1,32	4,42	3,44	12,00	89,00	71,33	0,022	0,14	0,11	0,029	—	—	—
	"	3,15	3,83	4,98	12,39	74,58	59,81	0,02	0,14	0,13	0,045	—	—	—
	goldgelb	8,34	5,13	10,65	20,15	58,61	47,15	0,130	0,813	0,349	—	—	—	—
Rußland	gelb	4,66	3,47	6,23	12,92	63,93	51,80	0,073	0,455	0,192	—	—	—	—
	dunkelgelb (1896/97)	7,78	6,00	10,42	21,45	63,74	51,39	0,147	0,922	0,358	0,148	3,13	4,52	0,21
	dunkelgelb (1894/95)	9,93	4,67	12,02	20,66	51,81	41,97	0,134	0,835	0,306	—	3,27	6,82	0,24
Türkei	dunkelgoldgelb	4,04	3,07	5,52	11,48	64,81	51,91	0,050	0,31	0,17	0,051	—	—	0,08
Japan	braungelb	3,92	4,17	5,85	13,85	71,7	57,8	0,084	0,528	0,21	0,072	0,77	3,29	0,12
Brasilien	hellgelb	3,90	4,56	5,76	14,48	73,76	60,15	0,093	0,56	0,29	—	—	—	0,14
	dunkel	5,52	4,43	7,29	15,79	65,04	53,19	0,10	0,625	0,30	—	—	—	0,14

Obergährige Biere.

Provenienz der Biere	Bezeichnung	Saccharometerangabe pCt.	Alkohol pCt.	Extrakt pCt.	Stammwürze pCt.	Vergährungsgrad a. scheinbar pCt.	Vergährungsgrad b. wirklich pCt.	Stickstoff pCt.	Protein pCt.	Asche pCt.	Phosphorsäure pCt.	Maltose pCt.	Dextrin pCt.	Milchsäure pCt.
Sachsen	Braunbier	1,31	2,19	2,33	6,70	80,45	65,23	—	—	—	—	—	—	—
	Weizenbier	5,12	1,44	5,74	8,56	40,33	33,10	—	—	—	—	—	—	—
	"	2,89	2,85	4,21	9,80	70,51	57,04	—	—	—	—	—	—	—
Westfalen	Weizenmalzbier	4,80	1,12	5,38	7,60	36,84	29,21	—	—	—	—	—	—	—
Westpreußen	Braunbier	4,81	2,71	5,79	10,11	52,42	42,72	—	—	—	—	—	—	—
	"	6,73	1,74	7,54	11,08	38,99	31,64	—	—	—	—	—	—	—
Berlin	Weißbier	3,00	2,42	4,08	8,85	66,10	53,90	—	—	—	—	—	—	—
	"	1,75	2,64	3,01	8,24	78,76	63,47	0,05	0,31	0,116	0,05	—	—	0,306
	"	1,53	2,72	2,83	8,21	81,86	65,53	0,042	0,264	0,109	0,048	—	—	0,348
	"	1,40	2,57	2,56	7,66	81,72	66,56	0,045	0,279	0,095	0,034	—	—	0,216
	"	2,12	2,15	3,04	7,32	71,08	58,39	0,032	0,196	0,085	0,048	—	—	0,216
	Kraftmalzbier	7,80	2,98	8,95	14,64	48,1	38,5	0,075	0,45	0,236	0,060	—	—	0,165

FIGURE 3.3 Chart of beer (analyses by style) for 1899, *Wochenschrift für Brauerei*, June 15, 1900. Courtesy of Bayerische Staatsbibliothek, Munich, Germany.

Reliance on scientific methods had widespread social consequences beyond industrial efficiency. Professionalization provided a measure of status in opposition to supposedly backward traditional brewers. The exclusion of women from technical education contributed further to their marginalization in the industry, although the devastating loss of young men in World War I briefly reversed this trend and drew women back into the brewhouse. As armies mobilized in the fall of 1914, Christel Goslich, the daughter of

Professor Walter Goslich, became the first woman to complete courses at the VLB, and in 1919, Elise Auer, another brewer's daughter, studied brewery accounting at Weihenstephan. Finally, the proudly national techniques of the brewhouse translated into sales of industrial machinery and raw materials. World's fairs and brewing journals publicized the latest equipment from Maschinenfabrik Germania of Chemnitz, refrigerators from the Société du Froid Industriel of Paris, and brewing architecture from Oscar Beyer of Chicago. Meanwhile, brewers debated whether German or American hops could be used to make a proper Pilsner.[45]

Even as technological innovation and commodity chains forged an international beer industry on the eve of World War I, brewing professionals insisted on distinctive national styles. For the British, the national character of ale arose from the diversity of local tastes, in opposition to the bland uniformity of Continental European lagers. Brewers in the United States promised to make beer widely available through the progress of giant firms rather than local pubs. The German national beer identity combined pride in the advance of brewing science with a rejection of perceived American excesses. The codification of beer styles through analytical chemistry further distanced lager beer from its Bavarian origins, as did trends in marketing beer.

Marketing Lager

Beer drinking cultures, like industrial production methods, changed radically in the nineteenth century. Although porter had been a favorite of London workers since the eighteenth century, an estimated 20 percent of British beer was still homebrewed as late as 1850. Across continental Europe and North America, shopkeepers and factory workers embraced the sparkling, clean taste of lager beer as a privilege of modern life, alongside white bread and sugar, refrigerated meat, and other foods made available by new technologies and expanding empires. Nevertheless, capitalist modernity also inspired a romantic nostalgia, which brewers satisfied by creating bucolic beer gardens and glittering beer palaces. Even in these spaces, commerce beckoned through the brand names on bottle labels and beer coasters. Thus, nineteenth-century marketing innovations complemented new production methods in making beer a modern commodity.[46]

Brewing journals cited growing consumption statistics as an indicator of the advance of civilization. By 1900, German beer drinking had risen to 134 liters of beer per capita, with the working classes having tripled their consumption over the nineteenth century. British intake grew more slowly, albeit

FIGURE 3.4 World War I-era manpower shortages opened spaces for women to work in breweries. A worker returning empty beer bottles to the Hoschschul Brauerei, a commercial brewery attached to the Berlin Versuchs- und Lehranstalt für Brauerei, 1916. "Mit Vollem Kasten" eine arbeiterin in einer Berliner Brauerei." Bild 183-R28458. Courtesy of Bundesarchiv, Koblenz, Germany.

from higher levels, and stood at 143 liters annually at the turn of the century. Belgians remained the world champion beer drinkers, downing more than 200 liters per capita. The most dramatic changes took place in nontraditional beer drinking lands. Americans drank just 5 liters of beer per capita in 1840, on the eve of the lager revolution, compared to 60 liters in 1900. Beer was also more widely distributed across the United States; in 1875 just over 100,000 hectoliters of beer were sold in the former Confederacy, but in 1902 southerners purchased 19 million hectoliters. Per capita beer consumption rose steadily in the wine republic of France, from 21 to 28 liters per capita, and more slowly in the vodka empire of Russia, from 3 to 4 liters over the last fifteen years of the century. Price was still an important factor in consumer choices. Italian beer consumption sank when the government imposed a heavy tax in 1892. Overall, the world's production of beer increased an estimated 45 percent from 1885 to 1900.[47]

Brewers sought to dignify their product with lavish spaces for upper- and middle-class drinkers, especially in Munich, where traditional Bavarian beer culture came to exemplify the spirit of Romanticism.[48] An 1890 illustration in *Schorers Familienblatt* (Schorer's Family Paper) portrayed the respectable nature of Munich beer halls. In one corner, artist P. F. Messerschmitt placed the ritual beer stein, newspaper, and pipe of the *Stammtisch* (reserved table). Regulars had started keeping their personal mugs at the beer hall, and the artist also included tiny, knitted figures of a priest and a soldier that served to identify them. A scene from the Hofbräuhaus included a customer searching a cabinet for his mug, while a band struck up a tune on the mezzanine of Löwenbräu's great hall. Waitresses in long black dresses and white aprons served their smartly attired clientele. Beer culture varied across regions, in the choice of drinking mugs as well as beer styles. Bavarian traditionalists clung to their elaborately lidded ceramic tankards, while elsewhere people drank from glassware such as the squat Vienna Kindl, the tall, thin Potsdamer Stange, and the inward-sloping Pilsner Seidl.[49]

The Wirtshaus or tavern in working-class neighborhoods similarly offered long tables for regulars to gather with friends, if not the same fine veneers. These spaces encouraged sociability outside of the workplace and provided meals for single men as well. Tavern keepers hosted the meetings of sports, music, and fraternal societies, with the expectation that members drank at least one round. Union organizers and socialist politicians also frequented bars to meet their constituents. Yet as Heinrich Zille's drawings of Berlin taverns show, these were not entirely masculine spaces, and women and children at times shared in the socializing. Workers also drank on the job, carrying venerable craft traditions into the modern factory. Some crews sent apprentices out for growlers of beer to share on break, while other laborers tucked bottles with resealable corks into their pockets for refreshment on the job. Although workers looked down on habitual drunkenness, they expected social drinking and tolerated the occasional binge. As unions secured better pay packages, large breweries began to invest in improvements for taverns in working-class neighborhoods, making them more attractive spaces for leisure and entertainment.[50]

Inventing Pilsner

FIGURE 3.5 Heinrich Zille's drawings portrayed the boisterous, gender-mixed sociability of Berlin's working-class taverns around the turn of the century. *In der Kaschemme*, 1910. My thanks to Mareen Heying. Wikimedia Commons.

Beer gardens, unlike the more segregated taverns and beer halls, offered public spaces for all, men and women, bourgeois and proletarian. Since medieval times, townspeople had ventured out to villages and monasteries to drink tax-free beer. Beginning in the eighteenth century, Munich brewers brought the countryside into the city, selling beer beneath the chestnut trees that shaded their lager cellars. Beer gardens survived even after mechanical refrigeration replaced caverns, if only as a tree-lined corner on the grounds of a sprawling factory. In some places, patrons were entertained by brass bands and watching laborers wheel beer carts to nearby railroad sidings. A Sunday afternoon visitor to the enormous Tivoli beer garden in suburban Berlin observed everyone "from the government official and well-to-do merchant down to the shopman and servant girl."[51]

Beer halls and gardens became an international phenomenon in the second half of the nineteenth century. Immigrants to the United States recreated both elaborate, brewery-sponsored, and gender-mixed beer palaces and gardens as well as masculine, working-class taverns. In Milwaukee, Schlitz Park attracted visitors with a bandstand, bowling alleys, restaurant, and lookout tower, while Pabst asserted its national preeminence with a theater and restaurant at Columbus Circle and a grand hotel on the future site of Times Square in New York City. Ordinary saloons numbered almost 300,000 by 1900 and attracted workers with free lunches and nickel beers. In the United Kingdom, the gender and class mixing of eighteenth-century inns gave way to strictly masculine, working-class pubs by the mid-nineteenth century. Respectable women were still excluded from public drinking even as rising incomes encouraged late-Victorian brewers to renovate centrally located pubs in a garish, glittering fashion considered appropriate for the working classes, as distinct from the tasteful decor of the gentleman's club. Lavish displays also spread across the channel to Parisian cabarets, the most famous of which was portrayed in Édouard Manet's 1882 masterpiece, *Un Bar aux Folies-Bergère*. The great mirror behind the barmaid reflected spectacular entertainments and diverse clients, "the calico sitting at the table next to the *hommes d'affaires*, taking care not to spill beer on his best suit or miss the words of Thérésa's latest song."[52]

New forms of print advertisement also helped to place beer in the public view. Bass, the great Burton-on-Trent ale brewery, designed its red triangle logo in the 1850s and, after two decades of rampant forgery, registered it under the Trademark Act of 1875. The ubiquitous label anchored both ends of the bar in Manet's *Folies-Bergère*. Trademarks became common among German brewers in the 1880s, and brewing journals reported the patent office's latest filings. A German printer also had the idea of reproducing his customer's labels on absorbent, pressed paper, thereby inaugurating the *Bierdeckel* (coaster). Alongside fancy labels, brewers conveyed luxury with flourishes such as champagne-style bottles and, in the case of Pabst, a blue ribbon around its Select-brand bottles, starting in 1882. Lithography, another German printing invention, allowed the mass production of advertising posters for decorating beer halls and taverns. By the 1880s, Germany also pioneered the picture postcard, and brewery and beer garden scenes over the "*Gruss aus*" (greetings from) caption were distributed widely through the mail. The promotional literature of labels and postcards often combined nostalgic pastoralism with industrial progress; for example, pristine alpine vistas evoked the purity of ingredients, while factory smokestacks demonstrated the modernity of production. Brewers also used patriotism and sex to sell beer from an early date. Anheuser Busch placed images of "Washington Crossing the Delaware" and "Custer's Last Fight" in saloons across the United States.

FIGURE 3.6 Édouard Manet's *A Bar at the Folies-Bergère* (1882) portrays the mixed society in a renowned Parisian cabaret, where wealthy bohemians rubbed shoulders with plebeian customers, even as bottles of champagne and cognac sat on the bar alongside Bass Ale, with its distinctive red triangle trademark. The Courtauld Institute of Art, London. Smith Archive / Alamy Stock Photo.

Classical Greek mythology added a fig leaf of respectability to nude scenes such as "Andromache at the Bath." Beginning in the 1890s, the matronly skirts of beerhall servers were replaced by folkloric *Dirndls* (peasant dresses), at least in Munich beer advertisements.[53]

Brewers also promoted their brands to the many attendees drawn to world's fairs. Eighteen-year-old Anton Dreher, Jr., showed himself a worthy heir to the Viennese brewing dynasty through his charismatic performance at the 1867 Universal Exposition in Paris, where he handed out miniature glasses of beer at a Châtelet pavilion. A German observer later recalled: "A 'bock,' as the Parisians called such a beer glass, became a beloved and overwhelming fashion in Paris."[54] Brewers from the Americas returned to the old country to learn about new technology, but they often felt discriminated against by contest judges. The *Tageszeitung für Brauerei* (Brewers' Daily Newspaper) complained about the proliferation of "medals awarded, or even just purchased, to deceive the public about the value of goods."[55] One such practice occurred at the 1893 Chicago Columbian Exposition, when Pabst used a controversial reading of the judges' rankings to declare victory over Anheuser Busch. The Milwaukee brewer awarded itself a "Blue Ribbon," thereby transforming a decade-old marketing gimmick into a seemingly official validation.[56]

Physical infrastructure and business networks were also essential for marketing beer. Sedlmayr purposely located his factory near the newly built Munich train station, while the Andwanters constructed theirs on the waterfront to ship beer up the long Chilean coast. Dreher pioneered ice-chilled railroad cars to deliver his Viennese beer to Paris in the summer of 1867, and Busch was an early adopter of pasteurization to be able to serve markets in the American South. Brewers from all lands employed local agents to market and at times bottle their beers. Arrangements with such agents varied, from company-owned stores operating in large markets to independent commission agents handling more occasional sales. Branch warehouse managers in the United States had considerable agency to sign up taverns, oversee deliveries, return empties, and maintain customer relations.[57]

The first major beer-marketing battleground was Germany, a patchwork of states and tariff regulations before unification. Already by midcentury, the Prussian and German Custom Union (*Zollverein*) imported large quantities of Bavarian beer, and in 1872, the first year for which national statistics are available, the southern kingdom led the empire, brewing 10 million hectoliters. Northern Germans also consumed smaller amounts of Burton ale and London porter. The removal of tariffs on beer from the Austro-Hungarian Empire in 1865 unleashed a flood of Bohemian imports. Spurred by this competition, northern German brewers quickly mastered the art of bottom fermentation, and in the last two decades of the century, doubled their production to 32 million hectoliters. Bavaria continued to export a million hectoliters a year, mostly to other German states, alongside 400,000 hectoliters from brewers in Habsburg lands. Nevertheless, after decades of growing international trade, German brewing was once again becoming a local business.[58]

A nineteenth-century version of the trickle trade that carried hopped beer across early modern Europe channeled lager to countries that were not traditionally consumers of beer. In France and other wine-drinking countries, as a vine-eating louse called phylloxera devastated the industry from the 1860s, workers substituted beer and distilled spirits such as absinthe. The brewing industries of Lille, Paris, Nancy, and even Marseilles surged after the loss of France's traditional beer region of Alsace-Lorraine during the Franco-Prussian War. In the mid-1880s, many Frenchmen declared the substitution of domestically brewed beers for imported German brands to be a patriotic duty. By contrast, German migrants drove the expansion of the Russian beer industry, replacing the former predominance of English ales and dark native beers with Munich and Pilsner-style lagers. Pasteurized beer shipped from Moscow and St. Petersburg competed for the Siberian trade with German brewers who settled in Irkutsk and Blagoveshchensk. Beer also trickled through the Balkans, courtesy of Hungarian brewers, who learned their trade in Austria, and of Serbians, who exported it to Macedonia and Salonica.[59]

Industrial modernity transformed the beer-drinking cultures of Europe and North America, even though marketing was often inspired by rural nostalgia. Despite the efforts of Central European brewers to advertise the high quality of their products, over the long run consumers were generally unwilling to pay more for imported goods when they could buy a similar product brewed locally. In Amsterdam, for example, Bavarian beer had cost four cents more per liter than domestic beers in the 1880s but a decade later the difference had fallen to only one cent. Likewise in the United States, although imported Bohemian beer sold for double the price of local beers about 1880, the premium also declined over time. Brewers and consumers alike thus questioned the meaning and value of genuine beers from cities such as Munich and Pilsen.[60]

A Golden Age?

Parisians flocked to drink a bock with the dapper young Anton Dreher at the Universal Exposition of 1867, but the popularity of his amber Vienna lager was already being challenged by its golden Bohemian rival. Even before the fair opened in Paris, Austrian official J. John observed: "In the struggle between light and brown beer, it appears that the light is gaining more followers day by day."[61] Just six years later, when the Austrian capital hosted its own World's Fair, the *Bayerische Bierbrauer* reported that Pilsner was "preferred to the famous Viennese beers, even in Vienna."[62] But Pilsner spread not only as a commodity in trade but also as a recipe made by brewers far beyond its Bohemian home town. As it traveled, the meanings of the style continued to change, in part because improved technology and consumer preferences drove a convergence of other beers toward the light, clear qualities of Pilsner. Brewers in Pilsen responded to this competition by seeking legal protection for their trade name, but they faced an uphill battle defending their claims in distant courts.

Despite brewing professionals' attempts to quantify beer through analytical chemistry, styles remained loose categories that varied widely. Nineteenth-century Germans recognized an entire taxonomy of beer, ranging from the most general *Bier-typus* (bottom- or top-fermentation, in English, lager or ale), through the mid-level *Bier-arten* (regional styles such as Bavarian, Bohemian, and Vienna), down to the most specific *Bier-sorten* (particular brands such as Spaten and Dreher as well as local variants like Märzenbier and Bockbier). These categories had accumulated through the centuries, and Bavarians still distinguished between summer and winter beers even after the advent of refrigeration. The arrival of new styles compounded the confusion in regions such as Saxony, where Lagerbier became conflated with Doppelbier, which meant that a top-fermented, double beer was considered a lager. When Saxon tax officials sought to clarify the situation in 1862, they categorized light Bohemian beers as Doppelbier, while dark Bavarians and English porters were declared Lagerbier.[63] Beer names also changed with the whims of fashion, as a journalist discovered when investigating the sudden disappearance of bock beers in Belgium around 1930. "The public was tired of the word 'bock' and so brewers had no alternative: find a new name for the blonde beer," a brewmaster explained. "But they're still 'bock.'"[64]

The Paris Exposition of 1867 illustrated how shifting fashions drove international competition among brewers. Dreher's performance inspired a surge of Austrian beer exports to France from a token 500 hectoliters the previous year to 16,000 the following year. But the market proved short lived, according to Dr. Carl Rach, a Weihenstephan alumnus working in the United States: "Bavarian brewers noticed the large consumption of the Vienna beer and made great exertions to compete with it, pushing their beers to the front and a large export business was the result."[65] The campaign had received inspiration from an ironic source, the Austrian official John, who advised brewers "not to throw ourselves exclusively into a single type of beer, but rather we must study the needs and tastes of other countries and direct our production accordingly."[66] Bavarians learned the lesson, and as the public taste for beers grew progressively lighter, they brewed first Vienna and later Pilsner-style lagers, at least for export.[67]

Mass-market Pilsner also spread across northern Germany in the final decades of the nineteenth century. Bismarck may have encouraged the Prussian fashion for Bavarian beer as a ploy to smooth the southern kingdom's entry into the German Empire, and by 1882 it had become "the most beloved drink in all the elegant beer restaurants."[68] But even as Junker aristocrats quaffed dark beers, Berlin's working classes were seeking out the light, making the Böhmisches Brauhaus (Bohemian Brewery) the capital's leading producer. Responding to this competition, many northern German brewers took the easy route of labeling their products "Pilsner." Others pursued the more difficult task of carving a regional identity for themselves between the Bavarian and Bohemian giants. One problem was that nobody within the vast area from Bremen and Hamburg to Berlin and Danzig really identified primarily as northern German. When pressed to name such a beer, authors often pointed to the North Rhine-Westfalia town of Dortmund, whose beers were described by one expert as a "very light, well-lagered, medium-hopped, alcohol-rich, and somewhat highly attenuated beer . . . that in almost all places at home and abroad is next as a beer style (*Charakter-Bier*) after Munich and Pilsner."[69] Nor did Pilsner brewers sit idly by while others encroached on their market. John had astutely predicted that Bohemian beers would sell better in Saxony and Prussia with a slightly stronger roast, and as the competition intensified around the end of the century, the brewers of Pilsen adjusted their recipe accordingly.[70]

To dispel the mystique around Pilsner, rival brewers studied the style carefully to match or surpass its qualities. Beer analyses had been available since the 1870s, but quantification failed to capture the beer's subtle aromas. VLB researcher Wilhelm Windisch ventured to describe it as "a sum of hop bitterness, hops and herbal spelt, yeast itself and yeast residuals, and a tiny little bit of pitch."[71] Julius Liebmann observed that the Pilsner brewery's practice of storing beer in small casks and re-pitching them for every use could never be adopted in the United States because the "flavor and odor of pitch in the beer is generally abhorrent to the taste of our consumers." He also emphasized that brewers "used not only the best obtainable Saaz hops, but plenty of them" and described the city of Pilsen "as steeped in hops and redolent of hop aroma." Alexander Bain, having worked there for a time, recalled that the beer was "strong in narcotic principles"—hops being related to cannabis.[72] While Americans drew allusions to drugs, some in Berlin equated competition with Pilsner as a nationalist struggle. One author denounced the Citizens' Brewery managers as "the most dangerous agitators" against ethnic Germans in Bohemia.[73] Delbrück, in writing the history of lager brewing, ignored archival references to fifteenth-century Bohemians and attributed the invention of bottom fermentation to eighteenth-century Bavarian monk Benno Scharl. Meanwhile, Windisch concluded that only the prejudice of an unthinking public could allow "Pilsner brewers to produce a weak beer, excessively foamy, unfiltered, unclear, sometimes quite cloudy, and yet when served it is declared the best beer in the world."[74]

Brewers made such ardent nationalist claims at a moment when the beers themselves were converging in character due to international advances of science and industry, a trend debated by brewers themselves around the turn of the century. When Carl Rach decried that brewers were foisting off Pilsner on an unsuspecting public and called for a return to dark Munich lagers, his colleague Francis Wyatt rejected the claim that American consumers were duped into drinking pale lager.[75] A similar pattern emerged in the United Kingdom, with the popularity of so-called running ales that matched the qualities of lager. Alfred C. Chapman observed: "What is demanded at the present time (more particularly in large towns) is a light, brilliant beer, not too heavily hopped, but highly charged with carbonic acid gas—a stimulating, thirst quenching beverage, devoid of marked narcotic properties, which can be drunk freely in hot weather."[76] Like Rach, W. L. Hiepe wondered if this change was driven by popular tastes or nefarious capitalists. "It does not seem clear what is the exact course of events, viz., whether a taste for lighter beers has developed in the public, compelling the brewers to follow it, or whether the brewers began to brew a lighter beer and, as it were, educated the public." Ultimately, the British brewing scientist reached a very different conclusion from the Bavarian. "I believe that both processes went on at the same time, and that the taste of the public has received an impulse in the direction of lighter beers by increased facilities of travelling and the increased importation of Continental beers of the Lager type."[77]

Lager beers also influenced the production of top-fermented ales in the United States and Germany. In New England, the use of ice and filters made it possible to produce "cold sparkling ales," like British running ales, which slowed the spread of lager through the region. California's unique "steam beer" used lager yeast without the chilled lager; the mild San Francisco Bay Area temperatures produced an effervescent beer described by one German traveler as "somewhat different from lagers but seemingly the same."[78] Many small German brewers likewise sought to meet their customers' growing expectation for lager without the expense of large cellars or refrigeration. In answering one reader's question, the VLB's *Wochenschrift für Brauerei* (Brewers' Weekly) explained: "Cold temperatures can achieve a similar taste to Bavarian beer when using top fermentation."[79] Brewers often deliberately switched back and forth between bottom and top fermentation, as they had inadvertently during the early modern era. In Cologne and Dusseldorf, lager-like ales evolved into distinctive styles, known respectively as *Kölsch* and *Altbier*. As late as 1880, top fermentation still accounted for as much as half of beer production across large parts of northern Germany, from the Rhineland through

Saxony, and large parts of Prussia. By 1910, the continued spread of lager had reduced ales to about a quarter of the production in Brandenburg, Posen, and East Prussia; only in Oldenburg did it remain over half.[80]

Nevertheless, exceptions remained to the convergence of beers around the Pilsner style. Arthur Guinness & Co. built the world's largest brewery, surpassing even the Midwestern American shipping brewers, by selling Dublin stout throughout the British Empire and its former settler colonies. In Belgium, spontaneous-fermenting lambics enjoyed a *fin de siècle* heyday, while the country's first lager factories struggled to build markets. Likewise in Germany, brewers continued to produce styles from the early modern era such as Broihan, Mumme, and Gose, a salty, sour beer made in the Leipzig suburb of Döllnitz. One particular sour wheat beer, Berliner Weisse, enjoyed a revival in the late nineteenth century. With technical support from researchers at the

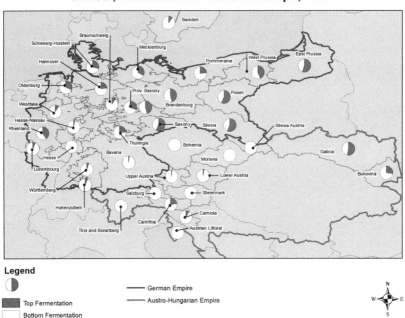

FIGURE 3.7 Southern Germany, Bohemia, and Austria had already made the transition to lager beer by the 1880s, but top-fermenting beers remained popular for decades thereafter in Prussia, the Rhineland, and parts of the Austro-Hungarian Empire. Source: "Der Biererzeugung und der Bierbesteurung während des Etatsjahres 1881/82 (Beer Production and Beer Taxation during the Fiscal Year 1881–82)," *ABHZ* 18, no. 22 (December 14, 1882): 924. Drawn by William Sturm.

VLB, the historic Heinrich Bolle factory expanded production of it to an industrial scale, even as new corporate breweries were founded by entrepreneurs like Carl Landré. Berliner Weisse was traditionally drunk from wide bowl glasses, straight or flavored with a red or green *Schuss* (shot) of raspberry or Waldmeister (woodruff) syrup. Wilhelmine court painter Adolph Menzel included Berliner Weisse in his 1878 masterpiece *Das Ballsouper* (Dinner at the Ball), which chronicled a gala party at the Berlin Stadtschloss (City Palace). A pair of old generals in the bottom left corner nursed the distinctive bowls, one a *kühle Blonde* (cool blond), the other red, while the rest of the smartly dressed crowd drank champagne. To highlight still further the disdain for Berliner Weisse among the capital's haute bourgeoisie, a pair of glasses, *mit Schuss*, red and green, sat discarded on a mantle to the right.[81]

Behind the pleasures of consumer society lay structural changes that threatened this golden age for many brewers. Mergers and bankruptcies consolidated the industry across Europe and the Americas. Independent

FIGURE 3.8 In Adolph Menzel's *Dinner at the Ball* (1878), two aging Prussian generals stand out in the bottom left corner with the distinctive bowl glasses of Berliner Weisse, amid a sea of haute bourgeois champagne flutes. Two other beer glasses sit discarded on a mantel under the mirror to the right. Alte Nationalgalerie, Staatliche Museen zu Berlin, Germany. Google Arts and Culture.

publican brewers still numbered 18,000 in the United Kingdom in 1880, but declined drastically, and by the end of the century, 75 percent of pubs had been tied to major breweries. Flush with profits, fifty of these industrialists sat in the House of Commons in the 1880s, plus four in the House of Lords. British investors also drove consolidation in lager breweries overseas through the purchase of brewing syndicates in numerous cities. The largest shipping brewers in the Midwest maintained their independence, each one producing as much as many syndicates; Pabst was the first to surpass the million-barrel landmark by 1893. The Chilean Compañía Cervecerías Unidas (United Brewing Company), founded in 1891 under an earlier name, had absorbed all but two competitors each in Valparaiso and Santiago by 1914. In Germany, thousands of small breweries closed in the final decades of the century, while the *Wochenschrift für Brauerei* pleaded simply: "No new corporate breweries!"[82]

Brewery owners were not alone in feeling the squeeze. Mechanization displaced many workers, while those who remained on the job feared steam kettle explosions and other industrial accidents. Laborers particularly resented the loss of workplace independence, and many migrated in the hopes of founding their own businesses, thereby helping spread beer around the world. Corporate consolidation also continued the longstanding trend of excluding women from brewery management. Nineteenth-century businesswomen such as Therese Wagner, Walburga (Wally) Hierl, Margaretha Zapf, and Marie Wolf owned prominent breweries in Munich, Schwabach, and Prague through the mid-nineteenth century, but such female leadership increasingly disappeared with corporate takeovers.[83]

The legal codification of beer styles meant that even the leading brewers in Pilsen and Munich were powerless to prevent distant rivals from using their place names. In 1896, responding to a growing number of requests for trademarks with the phrase "Pilsener Bier," the Berlin patent office essentially inverted the taxonomy of German beer names, declaring "Pilsner" to be a generic beer type rather than a specific geographic designation. When challenged, the trademarks were upheld in Hamburg commercial courts in what the *Böhmische Bierbrauer* (Bohemian Brewer) described as a "remarkable ruling" that "genuine Pilsener" need not actually come from the town of Pilsen.[84] The Citizens' Brewery promptly registered the trademark for Pilsner Urquell (from the source) and continued to file suits to stop the flood of ersatz beers. A stalemate of sorts emerged around 1911 over a pair of cases involving Englehardt Pilsener from Berlin and the Radeberger Pilsener of Leipzig. The label was required to indicate "Bier nach Pilsener Art" (beer in the style of

Pilsener) along with the location of brewing, but this was cold comfort for the citizens of Pilsen.[85]

The turn of the twentieth century was arguably a golden age for beer drinkers, as ever greater supplies of beer became available. Moreover, that beer increasingly followed the characteristics of Pilsner. Even in Munich, brewers began producing a *helles* (light) lager for domestic consumption in the 1890s, and it had largely displaced dunkel by the 1920s. But the brewing landscape became increasingly uneven, although surviving small brewers continued to compete successfully for local markets with continental giants. Among the large brewers, Austrians fared the worst, and Vienna lager had largely disappeared as a distinct style by the end of the century. Even the giants of Pilsen faced a difficult future without the right to protect their trade name.[86]

"That mysterious legend woven around the *old Pilsner beer*," declared Karl Dubský in 1899, "was nothing more than the exemplary purity of taste that put it at the forefront of all other beers."[87] Seen in the context of nineteenth-century industrial food production, which promised purity above all, the invention of Pilsner was neither the sudden inspiration of the brewer Groll nor the fortuitous combination of Bohemian hops, malt, and water, but rather an ongoing process of industrial innovation responding to technological change and consumer taste. Gabriel Sedlmayr and Anton Dreher likewise crafted their distinctive Munich and Vienna lagers through a conscious strategy of market segmentation within emerging pan-European markets. Scientific brewing made it possible to standardize those styles, and consumers in turn came to expect such predictability when they purchased beer.[88] Capitalist interests even determined the very meaning of beer styles. Whereas aristocratic French winemakers lobbied successfully for legal protection of regional designations in Bordeaux and Champagne, the imperial government in Berlin and commercial courts in Hamburg ignored the pleas of Bavarian and Bohemian brewers, granting trademarks to northern German industrialists for beers labeled "Munich" and "Pilsner."

The social consequences of industrial modernity also shaped the taste preferences for light, clear, mild, and fizzy Pilsner beers, which in turn transformed the meanings of beer. Low alcohol content made it easier for industrial workers to quench their thirst without risking accidents, while also deflecting the ire of the growing international temperance movement. Well-fed urban consumers no longer needed the calories of the full-bodied Munich lagers and London porters that had nourished them through the lean years before midcentury. Instead, they came to prefer a sparkling, light beverage that did not slow them down in sports, dancing, and other leisure activities. Finally, mild flavor and clear appearance exemplified the hygienic promise of nineteenth-century food processing. To put it another way, the pungent smell and taste of wild yeast and strong hops that are prized today as authentic and natural were perceived at the time as distasteful and potentially hazardous defects resulting from antiquated brewing methods. All of these trends culminated in the transformation of beer from a traditional source of sustenance to a modern form of entertainment.[89]

Even while celebrating "our modern beer," Bohemian brewmaster Dubský was enough of a modernist to recognize that modernity lay not in a particular style but rather in the choice among numerous options. "Where would our brewing industry be today, if it had only *one* taste to satisfy; so every taste finds its agreeable beer and every beer its admirer—the Pilsner like the Munich, the Culmbacher like the Gose."[90] The desire to express individual identity and social distinction in consumer choices sat uneasily at the heart of industrial capitalism with the soul-crushing standardization of factory labor and mass production. Consumers were not limited to a single taste and could tailor their beer styles to the moment, a light Pilsner for a carefree afternoon with friends or a sour Gose for a more sophisticated occasion. The choice of an exotic beer from a distant land likewise offered the opportunity to demonstrate social status. Dr. Max Wallerstein spoke for many brewers when he lamented the snobs who "like genuine imported beer, and prefer to drink beer which may be cloudy and spoiled."[91]

Nineteenth-century capitalist modernity created a beer world that we still inhabit, anchored in an imaginary geography of golden Pilsners and dark Munich lagers. But at the same time, brewing styles were a very real product of biology and technology, as well as global commodity chains and migration networks. Founded in capitalist and nationalist competition, these beer styles were carried even more widely during the age of empire.

4

Imperial Hops

JUANA CATARINA ROMERO spared no expense when the Archbishop of Oaxaca, Eulogio Gillow, visited her town of Tehuantepec, Mexico, around 1910. She served the prelate a lavish dinner of meat and seafood with European wine and "abundant beer imported from Saint Louis."[1] Located on the isthmus connecting central Mexico and the Yucatán peninsula, Tehuantepec was renowned as a Zapotec matriarchy, whose proud women wore embroidered silk skirts and *huipiles* (bodices), gold coins strung together as necklaces, and face-framing headdresses of pleated muslin. Juana Cata, as she was known to friends, had worn this indigenous dress as a young, illiterate merchant in the 1860s, driving mule trains of indigo and cacao up the mountain trails to Oaxaca City. When she received the archbishop, however, she dressed in a matronly Victorian gown, perhaps purchased while traveling on business to London or New York City. Although Tehuantepec may have appeared remote and exotic to intellectuals in Mexico City, the railroad across the isthmus formed a vital link for global commerce. In her store near the train station, Juana Cata sold huipiles made to order in Manchester and refreshed herself from the tropical heat with cold beers from St. Louis. She thereby connected her community with global capitalism and consumerism. But beer's global spread owed as much to its refreshing taste as to the merchants who transported it.

Among indigenous communities of postcolonial nations and in newly colonized societies of Africa and Asia, beer manifested the spread of European empires in the nineteenth and early twentieth centuries. To take just one example, British Lieutenant Ralph Patteson Cobbold, stationed near the Hindu Kush Mountains of Central Asia in the 1890s, came upon a "wine and spirit store where I spied, gently to my delight, the magic harp of Guinness."[2] At times, beer offered moments of fellowship between Europeans and locals, as when a Cambodian official delivered supplies to European engineers surveying near Angkor Wat in 1880. Frenchman Edgar Boulangier recalled: "With great joy I had him drink one of the bottles of beer that he brought us."[3] More often, colonists distanced themselves from local people and viewed beer as an expression of their own technological and moral superiority. The *Schwäbische Bierbrauer* (Swabian Brewer) praised "those apostles of German brewing culture, whom we meet in all kingdoms, from the Neva to the Nile, from the Ganges to the Amazon River, and where the breweries begin to serve the people the refreshing, splendid, and most welcome luxury." The author emphasized the imperial status of beer and the nationalist qualities of these brewers, "as German masters and managers, pioneers of German ethos and culture, fulfilled their duties with German diligence and German craft."[4]

In addition to its civilizing mission, beer joined in the flows of imperial commerce intended to further capitalist expansion by ensuring European powers with supplies of raw materials and markets for finished goods. These colonial relationships extended beyond the formal empires of occupied territories to include informal empires of economic domination. Despite Juana Cata's status as a Mexican citizen, not a colonial subject, her taste for beer was informed by daily interactions with British and American imperial agents, including staff at the Tehuantepec railroad. By the end of the nineteenth century, beer had become an object of competition between rival empires, as English ale and porter vied with continental lagers for the profits from colonial markets. Although Germany was by some measures the least successful of imperial powers, its light, refreshing beers were the most widely desired in tropical climates, even by the British overseas. Lager gained a foothold because of Britain's adherence to free trade in the nineteenth century, for such a transimperial trade that would have been impossible among early modern mercantilist empires.[5] Yet ultimately, Europe's export brewers lost out to European migrant brewers, those apostles praised by the *Schwäbische Bierbrauer*, who transplanted barley and hops, installed refrigerated machinery, and freed settler colonists from their reliance on beer from the metropolis.

Native people were not simply the passive subjects of European domination. While some such as Juana Cata incorporated beer into local drinking cultures, others clung to indigenous brewing traditions, in defiance of imperial prohibitions. Many people around the world enjoyed European beers as a sign of modernity, in defiance of traditional social restrictions based on gender, age, and status. The most avid consumers of western beer were the Japanese, who sent young technicians to learn the skills of European brewing and built their own empire of beer in East Asia. Elsewhere, native brewers resisted the competition from European imports and preserved their taverns as centers of sociability. Despite its exotic origins, European beer was incorporated into local cultural practices and medical beliefs; lager was often perceived as a cooling drink in the tropical sun, while Guinness stout offered strength and health. These taste associations gave visceral sensory expression to social signifiers of modernity and exclusivity. Regardless of whether local people embraced or rejected European beer, its arrival heralded the sweeping transformations of colonialism and capitalism. The appeal of the commodity, rather than the power of the empire, predominated in the spread of beer, for regardless of Britain's head start marketing ale in formal and informal colonies, the lager beers of German brewers ultimately conquered the world.

A Trade Empire of Ale

Merchants such as Juana Cata played a vital role introducing consumer goods to local communities, but they were only the final link in commodity chains that spanned the globe by the late nineteenth century. Companies hired specialized staff to ensure the quality of their perishable product through the travails of shipping, storage, and sales. In 1898, for example, Guinness hired a "world traveler" named Arthur T. Shand, who had been born in Scotland in 1853 and settled comfortably in New York, where he married a wealthy merchant's daughter. Having worked as a wine store clerk and an agent of Bass, the Burton ale exporter, Shand possessed the business experience and cultural savoir faire to survey market conditions, test quality, and guard against fraud and imitation.[6] For fifteen years, at the height of Britain's global reach, he visited pubs throughout the empire, and his travel journals provide unique insights on the international trade in beer. Although intended primarily to sustain European soldiers and settlers in distant lands, Guinness Stout, Bass Ale, and continental lagers found a ready market among native peoples, as Shand recorded. Flowing over the territorial boundaries drawn by European powers, beer belonged to a global trade empire defined by capitalism.

For centuries, European merchants carried beer as both a source of sustenance and an article of commerce. Medieval sailors of the Hanseatic League received a daily ration of 5 liters of beer, about the same as English and Dutch naval crews in the seventeenth century. Ship's beer was typically weaker than products intended for paying customers, and sailors on long-distance voyages complained about sour beer, although it kept better than water. As late as the eighteenth century, the Dutch East Indies Company shipped 3,000 liters of beer to Batavia annually. In the British Empire, commercial cargoes of beer were likewise small in scale, "adventures" undertaken by individual merchants such as Thomas Frankland, who in 1718 requested permission from the East India Company to send a hogshead of beer to his son, Henry, in Bengal. Europeans attributed racial differences to environmental conditions, including food and drink, and colonists went to great lengths to obtain familiar foods to avoid the risk of going native. The distilled spirits rum and gin had become common rations in the British army by the eighteenth century, but medical officers sought to replace them with beer. After one such substitution in India in 1840, the "men were remarkably well conducted because, as observed by their commandant, Major Mountain, 'they were sober.'" The surgeon in charge had "never witnessed so little disease as with this detachment tho' the season was particularly unhealthy."[7] Beer was so important to overseas Brits that G. I. Wolseley commented in 1878, "were we driven from [India], no trace, no monument, of our rule would exist ten years afterward, beyond the empty beer-bottles we had left behind us."[8]

India Pale Ale, the legendary beer that sustained the British Empire, has its origin myth in the experimentation of a London brewer. George Hodgson reportedly added an extra dose of hops to preserve his pale ale for the arduous voyage to Bengal undertaken in 1793 by his relative Thomas Hodgson, an East India Company ship captain. Hodgson's Pale Ale came to dominate the India trade for decades, until the Burton brewers Allsopp and Bass muscled into the trade. In fact, heavily hopped ale had been common in the overseas trade since at least the 1770s. Moreover, domestic consumption vastly outweighed exports, particularly after railroad lines connected Burton to London in 1839. Historian Alan Pryor has argued that the legend of India Pale Ale served mostly to market imperial nostalgia, allowing metropolitan clerks and shopkeepers to experience vicariously the adventures described by a Lieutenant Colonel Leach: "living in *bungalows* ventilated by *punkahs*, drinking therein, sundry bottles of Hodgson's pale ale; riding on elephants, shooting from the *howdahs* everything from tigers, boa-constrictors to buffalo."[9]

Whether shipping around the world or just to London, export brewers in Burton, Edinburgh, and Dublin employed local agents to bottle and market their products. While Bass is credited with pioneering these arrangements, Guinness exploited them most fully, employing thousands of firms in the United Kingdom, although only about thirty exported internationally. The brewer introduced its trademark harp in 1862, but independent bottlers applied their own private trademarks, a menagerie of cats, dogs, wolves, bulls, and monkeys. In addition to bottling, these merchants managed shipping, warehousing, distribution, wholesaling, and advertising. The Dublin brewer only began to oversee these far-flung commodity chains at the end of the nineteenth century with the appointment of world travelers Arthur Shand and J. C. Haines. By that point, however, the shifting tastes away from heavy porters and ales toward lighter and brighter beers, already observed in Europe and North America, had also reached the colonies.[10]

An Anglo-German trade rivalry arose in the sale of beer, in which lager brewers eclipsed the British trade empire of ale. The leading export brewery, Beck's, was founded in Bremen in 1873 by Heinrich Beck, who had migrated from his hometown of Eislingen, Württemberg, to work in an Indiana brewery. Returning to Germany in 1864, he introduced North American industrial methods to the St. Pauli Brewery of Hamburg before starting out on his own. Already by the mid-1880s, Beck's was outselling Bass in the Calcutta market. British administrator J. E. O'Conor attributed the growing preference in India for German lagers over British ales to their lighter taste. Meanwhile, fuller-bodied Munich lagers came to dominate exports to southern Africa and remained fashionable for decades in hotels, clubs, and restaurants. Of the German export breweries still operating on the eve of World War II, about a third were from Bavaria, another third from the northern cities of Bremen, Hamburg, and Berlin, and the remainder from the Rhineland, especially Dortmund. German brewing journals displayed their own imperial nostalgia by trumpeting the sales of lager beer in rival ports such as French Saigon and Dutch Makassar. O'Conor and other British officials regularly complained that Germans had been allowed to capture colonial markets, but Britain held firm to the doctrines of free trade and the mobility of migrant brewers, despite the competition.[11]

Germans were not the only lager brewers scrambling for overseas markets at the end of the nineteenth century. Companies often capitalized on their connections in nearby markets to spread their products and tastes. Austrian breweries at Trieste gained an advantage in sales to the Ottoman cities of Istanbul, Damascus, and Cairo, while Russian brewers at Odessa won a following in Jaffa and Jerusalem. Some British soldiers stationed in Cairo continued to drink Bass, but many others switched their allegiance to the Scottish lagers of Tennents and Youngers. Belgium's leading exporter, Brasseries de l'Etoile, leveraged its advantage in King Leopold's colony of the Congo to build African markets. Meanwhile, brewers from the United States began exploring potential markets in the Americas and Asia. Pabst landed in the Philippines in 1898 with the occupation of Manila and then used it as a springboard for the vast potential market of China. Anheuser-Busch,

FIGURE 4.1 Munich lager beer provides the comforts of home for colonial defense troops at leisure time, German East Africa, 1914–18. Bild 105-DOA6076. Courtesy of Bundesarchiv, Koblenz, Germany.

conscious of potential legal problems that could arise because its Budweiser brand was not actually made in Budweis, exported under the label "St. Louis Lager Beer." This place name was ironically appropriated by a New York City rival, and as a result, Juana Cata might not have been drinking an authentic beer from Missouri, but rather a New York knockoff.[12]

Despite the growing preference for light, refreshing lagers, Guinness retained a niche market due to its curative reputation. In India, the company's world traveler J. C. Haines characterized the typical stout drinker in bold masculine terms as "people who are continually on horseback, Europeans, Travelling Eurasians, Railway Officials, Planters, and Regimental Messes."[13] But when marketing to the tea plantations of Ceylon (Sri Lanka), he described a more feminine drinking culture of planters' wives sipping Guinness kept cool in ice chests. The spread of imperial tourism offered another market for the company. Arthur Shand observed that Mediterranean hotels stocked the product during the winter months when European travelers flocked there on holidays. He explained, "Guinness' Stout [in Malta], as in many other places, is not used as a beverage, but almost exclusively when ordered by a doctor."[14] Shand also had high hopes for sales at resorts near Victoria Falls, in present-day Zambia. "As the country increases in population and the Falls draw Tourists, our business will increase. Stout is a suitable drink, the Valley of the Zambesi being debilitating."[15]

Although European colonists often considered beer as a mark of distinction between themselves and indigenous peoples, Guinness and Bass welcomed native customers in Britain's informal trade empire of the Americas. As sociologist Gilberto Freyre explained: "Importing English beer into eighteenth-century Brazil was strictly forbidden hence it was considered the greatest luxury."[16] After independence, in 1822, beer was sold in stores along Rua da Alfândega near the Customs House of Rio de Janeiro. Spanish American patriots Simón Bolívar, Francisco de Miranda, and José María Fagoaga acquired a taste for beer while in exile in London. In Mexico, elites organized politically through York and Scottish masonic lodges (for liberals and conservatives, respectively), where they drank ale and porter (*blanca* and *colorada*).[17]

Nevertheless, alcohol sales to occupied territories raised colonial powers' worries about unrest by drunken natives. The Brussels Act of 1890 explicitly outlawed the export of intoxicating liquors to large parts of Africa. In South Asia, imperial concerns about temperance and civilization often intersected with local struggles over alcohol and hierarchy. Hindu priests and Muslim clerics had long sought to suppress palm toddies, fruit wines, and rice beers. Although these drinks were associated with the lower classes and tribal peoples such as the Santhals of West Bengal, Brahmins and Mughals often indulged as well. At first, European beer appealed mostly to small segments of Indian society with ties to the British, such as Sepoy soldiers and Lascar sailors. The modernist movement known as Young Bengal also adopted European customs to liberate themselves from generational and caste restrictions within Indian society. A leader of the group, poet Michael Madhusudan Dutt, who converted to Christianity in 1843 and married a Eurasian woman, declared himself to be "wading to liberalism through tumblers of beer."[18]

Native merchants, especially those outside the Hindu and Muslim majority, introduced European beer more widely through Indian society. Much of this commerce was handled by Parsis, descendants of Persian Zoroastrians who took refuge in India. H. J. Rustomjee of Karachi, for instance, imported Guinness, Youngers, and Coopers by 1880. After touring their main office and three retail bazaars in 1900, company traveler J. C. Haines declared: "Their 'Godown' is the finest in India."[19] Rustomjee & Co. also distributed beer and other European goods to so-called refreshment rooms along the railroad lines as well as through the interior provinces from Delhi to northwestern India. The merchants' local knowledge was invaluable for coming up with novel ways to advertise products. For example, lacquered trays decorated with the Guinness harp trademark were considered far more effective than billboards at the time. Such knowledge helped to grow local markets rather than rely on European colonists. Rustomjee apologized to Haines that the 1899 arrival in Karachi of a teetotal regiment, "The Prince of Wales' Own," had caused Guinness sales to drop by half, but his success in winning local demand ensured that consumption did not fall even further. Indeed, to restrict native drinking, in 1908 the colonial government doubled the customs duty on imported beer and liquor.[20]

Egypt also became a rising market for European beer, despite Islamic restrictions on alcohol. The taste for alcohol has been attributed to the nineteenth-century Ottoman reformer Muhammad 'Ali, whose modernization policies created a development-minded elite of western-oriented professionals. Particularly after the British arrived in 1882, these urbanites drank alcohol to distinguish themselves from traditionalist shayks and peasants. By the turn of the century, the British consul reported more than 4,000 bars, restaurants, and shops selling alcohol. Although many were owned by foreigners, 40 percent of the licenses were held by Egyptians, including Muslim pashas, beys, and even princes. J. C. Haines estimated that native consumers accounted for 60 percent of the market for Guinness in Cairo and 80 percent in Alexandria. He also described the drinking cultures in local cafes. "The peculiar habit exists of serving small pieces of bread, biscuit, cheese, meat, etc., with each bottle. In one case I saw three Arabs thus engaged, one was eating an orange between sips of stout, and the others little morsels of cheese."[21] Consumers were not limited to modernizing urbanites, as peasants began to exchange homebrewed *būza* for European beer. A postal clerk and social critic named Muhammad 'Umar complained about heavy drinking among the poor, particularly at *mulids*, Muslim saint's day celebrations. The most prominent such fair, dedicated to the twelfth-century mystic Ahmad al-Badawi, drew hundreds of thousands of devotees each year to the town of Tanta, which was identified by Shand as an important market. Pilgrims sought the saint's blessing to cure physical ailments, or in the case of women, to ensure fertility, and so a pint of Guinness made a natural accompaniment to the customary toasted chickpeas eaten at these fairs.[22]

While visiting India, Haines declared the stout to be "first rate," but he and Shand often lamented the poor quality of Guinness served in overseas markets. Lengthy voyages through the tropics to Australia and, before the opening of the Panama Canal, to San Francisco often left the beer "quite flat," "very acid and unpalatable," or "tasting of the wood."[23] Packaging and inferior corks could result in losses of 10 percent or more of the stock shipped. Some of the worst problems lay in the lack of care taken by bartenders, especially in tied houses that had financial incentives for promoting local brands over imported Guinness. Shand concluded: "The ignorance displayed by most Dealers in regard to our Stout is astonishing. Missionary work is necessary."[24] Bottlers such as the Liverpool firm of W. E. Johnson & Co. developed protocols to avoid common problems such as "overripeness" by rebottling in the morning and then corking in the afternoon. In response to complaints that the head took too long to fall, bartenders were encouraged to stand the bottle in ice for a couple of hours before pouring. Decades of missionary work were needed to convince customers that a long head was a desirable feature of Guinness.[25]

Representatives for Bass and Guinness also spent considerable time combating forgery and other trademark violations. In the 1860s, less than a decade after Bass had created its red triangle trademark, forgeries appeared in markets from Rio de Janeiro to Rotterdam. Many of the imitations were crude, but a particularly skillful label printed in Hamburg continued to circulate for the better part of a decade. One of Shand's first duties for Guinness was traveling across the United States filing lawsuits against imitators from New York to San Francisco. In a particularly brazen case, the Castlemaine Brewery of Queensland declared its stout to be the "Guinness of Australia" and sought to register the harp trademark as its own. Shand filed suit, and the local brewer withdrew its application, but had the agent not coincidentally been passing through, the local trademark would have gained legal standing. Even more common were the small-time frauds of refilling and recorking empty bottles of Guinness by "ill-intentioned bar tenders."[26]

Native markets for Guinness continued to grow in Southeast Asia and West Africa during the interwar period thanks to local dealers and distribution networks. Demand from the Chinese diaspora was second only to Australia in the region, and the company created Chinese language labels for sale in the Malay states. A memo from 1927 recorded that "the trade is almost entirely a native one."[27] Wholesalers in the region such as the Bhen Bark firm of Bangkok bypassed the bottling agents and sought to purchase directly from Guinness. West Africans had been drinking European liquors since the days of the early modern Atlantic slave trade, and beer was introduced in the nineteenth century with the shift to African agricultural commodities like palm oil. As elsewhere, Löwenbräu and other German brewers assumed a dominant role, shipping more than half a million gallons of lager annually on the eve of World War I. This volume prompted a colonial official to complain that "the trade appears to have been allowed to pass almost unchallenged into foreign hands."[28] On a visit in 1927, Guinness executive R. E. Goddard observed the continued growth of German lagers but nevertheless gave a more nuanced description of the market. Even on the coast, there were few bars or hotels, and consumers drank directly in the stores of firms like the Niger Co. and La Société commerciale de l'Ouest africain. In Nigeria, many locals considered Guinness to be good for virility and nursing mothers, while stout found little demand in the neighboring colony of Cameroon, where French tonic wines had captured the medicinal market. In Sierra Leone, Goddard found the market to be fickle, switching between lager, stout, tonic wine, and gin. The customer "gets occasional whims, so they tell me, for no apparent reason, and for a period drinks one thing and then just as suddenly switches over to another."[29] Clearly, consumer fashions were not limited to European modernity.

British territorial supremacy offered no guarantee that its porters and ales would retain their following among their own agents, much less indigenous people in colonial markets. Yet even as the light, sparkling taste of lager beers displaced heavier British pale ales, Guinness Stout was able to hold on to a market by having established a reputation for healthy properties. Despite European control of imperial shipping and ports, locals held considerable power over the success of the commodity in their markets. Native dealers provided essential distribution networks, especially in the interior. In India, for example, bazaar dealers competed fiercely for urban markets, then made up for losses by selling at inflated rates to consumers in the upcountry. As historian Rajat Kanta Ray explained: "Only the bazaar could 'deliver' the goods from the bottom to the top by virtue of complex financial arrangements that interlocked its own numerous successive layers."[30] Ultimately, the transfer of brewing technology to the colonies ensured the widespread triumph of locally produced pale lager.

The Civilizing Taste of Lager

Beer drinkers had many options in *fin-de-siècle* Istanbul. The city's Viennese and Swiss beerhouses served imported brands, while the hometown Bomonti Brewery operated a scenic beer garden on Çamlıca Hill overlooking the Bosphorus. But the most fashionable place to savor a pint was the hotel and theater district built on the former cemetery of the Petits Champs des Morts. A young Muslim man described the appeal simply: "it was full of women.

Wearing no veil, headscarf, but tailored suits or dresses."[31] Beer was sexy and modern, unlike the *rakı* (anise spirits) consumed by aging men in back-alley taverns. The cool, clean taste of lager embodied the triumph of refrigerated technology over insalubrious climates, and the contrast with strongly flavored indigenous drinks such as rakı and pulque further heightened beer's civilizational aura. In ancient cities and newly built industrial districts around the world, settler colonists and progressive natives founded breweries to provide a refreshing sip of European cosmopolitanism.

From the earliest days of colonial expansion, Europeans carried barley and hops as part of their civilizing mission, but brewing traditions took root only in favorable soil. Alonso de Herrera founded Europe's first overseas brewery in 1544 in the colony of New Spain. Beer enjoyed a moment of fashion in the court of Charles V, who had grown up in Flanders. Nevertheless, Philip I restored the primacy of wine among the Spanish elite, and Mexican natives continued to drink pulque. In 1659, Jan Van Riebeeck ordered the construction of a brewery for the Dutch settlement at the Cape of Good Hope, but despite the temperate climate, early attempts at brewing foundered. The Dutch East India Company sent an Amsterdam brewmaster, Rutgert Mensing, to put the industry on a sound footing in 1694. Settlers at New Amsterdam had established the first barley beer brewery in the future United States about 1612, although the English had experimented earlier with native maize. Even the most highly trained professionals could not brew successfully in the Dutch colonies of Batavia and Makassar, where licensed beer tappers sold imports from Holland or the Cape. South of the Tropic of Capricorn, retired soldier James Squire reportedly brewed Australia's first ale in 1795, less than a decade after the British occupied Botany Bay. John Molson founded Canada's oldest brewery in 1786 at Montreal, but brewing in Ontario remained a frontier industry well into the nineteenth century. John Sleeman's Guelph brewery struggled to source hops through the 1870s.[32]

In India, both British and natives overcame the challenges of warm weather by brewing in the highlands. Henry Bohle established the first brewery about 1832 at Mussoorie, a hill station north of Delhi, and another a few years later at nearby Meerut. The regimental commander Lt. Col. Bratton pronounced the beer "pleasant and palatable and no doubt wholesome when fresh, but it soon turns sour in the hot season."[33] The Mussoorie brewery even inspired a pilgrimage by renowned Urdu poet, Mirza Ghalib, a devout but skeptical Muslim. Encouraged by these early successes, the British developed local supply chains for brewing. When Bohle was unable to find indigenous hops, the Commissary General sent away for seedlings from the Cape Hope colony. By the 1880s, a dozen breweries operated in the northwestern province of Punjab, and on a smaller scale at Bangalore, Bombay, Lucknow, and Madras. Indigenous entrepreneurs also tried to compete for the trade; the Rajah of Kashmir maintained a 100-acre hop plantation, and the Sabapathy Moodelliar and Co. Brewery unsuccessfully bid for the contract to supply troops at Madras and other garrisons. The failure to establish local breweries resulted in part from lack of official favor. J. C. Haines wrote disdainfully: "Indian breweries have little or no civil trade. They all brew under the protection of the [British] government."[34] Nevertheless, the Murree Brewery, established in 1860 in the Pir Punjal Range of the Western Himalayas, won a medal in 1876 at the Philadelphia Exhibition.

The Ottoman Empire had greater contact with European brewing traditions than India, and it became an important brewing center. In the 1830s, an Austrian woman named Anna Forneris sold homebrew in the port town of Galata, across the straits from old Istanbul, until authorities closed down her establishment after a brawl between her German customers and Greeks drinking in a nearby wine bar. By the 1870s and 1880s, beer gardens flourished near Taksim Square, although the Viennese and Swiss beerhouses were actually operated by Greeks. In 1893, the Bomonti brothers, Swiss businessmen, established the first modern beer factory on the outskirts of Istanbul, and a short time later, the Allatini brothers founded the Olympos Brewery down the coast in Salonica. Across the Aegean, in Smyrna, the Aydin Brewery transformed a bucolic riverfront site known as Diana's Bath into a popular beer garden. Bomonti quickly established itself as the market leader, even winning an appointment as supplier to the Ottoman imperial court. Like many progressive Muslims, Sultan Abdülhamid II held the view that since lager beer had not existed in the time of the Prophet, it could not have been banned. In 1912, Bomonti merged with the rival Nektar Brewery, a London-based company, and in the 1920s, it expanded into Egypt by buying up the two leading breweries, Crown in Alexandria and Pyramid in Cairo, which had been founded by Belgian entrepreneurs.[35]

The St. George Brewery in Addis Ababa had an even more multinational character than its Ottoman counterparts, in part because of Ethiopia's success in modernizing its army and repelling European invasions. Businessman David Hall obtained the original government concession for the brewery in 1923 with the help of family connections. His Polish father, Moritz Hall, had made artillery for Emperor Tewodros II, and his Ethiopian German mother, Wälättä Iyäsus Zander, also known as Katharina, was prominent in the imperial court. In 1928, David Hall assembled a consortium of Berlin investors, including Paul Schubert, who began work on the brewery through his Milan-based construction firm. Schubert may also have recommended brewmaster Josef Pfeffer, a native of Mainz working in Milan. The project stalled in 1929, and in the process of refinancing, French investors led by Jean Laverny gained a majority shareholding. The brewery finally opened in June 1930 to glowing newspaper reports about the modern machinery and the high-quality helles lager.

Nevertheless, problems continued behind the scenes. A brewing engineer named Dietsche inspected the plant in May 1931 and condemned the poor state of the equipment. The French syndicate bought out Hall in January 1932, but Pfeffer contested the transfer of the concession and reportedly refused to obey orders. Franco-German rivalries may have aggravated the dispute, since the manager, Pierre Guillaumin, had served as a captain in the Algerian colonial army. The following January, Guillaumin sought to break the impasse by installing a Belgian brewmaster, René Hutois. With support from Ethiopian workers, Pfeffer and his wife refused to hand over the keys to the factory. The standoff finally ended on February 9, 1933, when a French consular tribunal ordered the brewmaster and his wife to leave Africa within thirty days. Hutois later published a brief account of his time at the St. George Brewery, without mentioning the scandal. The staff included a French administrator (Guillaumin) and bookkeeper, a Belgian brewmaster (himself), an Italian foreman, Armenian technicians, Greek delivery men—and no Germans. The Ethiopian employees had likely been purged, and to limit potential organizing, their replacements were divided between two rival ethnic groups, Semitic Ahmara and Cushitic Oromo. Hutois recalled: "What a Tower of Babel!"[36] Nevertheless, his tenure lasted only two years. Shortly after Mussolini's invasion of Ethiopia in 1935, the French sold the St. George to another German syndicate led by the Hamburg bank M. M. Warburg and the Bremen exporter Beck's.

The colonial transition from ale to lager brewing was likewise driven by European migrants and investors in British South Africa. Large-scale European migration to the colony began with the discovery of diamonds in the Northern Cape in 1869, followed by gold in 1886. The first modern breweries had been established by Swedish immigrants—Jacob Letterstedt, in the 1830s, and Anders Ohlsson, in 1880—although both produced British-style ales. Even Charles Glass of Johannesburg, the supposed inventor of Castle Lager, modern South Africa's leading brand, marketed ale and porter that was actually brewed by his wife. The couple sold out a few years later to Frederick Mead and George Henry Raw, who established South African

Breweries (SAB) as a lager brewery in 1895 with financing from British investors and machinery imported from the United States. Around the turn of the century, SAB expanded into the Cape Market, driving Ohlsson to update their own facilities to brew lager beer and also produce malt. In their competitive struggle, the two rival firms tied houses through contractual arrangements and created elaborate advertising campaigns based on patriotism, thereby closing off access to imported beers.[37]

Nevertheless, the imperial triumph of lager was not universal, and settler ties to the British homeland preserved a taste for ale in Australasia, even as distinctive local styles and drinking cultures took shape. German export brewers perceived Australia as a vast potential market, worrying only that American brewers would beat them to it. Beer imports reached 2 million gallons in 1908 but then fell to under 400,000 by the end of World War I and remained low throughout the century. Protectionist policies, tied houses, and ready supplies of malt and hops from Tasmania and New Zealand ensured the dominance of local brewers, while the small number of German residents limited the migrant marketplace for lager. As in Britain, the introduction of light, sparkling ales with a distinctive local taste may also have contributed to the failure of continental-style brewing. A visiting expert from the United States, B. Schirmer, observed in 1906: "Still, or crystal, or iced, or brilliant ale is rapidly coming into favor . . . this hybrid ale, when properly made and stored, has all the qualifications of a lager beer and yet retains the attributes of an ale." He commended the brewers Down Under that "with all the foul air and varied bacteria, the beer is rather clean in flavor, though much sweeter than is commonly liked here [in America]."[38] Guinness traveler Haines likewise noted the sweet character of colonial ales in Australia while describing some of the particularities of local drinking habits: "In numerous bars the custom is to have several bottles open on the counter at lunch time and a glass is poured out at a time."[39] National differences arose within the region, as Australian expert August J. Metzler explained: "The ales brewed in New Zealand are of a totally distinct character as compared with those produced on the Australian continent. They resemble the English ales very much more than the Australian."[40]

In contrast to the top-fermentation exceptionalism of Britain and Australasia, early lager adopters in the Americas built their own spheres of influence through the process of trickle trade. Chilean brewers had taken an early lead in South America, winning honors in world's fairs, as well as the respect of Arthur Shand, who declared Chilean lager a "very good tasting beer."[41] In Mexico and the Spanish Caribbean, Swiss and German immigrants founded the first lager breweries around 1890, but Mexican conditions favored the example set in St. Louis and Milwaukee of labor-saving machinery and maize adjuncts. The Cuauhtémoc Brewery's master, Joseph Schnaider, had formerly worked in St. Louis while the owner's son, Luis G. Sada, studied at the Wahl and Henius Brewing Academy of Chicago, as did the French-born manager of the Moctezuma Brewery, Philippe Suberbie. Likewise, the preferred variety of brewer's yeast in Mexico was Wahl and Henius's pure lager culture, known as Chicago Number 1. A school brochure declared: "The brewing industry of Mexico, which had been conducted strictly according to German models, was Americanized, adopting infusion methods, and at the present time nearly all Mexican breweries are operated by American brewmasters."[42]

Beer embodied the attachment of Mexican elites to the ideal of European modernity. The Dos Equis brand, introduced by the Moctezuma Brewery in 1897, originally referred to "Siglo XX" (Twentieth Century), heralding a progressive future of European-style consumption, while nevertheless maintaining patriotic ties to the past with an image of the Aztec emperor on the label. Legend has it that the Dos Equis Amber was modeled on Vienna lager, a nod to the Austrian archduke Maximilian, who ruled briefly as emperor of Mexico during the French intervention (1862 to 1867), but contemporary accounts described XX as a pale lager, while the XXX brand introduced in 1906 followed the style of Munich. The clean taste of lager, ensured by pure yeast, appealed to Mexican elites as a contrast to the sour, rank flavors of indigenous pulque. Advertisements emphasized the strict hygiene of industrial beer production in modern factories. Drinking cultures also contributed to the associations with European sophistication. The Toluca y México Brewery established a beer garden in Mexico City for the enjoyment of the rich, while North American–style saloons appeared in the north, where scarce labor raised factory wages. In Yucatán, the elite socialized with the novel "lunch-cerveza," using cold beer to alleviate the streamy midday heat.[43] Minister of Education José Vasconcelos declared: "Mexico will begin on the path of a great nation when the people, in place of consuming toxic beverages, drink beer."[44]

Yet not all Latin Americans viewed the native culture with such disdain. Admittedly, the European-descended elite of Bolivia made up a small but profitable market for lager breweries, including Otto Richter's Cerveceria Nacional of La Paz and the Germania brewery, in Oruro, which reportedly produced a Pilsner beer using as a fuel "the dried excrement of the llama."[45] Nevertheless, the indigenous-descended majority remained loyal to the native chicha. Seeking to modernize this ancient Inka beverage, chemist Manuel

FIGURE 4.2 An advertisement for the maker of Dos Equis beer, the Moctezuma brewery of Orizaba, Mexico. The Aztec emperor provided the brand with nationalist authenticity, while the factory, railroad, and ship emphasized the modernity of beer. J. R. Southworth, *Mexico ilustrado: Distrito Federal* (Liverpool: Blake & Mackenzie, 1903), unpaginated advertisements. Courtesy of the New York Public Library. My thanks to Stephanie Borkowsky.

Forgues conducted a study of regional variations among chicha producers in 1909. He tested saliva samples for chemical content and recorded sensory descriptors to map the terroir of chicha. Some of these reactions were quite negative, including one from the Valley of Cliza that had "yellowish white color and nauseating smell," and another from the town of Quillacollo with "no smell, appearance of chicken shit." Forgues deduced that lower levels of glucose produced more pleasant flavors such as the "dark yellow color, grain smell" from Valley of Taranta and the "white color and indefinable smell" of a Cochabampa sample. Although his plans for mass-producing chicha never came to fruition, Forgues's attempt to modernize the local culture rather than imposing European norms fit with the vision of progressive Bolivians such as Alfredo Bignon, who developed an export industry for another national commodity, coca.[46]

Europeans justified their imperial conquests based on the supposed civilizing influence of culture and technology, and beer, particularly the clean, cool taste of lager beer, exemplified these seeming advantages. As in the case of Ethiopia's St. George Brewery, this industry depended on the collaboration of cosmopolitan elites, European investors, and migrant brewing professionals. Once again, trickle trade led ultimately to import substitution within the colonies. Although many ventures failed, the appeal of beer's European associations remained strong, nowhere more so than in Japan.

Japan's Beer Empire

Magoshi Kyōhei was the acknowledged "Beer King" of Japan, although he had no professional training as a brewer. He was a company man at Mitsui, one of the industrial conglomerates (*zaibatsu*) that dominated Japan's twentieth-century development. After two decades running the Yokohama office of Mitsui's shipping line, he was named to head the industrial group's newly purchased brewery in 1892. He guided the business through a period of rapid growth and consolidation, merging the regional Sapporo, Asahi, and Yebisu brands into a single national firm, Dai Nippon or the Great Japan Brewery, in 1906. Though surrounded by western beer during the day, he devoted his leisure time to the traditional Japanese tea ceremony, *cha-no-yu*.[47] Magoshi exemplified the Japanese drive to adopt western technologies to survive in a world of empires while also adapting foreign novelties to national culture. After all, who could be trusted to assimilate beer to local tastes better than a tea ceremony master? Dai Nippon and its rival Kirin, a subsidiary of the Mitsubishi zaibatsu, built an industry from the ground up, training technicians, sourcing equipment and raw materials, winning over customers, and eventually conquering an empire for beer that spanned East Asia.

The brewing industry formed part of a top-down modernization campaign under the Emperor Meiji (r. 1868–1912), and early on, the foreign product evoked little enthusiasm. Japan's first recorded tasting of European-style beer came in 1854 at the signing of the Treaty of Kanagawa, which opened trade with the United States. After sampling from kegs of ale presented to the Shogun by Commodore Matthew Perry, one official compared the exotic liquid to "bitter horse piss."[48] Nevertheless, reformers were willing to swallow many unfamiliar tastes if they thought it would strengthen the nation and avoid the colonial fate of India and China. The initial demand for beer came primarily from visiting sailors, and in 1870, a Norwegian American named William Copeland opened the Spring Valley Brewery in the port of Yokohama to service this itinerant but thirsty market. Japanese entrepreneurs soon followed suit, copying trademarks as well as recipes. One traveler observed "a unique lot of foreign signs and labels, such as 'Bottled by Pale Ale

& Co' on an imitation of a famous English stamp."[49] In 1890, a foreign traveler found the Bass red triangle emblazoned on a flag above a teahouse in the sake town of Kobe, although he did not record whether the ale served inside was genuine.[50]

After a decade of experimental homebrewing, the industry was set on a more professional path with official backing and German technical support. The Meiji government took the initiative in setting up what became the Sapporo Brewery at the Hokkaido Agricultural Research Station in 1876 and in hiring German specialists to manage the plant. An American agricultural expert and temperance advocate, Horace Capron, advised on the cultivation of hops. Kirin, successor to Copeland's Spring Valley Brewery, sought to remain loyal to German traditions by hiring a brewmaster named Moritz Hermann Heckert and sourcing ingredients and machinery from Germany. Japanese technicians studied in Berlin at the Brewing Institute (VLB) and gained practical experience at the Tivoli Brewery. Kuroda Kiyotala, original director of the Hokkaido development plan and later prime minister, declared beer to be the "beverage of the new era."[51]

By the 1920s, Japanese brewers had nationalized the industry, led by Dai Nippon, with its origins in the Hokkaido Research Station. Agronomists rejected local hops and sought to acclimatize European varieties, but despite the breeders' careful efforts, genes from Japanese wild hops infiltrated commercial strains, imparting unique flavors. Brewers also contracted with farmers to supply barley to supplement imported malts. After World War I broke out, Kirin's brewmaster returned home and was replaced by a Japanese expert, Osamu Imaida. The company hired a Wisconsin maltster, August Groeschel, to build a plant in Yokohama using Japanese barley. Kirin also began fabricating equipment at Mitsubishi's shipbuilding plant. By the late 1920s, brewers had largely freed themselves of expensive foreign malts, although they continued to import hops from Europe and North America. Japanese brewing scientists also began to publish original research, at first in the Fermentation Institute's *Journal of the Brewing Society of Japan* and later in international journals as well. In a single generation, Japanese brewers had gone from counterfeiting labels to matching the quality of European beers.[52]

But technical skills alone were not enough to ensure success; a revolution in marketing was also needed. Tokyo brewery Ebisu opened a European-style beer hall in 1899 in the fashionable Ginza shopping district. An early cartoon with two people drinking beer and eating curry in a beer hall was captioned, "Big brother, if we don't eat this, people will think we're hicks."[53] Trains offered another venue for sampling this new beverage, and vendors sold beer along with bento box lunches to travelers. By the 1920s, cafes served beer and other western products to that denizen of modern Japan, the *salaryman*, or low-level office worker. Military service provided yet another opportunity for localizing beer, which served as rations along with beef. During the Russo-Japanese War of 1905, a journalist following the army at Port Arthur observed: "The path of the army can be traced by beer bottles—Asahi, Yebisu, Kabuta and Saporo [sic]."[54]

Although drinking was considered a masculine activity, appropriate for soldiers and salarymen, women outside of traditional family structures facilitated these new drinking cultures. One industry old-timer recalled: "In the beginning, Japanese people didn't appreciate beer at all. So [brewers] had to run around visiting waitresses and geishas in places such as cafes and hotels and charm potential buyers."[55] Geisha also played a prominent role in print advertisements for beer, such as the women shown offering a basket of Dai Nippon–brand beers from the window of a railroad car, prominently marked "First Class" in English. The company's factory, with its imposing smokestack, appeared in the background. Marrying Japanese tradition with western consumerism, it reassured consumers that tradition and modernity could be effectively combined. Geisha were beyond the reach of young salarymen, who fantasized instead about cafe waitresses with their flapper-style bobbed hair. Women did not become regular consumers of beer until after World War II, but the beverage could nevertheless enter domestic spaces on special occasions. Nakano Makiko, a merchant's wife from Kyoto, recorded in her diary the celebration of her brother's wedding in 1910: "We went 'modern' this time, and entertained them with München beer and bananas."[56]

In Japan as elsewhere, brewing professionals helped to create a new taste community around beer, mediating the sensory experience of drinking with the associations of modernity and status. As one brewer declared, "people said that to be civilized and enlightened, you should drink beer or that beer itself is a characteristic of the civilized."[57] Such experts were vital in shaping the shared understandings of this new product, combining chemical analysis with sensory experience. A Japanese sales agent described a blind tasting comparison with a Lipton Tea representative in British Calcutta: "Now, I knew the taste of Kirin Beer more than any, especially because the beer sample was fresh. At any rate, both the manager and I drank and drew the same conclusion as to which one was the best."[58] The agent's seeming relief about freshness suggests early industrial limitations on quality control and preservation. One industry professional lamented that often "the beer is cloudy, and some batches don't even have bubbles."[59]

FIGURE 4.3 Advertisement for Dai Nippon beer brands juxtaposing traditional and modern symbols of luxury. A geisha offers beers from a "first class" railroad car with the brewery's imposing smokestack in the background. Courtesy of Sapporo Breweries.

Yet the untrained responses of non-professional judgments are also valuable in explaining the Japanese preference for continental lagers over English ales. One hint about local taste perceptions appears in the Tokugawa samurai's comparison of European beer with "bitter horse piss." This may have been simply a metaphoric reference to the cultural indigestibility of foreign foods and, by extension, of foreigners. And yet, a stale keg of export ale may well have resembled equine urine—beyond just the color. The samurai had not likely tasted it, but he certainly had seen and smelled it. Draft horses were part of everyday life, and the yellow streams and ammonia fumes were a public nuisance that, if concentrated, posed genuine health hazards. The contents of India Pale Ale made this comparison even more probable, as brewing scientist Charles Bamforth observed: "Hop bitter acids by no means kill all organisms, and the most prolific inhabitant of those casks bouncing on the ocean waves was *Brettanomyces* (a genus of yeast). The typical flavor notes produced by this organism are 'barnyard' or 'mousy.'"[60]

Although "Brett" is still common in Belgian farmhouse ales, barnyard flavors were likely perceived by the Japanese as backward and inferior, contributing to the preference for lager beers. Even the British editors of the *Brewers' Journal* recognized their ales contained "too much alcohol, too much sediment, too much hops and too little gas."[61] By neutralizing off flavors and offering a crisp, clear product, Central European brewers imbued lager with a taste of purity and modernity that fit Japanese cultural taste preferences. The newspaper *Jiji Shimpō* (Current Events) explained in 1900: "To put it simply, British beer is rich and bitter. German beer is light and easy to drink."[62]

Even as Japanese brewers domesticated beer, they also looked abroad for raw materials and potential markets within the nation's growing sphere of commercial and military influence. In the 1890s, merchants sent beer samples on commercial missions throughout East and Southeast Asia, as far away as Thailand and India. Such efforts paid off within a decade as Japan began exporting beer from Singapore to Vladivostok. The Kirin representative's deal with Lipton Tea in Calcutta contributed to the growth of those markets, which, while insignificant compared to German beer exports, was quite a remarkable achievement for a new industry.[63]

Japan reached beyond trade connections to establish a territorial empire in Korea, beginning with a protectorate in 1905 and formal annexation in 1910. Japanese beer was used as a sign of the colonizers' superiority over the colonized peoples' local fermented rice beverage, *makgeolli*. Korean literature scholar Theodore Jun Yoo has described the stereotype of an "unrefined, milky colored, pungent, and slightly carbonated fermented rice drink, notorious for causing major headaches, chronic belching, and nasty hangovers."[64] The occupation government began to restrict production, shutting down a hundred thousand home breweries and revoking the manufacturing licenses for three times that number of professional operations. Even while suppressing the homebrew favored by farmers at weddings and funerals, Kirin led the way in marketing beer to urban elites. A foreboding advertisement in a Korean newspaper from 1929 depicted a muscular figure with a giant beer bottle casting a shadow across all of Asia. The text, written in a combination of Korean and

Japanese characters, listed Kirin's breweries and sales offices, placing Seoul alongside Tokyo and other Japanese cities. The Pan-Asian implication was that Japanese settler colonists and Korean elites would grow strong together by drinking Kirin. Both text and imagery echoed the aspirations of Japan's imperial Greater East Asia Co-Prosperity Sphere. Kirin had planned a Korean factory but proceeded only when rival Dai Nippon began construction of its own plant outside Seoul. In keeping with the imperial goals of self-sufficiency, Korean subsidiaries set about planting local barley and hops, although they achieved only modest results until the loss of Japanese shipping during World War II forced them to ramp up production.[65]

China presented an even greater potential market for the Japanese brewing duopoly. Territorial occupation began in Taiwan and Manchuria, as Japan defeated China and Russia in wars of 1895. The Dai Nippon Brewery took advantage of these inroads, establishing a factory at Shenyang in 1910, taking over the German Tsingtao Brewery in 1916, and founding the Takasago Brewery in Taiwan in 1922. Japanese advertisers displayed their international pedigree by using text in three languages—English, Japanese, and Chinese—thereby combining a modern lifestyle and European quality with Chinese cultural references. After the Japanese invasion of Manchuria in 1931, Dai Nippon and Kirin jointly established the Manshu Beer Company to refurbish and expand Russian breweries. Perhaps responding to nationalist resistance, in the early 1940s, the Japanese management at Qingdao created an advertisement recalling the classic *Romance of the Three Kingdoms*, in which three ancient Chinese folk heroes swore an oath of brotherhood while drinking.[66]

The nationalization of Japanese brewing culminated during World War II. Through the 1930s, beer had remained something of a luxury good, reserved for the upper and middle classes, but as the fighting in Asia intensified in the late 1930s, the Japanese government banned sake brewing to save rice for military consumption. At the same time, soldiers received rations of barley beer throughout the war, helping to inculcate a wider taste for the beverage. The preference for lager beer over British ale also signals less about German cultural domination than an expression of Japanese taste preferences for light products, a trend that continued in the postwar era.[67] Thus, local tastes and native investors drove lager's hegemony in Japan, while that nation's territorial empire spread lager more widely throughout Asia. Although the Japanese had considerable autonomy in their encounter with western products like beer, societies dominated by colonial powers had to struggle far more to accommodate the transformations of capitalist modernity.

FIGURE 4.4 A dark, muscular figure with a giant Kirin bottle looms ominously over Asia in this Korean newspaper advertisement. The text, written in a combination of Korean and Japanese characters, listed Kirin's breweries and sales offices, placing Seoul alongside Tokyo and other Japanese cities. The Pan-Asian implication was that Japanese settler colonists and Korean elites would grow strong together by drinking Kirin. Both text and imagery echoed the aspirations of Japan's imperial Greater East Asia Co-Prosperity Sphere. *Donga Ilbo*, March 11, 1927.

"Drinking in a Cage"

Native drinks were often caught between the prohibitionist impulses of empire and the supposed cultural superiority of European beer, but they survived nevertheless in hidden spaces of sociability and refuge. In 1930s Johannesburg, migrant workers from across southern Africa thirsted for sorghum beer after hard shifts in Witwatersrand gold mines, and women satisfied that demand, in defiance of colonial bans on the making and sale of alcohol. The covert homebrewing of an unnamed but entrepreneurial Zulu woman, living in a crowded slum called Rooiyard, was described by an early social anthropologist. Husbands expected beer for themselves and their friends, regardless of wives risking arrest to provide it. The production of beer also enabled women to challenge patriarchal authority by providing them with an independent income from selling beer to unattached males, often including those same friends. In the competition for weekend customers, the Rooiyard businesswoman "engaged choirs of four Zulu boys each to sing till the early hours of Sunday morning." Paid in beer instead of cash, the youths brought traditional Zulu harmonies from the countryside to the city. The Zulu brewmaster "sold three varieties of beer," changing the style as "these beverages become the 'fashion' for varying periods."[68] Fermenting the beer in underground chambers, she hired relatives to keep watch for white police and native informants. The cat-and-mouse closing of illicit bars, known by the Irish term "shebeens," became a perennial site of struggle under the Apartheid regime, even as the commodification of native beers unsettled traditional social relationships.

European observers often depicted African brewing traditions as primitive, but their technologies were in fact diverse and historically evolving. King Cetshwayo declared in 1881 that beer was "the food of the Zulus; they drink it as the English drink coffee."[69] A lithograph published in 1849 by George French Angas illustrated the basic procedures for brewing among the Zulu. "The large earthen jars over the fire contain the beer, which, after boiling, is set aside for some days to ferment," he explained. "One woman is stirring the millet with a calabash spoon, while another is testing its quality in a little cup, a third woman is advancing with a basket of millet on her head, and a fourth is pouring out the liquor in waterproof baskets."[70] Angas clearly left out some steps in the brewing process, including malting the millet that the third woman carried in the basket over her head, perhaps to grind on the stone at her feet, just to the right of the fire. Nevertheless, this family brew was far less elaborate than the community festivals observed among the Xhosa people by anthropologist Patrick McAllister. Formerly a pastoralist people, the Xhosa drank milk rather than beer on ceremonial occasions in the early nineteenth century. The loss of cattle to Zulu raiders forced them to begin brewing on a regular basis, and by the time McAllister arrived in the 1980s, brewers had created a week-long schedule of soakings, grindings, and boils. The Swazi, yet another group living in southern Africa, preferred to make beer from sorghum, although when grain was scarce in the dry grasslands of the lowveld, they fermented marula fruit.[71]

Ethnographers have also described elaborate languages of status, sociability, culture, and taste around beer and brewing in diverse African cultures. A Zulu king's beer was considered too strong for ordinary men to drink, for example, while a commoner who brewed ten times in one year was described critically to anthropologist Audrey Richards as "a woman who likes beer."[72] Among the Bemba and Zulu, sharing beer represented the height of neighborliness, and senior women carefully distributed beer, offering generous servings to honored guests while snubbing those who had fallen out of favor. Guests in turn shared their cups with others around the hut through an elaborate ritual of reciprocity. Offerings of beer also ensured good relations with the ancestors and spirits. The Maane people of West Africa varied their recipe across the life cycle, from sweet (happy) beer brewed for weddings to bitter (sorrow) beer for funerals. Connoisseurship of beer was also present among the Swazi, as geographer Jonathan Crush reported: a "light hand" was needed to make good beer, while less skilled brewers made beer "which is only water."[73]

FIGURE 4.5 An 1849 lithograph illustrated the basic procedures for brewing among the Zulu. George French Angas, *The Kaffirs Illustrated* (London: J. Hogarth, 1849), plate 26. Coloured lithograph by G. F. Angas, 1849. Attribution-NonCommercial 4.0 International (CC BY-NC 4.0). Wellcome Collection, Wellcome Library, London.

Imperial Hops 133

Alcohol became an important source of political power and labor control under the colonial economy. Afrikaans and British territorial expansion had already undermined indigenous economies, even before the mining bonanzas of the 1860s and 1870s. Restricted to precarious tribal "homelands," natives became a labor reserve for the development of extractive industries. European managers learned to offer beer as well as wages to attract workers to the Northern Cape diamond mines and the Witwatersrand gold fields. This appealed not just to the workers' desire to get drunk; a British medical officer testified to the nutritional value of the native brew: "Eggs and milk are nothing compared to the value of Kaffir beer as a pick me up."[74] Labor recruiters at many mines and factories hired native women to brew for the workers, while others sought to create a more stable workforce by encouraging workers to bring women from home to cook and brew for them. The so-called married quarters often became sites of illicit alcohol sales. Brewing provided an important business opportunity for African men and women alike, converting agricultural surpluses into cash and freeing them from the need to work as migrants on European farms, mines, and factories.

While Europeans viewed the native beer as a source of licentiousness and poor hygiene, for the natives themselves it offered a means to preserve social stability against the upheavals of colonization. A magistrate reported in 1906 that hundreds of native women traveled by train each weekend to Durban carrying beer for the port town's 20,000 African laborers, mostly dockworkers. As the urban market grew, women stopped commuting and set up houses in the suburbs. Local newspapers decried these informal taverns as "hotbeds of immorality" and "rendezvous of native women of loose character." Police reports summarized: "The beer is produced in kitchens, bathrooms, open dusty yards, behind sanitary conveniences, and in fact in any recess, shanty, or space which affords a convenient standing place of the open receptacles."[75] But the native homebrewing and drinking, singing, and dancing that Europeans perceived as licentious were simply expressions of communal solidarity. Sex work certainly existed, but many women brewed as familial duty for husbands, brothers, or fathers. Men could also commercialize the production of their female relatives. A sixty-year-old, mission-educated man named Mashikiyana Gumede reportedly earned more than a thousand pounds from his popular tavern.

To assert control over native drinking, the British adopted municipal monopolies on the sale of indigenous alcohol. Even while banning the sale of spirits, wine, and hopped beer to natives in the late 1890s, colonial governments had tolerated native brewing as a traditional practice. At the height of the moral panic in Durban, the provincial government passed the Native Beer Act of 1908 granting town councils exclusive authority to brew native beer. Inspired by the Gothenburg system of Sweden, Natal beer halls sought to limit the consumption of beer by making it as unpleasant as possible. Durban's first beer hall set a model for future construction, with a layout inspired by prisons and divided by wire fences. Only men could enter, and after purchasing a ticket from the manager, they passed through a turnstile and presented the ticket to the barman. After finishing their beer, they left through another turnstile. A European observed with satisfaction: "This method prevents natives from getting more than one drink and is most effective in preventing *indiscriminate drinking* and *idling*." Workers dubbed it "drinking in a cage."[76]

Despite the discomfort, the municipal beer halls proved highly profitable, and colonial administrators had opened them across southern Africa by the 1930s. The town of Durban built a two-story brewery to ensure regular supplies and also used beer revenues to construct prison-like barracks. Workers complained about the quality of the beer, which was sour, made with impure water, and often included harmful additives such as aloe ash, which was believed to make people thirsty and inspire more drinking. Even if the beer arrived in a decent state from the municipal brewery, bartenders watered it down and pocketed the difference. The beer halls were often built in a shabby manner, and even as the numbers of drinkers grew, managers refused to improve the facilities, using the profits to administer township governments, including police salaries.[77]

Native responses to the colonial regime took many forms, from grudging accommodation to outright rebellion. Beer-drinking rituals were central to the so-called Maji Maji uprising of 1906 in German East Africa and the millenarian movement of Wellington Buthelezi, who preached in the Transkei region in the late 1920s that African Americans would come with airplanes and western goods to liberate the native people. Others believed that giving up alcohol would help Africans liberate themselves from colonial rule. Indigenous temperance movements included Muslims and evangelical Christians as well as the African National Congress leaders Sol Plaatje and Modiri Molema. There was even a black South African section of the international Women's Christian Temperance Union organized by a Mrs. Ncamu, although it is not clear what the group's North American founders would have thought of her 1914 petition to abolish the municipal beer monopoly, which gained the signatures of 4,000 black women.[78]

Opposition to the beer halls also fed into the growing unionization movement among African workers and culminated in a mass boycott in 1929. The Industrial and Commercial Workers Union arrived in Durban in 1925 and within three years had signed up 37,000 worker members, who were dissatisfied with their low wages and poor treatment. The union scored legal victories against firing workers without notice but did not consider the beer monopoly a major concern until 1929, when popular protests broke out against the construction of a beer hall in a black neighborhood outside Durban. Local brewers organized a Women's Auxiliary and called for a boycott against the beer halls, winning the support of male dock workers. Brandishing cudgels, they marched through the streets, stoned beer halls, and fought with police. When white vigilantes besieged the union hall in June, a woman named Ma-Dhlamini led the resistance in a struggle that killed six Africans and two whites. Thousands of workers were arrested, but the boycott continued for eighteen months, crippling the government's finances. When police in the town of Estcourt arrested a group of protesting women, their husbands "threatened to lodge the babies in the Magistrate's garden for him to look after."[79]

Vice raids sparked occasional beer riots from Waaihoek in the Free State to Worcester in the Western Cape, but the resistance usually remained low-key. Protests against beer halls were most strenuous when they opened near black townships. Many colonial officials tacitly accepted a so-called moral contract with the native subjects, tolerating minor infractions and granting them autonomy in their private lives. One Salisbury magistrate was considered permissive because he refused to convict defendants who had been dragged out of their own homes by police on charges of drunkenness. Nevertheless, liquor laws imposed a heavy burden; by the 1950s, more than 200,000 people were convicted each year.[80]

Illicit shebeens serving homebrewed native beer became central to the urban culture of townships that sprang up around Johannesburg, Durban, and other industrial cities. In oral histories, workers described gathering with friends from their home community to drink beer and talk about girlfriends and life at home. Despite the ties of communal solidarity, workers also made friends with migrants from different regions, and multilingualism became common in the cities. The popular culture of singing and dancing likewise mixed traditional choirs and drum rhythms from the countryside with new art forms such as a jazz subculture that emerged over shared cups in the shantytowns.[81]

FIGURE 4.6 The police in a scuffle with women demonstrators from Cato Manor outside the Victoria Street beer hall, June 18, 1959. Courtesy of Durban Local History Museum's Collections.

Native beers likewise adapted under colonialism, becoming more alcoholic with new ingredients and brewing techniques. European agronomists encouraged the planting of maize and sugar cane, although many African consumers preferred the taste of beer made with native grains like sorghum and millet. Already by 1900, many Africans had begun to brew with hops, perhaps in part because it was forbidden by colonial authorities. Regional styles developed with the availability of market ingredients. Mozambican migrants who worked in South African mines insisted on a particular brand of golden syrup, Lyle's, which they believed made a stronger brew than those made with local Natal brands. Other additives included tobacco, methylated spirits, and even cologne. European brewers and municipal factories often sold yeast and hops to the shebeens. Brewers in the shantytowns made use of any available materials, such as surplus metal drums and mechanical grinders that eased the labor.[82]

The conditions of urban brewing also affected family and gender relations, as women gained opportunities to earn income. While traditionalists felt women should brew for their husbands, some men preferred to drink with their friends in beer halls in order to get away from the constraints of domestic life. Women brewers needed the assistance of family members or friends for the brewing process, especially to watch out for the police. Such brewing circles were also valuable in case a woman was arrested for bootlegging, since companions brewed for her family while she was imprisoned. Some cultures drew strong connections between brewing and sexuality, for example, believing that intercourse spoiled fermentation. A beer hall manager declared: "Home brewing is invariably associated with women of bad repute."[83] Many women from the countryside did indeed engage in sex work to support themselves until they could either marry or set up a brewing business. Colonial officials imagined that brewing was a lucrative business for women, but in fact it was often a marginal pursuit for which women were not always fully compensated.[84]

The commodification of beer and family life also spread to the countryside under colonial rule. Homebrewing and drinking of native beers was prohibited on the reserves under the Natal Liquor Act of 1928. Nevertheless, the wages of migrant workers and the availability of consumer goods provided an incentive for rural women to brew more often, while the availability of grain markets made it possible for them to do so without having to rely on surplus grain controlled by male relatives. Women used the extra income to purchase factory-made clothes, soap, and housewares, in addition to feeding their families. Men responded to the women's commercial brewing by trying to ensure access to beer through traditional family relationships. The colonial state shared in attempts to maintain patriarchy in rural communities by ensuring male control over marketable goods. "I did it to earn my dowry," explained a young Kenyan woman on trial for illegal brewing in 1952. "My parents wish me to marry but I will not be an old man's donkey."[85]

Brewing festivals were adapted, and at times invented, to fit with the changing social conditions arising from migrant labor. The Xhosa "beer drink festival" (*Umsindleko*), in which families thanked the ancestors for the safe return of a relative, emerged in the 1930s as an adaptation of an earlier festival involving the slaughter of a goat after a long absence. The involvement of neighbors in what had formerly been a family affair served to reinforce the role of migrant labor as a means of support for the entire community, and elders from beyond the family served beer to guests. Public speeches likewise sought to emphasize the authority of elders and to resist the temptation to view wages as personal property of the worker rather than a resource for the entire community. Finally, the act of brewing illustrated the work of women as a source of communal solidarity. Nevertheless, the disruptive potential of drunkenness also provided a constant reminder of the dangers of modernization.[86]

Commercial brewing indeed had a disruptive influence on African life, although tradition itself was at times an artifact of colonial rule, constructed to hold native people in the countryside except when their labor was needed for capitalist enterprise. Young men who worked in the mines, factories, and docks were no longer dependent on their elders for beer and other consumer goods. In South Africa, even the native brew served in municipal beer halls became associated with Apartheid after 1948, as the national government used profits to administer segregated township governments.[87] The forbidden nature of bottled beer, by contrast, made it a desirable symbol of modernity and freedom.

Encounters between mass-produced beer and traditional drinking cultures helped to integrate diverse societies into modern networks of commerce under the unequal power relations of imperialism. This world of beer was shaped by countless individuals, from Tehuana textile merchants, Parsi bazaar traders, and Guinness world travelers to modernist Muslim youth, Japanese brewing magnates, and Zulu homebrewers. Even as metropolitan brewers improved commodity chains to distribute beer around the world, migrant brewers transplanted the raw materials and technology needed to supply colonial markets. Often financed by British capital, these settler enterprises upended the colonies' dependency on the metropole. To brew in diverse climates, settlers employed technologies of refrigeration and attemperation that had been developed in Europe while also innovating to adapt to local conditions and ingredients. In doing so, they continued the evolution of pale lager from a Central European product to a global style.

Whether imported from Europe or brewed locally, beer contributed to the civilizing mission of colonialism, even as the threat of drunkenness posed challenges to that same project. Lager beer's purity of taste became associated with European racial ideology, and it was also adopted as the drink of choice by the Japanese in their own quest for empire. Yet beer was not simply an ideological tool of empire; it also carved commercial inroads into subsistence societies. Such transformations succeeded because marginalized people within those societies, especially young men and women, were eager to escape the control of elders. Purchasing beer with the wages from migrant labor provided men a measure of autonomy, while women used homebrewing as a means of acquiring independent incomes. Alcohol represented both opportunity and danger for imperialists, as it mobilized native labor while threatening social stability through drunken revelry.

Finally, the widespread preference of British settlers for German beer illustrates how taste could confound the imperial enterprise. Accustomed to heavy ales from the homeland, Brits came to appreciate the lighter flavors of lager in the tropics. Pale lager became even more ubiquitous with the growth of national brewing industries in the twentieth century.

5

National Beers

IN 1901, HENRI Van Laer, director of the Ghent Institute of Brewing, proposed a contest to invent a Belgian national beer style. Some found the idea absurd for a country that already had diverse regional beer styles, but according to this renowned brewing scientist, regional fragmentation was precisely the problem with Belgian beers and, it went without saying, for the Belgian nation, which was split between Dutch-speaking Flanders, French-speaking Wallonia, and the officially bilingual capital of Brussels. Van Laer had spoken frankly about the national industry's limitations five years earlier on a North American tour. Most Belgian breweries were small in scale and used top-fermenting yeast and low-quality malt to produce beers with a "peculiar taste"; a handful of large, bottom-fermenting breweries made high-quality lagers but found limited markets; and the spontaneously fermented lambics of Brussels he described as "a remnant of the ancient ways of beer brewing."[1] Van Laer hoped that a grand contest would spur innovation within the national brewing industry, not only to counter the popularity of imported Munich and Pilsner lagers, but also to help Belgian exporters compete in international markets. However contrived this campaign may have been, brewing industries around the world became increasingly nationalized in the first half of the twentieth century through industrial concentration, import substitution, and mass marketing. But this wave of nationalism threatened to drown regional diversity beneath a flood of pale lagers.

The twentieth-century nationalization of beer, like nation building more broadly, took different forms depending on historical circumstances. At an ideological level, nationalists, who insisted on the unity of a particular group of people, often signaled their ideal community and right to political self-determination through consumer goods such as a shared beer style. That rival nations or minorities considered unfit for citizenship might drink essentially the same beer made little difference in their efforts to attach tangible form to diffuse and often conflicted communities. This political ideology was often separate from economic forms of nationalization that arose through the consolidation of beer markets within national boundaries. Brewers around the world took advantage of government infrastructure projects to expand beyond local and regional markets, utilizing newly built highways to transport their products and advertising through mass media. Technological advances of chemical and biological control as well as refrigeration, pasteurization, and bottling created economies of scale that also contributed to market concentration. The growth of contract brewing meanwhile relieved factory bottlenecks, allowing the production of individual brands in multiple factories, a controversial undertaking at the time. While political forms of beer nationalism dominated in continental Europe, economic versions were more pronounced in the Americas. The political and economic nationalization of beer was mutually reinforcing in postcolonial Africa and Asia, where governments encouraged national beer industries through subsidies and tariff protection to provide citizens with a modern, affordable luxury. Even socialist economies dedicated scarce resources to supplying beer for the proletariat, both in established brewing nations of Eastern Europe and in newcomers such as China. Wherever nationalists sought to use beer, they engaged with regional diversity within the nation and with transnational flows of technology, capital, and raw materials.

Pale lager continued to evolve around midcentury by becoming ever lighter. Improved brewing techniques enabled brewers to identify and avoid a wide range of potential contaminants, from traditional scourges like bacteria and wild yeast to unanticipated byproducts of modernity such as chlorinated water and compressed air. Changing consumer tastes also favored light beers, even in societies with long traditions of drinking strong ales such as Belgium, Britain, Canada, and Australia. Younger generations who grew up on soft drinks and industrial processed foods rejected their parents' tastes, while migrants from the countryside associated factory-purchased goods with modernity and upward mobility. Homebrewed memories of rural poverty existed not only in marginalized regions of Europe and North America but also in industrializing nations. Mexico City factory workers switched from sour pulque to sparkling Corona, and Nigerian oil roughnecks abandoned gritty sorghum beer for smooth Star lager. For those modern souls who stood apart from the crowd, Guinness Stout offered a mark of distinction. But those who preferred traditional beers were overwhelmed by a flood of cheap pale lager.

European Beer Nationalism

In beer-drinking lands across continental Europe, from Belgium to the former Austro-Hungarian Empire, industrial beer brands became a source of communal solidarity and national competition, reversing the nineteenth-century integration of pan-European beer markets. Henri Van Laer's proposal to invent a national beer style responded not only to the threat of imports but also to profound divisions within the Belgian nation and its signature industry. As the working classes came to prefer the clean taste of Pilsner, bourgeois society invented traditions around lambics and Trappist ales. Meanwhile, legal conflicts over the Pilsner name were caught up in political struggles between Germany and the newly independent Czechoslovakia, heightening tensions on the eve of World War II. Perhaps because of the intense ideological focus of European beer nationalism and the desire to exclude foreign competition, industrial consolidation within nations remained relatively limited in the first half of the century, helping small brewers to retain local markets.

Few beer markets were as fragmented as those of Belgium at the dawn of the twentieth century. Newspapers advertised a host of regional styles, including the blondes, browns, double browns, and old browns of Flanders, whites and browns from Louvain, variations on lambic such as gueuze, sparkling lambic, kriek, and faro around Brussels, still more localized beers from the Flemish towns of Diest and Audenarde, and Belgian versions of English, German, and Pilsner beers—plus the myriad farmhouse beers that never came to market. The production and sale of beer were likewise dispersed, as foreign traveler William Griffis observed: "In some Belgian towns to-day one wonders whether the 'estaminets' (café taverns) do not outnumber the families."[2] Even with industrialization, Belgian brewing remained a largely local affair; when the quarries of Quenast expanded production in the 1870s, for example, a nearby farmer named Jules Lefèbvre built a brewery and opened cafes at every entrance to quench the thirst of stoneworkers.[3]

Many in Brussels sought to enshrine the local lambic as the national drink. Although the use of spontaneous fermentation made it a "remnant" of the past, the beer's commercialization was a novelty of the belle epoque, dependent on modern blending techniques and a secondhand market for champagne bottles. To assist the industry's development, Henri Van Laer and his colleagues conducted research on the nature of local yeasts, which turned out to be variants of the Brettanomyces common in Britain. Practical brewers meanwhile conducted their own experiments with newfangled ingredients. Turn-of-the-century journalists celebrated the invention of a raspberry counterpart to kriek, although the traditional version made with sour cherries was only a few decades old. Promoters also packaged new rituals of consumption in the flag of Belgian nationalism. In the Gothic splendor of the Brussels city hall, Prince Albert ceremoniously declined a glass of champagne and instead toasted Belgian National Day on July 21, 1901, with a "lambic of honor." Brewers touted their second-class beer, faro, with another beloved national symbol, Manneken Pis. In the fountain located a few blocks south of the Grand Place, the cherubic sculpture spouted beer rather than water from his penis for a day.[4]

Even partisans viewed lambic with a curious ambivalence and considered it to be simultaneously modern and ancient, omnipresent and invisible. Although the drink had achieved wide recognition only with the Brussels International Exposition of 1897, patriots ascribed to it a suitably ancient lineage. One author declared: "The composition of faro and lambic—or more precisely lembeck—date to about 950."[5] Others associated lambic with the anxieties of modern life, reporting incidents of anonymous cafe goers who ordered a lambic, perhaps in fluent French but with a foreign accent, and ransacked the establishment while the proprietor retrieved a bottle from the cellar. Journalists cheered exports to England, Germany, and even the Transvaal province of South Africa, but disputed the presence of lambic in Brussels. A self-described flaneur set one story "in the Grand Café of the Center, among the ecumenical pints of lambic and faro," while another writer insisted that to find a glass of lambic, one could not simply stroll down the fashionable boulevards or even take a tram to the suburbs, but rather had to take a train out of the city. "It's a real voyage."[6]

For the Belgian brewing industry as a whole, lambic's sour taste and erratic fermentation held little prospect for stemming the tide of imported lager. With such concerns in mind, Van Laer and a delegation of leading brewers petitioned the Ministry of Industry and Labor to sponsor a national beer contest as part of the International Exposition of Brewing, Food Industry, and Hygiene to be held in Brussels in 1904. The Ministry endorsed the proposal, but the contest soon ran into trouble. Two weeks after the call went out, a brewer named Van der Harten objected to the inherent conflict between the competitive advantage of individual firms and the collective benefits to the national industry: "I will not take part in a national contest for a Belgian style beer," he insisted, "because . . . it requires a perfectly detailed description of the methods of production, so that every brewer could produce that beer."[7] In the end, only twenty-one brewers considered the prize money sufficient to offset the loss of proprietary knowledge and submitted a recipe. But an even larger question remained as to whether Belgian beer styles should be chosen by a jury of experts or by the market as a whole. Brewing scientists generally advocated for the purity of bottom fermentation, but small firms could ill afford the transition from top-fermenting yeasts. Likewise, many connoisseurs preferred the rich flavors of dark beers, while the mass market was increasingly shifting toward pale, light beers. With the jury unable to reach consensus, Van Laer proposed running the contest again, but opposition from regional brewers, particularly in Flanders, doomed this attempt to decree a Belgian national beer.[8]

While top-down engineering of beer styles failed, innovation continued to bubble up from Belgian brewing kettles. About 1900, a new beer called Jack-Op became popular among students, particularly at the Catholic University of Louvain, as a regional and generational alternative to the lambic favored by the Brussels petit bourgeoisie. The meaning of the name is unknown, but a classified advertisement of 1902 reported a lost dog who "answers to the name Jack-Op"—perhaps he was confused by all the cafe goers calling him. Renowned brewing scientist Hubert Verachtert described Jack-Op as a brown ale with a dose of lambic to add sourness and extend shelf life. It was produced north of Louvain in the village of Werchter by a young brewer, Arthur Van Roost. His beer won an Honorable Mention in the Milan Exposition of 1906 and a coveted tap at the capital's Café Central. Rivals soon began to imitate Jack-Op, and to keep up with demand, Van Roost contracted out production to a second brewery, De Palmboom.[9]

Belgian beer production remained highly decentralized around the turn of the century, with more than 2,600 breweries for a population of around 7 million. Lambic brewers made little attempt at vertical integration or branding and used sales agents or simply classified advertisements to list stocks of gueuze, kriek, and faro available to merchants and cafes. Belgian Lion Gueuze, one of the earliest brand names, was marketed in about 1900 by A. J. Simon, the import agent for Bass. Although a few family firms like Cantillon have survived to the present, perhaps more typical of belle-epoque lambic breweries was Dewolfs Freres et Soeurs (Brothers and Sisters), located in the garden suburb of Boitsfort. The founding generation had built the three-story, red-brick brewery during the lambic boom of the 1890s. The most prominent of the brothers, Philippe, was a renowned horticulturalist and liberal mayor of Boitsfort. A younger brother, Henri-Édouard, was the family brewer, while an unmarried sister, Marie, and possibly the widowed sister Emile, participated in the business. The Dewolfs seem not to have chased after gold medals in world's fairs and instead focused on serving their loyal customers around

FIGURE 5.1 The Belgian brewer Arthur Van Roost, maker of the popular Jack-Op beer, would have seemed at home today in any hipster microbrewery, with undercut hair blending into the stubble of his beard, topped by a brush-up and handlebar mustache. *Le Petite Journal du Brasseur* 8, no. 323 (June 22, 1900): 359. Courtesy of Bibliothèque Royale de Belgique.

Boitsfort. The second-generation brewer, Jean-Henri Dewolfs, had taken over the firm by the 1930s and continued to serve the community.[10]

Despite this apparent prosperity, pale lager was already making inroads among younger generations and eventually came to dominate the industry. The Artois brewery of Louvain had made the transition to bottom fermentation in 1893, constructed underground caverns, and launched its Stella brand in the 1920s. Like other national brewers, it used advertising to bypass cafes and sell directly for home consumption. "Hello! Hello!" began one newspaper promotion, which then listed the telephone number of the company's agent. For those unfamiliar with telecommunications, the ad helpfully provided a script for ordering a twelve-pack. Artois rebuilt the brewery in the late 1920s, constructing an ultramodern landmark in the picturesque town of Louvain.[11]

The spread of lager beer coincided with campaigns to promote hygiene and modernity in the interwar years, but also spawned waves of nostalgia for more traditional beverages. A poster from the 1920s displayed two nursing mothers under the phrase: "Beer is Nourishment." On the left, an attractive, middle-class woman feeding a plump, blond baby held up a sparkling, foamy beer. The caption declared: "She buys her beer at the brewery." On the right, a squalling, emaciated infant refused to nurse from a haggard, plebeian mother with a cloudy, flat beer. "She makes the drink herself."[12] While progressive mothers could not afford to risk the health of their children, other members of the Belgian bourgeoisie celebrated the old-style beers as a mark of national authenticity. Newspapers evoked the seventeenth-century painter of peasant life, Pieter Bruegel the Elder, with photographs of people in rural costume pouring lambic from ceramic pitchers, while authors lamented the disappearance of faro, which had been replaced by lager as the drink of the working classes.[13]

The themes of nostalgia and health came together between the wars with the growing popularity of Trappist beer. This monastic order was founded in the seventh century and fled to Belgium in the 1790s to escape the secularizing campaigns of the French Revolution. Following the Rule of St. Benedict, the Trappists produced their own foods and marketed surplus cheese, chocolate, and chicory coffee. Trappist beers were sold from a Brussels drug store as early as 1893. The advertisement, likely written by the pharmacist rather than the fathers, promised: "Regenerate the blood. Fortify the pulmonary [system] and bronchi."[14] The ad did not specify the precise monastery that produced the beer. Indeed, the drink might have had no ties to actual Trappists, as the industry experienced fraudulent claims of religious affiliations. One monastery eventually sued a Brasschaat brewery in 1934 for using the Trappist name on their beers. Although not identified in news reports, the firm may have been the Drie Linden Brewery of Hendrik Verlinden, who in 1919 had acted as a consultant for the nearby monastery of Westmalle. Defense lawyers argued that the Trappist name was not a trademark but rather applied to many beers produced by different monasteries. The Antwerp judge admonished the fathers to stick to their good works, denied their request for 250,000 francs in damages, and ordered them to pay court costs. Encouraged by the ruling, brewers producing fake Trappist beers proliferated, marketing under brand names such as Cardinal, Kapittel, Stavelot, and Bia Bouquet. Belgian attempts to nationalize brewing around nostalgic and modern beers were repeated throughout Europe, fragmenting the continental markets forged in the late nineteenth century.[15]

The Bohemian brewing industry faced new opportunities and challenges with the breakup of the multiethnic Habsburg Empire. Emerging national loyalties splintered the formerly bilingual inhabitants of the renowned brewing town known as Budweis in German and Budějovice in Czech. The Citizens' Brewery was founded in 1795 by about 400 downtown property owners, whose shares in the brewery transferred along with the sale of their buildings. Enriched by dividends from the thriving business, shareholders generally voted for Liberal German politicians following the Revolution of 1848, although a growing minority identified with Czech nationalists. In 1895, insurgents founded a rival Czech Shareholders' Brewery, whose sales surpassed the established firm in just six years. Mismanagement contributed to the decline of the Citizens' Brewery, but beer drinking had also become an indicator of national identity, limiting local markets. Meanwhile, exports suffered as Austria imposed high tariffs on its former province, and Germans organized boycotts against Czech beer.[16]

The spread of tariff restrictions renewed the importance of protecting the designation of place names, a question left unanswered by courts and legislatures before World War I. When a German court ruling in 1920 reaffirmed that Pilsner indicated a quality description rather than a place of origin, the newly independent government of Czechoslovakia proposed a treaty granting German brewers absolute assurance of their naming rights in return for reciprocal treatment. Bavarian breweries had long fought against the abuse of place names, since many breweries across Germany produced a Munich beer alongside a Pilsner. Nevertheless, northern German industrialists protested that losing the trade name would threaten more than 500 breweries producing some 8 million hectoliters of Pilsner each year. The continued popularity of Pilsner Urquell already created a trade imbalance, and the German government refused to recognize Czech claims. A civil court in Prague retaliated by declaring that the name of the fabled German knife-making town of Solingen was a quality indicator that could be used by steelmakers anywhere.[17]

Anti-Pilsner sentiment also became associated with Nazi racial ideologies. The National Socialist movement had first gained notoriety with the Beer Hall Putsch of 1923, when a superannuated German general and an unhinged Austrian corporal plotted in a Munich tavern to overthrow the democratically elected government of Bavaria.[18] Two years later, Nazi agitators in Passau denounced Pilsner beer imports over insults supposedly suffered by Germans living in the Sudetenland of western Czechoslovakia. With the increasing polarization of German politics in the 1930s, the party inflamed its attacks on Pilsner as a threat to national sovereignty, offering the sarcastic invitation: "Drink Czech beer, demand a Pan-European state."[19] Even beer coasters became instruments of propaganda after the Reichstag Fire of 1933; when drinkers lifted a glass of one brand of Pilsner, they saw Czechoslovakia depicted as a sack opening into the side of Germany and spewing barley grains like an army of occupation. The image's caption declared: "Every Reichsmark that departs into foreign lands increases unemployment and imperils the national wealth. Therefore, German, drink German beer!"[20]

Beer nationalism extended beyond Pilsner, as the German government also sought to restrict French imports with an ironic attack on brands employing German-language names such as Prinzbräu and Schlossbräu. The French government responded by complaining about the illegal dumping of German beers on their market. During the Sudetenland crisis of 1938, as Hitler schemed to seize the industrial heartland of Czechoslovakia, Nazi party leaders in neighboring Saxony declared a "Beer War against Czech Breweries." To assist a planned boycott of Pilsner Urquell, identified as a "Jewish business," the flyer provided a list of "Good German Breweries" to patronize along with "Czech breweries" to avoid.[21]

At the outbreak of World War II, Germans took over the Czech brewing industry for the use of the Nazi military, but allied blockades and bombing devastated the supply chains for foods of all kinds. The Pilsner brewery's reputation as a Jewish business facilitated its expropriation under Aryanization laws. Even the Pilsner beer garden was symbolically Germanized as a Volkspark (people's park). More broadly, the government took control of food industries in occupied territories through marketing bodies such as the Bohemian-Moravian Federation for Hops, Malt, and Beer. A third of all Czech breweries were destroyed during the war, and international supply lines were disrupted as well. To obtain foreign exchange, German hops were exported along elaborate routes, disguised on neutral Belgian ships, through Istanbul, and even across the trans-Siberian railroad to Japan.[22]

Following World War II, chilled beers were deployed as weapons in the Cold War between capitalism and communism. The Czech Socialist Republic's Brewing Research Institute declared: "Comrades, our task is not to improve the quality of beer but to ensure that our workers have enough of it."[23] Belying that commitment to equality, the leading brands were exported to generate much-needed foreign exchange. Nevertheless, beer was important enough in German and Czech culture to ensure a basic commitment to quality, if only to prevent rioting. Women benefited from greater access to beer under Communism, since it was increasingly available bottled in grocery stores and not only in male-dominated taverns. Communist support of gender equality also led to a feminization of brewing, a shift already apparent to an American trade delegation to the Soviet Union in the 1930s. Before the construction of the Berlin Wall, instructors at the Berlin brewing academy (VLB) gave lectures in the Russian Zone to largely female classes. The women laborers remained active in the brewery workforce, though they were often shunted off to perform menial tasks.[24]

Belgian patriots during World War II used beer to voice their covert disdain for the German invaders, but even with the postwar return of cafe culture, the passing of an older generation accelerated the decline of lambic. In a pair of newspaper articles in July 1940, an anonymous author celebrated the "rebellious lambic" as an expression of Belgian spirit, while describing "le bock"—a veiled reference to the occupying soldiers, since the German-origin lager had been localized under the name "bock"—as automatons "accepting a rational regime, manufactured down to the last detail, and realized in a quasi-mathematical fashion."[25] Nostalgia persisted after the war, but the old-timers' memories did little to help lambic brewers pass their businesses on to the next generation. Classified ads to attract young brewers and salesmen lingered forlornly for months in newspapers, and storied firms were forced to close. After a series of industrial accidents, the Jack-Op Brewery was folded into an industrial conglomerate in 1954, two years before the last Van Roost brewer, Félix, passed away. When Jean-Henri Dewolfs died in 1960, the Boitsfort brewery was shuttered. As mergers and closures decimated the industry, Henry Lemaire provided an epitaph for a generation: "If lambic still hangs on around Brussels, faro, for its part, is dead and will not be resurrected."[26]

Although beer symbolized nationalist struggles in continental Europe during the twentieth century, the industry remained far less concentrated than its counterparts elsewhere. Tied houses and limits on advertising ensured continued small-scale production in West Germany, while in East Europe central planning dictated that breweries serve local markets and not advertise at all.[27] Industrial concentration increased most in Belgium, but from such a diffuse base that even the closing of large numbers of small breweries left a considerable base in operation. By contrast, the national consolidation of brewing in the Americas was more far-reaching.

Consolidation in the Americas

"Twenty million Mexicans can't be mistaken!"[28] With this brash slogan, the Modelo Brewery implied that Corona beer was preferred by every man, woman, and child, as enumerated by the country's 1940 census. Unlike the cosmopolitan clientele of the nineteenth-century brands Bohemia and High Life, Corona appealed to a mass market through a combination of nationalist symbolism (the combination of Spanish crown and indigenous feathered serpent) and modernist sensibility (art deco lettering painted on clear, glass bottles). By the 1940s, a booming economy and urban growth made beer an affordable pleasure for the middle classes and factory workers. The Modelo Brewery of Mexico City and Cuauhtémoc, its Monterrey-based rival, built national markets by taking over regional breweries, modernizing plant and equipment, shipping on newly built highways, and advertising in print and cinema, all under the protection of high tariff barriers that restricted foreign competitors. Technological innovation and economic development policies encouraged similar patterns of industrial consolidation throughout the Americas.

Decades of transnational research on malting, brewing chemistry, fermentation, and hop utilization gave brewers greater control over production and allowed them to extract more beer from existing equipment. Moreover, a new "cylindroconical" tank design allowed brewing and fermentation to take place in the same vessel, enabling faster and more hygienic production. Both the science and engineering crossed national boundaries; the cylindrical tanks, for example, were pioneered by Swiss and British brewers in the 1920s, and improved by the Dutch and Irish, before the Japanese added the sloped bottom in the 1960s. But theoretical models proposed by brewing science did not always work out on the factory floor. Continuous fermentation, long considered the holy grail of industrial efficiency, suffered in practice from microbial contamination and unpleasant flavors. Nevertheless, this research offered significant improvements in batch production. High-gravity brewing beckoned as another way to boost productivity; beer was brewed with high-alcohol beer and then diluted back to the expected strength. Although useful in some industrial applications, such as the "extreme beers" of craft brewers, it never quite tasted the same as traditional methods. Taken together, these technological advances had the paradoxical effect of increasing the so-called minimum efficient scale of brewing from 100,000 barrels a year to a million, creating economies of scale that favored the largest producers, while at the same time allowing small-scale brewers to match the quality and consistency of premium beers. This provided the foundation for the rise of craft brewing a few decades later.[29]

Brewing, like other industries, was transformed by marketing. The shift from drinking in exclusively male saloons to the gender-mixed domestic

FIGURE 5.2 "Twenty million Mexicans can't be mistaken!" This early version of a long-running advertising campaign from the Modelo Brewery implied that Corona beer was preferred by every man, woman, and child in Mexico, as enumerated by the 1940 census. The slogan was inspired by a Prohibition-era song in the United States about French drinking habits. Source: *El Nacional*, December 15, 1941, 4. Courtesy Biblioteca Miguel Lerdo de Tejada of the Secretaría de Hacienda y Crédito Público (SHCP), Mexico City.

consumption was facilitated by the spread of home refrigerators and the invention of canned beer in 1935. Canning technology did not achieve its full potential until the introduction of aluminum in the late 1950s and the ring pull lid in 1964. In the short term, delivery trucks had a greater impact by allowing distributors to reach beyond the major railroad lines to small-town markets. Improvements in bottling and canning favored large producers, since they could more easily afford the expensive systems required. Finally, advertising became an increasingly important factor in building brand loyalty, as the actual taste of most beer brands became ever milder and more indistinguishable.[30]

The mild, refreshing taste of lager beer ranks among the achievements of twentieth-century science, a tribute to the work of transnational brewing professionals and the food industry's larger project of quantifying flavor. In 1938, F. P. Siebel of Chicago summarized the problem in practical terms. "There has been much discussion as to whether the beer has the same flavor and aroma as in the days before Prohibition," he observed. "This is no way of telling if such a statement is right or wrong, for no methods, either subjective or objective, physical or chemical, have yet been developed for recording the flavor and aroma of fermented beer."[31] Yet even as Siebel lamented the failings of taste memory, brewing scientists at the Carlsberg Laboratory had developed a protocol for standardized taste testing. The Copenhagen system, also known as the triangular tasting panel, convened a group of experts and provided each with three unmarked glasses of beer, two identical and one different. Based on the number of tasters who detected the odd sample, researchers could calculate the probabilistic difference between the two beers. With a reliable means for testing samples, Jean de Clerck of Leuven, Heinrich Leurs of Munich, and other scientists methodically varied raw materials and brewing conditions to identify the complex chemical components of taste and smell that emerged from the myriad reactions in malting, brewing, and fermentation. A few women contributed to the industry's scientific development. For example, Elsie Siguen, a German émigré chemist at Siebel Institute of Technology in Chicago, published early research on flavor technology in the 1930s, and Joan Robblee headed the chemistry department at the Iron City Brewery of Pittsburgh in the 1960s.[32]

Given the financial costs that would arise from the contamination of enormous tanks, brewers sought to remove any possible flavor irregularities that might offend consumers. Like their forerunners fifty years earlier, midcentury brewers attributed the changes in beer tastes to market demand. Brewing professional Kurt Becker observed in 1951 the "definite trend in the United States towards beers of paler color, less satiating character, reduced bitterness, milder and blander flavor, more 'snap' in the sense of thirst quenching qualities, and with emphasis on either a 'drier' or 'sweeter' taste." Painstaking quality control was essential, Becker explained, because "even the faintest of off tastes and odors are likely to become manifest to the average consumer because the delicate beers of today and tomorrow have nothing to mask or hide irregularities."[33] If not strong flavors, what consumers did want was foam, and scientists probed the mysteries of carbonation. Researchers at Guinness discovered how to use nitrogen to stabilize foam, although lingering heads had previously been a source of consumer complaints. In an otherwise dry technical report, Becker waxed poetically: "In its creamy whiteness, seething with the forces of creation and destruction, foam has universal aesthetic appeal."[34]

Perhaps the first truly national brewing firm in North America was Mexico's Cuauhtémoc, which already held a commanding presence across regional markets by the mid-1930s. A branch of the Garza Sada industrial group of Monterrey, the company had offered to buy out the fledgling Modelo Brewery in the late 1920s, and when rebuffed, it purchased the Central Brewery of Mexico City. In the 1930s, Cuauhtémoc contracted with firms in Veracruz and Guadalajara to brew its brands for eastern and western markets, and a decade later it took over the failing Tecate Brewery in the northwest. Modelo responded with its own expansion plan, acquiring the Toluca and Mexico Brewery in 1935, followed by the west coast Estrella and Pacífico breweries in the 1950s, and building new plants across the north in Sonora and Coahuila in the 1960s. Cuautémoc's merger with Moctezuma and Modelo's purchase of the Yucateca Brewery in the 1980s cemented a duopoly within the Mexican beer industry.[35]

Nationalization had significant consequences for supply chains and consumer cultures. To provide skilled technicians for their industrial empire, the Garza Sada family established a brewing program in 1943 at the Monterrey Technological Institute, which was modeled on the Massachusetts Institute of Technology. A graduate of the program, Guillermo Ceballos Aguilera, devised new machinery in the 1960s to process and malt sorghum, thereby anticipating the demand for gluten-free beers. With the growth of mass markets, drinking occasions became more commercialized; for example, the Yucatecan "cerveza lunch" was transformed into the "Crystal Hour" (Hora Cristal), a popular radio program sponsored by a local brand. The sensory taste of beer also changed, not always for the better. Sorghum beers do not appeal to every taste, and Corona's clear glass bottles increased the risk of light exposure, which can cause "degradation of iso-α-acid bitter substances," a condition "referred to either as 'lightstruck,' or worse still, 'skunky.' "[36] National consolidation also led to the standardization of regional styles that dated in some cases to the late nineteenth century. After the takeover by Modelo, Yucateca's loyal customers complained that their familiar Montejo and Negra León brands did not taste the same.[37]

While brewing duopolies took shape in Mexico, Brazil, and Argentina, smaller Latin American countries fell under the sway of national monopolies.

The Foam Pourer in action.

FIGURE 5.3 "The Foam Pourer in Action. Watching the Results." Midcentury brewing scientists probe the mysteries of carbonation. James S. Wallerstein, "The Nature and Origin of Beer Foam," *Communications on the Science and Practice of Brewing* 1 (December 1937): 31–38.

The United Brewing Company essentially controlled the Chilean industry by the 1910s, while the Guatemalan-based Central American Brewery, with its Gallo (rooster) brand, dominated beer markets throughout the region. In Colombia, the Bavaria Brewing Consortium of Bogotá and the Continental Brewery of Medellín shared the national market until World War II, when the government expropriated Bavaria from its German and Dutch immigrant owners and sold it to the powerful Santo Domingo family. With the purchase of Continental in the 1970s, Bavaria gained an almost complete monopoly over Colombian brewing.[38]

Canadian beer markets were fragmented by province until after World War II, when three firms expanded to create a national oligopoly. Industrial consolidation began in the 1920s when the Quebec firm National Breweries bought up venerable brands like Dawes Black Horse and Dow Ale. Unfortunately, they did so just as the market was shifting away from old-fashioned, hoppy ales toward modern pale lagers. More successful was the Ontario-based Canadian Breweries Limited, run by E. P. "Eddie" Taylor. The son of an investment banker, he took over his grandfather's brewery and followed National's expansionist playbook. However, he closed ale breweries and focused instead on the lager brands Carling Black Label and O'Keefe's. Taylor overextended himself during the Great Depression but held the company together until his expansionist bets paid off during the postwar boom. By 1948, Canadian Breweries had surpassed Labatt as Ontario's leading brewer, and in 1952, Taylor bought out the failing National Breweries to gain a strong position in Quebec. He then headed westward, just in time to profit from the Alberta oil boom. When government attorneys lost a competition case against Taylor, Labatt and Montreal-based Molson rushed to build their own national presence. Whereas sixty-one breweries operated at the end of World War II, all within provincial boundaries, by 1962, the Big Three brewed almost 95 percent of the beer in Canada.[39]

In the United States, although Midwestern brewers Anheuser Busch, Pabst, and Schlitz had shipped across the country since the nineteenth century, local and regional firms remained competitive until after World War II. Prohibition has often been blamed for the downfall of regional diversity, but within just two years of its repeal, 750 breweries had resumed operation. Competition was subdued as many states and localities remained dry, and regulators kept a close watch in jurisdictions where beer was legal. With low demand during the Great Depression, brewers focused instead on cutting costs. Fears of a return to prohibition disappeared after the outbreak of World War II, as Congress jacked up taxes and ordered beer for the troops.

When wartime rationing finally ended, brewers rushed to acquire a national presence. Pabst planted the flag in the Northeast in 1945 with the purchase of the Hoffman Brewery of Newark, New Jersey, and Midwestern rivals closely followed. Regional brewers Ballantine, Schaeffer, and Rheingold fought back, sparking brutal advertising and price wars. Guinness unwittingly entered this vicious market in 1949 by opening a brewery in Long Island City, New York; five bruising years later they bid a retreat. Meanwhile, new rivalries erupted in California and Florida. Finally, in the late 1950s, as management scholar Anita McGahan explained: "A new type of rivalry began, with several of the largest shippers adopting advertising and distribution strategies to secure a stable national advantage."[40]

In the postwar era, national brands gained market power in consumer goods sectors, from household appliances to fast food. Among brewers, the relentless ambitions of industry leaders drove consolidation. August Anheuser "Gussie" Busch Jr. took over the family firm in 1946, determined to be number one, whatever the cost. To do so, he opened a succession of state-of-the-art facilities in Newark (1951), Los Angeles (1953), Tampa (1959), Houston (1966), and Columbus (1968). Meanwhile, the Frederick Miller Brewery of Milwaukee had been a regional player as late as the 1937, when Frederick and Clara Miller retired, leaving the firm to their daughter Elise as president and son Frederick as vice president. Through innovative advertisements, including in women's magazines, Miller had become a national brand by the early 1950s. Nevertheless, such unbridled growth was not always the most profitable approach in the short term. Anheuser Busch's St. Louis rival, Falstaff, built a highly profitable regional firm starting in 1936 with the purchase of the Krug Brewery of Omaha, Nebraska. Falstaff was the first American firm to brew the same brand in multiple locations, achieving a consistent flavor that many had previously considered impossible. A year later, the company bought the National Brewery of New Orleans and in 1954, the Berghoff Brewery of Fort Wayne, Indiana. By rationalizing production and limiting debt, Falstaff was actually more profitable than the nationals. Yet another successful model was the portfolio approach taken by Heileman, a regional brewer from LaCrosse, Wisconsin. As national giants began squeezing regional brewers in the 1960s, Heileman stepped in to buy their brands, consolidating production in a far more economical fashion than Anheuser Busch's expensive new factories.[41]

Even as breweries built nationwide markets, some people struggled for acceptance in the workplace and in spaces of consumption. White concerns about the supposed dangers of African American drinking had contributed to the political coalition that enacted Prohibition, and stereotypes lingered.[42] In the 1950s a brewing professional described a beer brand that had supposedly become popular "among the colored population of New Orleans" on account of its advertising the properties of lupulin (the agent in hops); "the rumor circulated that this substance, lupulin, increases man's sexual powers considerably, and sales of this beer have increased substantially."[43] Discrimination also followed blacks on the Great Migration northward; tavern owners in postwar Milwaukee charged them higher prices on the pretext that their beer mugs could not be reused by white customers and had to be thrown out. Race featured in union struggles, including a 1953 strike against Milwaukee firms and another in 1977 against Coors in Golden, Colorado. Boycotts in both cases united progressive whites with African Americans and Latinos, all of whom wished to withhold their consumer dollars from companies that refused to treat them fairly in the workplace.[44]

Technological advances facilitated postwar industrial consolidation, although the success of regional brewers like Heileman demonstrates that technology alone did not determine the structure of the industry. Industrial policies also contributed to the rise of brewing oligopolies throughout the Americas. But even while mass production made commodity beer more affordable for many customers, women and minorities struggled to gain access to jobs and bars. Those same trends also extended to the British Commonwealth.

A Commonwealth of Beer

Rasendra I. Mazumdar began each day "mashing-in" a batch of Kingfisher lager, then playing nine holes of golf before breakfast. "Mazzie" had taken up golf in Edinburgh in 1946 while completing the fermentation program at Heriot-Watt University, where he became the first native Indian to gain credentials as a master brewer. The British exodus from India the following year opened the position of general manager at United Breweries, a company founded in 1915 through the merger of regional breweries.[45] After independence, control passed to Vittal Mallya, who had likewise just returned at age twenty-two from a Grand Tour of Britain. Across the Commonwealth, politically connected businessmen and talented brewing professionals like Mallya and Mazumdar leveraged postcolonial development policies to build national brewing industries. The brewers' Anglophilia did not stop them from favoring Pilsner-style beers like Kingfisher. Even in the ale bastions of Britain and Australia, bottom fermentation gained ground in the postwar decades. The exception once again was Guinness; from its headquarters in a former British colony, the company embraced the new political climate with joint ventures and local factories, nationalizing the brand across Africa, Asia, and the Caribbean. Guinness also responded to taste trends by introducing a pale lager called Harp. As postcolonial migrations carried new beer brands and drinking cultures to Britain, the empire of lager struck back against the metropolis of ale.

Brash Canadian entrepreneur Eddie Taylor shook the British brewing industry out of complacency and drove a wave of mergers in the 1960s. Industrial consolidation had already reduced the number of breweries in the United Kingdom from more than 11,000 at the turn of the century to 567 in 1950, but most firms still catered to regional and local markets. The six largest brewers controlled just 16 percent of the nation's pubs and produced a quarter of the nation's beer. Taylor entered the market in 1952 through a joint arrangement with Hope & Anchor, whereby the Sheffield brewer sold Carling Black Label in Britain, while Taylor's company introduced Jubilee Stout in Canada. The deal proved mutually disappointing: Canadians had little interest in the heavy, dark beer, and Taylor needed more than a modest stable of Yorkshire pubs to achieve his national ambitions. In 1959, he bought out the failing Hope & Anchor and used it as a platform for growth, merging with Hammonds United Breweries in 1960, Charrington in 1962, and finally Bass in 1967. Taylor's negotiating failures proved as consequential as his successes; companies sold themselves in desperation to any British brewer that would take them rather than fall into colonial hands. Rising property values also contributed to the industry's consolidation, as real estate developers bought out breweries just to gain access to undervalued urban pubs. By 1967, the "Big Six" of Bass Charrington, Allied, Courage, Scottish and Newcastle, Whitbread, and Watney, Mann and Truman, plus Guinness dominated the industry. Further consolidation reduced the number of breweries in the United Kingdom from 524 to 142 by 1980, at which point they brewed 80 percent of the nation's beer and controlled half the pubs.[46]

Industrial change likewise had implications for the marketing of beer in postwar Britain. Guinness and Whitbread had developed highly successful advertising campaigns in the interwar period, even as large brewers improved their bottling and distribution networks. During World War II, the troops consumed bottled beer, a habit many continued after returning home. The modern cachet of bottles also appealed to women, who increasingly purchased beer in supermarkets. This growing domestic market threatened pubs. Having invested heavily in building chains, brewers sought to modernize traditional outlets by replacing antiquated and labor-intensive "engines," fed by lead pipes from musty cellars, with so-called keg beers that were brewery conditioned, meaning carbonated, filtered, and pasteurized. Despite industrial rationalization, British productivity lagged behind the United States and Germany, in part because the "Big Six" continued to brew in relatively small plants for variegated markets with distinct local tastes.

While British beer traditionalists were unhappy about keg beers, they looked with genuine horror on the spread of lager. Many blamed the brewers for foisting pale lager on an unsuspecting public as part of their modernization scheme, thus echoing claims made fifty years earlier about the triumph of pale lager over dark in the United States. But there was considerable demand for lighter beers from British veterans who had acquired a taste for lager while stationed in Germany, tourists who vacationed on the Mediterranean coast, immigrants from lager drinking colonies, and young people who rejected their parents' preference for heavier ales. Light lagers also went better with spicy Indian and Caribbean foods, which gained popularity in the postwar era. Although the first major brands, Carling Black Label, Allied's Skol, and Guinness's Harp, were only introduced in about 1960, lager had claimed a 30 percent share by 1980 and a full half of the beer market a decade later.[47]

With their seeming links to an ancestral England, pubs became a crucial battleground in struggles for national identity in a postcolonial era. Although the material trappings and social composition of public houses have changed radically from patrician Georgian inns to working-class Victorian pubs and the interwar "improved pubs," Britons imagined a timeless institution at the center of communal life. The image of English traditionalism was challenged by postcolonial migrants from Africa, Asia, and the Caribbean, who began to claim spaces for themselves in the pub. When the Indian Workers Association began to organize immigrants in the late 1950s, it recruited them in pubs as well as temples. West Indians likewise colonized locals in working-class neighborhoods. Violence broke out when immigrants tried to order pints in what were considered exclusively English pubs. The Notting Hill race riots of 1958 began with turf battles over pubs, as did the violent summer of 1981, when racialized youth and police fought for ten days across Britain.[48]

Postwar Australian brewing mirrored trends found in the United Kingdom, with industrial consolidation, the rise of lager, and racial tension. Australia's smaller, more concentrated population contributed to the establishment of state-level monopolies or duopolies. Economies of scale among larger firms and limits on the number of hotels, as pubs were known, deterred new competitors from entering the market. Brewers produced a full range of products, although ale remained the drink of choice as late as 1940. According to the *Australian Brewing and Wine Journal*, 67 million gallons of ale were consumed compared with 8 million of lager and 3 million of stout. As in Britain, lager swept the market in the postwar era.[49] Beer also played an important role in civil rights struggles in Australia. In 1965, the academics Rosalie Bogner and Merle Thornton chained themselves to a bar in the Regatta Hotel of Brisbane to protest discrimination against serving alcohol to women. Because the White Australia policy restricted immigrants from Asia and the Caribbean, racial animosity was often directed against Aboriginal peoples. Even after bans on alcohol sales to Native Australians were overturned in the 1970s, barkeepers often refused to serve non-white customers. Senator Neville Bonner, Australia's first Indigenous parliamentarian, made a habit of challenging racist publicans, and the negative publicity when he was denied a beer, for example, at a Warrnambool Hotel in 1975, contributed to the wider protest movement against discriminatory practices by whites.[50]

Unlike in Britain and its settler colonies, the challenges to nationalizing beer in South Asia lay in widespread moral condemnation and the difficulty of marketing to impoverished rural communities. The Indian Constitution enshrined prohibition, at least as a goal, while Pakistan and Bangladesh forbade the consumption of alcohol by Muslims. Vittal Mallya expanded United Breweries from its independence-era base in Bangalore, Madras, and Nilgiris through the construction or acquisition of eight new factories in the 1950s and 1960s. By the end of the century, the company operated nearly thirty breweries across India. Its chief rival, Shaw Wallace & Co., started in the 1880s as a Calcutta mercantile house specializing in tea, moved into liquor after independence, and began brewing in 1963 through a joint venture with Britain's Allied Breweries. Sheltered by tariffs from international competition, Indian brewers and other manufacturers faced their most significant challenge in building distribution networks to penetrate the vast up-country. Parsee wholesalers continued to dominate the sale of alcohol, as they had in colonial times, but even the most efficient networks could not overcome the low disposable incomes in rural India. Punjabi officials complained about persistent bootlegging of distilled spirits despite the government having spent large sums in the early 1970s to subsidize breweries, suggesting that price and potency remained important considerations for consumers.[51]

Throughout postcolonial South Asia, beer drinking remained associated with imperial nostalgia among particular communities. East Indians, an indigenous people living around Bombay who converted to Christianity, combined beer and cooking through the tradition of "bottle masala." In an annual summertime event, held over two or three days, families purchased their favorite spices from the *masalawallah* (spice man), and then stored them in empty beer bottles. In the north, Punjabis drank beer and wine at roadside stalls, perhaps using travel as a way to evade moral restrictions. These informal pubs were often decorated with Union Jack flags and other colonial memorabilia. Likewise, the survival of the Murree brewery in Muslim Pakistan has been attributed by newspaper editor Rashed Rahman to "vaguely affectionate memories of the British Raj. 'Everyone knows that when the gora sahibs ["white masters"] were here the beer... was the only thing that stopped them from going nuts in the heat,' [Rahman] jokes."[52]

Both the production and consumption of alcohol were associated with masculinity in India. It has been difficult for women to break into the industry. The daughter of United Breweries general manager Mazzie, Kiran Mazumdar, graduated at the top of her class at the Malting and Brewing program of Ballarat College in Australia and hoped to follow her father's profession. When sexism within the industry prevented her advancement, she founded a biotechnology company instead. For many Indian consumers, alcohol content was the primary selling point. Firms touted the strength of brands such as Mysore Breweries Limited's "Knock Out/High Punch/Strong Beer," which reproduced a famous photograph of Muhammad Ali knocking out Sonny Liston on the label. Brewers nevertheless carefully observed legal limits, which varied by state between 5 and 8 percent alcohol.[53]

Colonial-era breweries likewise provided the basis for national industries in Africa. The first brewery in French West Africa was built by Les Brasseries et Glaceries d'Indochine in Cameroon in 1948, while in the neighboring British colony, Heineken and Unilever established Nigerian Breweries Limited in 1946. East African Breweries Limited, a holding company of regional firms, began with Kenya Breweries, founded in 1922, followed by Tanganyika Brewery in 1936 and then with a stake in Uganda Breweries in the 1950s. After these colonies gained independence in the early 1960s, the firm split along national boundaries. Eager to show their nationalist credentials and build market share, brewers encouraged African entrepreneurship by offering credit for distributorships and bar owners. The companies also served as vanity projects for postcolonial elites; a publicity photograph of Kenya Breweries' headquarters displayed a row of matching, cream-colored Mercedes Benz cars in the parking lot and a nearby golf course. But at least this Kenyan company's profits could finance such extravagances. According to historian Justin Willis, the nationalization of brewing in Tanzania led to "an extraordinary decline, as mismanagement and shortages crippled production and distribution."[54]

As elsewhere, African drinking cultures of bottled beer became associated with middle-class modernity. After serving in Allied armies during

World War II, many blacks demanded equal rights, including access to European beer that they had enjoyed while in uniform. In Nigeria, the petroleum boom of the 1950s created demand for cold beers among thirsty oil workers. Pilsner beer was also sought after by black urban workers in South Africa, where the Apartheid regime, founded in 1948, used sales of so-called Bantu beer to finance segregated township governments. The association of manufactured native beer with racial oppression led rioters to target municipal beer halls during the Soweto Uprising of 1976. South African Breweries (SAB), which had merged with Ohlsson's Cape Breweries and Chandler's Union in 1956 to create a dominant national firm, began marketing covertly across racial lines to shebeens, whose owners spent less time homebrewing and more time sourcing commercial products. In 1966, the company obtained a license to brew Eddie Taylor's Carling Black Label and marketed it especially to black customers as an extra-strength beer for macho men. In contrast to municipal beer halls, which financed oppressive policing, SAB donated profits from sales in the townships to buy textbooks for local schoolchildren. Such goodwill was savvy marketing. In the 1980s, even before the fall of Apartheid, black consumers purchased 80 percent of South African beer.[55]

Nevertheless, indigenous beers remained widely popular, especially in rural areas, and industrial brewers sought to tap this market. Factories had been supplying Bantu beer to municipal beer halls in South Africa and Rhodesia since the 1910s, but the problems of scaling up from homebrewing to mass production had persisted for half a century. Beginning in 1955, Max Heinrich applied the technologies of modern biological control developed for barley beers to brewing with sorghum. In less than a decade, his Chibuku brand had gained a dominant share of the Zambian market, while also establishing footholds in neighboring Rhodesia, Malawi, Swaziland, and Botswana. Heinrich's company wisely chose a low-cost, high-volume strategy, sharing the profits with distributors, retailers, and municipal governments. As partners rather than competitors, shebeen owners often sold both commercial and homebrewed sorghum beer side by side. The factory version came in brightly colored cartons, helping to overcome its old-fashioned image. The slogan "shake shake"—distributing the contents evenly before each sip— charged the drinking experience with kinetic energy. In 1963, Heinrich sold out to a Rhodesian British transnational, Lonrho, which passed the Chibuku brand along to SAB in 1972. Within a few decades, subsidiaries of the South African brewing giant were marketing the drink across southern and eastern Africa.[56]

The growth of Commonwealth markets also caught the attention of Guinness, whose exports rose more than tenfold in the 1940s and 1950s, especially in Africa and Southeast Asia. Already in the 1930s, the Irish brewer had begun to take a greater interest in marketing by consolidating bottlers and increasing advertising. A subsidiary Guinness Exports Limited was founded in 1950, but officials feared that simply setting up local bottlers would not be sufficient to hold postcolonial markets. In 1949, after a visit to Lagos, Nigeria, an executive warned that "if the Club Brewery [of Accra] could be expanded sufficiently it would automatically close the market to imported beers."[57] Nevertheless, the challenges of reproducing the taste of Dublin stout in a tropical environment dissuaded investment plans for another decade. Not until 1960, when Nigerian Breweries Limited announced plans for its own stout, to be named for the Biblical strongman Samson, did Guinness finally take the plunge. Even then, it established Guinness Nigeria Limited as a joint venture with Unilever's African marketing subsidiary, which had been a major distributor of Guinness and also held a stake in Nigerian Breweries. The choice of an experienced local partner proved wise, and in 1963, the factory opened in Ikeja, a suburb of the capital Lagos. Perhaps the biggest challenge was not shortages or bureaucracy but rather brewing a Foreign Extra Stout that matched the product made by the factory at St. James Gate. To ensure a proper flora for fermentation, brewers inoculated the vats with material from Dublin. Ultimately, the company developed a system of brewing a high-gravity beer with low hop levels that could be mixed with locally produced beer. Aged before leaving Dublin to develop lactic acid, it "was originally known as 'acid beer', which was alright for internal use, but for several obvious reasons AHH [Arthur Hughes, overseas trade director] did not like this as a name for sending it to Nigeria, and the term 'matured beer' was substituted."[58]

The success of brewing in Nigeria led Guinness to expand its overseas operations rapidly. The company opened factories in Malaysia (1965), Cameroon (1970), Ghana (1971), and Jamaica (1973), while entering agreements for contract brewing with SAB in Southern Africa (1964), South Australia Brewing in Adelaide (1964), Labatt in Canada (1965), and East African Breweries (1966). A planned brewery in Bahia, Brazil, was never completed due to disputes with the local partner and the disappearance of a mash tun en route from São Paulo. Local brewing professionals were sent to Ireland to learn the company's manufacturing techniques. Even with reliable partners and skilled technicians, Guinness managers had to navigate geopolitical crises. Reflecting on the company's success building market share during the Nigerian Civil War of 1966–70, one of them ended his list of future tasks: "Buy a new prayer mat."[59]

FIGURE 5.4 Postcolonial encounters among Guinness Brewing School students in Dublin (from left): Maxwell Oteri, Paul Byrne, Silvia Lumor, Michael Kok Hoy Lim with instructor Lawrence Benge (second from left), 1974–75. GPR/PR02.02/0001/107.056. Courtesy of Guinness Archive. Diageo, Ireland.

A portion of mature beer from Ireland offered no guarantee that the final product would meet company standards, so overseas brewers regularly sent samples for review to St. James Gate. The tasting notes, on file in the company archive, provide a catalog of quality control failures: "Aromatic, harsh, caramelly," "Sickly, aromatic, unclean," "Horrid," "Yeasty," "Overseas," and, perhaps most damning of all, "Not Guinness." Perhaps colored by prejudice that true Guinness could never be brewed outside the British Isles, the comments did at times convey a grudging approval: "Much improved. I did not recognize it as overseas."[60] Such successes were all the more noteworthy given the difficulty of obtaining adequate raw materials. Nigerian import controls forced brewers to malt local sorghum and wheat instead of barley. Even with refrigeration, the tropical climate took a toll on equipment such as the aluminum-clad water mains used at a rival brewery. "The effect reminds one of popular television science fiction," observed the executive J. H. D. Hughes. "It is not water-tight and I have a suspicion that its main effect may be to conceal from the eye the horrors that are going on behind."[61]

Beer played an important role in shaping modern identities in Britain and the newly independent nations of the Commonwealth. Local ales retained their followers, especially among older generations in the United Kingdom, which slowed but did not stop industrial consolidation. The preference for lager among younger Britons, including postcolonial migrants, heralded the influence of outsiders, although, as with the Civil Rights struggles in the United States, these changes brought social conflict. In former colonies, beer offered a form of cosmopolitanism. Speaking of Africa, historian Justin Willis declared beer "the communion wine of responsible modernity."[62] Nevertheless, indigenous beverages still kept their dedicated followers, like the ales of the metropolis. With its headquarters in a former colony, Guinness was perhaps the most successful company in navigating the politics of decolonization, as it established a local identity throughout large parts of Africa and Asia. Beer's modern associations even reached beyond traditional drinkers and capitalist markets to Communist China.

Brewing under Mao

In January 1958, Chairman Mao called for a Great Leap Forward, a massive program of industrial modernization and agricultural collectivization. Intended to launch China to the top ranks of industrial nations, it resulted instead in a famine that killed some 30 million people. Although generally associated with heavy industry, particularly the disastrous attempt to build backyard steel mills, the Great Leap also sought to increase production of consumer goods such as beer. Unlike steel, which could only be efficiently forged in giant factories, beer could be made successfully in small-scale, communal breweries, and output peaked at 146,000 tons in 1960—in the midst of the great famine. The image of party cadres and factory workers drinking beer while farmers starved in the countryside offers a stark image of rural-urban inequality in Maoist China. Nevertheless, the presence of European beer in a socialist society dedicated to providing the "necessary" but not the "superfluous" represented a triumph of nationalization by Chinese intellectuals and brewing professionals.[63]

The Chinese had long associated beer with colonial powers that had introduced it in the nineteenth century and established breweries in the early twentieth. Although the Tsingtao Brewery, founded in 1903 in the German concession of Shandong, is the best known, Russians had begun brewing a few years earlier in the northeastern cities of Harbin and Mukden to supply workers on the Trans-Manchurian Railway. American investors financed an ill-fated Hong Kong brewery in 1909, and Shanghai had two plants by the 1930s, one held briefly by flamboyant real estate mogul Victor Sassoon and the other built by the British trading company Jardine Matheson. Meanwhile, the Japanese opened breweries in Manchuria and in 1916 took over the German factory in Qingdao. These early ventures were intended to produce goods for an expatriate market, but Chinese modernists also began to enjoy beer. Reform-minded mandarin Jiang Zhiyou loved drinking beer in Shanghai restaurants. Writer Zheng Yimei first tasted beer at a Russian brothel, another site of cross-cultural encounters.[64]

By the 1930s, beer had moved from foreign colonies to the intelligentsia and the working classes. Manual laborers, students, and clerks gathered at proletarian restaurants in Shanghai to eat porridge and noodles and to drink beer and Chinese alcohol purchased from nearby wine shops. Meanwhile, Chinese intellectuals traced a native genealogy for the beverage. Xu Ke, in his 1917 *Collection of Anecdotes and Romances of the Qing Period*, associated beer with *mai jiu*, a fermented alcoholic beverage made of wheat or barley during the Han Dynasty (25–220 CE). For example, it was brewed by one Fan Ran in honor of a friend's appointment to the bureaucracy. This native tradition was elaborated by later authors such as Cao Zongye, who identified another early Chinese version of beer known as *li*, a sweet, thin alcoholic beverage made from malt. Citing Ming and Qing dynasty scholars, Cao concluded, "we can regard China as one of the oldest birthplaces of beer."[65]

Chinese entrepreneurs began nationalizing the production of beer in the early twentieth century. The first native-owned brewery was founded in Beijing in 1914 by Zhang Tingge, or perhaps purchased from earlier Swiss owners. Zhang was born to a peasant family in 1875 and at the age of twenty-one moved to Vladivostok, where he learned Russian and opened a grocery store. Impressed by soldiers' thirst for beer during the Russo-Japanese War of 1904, Zhang began brewing Five Star beer. The company's success inspired Chinese businessmen to construct breweries at Yantai, Tianjin, and Hangzhou in the 1920s, but it was another decade before China had its first native brewmaster, Zhu Mei. Although little is known of his background, he studied at the Pasteur Institute in Paris in 1931, then transferred to the Belgian National Brewing Institute, where he graduated in 1935. After a year of practical training at the Brasserie Chasse Royale in Brussels, he returned to China in 1936 and began work at the Yantai Brewery near Qingdao. The company had originally employed an Austrian brewer, but financial problems led it to be taken over by the Bank of China in 1934. Zhu recalled later that he had saved the company money on spurious foreign expenses charged by the

National Beers　167

previous brewer, who had pocketed $5,000 annually for chemicals supposedly needed to produce carbonated gas, which was of course a natural product of fermentation. The Chinese expert also solved the problem of cold-weather cloudiness, eliminating winter returns from retailers.[66]

Images of beer in newspapers, whether intended as product placements or simply depictions of modern life, situated the western beverage within Chinese drinking rituals. A photo from 1948 of seven clean-cut young men sitting around a banquet table in matching workers' coveralls was captioned: "Fat chicken and beer are perfect for the Chinese Spring Festival." This jovial celebration contrasted with a menacing reference to competitive masculine drinking from a 1944 ad. A barrel-chested man in a gangster-style coat and hat, framed by two open beer bottles in the foreground and a full shelf behind, held up a mug to the camera and challenged the reader: "Twenty bottles of beer, let's empty them!"[67] When women did appear along with beer, they tended to be associated with production rather than consumption, such as one showcasing female factory workers affixing labels.[68]

Even while grounding beer in local traditions, Chinese authors emphasized its health benefits and sensory pleasures. Xu Ke differentiated the western drink from traditional Chinese liquors by emphasizing the lively bubbles, which aided digestion. Journalist Xiao Zu likewise introduced beer to Chinese consumers as a luxury beverage: "In a banquet, with snow white tablecloth and colorful lights in the air, the golden fluid is served in a glass." He also emphasized the beneficial effects of beer. "In early summer, a sip of beer makes one feel buoyant, like entering into a cool world in which all troubles are gone."[69] The advice to drink beer in the summer aligned with Chinese humoral beliefs that discouraged the consumption of cold food or beverages during winter. Bohemian poet Yang Sao's "Ode to Beer" offered a more earthy description: "If one of us got paid and had some money in our pocket, we would buy half a dozen [bottles] of beer or a bit more to drink. Once we had beer our eyes would gleam." But Yang's sensory delight did not stop with flavor. "When the fermented air came out of the throat from the stomach, we would try to make the burp as loud as possible, raise up our eyebrows, and pleasantly release a mouthful of air." He concluded blissfully: "The beauty of such an atmosphere cannot be imagined by anyone else."[70]

On the eve of the Communist Revolution in 1949, western beer had made only limited inroads among Chinese consumers. Of the dozen or so breweries founded in China during the first half of the twentieth century, only seven still operated, in the Northeast, Shanghai, and Guangzhou. Even these factories were in poor shape after two decades of foreign invasion and civil war. Total output from the national industry amounted to a mere 70,000 hectoliters, and consumption was limited to the urban middle classes, particularly intellectuals and well-paid workers. Nevertheless, Chinese brewers and modernists had succeeded in localizing the product sufficiently that the Communists sought to revitalize production rather than ban beer as a symbol of western imperialism and bourgeois decadence.[71]

In the first years of the revolution, beer was a low priority for the Chinese Communist Party, which did little more than nationalize existing factories. To develop the industry more fully required local supply chains and skilled technicians. Foreign-owned breweries had insisted on importing raw materials from Europe and North America, while withholding technical knowledge from Chinese workers. The economic embargo imposed on the People's Republic during the Korean War added new urgency to finding local sources of barley, hops, and yeast. Such efforts had begun decades earlier, when Beijing brewers had recognized the nearby province of Hebei as an excellent source of European-style, two-rowed barley. Likewise, in his time at the Yantai Brewery, Zhu Mei had begun breeding yeast to save the cost of importing it dried from the Carlsberg Laboratory in Copenhagen. During the occupation of Manchuria, the Japanese had begun processing hops near Yimianpo in Heilongjiang province. While expanding these initiatives, the government also sought to train a skilled workforce. In 1952, the Ministry of Light Industry transferred Zhu Mei from Qingdao to Shanghai to replace foreign technicians. He later recalled: "I felt it was my responsibility to teach the workers to operate the machinery and to explain the theory behind it. It was too slow to hold classes, so I worked together with them and taught them through actual practice."[72]

Like other commodities, beer was distributed through bureaucratic systems intended to maximize production with little regard for market demand. In practice, its consumption was largely reserved for party elites, which gave it a measure of socialist distinction. The Beijing Brewery's venerable Five Star brand became the official beer for state banquets at the Great Hall of the People, reportedly at the behest of Premier Zhou Enlai, who drank beer while studying in Europe during the 1920s. Marketing was also closely tied to Communist propaganda; the Beijing Brewery commemorated the revolution's tenth anniversary in 1959 by launching a premium brand called Beijing Special.[73]

During the Great Leap Forward, Chinese beer production more than doubled briefly, then collapsed by 40 percent in the subsequent famine (see Figure 5.5). The Ministry of Light Industry provided the impetus for the

National Beers 169

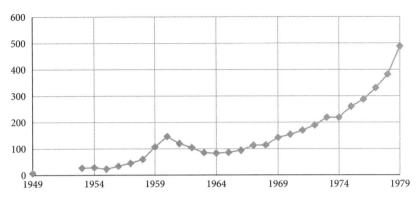

FIGURE 5.5 Chinese beer production, 1949–79 (million liters). Beer was an important component of the "Great Leap Forward" industrialization program, and production peaked in 1960, during a famine that killed an estimated 30 million people. After falling back, output rose gradually even during the upheavals of the Cultural Revolution. Sources: Zhu Mei and Qi Zhidao, *Pijiu jiangzuo yi* [Lectures on Beer], in *Heilongjiang fajiao* [Heilongjiang Fermentation] (Harbin: Helongjiang sheng qingongye yanjiusuo, 1981), 41–54; Guo Yuantao, *Global Big Business and the Chinese Brewing Industry* (London: Routledge, 2006), 185, 188.

initial growth in April 1958 by convening a conference at the Yuquan Model Brewery near Harbin with representatives from sixteen provinces and cities. The choice of Harbin rather than Qingdao carried symbolic weight as the site of an early brewery established by Russians, a Cold War ally. Yuquan also served as a model because of its small size and focus on domestic consumption, unlike the giant, export-oriented Tsingtao Brewery. Zhu Mei explained the goals of the conference in a short volume called *How to Run a Small-Scale Brewery*. After touting the health benefits and good taste of beer, he lamented the regional concentration of Chinese breweries and the difficulty of shipping beer to interior provinces. Zhu then explained the tasks involved in running a small brewery, including sanitizing equipment, boiling, mashing, fermenting, and packaging in bottles or kegs. He concluded: "Most Chinese cities need beer, and they need it urgently."[74]

Despite the surge in output, the Great Leap did not achieve the stated goal of the Yuquan Conference, and brewing remained limited to coastal industrial cities, mostly in the Northeast. By the mid-1960s, the only major brewery in the interior was at Xi'an, the ancient capital of China's first emperor. Such a geographical distribution fit with the unstated purpose of the Great Leap, exploiting agriculture to finance industrialization. In 1959 and 1960, China exported 6 million tons of grain, even as national production fell by more than 50 million tons. Admittedly, urban workers also suffered during the

Great Famine, although not on the scale of rural starvation. Even discounting exaggerated production figures, the Great Leap clearly made beer more available to privileged sectors of society—including party cadres, the military, and workers in strategic industries—at the expense of China's peasantry.[75]

Although beer production declined for the next five years, industrial consolidation set the stage for slow but steady growth throughout the Cultural Revolution. In 1964, the Ministry of Light Industry convened a second brewing conference at the flagship brewery, declaring: "The beer industry should learn from Qingdao."[76] The move from Harbin reflected in part the 1960 Soviet Chinese split, but equally important was the shift away from the small-scale ideal of Zhu Mei's 1958 pamphlet. The technicians assembled at Qingdao in 1964 produced a comprehensive volume titled *Operating Methods of the Tsingtao Brewery* as a handbook for the entire industry.[77]

By the 1970s, beer had become a typical consumer good in socialist China, with all the shortages, inequalities, and imperfections that entailed. Access to consumer goods was generally determined by workplaces, which distributed staple foods at the end of the week or before holidays. The Ministry of Light Industry also maintained a network of stores where shoppers could make purchases with ration books and coupons, if they could find anything on the shelves. The party paid lip service to rural consumers; for example, an advice manual for everyday life in the countryside, published in 1964, recommended storing beer and carbonated beverages in the shade to prevent temperature changes that could lower the quality and potentially cause bottles to explode. Although such statements may have encouraged curiosity about beer, or perhaps fear, rural dwellers had little to worry about in finding beer bottles in their everyday life.

Under Chinese socialism, the quality of goods was ranked by "fame" instead of price. Tsingtao Beer was declared a "famous alcoholic beverage" at the Second National Alcohol Exhibition in 1963 and therefore qualified for national distribution, although it was mostly reserved for export. Provincial bureaucrats distributed "locally famous alcoholic beverages" such as Shenyang Snow, Shanghai Seagull, and Beijing Special beers within the urban markets where they were produced. The Qingdao *Gazetteer* left a revealing record of beer's availability in the brewing capital of China: "After 1970, on the National Day and Spring Festival, every household could get five bottles of beer with their coupons. Draught beer was open for sale, though inconsistently."[78]

Low quality had been a tradeoff that China's original brewmaster, Zhu Mei, accepted to put beer in the hands of the proletariat. Although capable of brewing full-bodied Munich dark beers, he focused on the cheapest of pale lagers, and rather than spend valuable foreign currency on imported pure yeast, he propagated his own, overlooking any imperfections that resulted. His plan to build small-scale breweries foundered on the grain shortages of the Great Leap Forward, but he was nevertheless promoted to the rank of senior engineer in the Ministry of Light Industry, where he continued to develop the national industry. By the late 1970s, beer accounted for nearly a quarter of all the alcohol produced in China, a figure that has now grown to nearly 90 percent.[79]

The available evidence suggests that brewing was a rather ordinary industry in Mao's China, which is to say autarkic, backward, inefficient, politically fraught, and intensely nationalistic. With its modern, industrial production, beer appealed to the government as a mildly alcoholic and more grain-efficient alternative to the hard liquor produced in rustic distilleries throughout the countryside. But to achieve that promise required significant work, for the handful of factories that existed in China in 1949 had been neglected during two decades of warfare. Zhu Mei and his colleagues rebuilt the national industry with minimal outside assistance, improvising solutions to the myriad technical complications that arose. The failures of agricultural collectivization severely limited the volume of grain that could be brewed into beer. Nevertheless, communally owned enterprises founded during the Maoist period provided a base for the explosive growth of brewing that followed economic reforms in 1978. The experience of Maoist China also demonstrated that it was not mass advertising alone that made lager a ubiquitous global commodity. Although promotional campaigns and modernist intellectuals in prerevolutionary China collaborated to develop a genealogy of beer that made it seem both patriotically local and alluringly foreign, the taste for beer remained limited to a handful of cities before 1949. The Chinese Communist Party seems to have encouraged a much wider demand for beer through non-market forms of conspicuous consumption. Simply put, beer was an urban privilege in a society defined by scarcity.

As the nation became the fundamental political unit in the twentieth century, beer was pressed into its service as an expression of shared identities and a driver of economic development. On an ideological level, beer styles contributed both to a desire for modernity through the purity of pale lager and to a nostalgia for the past among adherents to the top-fermenting ales of Britain and Belgium as well as other indigenous beverages around the world. The spread of brewing technology contributed to import substitution policies intended to promote economic growth. Such technological advances made it possible to produce ever lighter versions of pale lager, a taste encouraged by food-processing industries and embraced as a form of social mobility by rural migrants. In many former colonies the goal of making even cheap pale lager available to all citizens was still an aspiration, although such production limits were largely overcome by the twentieth-first century, most dramatically in China.

In the mid-twentieth century, the national concentration of brewing industries and the move toward pale lagers seemed inexorable. Belgium's *Le Petit Journal du Brasseur* published a pair of articles in the spring of 1966 warning of the dangers that lay ahead for small and medium-sized firms. Traditional top-fermenting breweries had flourished in small villages before World War I through the support of their neighbors, "even when the quality of their [beer] left much to be desired."[80] But brewers could no longer count on such loyalty. The authors predicted that the survival of these firms depended on the adoption of new technology, as rising disposable incomes allowed consumers to demand higher-quality products. "We must ask ourselves, what type of consumer are we going to face, not today, but in 1975."[81]

Beer markets in 1975 turned out to be far different from the brewing professionals' predictions in the mid-1960s. A countercultural reaction against standardized pale lagers had begun to inspire a new generation of Belgian brewers to revitalize traditional ales. Meanwhile, economies of scale were making commodity brewing impossibly competitive for all but the largest firms. Even the craft beer revivalists of Europe and North America, alongside brewers of traditional beverages in other regions of the world, faced difficult years as these giants began to expand beyond their borders to build international brewing conglomerates in the final decades of the twentieth century. Although few industry observers predicted it, the advantages lay not with national champions of the Global North but with upstart brewers in the Global South.

6

Global Lager

ON MAY 31, 1986, the *Denver Post* reported, "Happy Hour has soured for those who trendily twist their fresh-sliced limes into long-neck bottles of Corona." The Mexican import beer had surged to popularity so suddenly that shortages broke out across the western United States, and Corona's distributor had "exactly *nada* cases" in the Denver warehouse. "Everybody's yelling and screaming, but we've been doing the best we can to fairly allocate what we have," explained regional sales manager Don Taylor.[1] With retailers sold out, "young people are offering double for the Mexican beer, and a black market has arisen. Anything goes to avoid the phrase no more beer."[2] The gentrification of a plebeian Mexican lager into a premium international brand revealed the paradoxes of global capitalism around the turn of the millennium. Corporate bosses splurged on advertising campaigns and cross-border mergers and acquisitions, but as the astonishing rise of Corona showed, the success of these ventures often bore little relationship to the money invested. Moreover, Corona's explosive growth heralded a tectonic shift in the industry away from traditional brewing centers in Europe and North America toward firms based in Africa, Asia, and Latin America.

The rise of a significant international trade in beer formed part of a larger transformation of the global economy beginning in the 1970s. Governments pursued an agenda that included removing tariff barriers and foreign exchange restrictions, deregulating environmental and consumer protection, imposing regressive tax codes, and criminalizing union organizing and migrant labor. Although often lumped together under the label "neoliberalism," a more accurate description might be corporate authoritarianism. Yet free trade and improved transportation cannot fully explain the growth of large-scale shipping in beer, a standardized commodity that is basically water. Demand for exotic beers responded to a glamorization of consumerism that facilitated and justified growing corporate power. Young urban professionals celebrated their material success through visible displays such as drinking beers they had discovered while on vacation. One importer evoked "the travel lust of the Germans . . . Water, sun, and palm trees . . . Now we import beer from Tahiti."[3] Consumers paid premiums for such brands more as fashion statements than taste preferences. Nor was it entirely clear where these beers came from, as technological advances made it possible to brew any given brand under contract in distant factories. The de-localization of beer, which had begun a century earlier with Pilsner, continued apace.

Advertising became ever more important with the standardization of pale lagers. In the 1950s, American psychologists found that consumers attached great loyalty to their preferred brand of beer but could not actually identify it in blind tastings. Informed by these findings, advertising agencies and marketing executives sought to endow brands with personalities to win customer loyalty and encourage greater consumption. Even as media technology advanced, actual sales pitches generally fell back on long-established tropes of masculinity, patriotism, modernity, and nostalgia. Because the most effective promotions were those that involved consumers actively with the brand, such as twisting limes into bottles of Corona, corporations promoted beer festivals and other invented drinking occasions. Taste proved a curiously difficult trait to sell, and not only because beers were largely indistinguishable.

Surging exports encouraged brewers to look beyond domestic markets, culminating around the end of the century in a race to achieve global domination. The internationalization of capital markets fueled a binge of highly leveraged mergers and acquisitions. Corporate raiders prized firms with unionized workforces, whose salaries could be cut to pay off the debts that financed buyouts. Transnational brewing firms were particularly eager to expand into emerging markets, where younger consumers offered greater potential growth than in many rich countries, whose declining populations increasingly preferred wine. In the twenty-first century, beer drinking grew by 50 percent in many Asian and Latin American countries and by as much as 100 percent in parts of Africa.[4] Firms with experience in managing the challenges of emerging markets flourished, while those accustomed to more stable conditions struggled to adapt. Legacy brands such as Budweiser often had little meaning for consumers in emerging markets.

The structure of the brewing industry changed dramatically in the second half of the twentieth century through revolutions in management, which shifted from brewing engineers to advertising executives and then to investment bankers. As a result, the technological mastery of brewing professionals served not to produce a better beer but rather to heighten the profits of financial speculators.

A Flood of Imports

International trade in beer has grown dramatically but unevenly as Table 6.1 shows; in the 1970s only 2 percent of all the world's beer was exported while by 2010 that figure was more than 6 percent. During the 1980s alone, cross-border shipping of beer increased more than 80 percent while trade in all goods increased by only about 25 percent. The rise of beer exports was particularly dramatic compared with the agricultural sector, which dropped from 77 percent of world trade in 1962 to 16 percent in 2015. The removal of trade barriers within the European Union encouraged a significant increase in cross-border sales, particularly in non-traditional beer-drinking countries such as France and Italy, which had some of the highest levels of imports as a percent of production, approaching 50 percent. Short-distance trade also predominated in North America; beer imports to the United States reached 14 percent of domestic consumption and came primarily from Canada and Mexico. By contrast, Australia had one of the lowest levels of beer imports in

Table 6.1 International Trade in Beer, 1961–2010. Beer imports as a percentage of total consumption reveals the dramatic but uneven growth of international trade. While imported beers became fashionable in the United States and United Kingdom, increasing steadily over the period, import substitution displaced foreign beers in Nigeria and China. European countries without a strong beer culture such as France and Italy showed the greatest increase in imports as a result of European Union integration. Source: https:fao.org/faostat.

	1961	1970	1980	1990	2000	2010
World	0.017	0.017	0.023	0.033	0.046	0.062
UK	0.056	0.051	0.041	0.081	0.080	0.179
US	0.005	0.007	0.024	0.043	0.100	0.140
China	0.036	0.127	0.067	0.011	0.013	0.007
Nigeria	0.400	0.013	0.011	0.000	0.009	0.000
France	0.014	0.057	0.126	0.159	0.232	0.471
Italy	0.030	0.049	0.120	0.215	0.371	0.510

the developed world. Trade plummeted in many new nations as postcolonial elites pursued policies of import substitution. At the time of independence in 1960, Nigeria imported 40 percent of its beer, but with the opening of Nigerian Breweries and a local Guinness factory, that figure fell to 1 percent or lower. China, likewise, rebuilt its brewing industry after shortages of the Maoist period to achieve beer self-sufficiency. To understand these trends, it may be helpful to begin with the leading exporter, Heineken.[5]

The company founded by Gerard Adriaan Heineken in 1864 achieved a global reach through technical acumen and imperial legacies. When he first purchased an aging Amsterdam brewery, Heineken intended to make English-style ale, but the popularity of lager at the city's International Exposition of 1869 convinced him to send his brewmaster to study in Germany and Austria. The company flourished, along with two other firms that switched to lager, the Royal Netherlands and Amstel breweries. Heineken modernized and expanded operations by installing Linde refrigeration equipment and a laboratory for making pure yeast using Hansen's method. Exports to the Dutch East Indies had begun already in the 1870s, but it was not until 1929 that the company employed Pieter Feith as the equivalent of Guinness's world travelers to develop overseas markets. His first step, in partnership with John Fraser and David Chalmers Neave, the Scottish owners of a Singapore bottled water company, was founding Malayan Brewers Limited and its Tiger beer brand. In the 1930s, Heineken began to actively manage overseas breweries that it held through investment funds to create a portfolio of factories stretching from Egypt and Angola to Java and Indochina, all overseen by technicians from its Rotterdam laboratory. After World War II, the company continued to expand, particularly in Africa, with ventures such as Nigerian Breweries Limited.[6]

Heineken's premium reputation depended on tireless promotion as well as technical mastery. In March 1933, Pieter Feith boarded the Holland-America liner *Statendam* to deliver the first shipment of import beer to the United States after Prohibition. On the voyage, Feith met a voluble steward named Leo Van Munching, who became the company's dedicated sales agent in the United States. Van Munching placed Heineken in some of the most exclusive bars in Manhattan, including the Waldorf Astoria Hotel and the New York Athletic Club, helping to create an elite reputation for the brand. The Heineken pavilion at the 1939 New York World's Fair served beer on the ground floor of a life-sized windmill, although wartime exigencies prevented the company from capitalizing on the publicity. After the war, 23-year-old Alfred Heineken did an internship with Van Munching, cementing ties with the American

Global Lager   177

distributor for another generation. He returned home two years later with an American nickname, "Freddy"; an American wife, Kentucky distilling heiress Lucille Cummings; and an American flair for advertising. After taking control of the company in 1954, he personally oversaw promotional campaigns, insisting on the brand's distinctive green bottles and controversial red star—often confused at the time with international Communism. Meanwhile in the 1950s, Heineken benefited from a global American presence, including the return of US troops from overseas who purchased imported beers they had tasted while stationed in Europe.[7]

Even while introducing its premium beer across Europe, Heineken learned the importance of maintaining local brands. To counter the plebeian image of beer in France, Heineken arranged for distribution through the champagne house of Moët & Chandon. By contrast, the company stumbled in purchasing the Spanish El Águila brewery, discontinuing successful local brands without building a market for its Dutch counterparts. Heineken did better in Italy, taking over the Dreher and McFarland brands in the 1960s and only later brewing its premium brand locally. The company boasted its greatest victory with the takeover of the hometown rival Amstel, which was relegated to a secondary brand. But a premium image could not simply be manufactured if the beer's taste did not satisfy local consumers. In Britain, Heineken acquired a down-market image favored by young consumers, in part because it was brewed under contract by Whitbreads to local levels of about 3.4 percent alcohol, below its usual strength. Even regular Heineken had little appeal in Central European nations accustomed to more full-bodied beers. As one Belgian brewer joked: "We already have water running from the taps."[8]

Heineken was not the only brewery profiting from the postwar rise in trade. Firms such as the Bavarian Löwenbräu and Bremen's Beck's worked to rebuild their international markets and brand associations, contributing to what historian Robert Terrell called a "larger reckoning with German identity on a global level—beer and gaiety rather than just Nazis and fanaticism."[9] Meanwhile, Guinness and Carlsberg, like Heineken, took advantage of their strong position in the relatively small national markets of Ireland and Denmark to finance export campaigns. They were followed by the French firm Boussois Souchon Neuvesel (BSN) and the Belgian Artois Brewery. In the British Commonwealth, Courage opened a Melbourne brewery in 1968, while South African Breweries (SAB) moved into Zambia, Botswana, and Angola.[10]

Whereas light imported lagers appealed to Britain's Beatles generation as an alternative to traditional ales, imports to the United States acquired a reputation for full body, in contrast to ever-lighter domestic lagers. The trend toward effervescence, already underway in the 1950s and 1960s, accelerated with the invention of so-called light beer by biochemist Joseph Owades. At the Rheingold Brewery, he experimented with using enzymes to break down starch more fully, reducing the residual malt that gives body—and calories—to beer. The new "diet beer" came out in 1967, though it was too late to save Rheingold from bankruptcy. Owades then brought his invention to the Peter Hand Brewery of Chicago, where it was marketed briefly as Meisterbrau Lite. Miller took over the brand in 1972 with the brilliant idea of selling light beer not as a way to lose weight but as an excuse to drink more. Owades explained in 1982: "Over the past decade American brewers have gradually modified their beers to make them more 'drinkable,' a term the industry uses to denote a product less harsh on the palate and lighter in body." An additional 20 percent reduction in malt content and hop bitterness during the 1970s, from already low levels, "made it easier to drink large quantities without feeling full."[11] Light beer was thus an early step in supersizing the American diet.

Flush with the success of Miller Lite, management took the logical next step of attempting to pair the status of European beers with the drinkability of domestic lagers. The fabled Löwenbräu, which Miller was already distributing, provided the ideal vehicle. In 1974 the American firm signed a contract to brew the beer in Milwaukee, which enabled them to save on freight costs while adjusting the recipe for American tastes. The only problem was that Miller continued to market the beer as an import using the original green bottle and German label. Anheuser Busch filed a false advertising case with the Federal Trade Commission, pointing out that the adjunct lager would not even qualify as beer in Munich. Miller was forced to withdraw the label, essentially killing the brand in the United States. Although the strategy failed this time, it foreshadowed the future associations of imported beer in America.[12]

Japanese brewers also contributed innovative technologies to the progressive lightening of the global lager. Beer sales in Japan surpassed sake in the late 1950s, driven in part by demand from young and female customers, many of whom, like their counterparts in Europe and North America, preferred a lighter beer. In 1967, the distiller Suntory entered the market with a new product called *nama* beer, meaning raw or fresh, achieved by replacing pasteurization with micro-filtration, a technology developed by the National Aeronautics and Space Administration to recycle wastewater for astronauts. The fresh, light taste proved enormously popular, and rival brewers adopted the method not only in Japan but around the world, in brands such as Miller Genuine Draft. Two decades later, in 1987, Asahi introduced "dry beer," a

Global Lager 179

highly fermented product they advertised as "rich in taste but also sharp and refreshing."[13] The "dry revolution" upended Japanese beer markets, rescuing Asahi from bankruptcy and eventually displacing the former market leader Kirin. The fad spread globally, although its meaning changed according to local tastes. Journalist Florence Fabricant explained that dry beer "appears to be an elastic concept that the beer industry is stretching over a batch of stylish selling points, suggesting a product that is clean, lively, refreshing, less sweet and has no aftertaste."[14]

Despite these market-shifting innovations, there were limits to the ability to engineer a better beer. The number two brand in the United States, Schlitz, sought to cut costs in the 1970s by reducing fermentation time, substituting barley malt with corn syrup, and stabilizing the foam with silica gel. This cocktail of ingredients produced a chemical reaction that left a haze of flakes in the beer, which became known among consumers as "Schlitz Bits."[15] Factory employees had noticed the problem immediately, but management ignored their warnings until it was too late. Sales plummeted amid federal investigations before the failing company was bought out by the Stroh Brewery Company in 1984.[16]

With concerns about the quality of industrial beers in the United States, imports surged in the 1970s. At the high end of the market, Heineken's sales rose from 3.5 million cases in 1972 to 25 million cases by the end of the decade, accounting for 40 percent of all imported beer in the United States. Meanwhile, Canadian brands Molson, Labatt, and Moosehead became popular among college students in border states such as Michigan and Vermont. The attraction of Canadian beer stemmed in part from its reputation for being stronger than American beer, although the difference was a statistical mirage created by Canada's practice of listing alcohol by volume rather than weight, as in the United States. Canadian brewers mounted advertising campaigns in the United States, but the most valuable promotional spots may have appeared on the Canadian Broadcasting Corporation comedy show SCTV. In a recurring skit called the "Great White North," Rick Moranis and Dave Thomas played Bob and Doug McKenzie, a bumbling pair who wore heavy winter clothes, drank beer, and called each other "hoser." While the brothers attracted many Midwestern university students to Canadian brands, Heineken faced an even greater challenge from imports across America's southern border.[17]

Corona has become a business school case study in how to create a bestselling brand "even if the beer is mediocre."[18] In fact, the Mexican beer's rise to fame and fortune was the product of neither visionary management nor clever marketing. Carta Blanca, Tecate, and Corona had been shipped across the border sporadically for decades, but it was not until 1979 that Modelo appointed an export manager, Carlos Alvarez, and formally introduced the brand in Southwestern markets. The company adopted the American practice of using brown bottles instead of the clear, glass longnecks familiar in Mexico. As a result, Corona's arrival went largely unnoticed, even by tourists who knew the brand from border-town bars and Baja beach vacations. A 1981 relaunch in Austin, Texas, and San Diego, California, using the traditional bottles sparked a beer-guzzling frenzy. Sales rocketed to more than 12 million cases in 1986, largely through word of mouth. Barton Brands, the Chicago-based distributor, specialized in distilled spirits and had little experience selling beer. During the boom years of 1985 to 1987, Modelo cut its advertising budget in half since the beer was selling itself.[19]

Astonished by the remarkable growth, industry insiders and journalists alike sought to explain the brand's popularity. Modelo's spokespeople repeated platitudes about the high quality of the beer and said nothing about its plebeian reputation in Mexico. Celebrity sightings of Irish rock musician Bono and beach-bum minstrel Jimmy Buffett nursing the distinctive longnecks contributed to the buzz around the brand. A shortage of the wildly popular beer in the summer of 1986 added further to the aura of exclusivity as fans vied to score a case. But the larger explanation for Corona's success lies in the bizarre ritual behavior observed by bartenders: young men asked for bottles, rather than mugs, along with a slice of lime. They pushed the lime into the bottle and drank the beer, leaving the lime at the bottom. Like the popularity of Bob and Doug McKenzie, this performance was inexplicable to outsiders but deeply appealing to initiates of the subculture.[20]

Competitors insisted that the craze would soon pass, given the fickle nature of Corona's young, male customers. To accelerate the brand's decline, they began spreading rumors that it was contaminated with urine. The *Los Angeles Times* reported the story on July 28, 1987, after some thirty-five separate retailers asked about the rumor on the same day. The claims were particularly inflammatory given the nativist outcry over Mexican migrants in the mid-1980s. Investigators traced the rumors back to a Heineken distributor, Luce & Son of Reno, Nevada, and Barton Brands obtained a settlement that included a written statement attesting to the beer's purity.[21] Modelo executives took the rumors very seriously, but they had inside information that had already been published in Mexican newspapers a year earlier. The company had commissioned a marketing firm to conduct focus groups with Corona's primary demographic, male university students. When asked to explain their

Global Lager

181

preference for the bright yellow beer in the clear glass bottles, large numbers responded, no doubt smirking: "It looks like another liquid."[22] Far from worrying about impurities, hip young consumers laughed at the scatological joke, and sales continued to soar.

Even if the urine rumors were not invented by distributors, the Corona shortage may well have been, at least in part. Admittedly, the brand's popularity caught Modelo executives by surprise, and they ran their factories flat out to meet demand. Nevertheless, the Denver wholesaler who claimed to be "doing the best we can to fairly allocate" beer during the summer of 1986 was reportedly profiteering from the black market. According to *Beer Blast*, a journalistic account by Philip Van Munching, the grandson of Heineken's American agent, the distributor was transshipping Corona—selling it without legal authorization—to more lucrative markets on the East Coast. The export manager Carlos Alvarez had negotiated the original contract with Barton for distribution in twenty-five Western and Midwestern states, never imagining that young people in New York, Boston, and Miami would suddenly clamor for Corona. In 1986, Alvarez left Modelo and founded the Gambrinus Company to sell in the remaining states. While the new company applied for state licenses and organized sales networks, western distributors hired independent truckers to deliver beer clandestinely to East Coast bars and bottle shops. Quality control may have suffered on these illicit supply chains, but if customers had discovered the underhanded dealings, they likely would have enjoyed the thrill of drinking bootleg beer.[23]

Over the next few years, Heineken and Corona battled not just for market share but for the very meaning of imported beer in the United States. By 1987, the Dutch beer had fallen from 40 percent of the market to 24 percent while Corona rose to number two at 17 percent, a bitter reversal for what Leo Van Munching derided as "Mexican soda pop."[24] A recession two years later knocked the bottom out of the market for all imported beers. Modelo responded by cutting prices, while Heineken, seeking to reclaim the higher end of the market, abandoned corn adjuncts and returned to an all-malt recipe. By this point, associations of quality were already passing from the import sector to the emerging craft beer market. Meanwhile, Corona introduced a new advertising campaign featuring lime-adorned bottles of Corona on idyllic beaches with the logo: "Change your whole latitude." By 1997, the Mexican brand had surpassed Heineken as the best-selling imported beer in the United States.[25]

Corona's "vacation in a bottle" image spawned endless copy-cats, not to mention alternate claims to have "invented" the lime ritual. Given that lime

FIGURE 6.1 Corona advertises a beach vacation in a bottle to Canadians eager for relief from a long winter. Photo by the author, 2015.

is widely used as a garnish across Mexico and had been added to Tecate since the 1950s, the idea of invention is absurd, but claimants include a British beer importer and American tourists in Mazatlán and Laredo. That people sought to claim credit, or assign blame, for this ritual indicated its importance to Corona's success. As Modelo struggled to keep up with demand in the United States, longtime Mexican rival Cuauhtémoc introduced its Sol brand to the British market. With a 1920s-vintage painted glass bottle and a "cabbagy aroma," according to beer critic Roger Protz, Sol ironically occupied the "premium import" sector in the United Kingdom, in contrast to the down-market image of Heineken.[26] In 1998, Anheuser Busch tried to compete with a tequila-and-lime flavored beer called Tequiza, which proved too sweet for beer drinkers and was quickly discontinued. Nevertheless, it spawned a new category of flavored malt beverages such as Bud Light Lime, introduced in 2009, along with many others around the world. Meanwhile, importers introduced Argentine Quilmes, Bahamian Kalik, Trinidadian Carib, and other brands, hoping to capture the newly discovered spring break market.

One aspiring entrepreneur even solicited investors for a factory in Aruba intended to create a "cult beer similar to that of 'Corona' brewed in Mexico."[27]

This brand identity of an anonymous beach, unattached to any nation, exemplified the political economy of beer in a world of mobile capital and labor restrictions. Modelo workers certainly did not share in the profits from the export boom. Although well paid by Mexican standards, brewery union members sought to renegotiate their contracts in 1989. One of their demands was a flexible retirement age, as many had worked around the clock to meet the export demand. When the company refused to negotiate, the union went on strike in February 1990. Picketing workers suffered two months of violent attacks by riot police before capitulating. Not only did factory workers not reap the rewards of Corona's success, but neither did the agricultural sector. Although Corona has been portrayed as Mexico's great success story under the North American Free Trade Agreement, its sales did little for the nation's farmers because the company imported malt and hops from the United States. Development scholar Timothy Wise compared breweries to the assembly factories set up along the border beginning in the 1960s to utilize cheap, generally female labor. "The country is basically a *maquiladora* for beer bottling. I guess Mexico contributes the water. Which it doesn't have enough of."[28]

By the end of the century, the international trade in beer had become a mature industry with an infrastructure of agents dedicated to maneuvering the byzantine national and local regulations controlling the sale of alcohol. The 1995 edition of the *Beer Directory* listed about seventy importers each in the United States and the United Kingdom, including company distributors such as Heineken's Van Munching and Molson UK; brewers with mutual import agreements, such as Anheuser Busch's contract with Carlsberg; and small firms like Vanberg & DeWulf and the Beer Cellar offering Belgian ales and other specialty beers. A journalist described boutique importers as "three or four people in a small office maintaining relationships with overseas brewers that have taken years to cement, shepherding their brands through the dark labyrinth of government regulations, waltzing with wholesalers one at a time, and making a lot of guesses about what will happen next."[29]

International beer exporters were able to overcome great hurdles and extended their reach into challenging markets such as the former Soviet Union and Muslim countries. The Turkish market leader Efes took advantage of the fall of Communism to move into Russian and Central Asian beer markets. Even in Iran under the Ayatollahs, the right contacts made it possible to drink beer. "One of the religious militia groups," the *Guardian* reported, "has the monopoly on beer imports from Turkey."[30] The Murree Brewery survived in

Pakistan through a court order protecting the minority rights of its Parsee owners. The head of quality control, Huma Zubair, a microbiologist who studied in the United States, swore she always spits after tasting. As the rise of fundamentalism closed off domestic markets, Murree reached out to the South Asian diaspora. "I would like to get this very famous name—it is, after all, a British legacy—on to the streets of the UK," said chief executive Isphanyar Bhandara. "My aim would be to put it in the ethnic restaurants and give the Indian beers, which totally suck, a run for their money."[31]

Exotic beers commanded a premium as the international trade in beer rose dramatically, while at the same time the meanings of import and domestic brands shifted. Before World War II, imports generally came from European countries with reputations for full-bodied beers. By 2010, pale lagers made up nine of the top ten import brands in the United States, excepting only Guinness. Apart from Heineken and Stella, the remaining imports came from Mexico or Canada. The identities of beer also became increasingly divorced from geography. Sapporo began brewing in Ontario to save money on shipping to the United States without losing its import label. The two top-selling beers in Canada were Budweiser and Coors Light, both brewed locally. Increasingly, the advertising of beer brands became more important than the technical skills of brewing.[32]

The Mad Men of Beer

During the 1970s stagflation, as cost-cutting at one major brewery produced unappetizing "Schlitz Bits," Gussie Busch chose instead to slash his company's advertising budget. His fanatic devotion to quality was understandable; in keeping with family tradition, his very first taste was Budweiser, a sacramental drop on the tongue before he received his mother's milk. There would be no "Bud Spuds" on his watch. But the decision had its perils, as tobacco executives from Philip Morris, who had taken over the Miller Brewery and understood the affinity between selling cigarettes and pale lager, took on nearly $1 billion in debt to purchase exclusive sponsorships on every available professional sports program for its Miller Lite "Tastes Great, Less Filling" commercials. As Miller challenged Anheuser Busch's market share, Gussie was hurried into retirement. His son, August III, proceeded to buy up the remaining sports television, including college athletics as well as the niche markets of the nascent cable network ESPN. Anheuser Busch reasserted its supremacy at the 1987 Super Bowl with an advertisement introducing Bud Light's new mascot, a bull terrier "super party animal named Spuds MacKenzie."[33] In the 1970s, management passed from brewing professionals to marketers and accountants, the so-called Mad Men of Madison Avenue, New York City's advertising district. As European and North American firms placed their bets on glitzy promotions, emerging-market competitors came to match them in production quality.

Guinness was an early pioneer in tailoring promotions to the cultural values of specific nations. In the 1920s, the company distributed a grab-bag of novelties, sending puzzles and pocket watches to India and Southeast Asia, menu cards to Java, and cigarette cases to Canada and Australia. In a 1949 tour of West Africa, executives sought to survey market conditions, while insisting that "Advertising should at all times be addressed to the African." The legacy of independent bottlers impeded efforts to create a unified identity for Guinness, since brand marks like the Boar's Head held greater recognition for African consumers than the Irish harp trademark. Nevertheless, local merchants and petty traders made effective use of poster advertisements and showcards. Company representatives estimated that half of African consumers considered Guinness to be medicine, while the other half drank it for strength and taste. Only 10 percent of consumers were thought to be women. Taste preferences and drinking cultures varied across the region. In Sierra Leone, consumers had a "decidedly dry palate" and took their Guinness neat. Residents of the Gold Coast were more likely to mix stout with beer, "half-and-half," while many Nigerians added palm wine as an economy measure.[34]

The Irish brewer launched its first British national advertising campaign in 1929 with the slogan "Guinness Is Good for You." Although such health claims are no longer permissible, scholar Brenda Murphy found that "the myth continues to carry great strength among many drinkers and non-drinkers."[35] Artist John Gilroy produced memorable advertising posters in the 1930s and 1940s, including a worker casually hoisting a steel beam on his shoulder over the caption "Guinness for Strength." A whole series of zoo-themed images followed with a hapless zookeeper exclaiming, "My Goodness, My Guinness!" while trying to recover a pint that had been pilfered by bears, sea lions, ostriches, and toucans.

Tailoring ads to local populations proved difficult at times. When the company shipped a consignment of leprechaun novelties in the 1960s, a Kenyan settler colonist, Eric Keartland, complained that the charm had brought him nothing but bad luck. He lost at cards, faced native union activism in his factory, and his housekeeper considered the charm to be "Bwana Mbaya (bad boss)" and refused to clean anywhere near it. The Guinness sales manager

FIGURE 6.2 "My Goodness—My Guinness." Artist John Gilroy produced a series of memorable advertising posters in the 1930s and 1940s featuring a hapless zookeeper trying to recover a pint that had been pilfered by bears, sea lions, ostriches, and toucans. GDB. MK10.02.0008.23. Courtesy of Guinness Archive. Diageo, Ireland.

commiserated with the misfortune, promised to look for a "wee psychiatrist," and recommended placating the leprechaun with a nightly tuck of Guinness from the bottom of an empty glass.[36] The company did adapt advertising posters replacing a British worker hoisting a steel beam with a black man carrying a tree trunk. The tagline was changed from "Guinness for Strength" to "Guinness Gives You Power," thereby alluding to a sense of masculine potency, although the image might have seemed condescending to Nigerian oil workers.[37]

FIGURE 6.3 "Guinness Gives You Power." Guinness Nigeria adjusted its advertisements to local conditions, replacing the steel girder carried by a British worker with a giant log and changing "strength" to "power." 1962. GOL.MK02.01.0012.0001. Courtesy of Guinness Archive. Diageo, Ireland.

In the United States, the oligopolistic concentration of beer markets saw a handful of firms competing through radio and television campaigns rather than price. The Theodore Hamm Brewery of St. Paul, Minnesota, created a series of animated commercials about a wacky bear who bumbled his way through log rolling, sky diving, and other outdoor activities. Accompanied by catchy tom-tom drums and the chorus "From the land of sky-blue waters," the Hamm's Bear was voted the best loved advertising character in America in 1965. Promotional budgets, which had been negligible in the 1930s, had risen to more than 6 percent of sales in 1958 and equaled the cost of ingredients by the mid-1970s. American advertising practices also began to exert a global influence. For example, South African Breweries sent its marketing director Peter Savory to Harvard Business School to learn how to "establish brand identity and generate brand recognition."[38]

Advertising agencies had their own internal divisions between departments labeled "creative," research, media, and accounts. Creative talent included Terry Lovelock, a jazz drummer and copywriter at London's Collett Dickenson Pearce agency, who in 1973 devised the Heineken slogan about refreshing "the parts other beers cannot reach." One installment showed the Star Trek character Mr. Spock with his Vulcan-pointed ears drooping. After drinking a mug of Heineken, his ears spring back up, which he declares, in a cartoon bubble: "Illogical."[39] The creativity of copy writers was informed—and often shaped—by research staff who used psychological theories to test out the effects of potential marketing campaigns. Ernest Dichter, a Viennese-trained psychiatrist who fled to the United States before World War II, pioneered focus group interviews to probe the motivations behind consumer purchases. In a 1952 study undertaken for the Hoffman and York Brewery of Milwaukee, Wisconsin, Dichter recommended that campaigns for their regional Berghoff and Gettelman brands target working-class consumers with sensual experiences and neighborly associations. Guinness developed its West African advertising campaigns based on similar market surveys conducted in Nigeria and Benin. Media executives placed these promotional campaigns in appropriate markets, the most prestigious of which became the American Super Bowl. Anheuser Busch spent $274 million on these annual television spots between 1988 and 2007. Nevertheless, the most important advertising consumers were not the public at all but instead brewery executives, with whom account managers worked to maintain agency-client relations.[40]

Targeting young males, considered the primary market for beer, advertisements featured masculine competition, often emphasizing sports. Firms went so far as to invest in professional athletics. Anheuser Busch bought the St. Louis Cardinals baseball team, and Molson purchased the Montreal Canadien hockey team. In Africa, the Holsten brewery of Hamburg sponsored the Bergedorf Cup for Nigerian football tournaments beginning in 1938. SAB sought to match its brands to targeted ethnic segments, Lion Lager was aimed at rugby fans, a largely white crowd, while Castle Lager appealed to the mixed-race followers of soccer. Sponsorship was not simply a matter of posting advertisements around stadiums and taverns; companies were expected to maintain fans' values, including their rivalries. One such grudge divided the two leading cities of Portugal, Lisbon and Porto, and their respective soccer teams, Benefica and Porto. The Lisbon-based brewer of Sagres beer and Benefica sponsor, Central de Cervejas, offered to pay for the renovation of Porto's cathedral. With this artificial display of philanthropy, the brewery implied that the rival townspeople were incompetent in maintaining their religious shrine. Outraged by the affront, Porto fans insisted their own team's sponsoring brewery, Super Bock, pay for the renovations, thereby upholding their honor as men capable of performing their civic duty.[41]

Another side to masculine domination—female submissiveness—has been explicitly used to sell beer. At least since the turn of the century, waitresses garbed in peasant dresses served in urban German beer halls, and geisha were employed as brand ambassadors for Japanese breweries. Bud Light's Spuds MacKenzie ads juxtaposed an ugly mutt with beautiful young women. Nevertheless, using sex to sell beer posed its own risks. In 1991, not long after Spuds's premiere, the Stroh Brewery created a campaign for its Old Milwaukee brand featuring an imagined Swedish Bikini Team of tall, blonde women who parachuted from out of the blue, bringing cases of beer to vacationing men. The advertisement backfired when women employees at Stroh filed a sexual harassment lawsuit, based not only on the actions of male coworkers but on the company's own promotional materials displayed in the factory. Stroh settled out of court for an undisclosed amount. For the rest of the decade, sexual content was subdued in beer advertising, which instead featured animal-themed promotions such as a trio of frogs who croaked "Bud," "Weis," "Er."[42]

By this point, Guinness had developed more nuanced portrayals of African masculinity for advertisements aimed not at the working classes but at a more aspirational black middle class. A campaign launched in 1999 by the Saatchi and Saatchi marketing agency centered around action hero Michael Power, whose last name recalled Guinness's longstanding African promotions. Filmed in Nigeria by a pan-African crew and starring the London-born and Jamaica-raised actor Cleveland Mitchell, the ads were a bargain compared to the €60 million reportedly paid by Heineken for the sponsorship rights to the James Bond spy franchise. Power worked not as a secret agent for authoritarian regimes, but rather as a reporter solving the problems of ordinary people and uncovering elite corruption. In one spot, a power outage threatened to cancel a music festival until he used his cellphone to call a fleet of taxis, who used their headlights to illuminate the party. The advertisements were so successful that Guinness commissioned a feature film, *Critical Assignment* (2003), filled with product placements, including a Guinness delivery truck that conveniently stopped the villains from escaping. Wearing black Armani suits, Power defied the image of the traditional Big Man and offered a modern ideal for urban Africans.[43]

Although generally focused on young men, brewers occasionally recognized the potential for marketing to women. After the repeal of Prohibition in the United States, brewers demonstrated their commitment to moderation by portraying domestic consumption, although women generally appeared not as consumers but rather as shoppers. By the 1950s a few commercials showed men and women, and a decade later, women were shown drinking together. In South Africa, advertisements depicted women drinking beer under the gaze of men. The sexual harassment lawsuit against Stroh finally broke through such myopia, and in 1992, Miller, Anheuser Busch, and Coors all began running advertisements in women's magazines and on daytime television.[44]

Like the pan-African, urban audiences that thrilled to the deeds of Michael Power, beer advertisements often evoked imagined communities of various kinds. In 2000, Molson packed as many nationalist tropes as possible into a sixty-second television campaign dubbed "The Rant." Every line from the young, white spokesman was focus-group tested for nationalist appeal, from "a beaver is a noble animal" to "Canada is the second largest landmass, and the first nation of hockey." As the music built up to a crescendo and a giant glass of Molson bubbled up on the screen behind him, he proclaimed: "I am Joe. I am a Canadian!" The advertisement struck a chord among young men, who gave "ritualized performances" of the script in public spaces.[45] Campaigns made similar claims for ethnic allegiances, including an SAB promotion for Castle Milk Stout featuring a Zulu war dance. Often these campaigns targeted diasporic audiences. Tsingtao Brewery granted American distribution rights to the Monarch Wine Company, maker of the Kosher Manischewitz brand. The company's New York Jewish owners promised to market the beer in Chinese restaurants, a seemingly obvious strategy but apparently one that did not occur to waspy ad executives, who were less likely to frequent such establishments.[46]

As the Jewish Chinese restaurant connection illustrates, nation-branding often appealed beyond the national community. Löwenbräu had long represented Germany abroad, having established a sales outlet in London in 1897. In 1965, the Munich brewer's English importer, J. C. McLaughlin, gathered local investors to finance a series of branded beer halls in cities across the United Kingdom, increasing sales from 10,000 to 100,000 gallons. In the 1990s, a Dublin-based developer, the Irish Pub Company, opened 2,000 pubs in cities around the world; Guinness supplied the beer but otherwise did not participate in the business. Sapporo's "Legendary Biru" television advertisement, created in Canada for North American audiences, imagined how beer might have been brewed in a mythical Japanese past. Using a seemingly uninterrupted tracking shot, the camera moved from a samurai riding across the landscape to peasants carrying buckets of spring water, geisha sorting barley, giant sumo wrestlers on the malting floor, dragons boiling wort, and a frozen lake for lagering, all to the beat of taiko drummers. At times, advertisers completely abandoned national associations, as with Corona's anonymous beach vacation. Heineken stripped away Mexican associations when distributing Dos Equis with the "Most Interesting Man in the World" campaign, featuring an Ernest Hemingway–like figure with improbable lines such as, "When he goes to Spain, he chases the bulls."[47]

The paired tropes of authenticity and modernity, present already in nineteenth-century images of factories and beer gardens, echo through contemporary advertisements. Anheuser Busch parades its Clydesdale horses to demonstrate tradition, while Asahi promoted its novel beer not with "elderly men gazing pensively over Japanese landscapes" but rather "good-looking young throats gulping down Super Dry."[48] At times, brewers simply attached traditional names to modern beers. In post-socialist Georgia, for example, a pale lager was branded as Aluda beer, supposedly made by mountain men with "traditional Khevsur methods," a folk-brewing tradition that has been described as "sweetened motor oil."[49] Helsinki shops sold cans labeled Sahti, the traditional Finnish rye and juniper beer, but they were simply English brown ales. In the 1970s, the Bavarian Brewers Association touted local brewing traditions with archaic-looking posters of Duke Wilhelm IV's 1516 decree, translated into multiple languages and labeled with the modern term, "Reinheitsgebot." Although popular with consumers, the campaign failed to deter rivals from calling their own beers "Bavarian."[50]

Brewers had a difficult time advertising the flavor of their products in terms beyond glib generalities. Industrial quality control depended on a technical device called the "flavor wheel," created in 1979 by Morton Meilgaard, a Danish flavor chemist working at the Stroh Brewery Company of Detroit. Intended to create a common terminology for chemical researchers, quality-control tasting panels, and other industry professionals, the flavor wheel avoided aesthetic judgments such as "good" or "bad" and instead provided chemical reference standards such as the organic compound 6-Nonenal responsible for a "melony" aroma. The flavor wheel was adapted for wine in the mid-1980s by University of California, Davis, oenologist Ann Noble, who popularized the tool for aspiring wine drinkers seeking to learn the arcane language of the industry. By contrast, Meilgaard intended the beer wheel for strictly professional use. He explained in a *New York Times* article: "Brewers don't want beer drinkers to be aware of beer's major and minor components, only its overall taste."[51] Not until 1989 did advertisers emblazon the flavor wheel across a pint of beer in the British newspaper the *Guardian* under the headline: "Perfect Draught Bass. A delicate balance of fruit, grass, and leather." The ad explained that skilled flavor testers offered "the only sure way to keep every pint of Draught Bass we make as distinctive as the original 1777 brew.... Naturally, we would never expect you to worry about the subtleties that keep our experts engrossed for hours."[52]

Despite the vast sums spent on media advertisements, participatory spectacles provided some of the most memorable promotions, as they had since the world's fairs of the nineteenth century. Even while staging Oktoberfest as a tourist attraction, Munich brewers encouraged its globalization. In 1956,

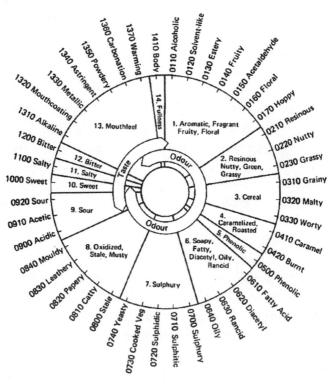

FIGURE 6.4 Beer flavor wheel created in 1979 by Danish brewing scientist Morton Meilgaard as an industrial quality control device, replacing aesthetic judgments such as "good" or "bad" with precise chemical reference standards. Morton C. Meilgaard, C. E. Dalgliesh, and J. L. Clapperton, "Beer Flavour Terminology," *JIB* 85 (January–February 1979): 38–42.

American veterans who had been stationed in Germany celebrated a local version in Monterey Bay, California, while the Blumenau Oktoberfest was first held in 1984 in Santa Catarina, Brazil, and the Qingdao International Beer Festival began around 1990. Guinness was long a supporter of Dublin's St. Patrick's Day celebration, but the company began to commercialize the event more widely in the late 1980s with the growing interest in Irish heritage among diasporic populations, especially white ethnics in the United States. Cinco de Mayo, celebrating Mexico's victory over French invaders on May 5, 1862, was largely ignored after a 1910 revolution overthrew hero-turned-dictator Porfirio Díaz. It remained popular among Mexican Americans, including Díaz's exiled followers, and was coopted in the United States as an excuse for drinking beer during the Corona boom of the 1980s.[53]

Beer companies also established more brand-specific tourist experiences through the creation of beer museums, which began as corporate archives and memorabilia collections and were repurposed for public relations beginning in the 1970s. The Bass Brewery of Burton-on-Trent founded perhaps the first major beer museum to celebrate the company's bicentenary in 1977. It was soon followed by the Cuauhtémoc Brewery Museum in Monterrey, which also housed the Mexican baseball hall of fame, and the Tiger Beer Museum in Singapore, with a taproom and promotional materials. At Bass, the museum functioned less as a tourist attraction than as a space for promoting corporate identity among globe-trotting managers, a mission that proved vulnerable to industrial consolidation. In 2000, Bass was taken over by the Belgian firm Interbrew, which kept the brand but sold the Burton factory to Coors in 2003. The new owners changed the name to Coors Visitor Centre, then closed it down due to lack of visitors. Although Burton's heritage meant little to executives in Golden, Colorado, the local Member of Parliament, Janet Dean, led a campaign to restore the museum, using tours and special events to keep the space viable as they raised funds for a National Brewery Heritage Trust.[54]

Conflicts within the Belgian brewing industry frustrated attempts to open a national museum of beer in Brussels. The spontaneous fermentation of lambic was already considered a museum piece, and to showcase it in 1978, Jean-Pierre Van Roy invited the public to tour his Cantillon Brewery, near the capital's train station, as a Museum of Gueuze. The Belgian Brewers' Federation was divided between the conglomerate Interbrew, best known for Stella Artois lager, and hundreds of suspicious small brewers making diverse varieties of beer. In 1990, at the request of the Brussels tourism office, it opened a public museum in the cramped basement bar of its otherwise ornate headquarters on the city's Grand Place. Determined to do better, Flemish politician and sometime Brewers' Federation head Sven Gatz spent a decade trying to reconcile the industry's conflicting groups to build a temple worthy of Belgium's historic beers. In 2015, the Federation leased the old Brussels Bourse and began planning a Belgian Beer World, complete with historic exhibits, tasting rooms, and restaurants, although delays plagued the project.[55]

Like other public history exhibits, beer museums allowed corporations to narrate their heritage and situate their brands. The SAB World of Beer in Johannesburg foregrounded Africa as the home of brewing, with the first two rooms dedicated to ancient Egyptian and sub-Saharan brewing traditions, including a tasting of sorghum beer. The Oktoberfest Museum in Munich derived its authenticity from its fourteenth-century building, reputedly the city's oldest townhouse. Curators saw no need to acknowledge that beer might be brewed anywhere else and displayed historical rooms, Oktoberfest posters, and commemorative beer steins above a ground-floor tavern crowded with people in folkloric costume. In Copenhagen, the Carlsberg Brewery tour prominently displayed Hansen's original pure yeast machine, while the World of Tsingtao proudly exhibited rice alongside barley, unlike many other breweries that sought to hide their use of adjunct grains. Over time, brewery tours grew into sophisticated forms of experiential branding. In 2000, Guinness converted a storehouse into a stout extravaganza, with an academy for pouring the perfect pint, a life-sized menagerie of Gilroy cartoon characters, and a rooftop "Gravity Bar" overlooking Dublin. The following year, its Dutch rival converted an old brewery near Amsterdam's museum district into the Heineken Experience. Tour guides explained that the goal was to turn Heineken drinkers into brand ambassadors, and every step along the way provided selfie spots for visitors to pose with green bottles while engaging in their favorite pastimes. Free wifi throughout the building ensured immediate social media postings.

Experiential advertising did not require huge investments. African brewers simply painted tied houses in trademark colors. This low-tech approach to marketing required only a few cans of paint, but it engaged consumers in a lively fashion. In Dar es Salaam, the market leader Tanzania Breweries Limited and rival Serengeti, a subsidiary of Diageo, captured pubs and repainted them like sporting teams in red and yellow, respectively. Shifting hues therefore mapped the battle for market share across the urban landscape. Heineken took this practice a step further by donating money to African schools in return for painting them the brand's distinctive green, claiming a charitable tax deduction while encouraging customer loyalty from an early age.[56]

Advertising played an increasingly prominent role in marketing beer across the twentieth century, but the tropes behind these promotions have not changed significantly from the early modern era, when masculinity and community drew customers to the pub. Nor were high tech media spectacles necessarily more effective at building brand loyalty than the communal work of repainting a pub in Africa. The seemingly primitive nature of such advertising reassured managers in Europe and North America that the real value of firms lay in intellectual property, even as brewers in Latin America, Africa, and Asia came to match their production efficiency.[57] This faith in legacy brands was tested in the decades around the turn of the twenty-first century, as commodity brewers battled for global supremacy.

The Dance of the Elephants

For countless people around the world, the late 1980s and early 1990s were a time to crack open a beer and celebrate. The fall of the Berlin Wall heralded the collapse of Communist dictatorships in Eastern Europe; economic reforms spurred rapid growth in China; civilian governments replaced military regimes across South America; and multiracial elections spelled the end of Apartheid in South Africa. The apparent triumph of capitalist liberal democracy after decades of Cold War launched a new wave of globalization, and brewers ventured out from their national markets in search of new customers. Established giants such as Heineken, Guinness, and Anheuser Busch held advantages built on centuries of accumulated capital and colonial rule. But investors increasingly scorned the stability of mature industries and family management in favor of rapid growth and market disruption. Investment bankers and leveraged buyouts provided weapons for upstart firms to bring down complacent managers. In 2003, as established giants like Bass and Miller fell, Graham Mackay, the chairman of South African Breweries, predicted that just three or four big firms would survive what he called "the dance of the elephants."[58] With Goldman Sachs tapping the keg, there were fortunes to be made, but would the beer still be worth drinking?

As late as 1990, the international brewing industry reflected the legacies of postwar Fordist industrial organization. The United States remained the largest market by far, and half of that was held by the family firm of Anheuser Busch. But the deregulation of financial exchange in the 1970s brought a wave of change. Corporate raiders borrowed heavily to purchase established firms, selling assets and cutting unionized workforces, while new investments in emerging markets promised to satisfy growing populations. China had already become the second leading consumer of beer by 1990, and its Maoist-era machinery could scarcely keep up with demand. In their quest for international growth, firms adopted various models. Managers at Anheuser Busch dreamed of extending their American dominion under the motto, "Budweiser: One World, One Beer." By contrast, the Belgian firm Interbrew aspired to become the "World's Local Brewer." Anheuser Busch was betting on Americanization at a moment when the world was turning away from such models, as management scholars Martin Stack, Myles Gartland, and Tim Keane observed: "Internationalization has occurred, but it has been at the level of the brewery, not the brand."[59]

Australian financiers were among the first corporate raiders to target the beer industry in the 1980s. The pickings were ripe, with just eight breweries in the entire country, each comfortably ensconced in a state-level monopoly or duopoly. In 1983, former McKinsey consultant John Elliott added Carleton and United, the Melbourne brewer of Foster's Lager, to his agribusiness conglomerate, Elders IXL. Two years later, Alan Bond, a boardroom buccaneer with a penchant for yacht racing, took over the venerable Tooheys and Castlemaine XXXX brands. By the end of the decade, the pair held 85 percent of the Australian beer market and had begun to look abroad. In 1985, Elliott made a hostile bid for Britain's second largest brewer, Allied-Lyons, offering £1.8 billion, four times the value of Elders IXL. Rebuffed by the board, Elliott bought Courage instead, along with the Canadian firm Carling O'Keefe. Meanwhile, Bond purchased Pittsburgh Brewing and G. Heileman. Corporate loot, like pirate's treasure, often vanished as quickly as it came. Bond liquidated his brewing interests, with the Australian holdings going to the New Zealand conglomerate Lion Nathan in 1990, shortly before his A$1.8 billion bankruptcy and imprisonment for securities fraud. Elliott was cleared of similar charges, but he too eventually filed for bankruptcy. Regardless of their fate, these raiders revealed the potential windfalls available in the brewing industry.[60]

Brazilians also took an investment banking approach of consolidating firms and cutting costs to brewing. Jorge Paulo Lemann, the son of a Swiss businessman and a Harvard Business School graduate, purchased the Brahma Brewery in 1989 through an investment bank he had founded on the model of Goldman Sachs. A decade later he merged Brahma with the Antarctica Brewery to form the Drinks Company of the Americas (Ambev), thereby controlling 70 percent of the Brazilian market. President Fernando Henrique Cardoso waived competition rules in the hopes of building an international giant, and Lemann did not disappoint, purchasing breweries in Argentina

(Quilmes), Uruguay (Salus), Ecuador (Sur Americana), and the Dominican Republic (Dominicana). Squeezing profits out of the takeovers was the job of Carlos Alves de Brito, a mechanical engineer and Stanford Business School MBA with a "fanatic attention to detail." When the Brazilian government demanded energy cuts during a hydroelectric crisis in 2001, Brito developed a plan to boost efficiency in the storage of chilled drinks and snacks, personally explaining it at bars and corner stores. He later recalled: "The ice cream boys (tipos de los helados) who didn't get with the plan suffered big time."[61]

South African Breweries also used its domestic monopoly as a springboard to regional and global expansion. Opportunities abounded in Africa during the 1990s, as International Monetary Fund structural adjustment programs privatized national breweries founded at independence. Nevertheless, competition was fierce from Heineken, Guinness, and France's Castel. The election of Nelson Mandela in 1994 opened capital markets, and SAB quickly struck deals in Botswana, Ethiopia, Ghana, Mozambique, Tanzania, Uganda, and Zambia. Not all ventures were successful; a new factory in Kenya was shuttered due to competition from the local leader, East African Breweries. In Nigeria, dominated by Guinness and Heineken, SAB risked only a modest presence, well away from the capital, Lagos. In 1999, the African company listed on the London stock exchange to facilitate global expansion.[62]

The fall of the Iron Curtain provided access to historic brands and devoted beer drinkers in Eastern Europe. Anheuser Busch wasted no time in making an offer for the Budejovicky Budvar brewery, hoping to gain universal rights to the name of Budweiser. In 1939, the American brewer had reached an agreement with Budvar that each would have the Budweiser name in its home territory. Anheuser Busch spent heavily in the Czech Republic to build goodwill, but its offer was rejected. Meanwhile, European firms went bargain hunting to build market share across the region. Carlsberg moved into the neighboring Baltic countries of Estonia (Saku) and Lithuania (Svyturys), while Heineken bought breweries in Slovakia (Zlaty) and Bulgaria (Ariana). SAB was the most aggressive buyer of Eastern European breweries, a strategy explained by Graham Mackay: "They were the only ones that were affordable."[63] The African company acquired firms in Slovakia (Saris), Hungary (Dreher), Poland (Tyskie), Romania (Timisoreana), and the storied Czech brewers of Pilsner Urquell and Gambrinus. Russia's markets offered rich pickings for politically connected oligarchs. Eugene Kashper, an Ernst & Young consultant who had emigrated as a child in 1969, joined local business partners to build a brewing empire that spanned Russia and other post-Soviet republics.[64]

Beer consumption grew 25 percent annually in China during the late 1980s, as the Maoist-era thirst could suddenly be satisfied thanks to economic reforms. "Literally hundreds of small breweries emerged from the rice paddies," observed economist Bai Junfei. "Most were state owned at the country level. A county's beer factory frequently was its status symbol."[65] In the rush to increase supply, production remained rudimentary, and as late as the 1990s, more than half of all domestic breweries reportedly failed quality-control tests. Shopkeepers and customers alike faced a game of Russian roulette, as by some estimates, roughly one glass bottle in every case exploded before it could be consumed. Wary drinkers filled plastic bags with beer from corner-store kegs. The situation seemed ripe for western firms with capital and technical knowledge, but challenges abounded, not least from Communist Party bureaucrats.[66]

Dreams of a billion beer drinkers inspired a rush of foreign investment in the 1990s. Experienced Asia hands Heineken and Beck's competed with regional rivals, including the Australasian Foster's and Lion Nathan, the Japanese Kirin and Asahi, and the Philippines' San Miguel. Many companies sought local knowledge through joint ventures; Miller took a stake in Beijing's Five Star Brewery, prompting Anheuser Busch to partner with Tsingtao. Bass, Carlsberg, Interbrew, and SAB also made significant investments. The gold rush for Chinese beer even attracted a Canadian mining company, Noble Mines and Oils, to buy three breweries. Many investors fulfilled their operational goals of building state-of-the-art factories and creating brand awareness through advertising campaigns, earning the respect of Chinese rivals for the quality of their beer. Nevertheless, to support fixed investment costs, the foreigners had to sell at up to five times the price of local brands, and plants ran far below capacity. Consultant Norman Sze shrugged: "They would rather lose money than not come into China at all."[67]

Reckless investments offered windfall gains to more cautious outsiders and locals. Even while writing off $200 million, Foster's doubled down with new capital, as did Lion Nathan and Heineken. Anheuser Busch likewise poured money in, acquiring 29 percent of Tsingtao before realizing that Chinese authorities would never cede control of this iconic firm to foreigners. SAB had more success in its joint venture with China Resources, having become "accustomed to managing factories with unreliable energy sources, inconsistent supply and delivery of inputs, unskilled labour pools, and the use of older technology and plant infrastructure."[68] As foreigners began cutting losses, SAB and Tsingtao bought up plants on the cheap, including the Five Star Brewery. Yanjing, Beijing's municipal brewery, made its own series of acquisitions, including three factories in Shandong province on Tsingtao's turf. Foreign brands continued to be available, but domestic companies controlled the market. Foster's former marketing manager, Tim Murray, called the Chinese beer rush a "corporate Vietnam."[69]

Consolidation also accelerated in mature markets of Europe and North America, although export leaders took a relatively minor role. As privately held companies, Heineken and Carlsberg were immune from hostile takeovers but also had limited opportunities to raise money for acquisitions. Guinness likewise stood apart, having merged in 1997 with the distilling giant Grand Metropolitan to form Diageo. The driving force in European buyouts came from Interbrew, which had been founded in 1971 as an alliance between the Belgian lager brewers Artois and Piedboeuf. The agreement was kept secret until 1987 to forestall Belgian competition regulators from investigating price fixing among the leading brands Stella and Jupiler. Rivalries among the owners, the grand families of De Spoelberch, De Mévius, and van Damme, made management difficult, although the company was able to grow by purchasing small specialty brewers. Global expansion began in earnest through a 1995 merger with the Canadian firm, Labatt. When no leadership candidate emerged in Brussels, the combined firm Interbrew was handed over to Labatt's chair, Hugo Powell. The cosmopolitan Englishman moved swiftly to shake up the staid Belgian company, taking it public to raise funds and, in the spring and summer of 2000, purchasing Whitbread and Bass, the latter for £2.3 billion. British competition authorities promptly ordered the divestment of factories, which Coors purchased at fire sale prices.[70]

The mergers vaulted Interbrew to number two in the industry, with 13 percent of the global market, still far behind Anheuser Busch at 25 percent, but ahead of Heineken at 12 percent and the Brazilian Ambev at 10 percent. Losses from Bass did not slow Powell, who proceeded in August 2001 to buy the German exporter Beck's for an inflated price of $1.6 billion. That fall, business newspapers reported yet another imminent acquisition, SAB. The story read like a spy novel, with Interbrew referred to by the code name Ice and the target company called Zulu. A Belgian spokesman blamed the intrigue on "fee-hungry investment bankers at Goldman Sachs and Lazard, with too much time on their hands, exploring different strategic options," but refused to rule out an offer. The *Independent* declared the plans to be "a complete joke. SAB is a smaller company by market capitalization, but in terms of strategy and management it is streets ahead of Interbrew."[71] Insiders speculated that Powell's enemies on the board had leaked the plan to push him out. The company's share price had fallen 40 percent by the time he retired the following year.[72]

By this point, brewery managers everywhere were desperately seeking partners. SAB's chairman Mackay indeed felt vulnerable, as the devaluation of the South African rand caused the share price to tumble, risking expulsion from the London FTSE 100 ranking. In 2002, the company launched a bold takeover of Miller, offering $3.6 billion in stock and $2 billion in debt. The South Africans cleaned up operational troubles at the American firm and set about increasing market share. Meanwhile, Coors, having gained a European presence on the cheap with the second-hand purchase of Bass's factories, partnered with Molson in 2005 to create the world's fifth largest brewery, capitalized at $6 billion. These mergers revealed the growing vulnerability of Anheuser Busch, despite its continued dominance in America. The company's attempts at international growth in the 1990s had led to costly failures in China and ongoing litigation with Budvar over the Budweiser name in some eighty countries. Anheuser Busch had seemed an obvious buyer for Beck's in 2001 but lost out to Interbrew. The St. Louis firm's most successful international venture was acquiring a 50 percent stake in the Mexican brewer, Modelo, which boosted Corona's global presence.[73]

Meanwhile, Interbrew continued its inexorable growth through a 2004 merger with the Brazilian firm Ambev worth a combined $11.4 billion. On paper, Interbrew remained the senior partner, with 85 percent of the voting shares. Ambev's management oversaw operations in the Americas, while Interbrew executives retained control elsewhere. The combined company, called InBev, retained its Leuven headquarters and Brussels Stock Exchange listing. But those who knew the banker Lemann and his partners may have wondered about this division. A former associate from the 1970s, Luiz Cezar Fernandes, observed: "They like control when they invest."[74] Lemann's protégé Carlos Brito promptly fired a fifth of Labatt's management and closed the flagship Toronto brewery, then turned his attention to the home office in Belgium. The incumbent chief executive, John Brock, who had negotiated the merger for Interbrew, was ousted in 2005, like Hugo Powell before him. Yet Belgians did not sit passively by as Brito and his accountants set to work cutting costs and raising prices. Competition regulators opened a price-fixing investigation, acting on suspicions that had lingered for decades but acquired urgency under the new management. Meanwhile, brewery workers launched a wave of strikes, and in Belgium, unlike in Latin America, they could not be silenced by riot police. One particular focus of protest arose from the closing of the Hoegaarden brewery, a beloved maker of *witbier* (wheat beer) that Interbrew had purchased in 1985 at the dawn of its merger campaign. In response to popular demand, the plant was restored. On a global scale, the merger catapulted InBev past Anheuser Busch to number one, followed by SABMiller, Heineken, Molson Coors, Carlsberg, and Scottish & Newcastle, with three emerging-market firms, Modelo, Asahi, and Tsingtao, rounding out the top ten.[75]

Having gained control in Belgium, Brito set his sights on an even bigger takeover: Anheuser Busch. The St. Louis brewer had slipped below its peak of 50 percent market share in the United States, and it faced growing competition from MillerCoors, a 2007 joint venture of the American operations of SABMiller and Molson Coors. Apart from the deal to distribute Corona, Anheuser Busch lacked the premium brands to finance a price war at the low end of the domestic market. Nor was the company's leadership equipped to navigate these hazards; August Busch III had grudgingly relinquished the chairmanship in 2003, but he retained his seat on the board and questioned every move by August IV to cut costs and update operations. The elder Busch was particularly outraged when his son struck a deal with InBev in 2006 to import the Stella and Beck's brands. Within a year, investment bankers had begun to consider a merger between the two companies inevitable, and Brito tried to smooth the waters by touting his Stanford MBA and American management style. The Anheuser Busch board cast about for possible defensive strategies, alighting on a merger with Modelo, which could add $10 to $15 billion to the combined company's price, making it impossible for InBev to swallow, but the negotiations foundered. While outwardly confident, Brito was desperate to close the deal in the summer of 2008 and offered $52 billion. Guided by August III, the board accepted the bid on July 13, although financing was not secured until November, in the midst of the banking collapse. Journalist Julie MacIntosh later reported that the deal would have fallen apart if it had taken another month or two to close.[76]

As it was, Brito worked desperately to pay off loans before they came due. Industry analyst Tom Pirko explained: "They did the right deal at the wrong price at the wrong time and now they're choking for air."[77] To meet the first year's installment of $17 billion, the Brazilians immediately sold off the company's entertainment unit as well as its Asian holdings. With staff cuts of 40 percent at the St. Louis head office, atrade journal reported: "It's like a bomb went off at One Busch Place."[78] Those who remained faced a very different working environment under the famously spartan Brito, who bragged about "unplugging mini-refrigerators." Recalling the early days of energy savings in Brazil, he did not seem to wonder if employees would lose focus on quality control while drinking warm beer. Advertising and sponsorships also fell by the wayside, including the Super Bowl, a perennial source of excitement for the brand. Distributors were asked to provide "100 percent share of mind," essentially playing one off against another to ensure greater profits at the top. Efficiency measures on the factory floor included "replacing higher cost inputs with lower cost ones—thinner glass bottles, cheaper ingredients—and pressing suppliers to give them twice as long to pay for goods."[79] At the same time, the company began raising prices, beginning a steady erosion of market share. Recalls and contamination scares brought back memories of Schlitz. Even a competitor sighed: "It's hard to watch them gut a great American brewery."[80]

After a brief pause to mop up independent firms, bankers began salivating over the prospect of a marriage between AB InBev and SABMiller. Brito paid down the astronomical debt before purchasing the remaining stock in Modelo, while Mexican rival, FEMSA, fell to Heineken, and Kirin and SABMiller took over the Australasian firms Lion Nathan and Foster's. But all eyes were on AB InBev, which still earned 90 percent of its revenue in the Americas and hoped to gain geographical diversity. Unlike Heineken and Carlsberg, with their family control, SABMiller was considered vulnerable because of its open shareholder base. Graham Mackay rejected the deal as one that "only makes sense to investment bankers."[81] He argued instead for organic growth by making better beer, but like his predecessors in St. Louis, he realized that SAB could raise the price of a takeover but not hold it off indefinitely. The company's fate hinged on another Latin American family, the Santo Domingos of Colombia, who had acquired a holding as part of SAB's 2005 merger with Bavaria. In 2013, Mackay died of cancer, and two years later, the offer duly arrived, for $104 billion. Competition authorities picked over the deal, requiring the sale of SABMiller's stake in MillerCoors, and the transfer of its Chinese holdings to the local partner. Asahi picked up Anheuser Busch's former share in Tsingtao as well as Central and Eastern European brands divested to satisfy European Union regulators.[82]

But even as AB InBev cemented its standing as a global leviathan, the long-term viability of its strategy was already coming into question. David Peacock, the last Anheuser Busch executive to leave the company, declared that "while famous for cutting costs, [Brito and his team] have yet to demonstrate that they can grow without acquiring other companies." Such a strategy could not continue indefinitely, "because once you buy SAB, you're kind of done—there's not much else to buy."[83] Lemann's attempt to diversify through the purchase of Kraft Heinz with investor Warren Buffett had begun to unravel by 2019, as cost cutting undermined the company's reputation for quality. Brito sought to distance himself from the woes at Kraft Heinz, but the *Economist* observed: "Exclude acquisitions and ABI has not increased beer volumes in over a decade. Sale growth, of 4.7% a year since 2008, is largely thanks to what Mr Brito calls 'revenue management initiatives'—or, in plain English, selling ABI's existing beers at higher prices."[84]

As the dust settled from the dance of the elephants, the European and North American domination of international beer production had been turned upside down. Anheuser Busch was tripped up because of its inability to build a global strategy, while other national brands lacked the resources to survive the merger frenzy. The undisputed leader, producing one-third of the world's beer, AB InBev retained its nominal Belgian headquarters, but it was run from New York by Brazilian executives. Heineken and Carlsberg also held their rankings in the top four, leaving Molson Coors as the last major brewer owned in North America. Projections of future market growth meant that five of the top ten were Asian, including the Chinese Snow, Tsingtao, and Yanjing and the Japanese Asahi and Kirin. The French multinational Castel, with its African and Asian holdings, rounded out the industry leaders. Throughout this flurry of global consolidation, the names on the bottles scarcely changed.

Scientific research of the early twentieth century intended to brew a better beer culminated at the century's end with the goal of making a more profitable one. While brewers and consumers might debate the relative merits of pale lagers and hearty ales, only accountants could see the beauty in chemical stabilizers and discount packaging. In the twenty-first century, brewing professionals held little voice in management, having been displaced first by advertising executives and then by investment bankers. The political economy of financial deregulation facilitated the global consolidation of commodity brewing, while the size of the resulting firms was limited, in any given market, only by the increasingly lax enforcement of competition authorities.

Despite these structural constraints, technological advances in brewing did plant the seed for the displacement of brewing professionals. The standardization of pale lager and the consolidation of national firms at midcentury dictated an increasing reliance on the narratives of advertising to build market value. The rise of imports as a market segment offered simply another such form of distinction. Heineken achieved a premium status as a better beer in the United States through the savvy marketing of Leo Van Munching. By the end of the century, even the pretense of quality had been largely abandoned, as the import sector came to be dominated by pale lagers from Canada and Mexico. With the advent of flavored malt beverages such as Bud Light Lime and Chinese clam and passion fruit beers, the art of brewing was taken over by food industry formulators, reducing beer to the level of Nacho Cheese Doritos. But despite the cachet of imports, most consumers remained loyal to local brands, even if they had been taken over by remote conglomerates.

The long-term transformation from communal imbibing to drinking alone at home had its limits, for beer is the most social of beverages. Advertisers sought to profit from this image of community, through both media and manufactured drinking occasions such as Cinco de Mayo and the Heineken Experience. Nevertheless, in an age of corporate domination and mass production, as the ownership of breweries became ever more globalized and distant, many people sought to regain a sense of personalized experience and community. The craft beer movement promised a return to such values but struggled to escape the constraints of the capitalist marketplace.

7

Peak Hops

WHEN GREG KOCH announced plans in 2014 to open a California-style brewpub in Germany's capital, the *Berliner Kurier* dubbed him the "Beer Jesus from America."[1] Koch looked the part of a craft beer evangelist—tall and thin, with long blonde hair and beard—but he didn't turn the other cheek. Selling bitterly hopped IPAs, with names like Arrogant Bastard and Ruination, the muscular gargoyle mascot of Koch's Stone Brewery sneered: "You Are Not Worthy." The irony of a descendant of German migrants returning to the ancestral homeland to preach about beer was not lost on Berlin journalists. Although Koch was crucified in print, the venture failed not from lack of interest by German youth but rather because of the mundane challenges of trade unions and building codes. Indeed, the Mariendorf taproom was taken over by Brewdog, a Scottish craft brewer with an equally irreverent attitude toward the Reinheitsgebot. The episode illustrated a fundamental contradiction between the rhetoric and practice of craft beer, whose advocates may have imagined themselves as prophets casting commodity beer from the temple but nevertheless traded in the silver coins of capitalism.

Whereas some Germans saw craft beer as a cult, the movement's story in the United States has often been narrated using the patriotic language of founding fathers. Sharing a passion for good beer and a dissatisfaction with bland corporate products, Fritz Maytag, Jack McAuliffe, Ken Grossman, and Jim Koch pioneered a new microbrewing industry. Koch even made the revolutionary link explicit by naming his signature lager after the patriot Samuel Adams. Except for the cantankerous McAuliffe, all were rewarded with enormous wealth. Such origin stories conferred authority and legitimacy on these exceptional individuals, justifying their supposed revolution against the corporate power of so-called big beer, even as they exemplified the capitalist system.[2]

As a tale of American exceptionalism, the founding father narrative of countercultural rebels also obscured the global nature of the craft movement. Although the homebrewers who pioneered the industry traced their lineage to Prohibition-era outlaws, the hobby would have remained a fringe pursuit without international supply chains of high-quality malt, hops, and yeast, which became available in retail shops after the United Kingdom legalized homebrewing in 1963. The narrative also depicted the brewer as mad scientist, tinkering with chemistry sets and assembling breweries out of junkyard surplus. In fact, entrepreneurs depended on a technological infrastructure constructed by the giants. Much of the surplus equipment that ran early microbreweries came from regional firms that had been bankrupted by industrial consolidation in Europe and North America. For this reason, Jim Koch and other contract brewers, whose business model employed the industry's skilled personnel and excess capacity, elicited scorn from rivals within the movement.

The rugged individualist narrative also concealed the role of professional organizations and knowledge networks of beer writers and internet forums. Trade groups circulated technical advice and ran the beer festivals that served to educate consumers and promote brands—an essential service for firms without large advertising budgets. These organizations and networks also devised and disseminated a shared vocabulary of taste that enabled aficionados to assert their rugged individual preferences for big, flavorful beers. These supply chains, professional organizations, technical infrastructure, and knowledge networks were thoroughly globalized. When craft breweries languished in the United States and Britain for a decade around the turn of the millennium, the movement spread from Prague to Perth and from Beijing to Bogotá.

Craft beer developed through three periods, each exemplified by a particular beer style. It began in the 1970s among British and Belgian brewers and consumers seeking to revive regional ales whose full, sweet flavors were being displaced by light, dry lagers. By the 1980s, craft beer had spread through the British Commonwealth and the United States, although with very different meanings. Whereas a revivalist movement anchored on the communal pub inspired Anglo craft beer, a sense of individualism and innovation drove the American version. During the second period, from about 1990 to 2010, the microbrewing industry consolidated in its original Anglo-Belgian homelands while enthusiasts introduced homebrewing and brewpubs to new markets around the world. India Pale Ale, the iconic beer of this period, constituted less than 8 percent of US craft sales as late as 2008, but its intensely bitter hop profile influenced the taste of beers across the craft market. The internet promoted this preference through "imagined communities" of connoisseurs around the world.[3] During the third period, beginning about 2010 and running at least through 2020, craft brewing became a stable, mature industry, not just in Anglo-Belgian countries but in non-traditional markets as well. While some brewers continued to unleash ever more bitter beers, others followed a Zen path of spontaneous fermentation and barrel-aging in pursuit of mellow, sour beers. In seeking to expand beyond a niche market, the industry had to confront the craft movement's reputation for white, male exclusivity, a process of reconciliation that may have left a sour taste for some who had cultivated this beer for its aura of individuality and status. In short, the global evolution of the craft beer movement can be traced not only through its growth from nimble startups to corporate giants but also through its shifting flavor profile, from sweet to bitter to sour.

The Sweet

On March 5, 1976, a rumpled British journalist named Michael Jackson called on the Liefmans Brewery in the town of Oudenaarde and met with the elegant brewmaster, Rose Blancquaert-Merckx. In his letter of introduction, Jackson had declared himself eager "to learn something about the traditional beers of Belgium!"[4] They toured the "sparkling copper kettles and well-racked cellars," then tasted the beers, including Gouden Band (Golden Band) Special, "a medium-strength brown ale, with a dry palate and a slightly sweet aftertaste."[5] A photographer captured Blancquaert in a tartan skirt that coordinated smartly with a jeroboam of Kriek beer and the green Flemish landscape. The tasting notes and portrait appeared prominently in Jackson's *World Guide to Beer* (1977). Although the text focused on taste, Jackson's readers may also have been interested to know that the brewery had been purchased a few years earlier by the British firm Vaux as a tax write-off when the United Kingdom entered the European Economic Community. While Liefmans was portrayed as quintessentially Belgian, its beers were available in London bottle shops. Such linkages formed part of a larger consumer movement spreading on both sides of the English Channel dedicated to the revival of sweet, regional ales. The commercial and educational efforts of the Anglo-Belgian craft beer movement in turn inspired and facilitated the founding fathers of home- and microbrewing in the United States and the British Commonwealth.

Publication of the *World Guide to Beer* established Jackson as the prophet of craft brewing. Born in 1942 to a working-class, Jewish family in

Huddersfield, West Yorkshire, he loved modern English literature and Samuel Smith's beer, which led naturally to a career in journalism. His first story, published in a local paper at the age of sixteen, was titled "This Is Your Pub," and after twenty years as a London reporter and foreign correspondent, he returned to his original muse. He thereby helped pioneer the field of lifestyle journalism, which served to guide cosmopolitan tourists to the world's best hotels, resorts, food, wine, and of course beer. Unlike the Oxbridge-educated Hugh Johnson, whose lavishly produced *World Atlas of Wine* was published in 1971, Jackson researched his beer guide on a shoestring. With journalistic inventiveness, he sent a mass mailing to the publicity departments of breweries around the world requesting information on beer types, flavor profiles, and, most importantly, labels. The volume focused heavily on Europe; for Czech breweries, which did not have publicity departments under Communism, he commissioned journalist Jaroslav Kořán to compose the text and gather illustrations. Elsewhere he may have raised hackles with his Orientalist search for "anything on the 'romance of the East' aspect" and a request to South African Breweries for publicity materials from regional competitors.[6] He met resistance with equanimity, explaining in the preface: "Some of the brewers whose products I most admire have been recalcitrant to the point of discourtesy. I have made every effort, nonetheless, to do justice to their beers."[7]

Jackson's volume received a clamorous reception from a growing consumer movement in Britain. In 1971, three journalists and a brewery office worker had founded the Campaign for Real Ale (CAMRA), which challenged a tightening oligopoly of national breweries. The Big Six had cut costs in their chains of brewery-owned pubs or tied houses by replacing hand-pumped cask ales with keg lager. CAMRA staged public demonstrations, marching through towns and villages dressed in funeral garb and "carrying wooden casks on biers."[8] One of the six, Carlsberg Tetley, dismissed the group as "bearded, be-sandaled, and with a generous girth from sampling a 'tad' too much fine ale."[9] Nevertheless, they attracted 40,000 visitors to the Covent Garden Beer Exhibition in September 1975, which became an annual Great British Beer Festival. The organization's *Good Beer Guide* got off to a difficult start in 1974, when the publisher withdrew the first edition for fear of libel suits from the Big Six. Journalist Roger Protz took over the *Guide*, updating it annually, while expounding on CAMRA's ideals. "Traditional Draught Beer, often called 'Real Ale' in common parlance," he explained with Victorian flourish, "can be dispensed by genial hosts straight from the Cask, by Beer Engine, or even with the aid of Electrical Power, but all these Systems eschew the Noisome Carbonic Gas, which the Purveyors of Inferior Brews use to

FIGURE 7.1 The British lifestyle journalist Michael Jackson helped create a new culture of beer connoisseurship through his prolific writings. Courtesy of Paddy Gunningham and Sam Hopkins.

mask the Lacklustre Taste of their Dubious Products."[10] The organization did not imagine that good beer alone would save pubs. In 1979, chairman Christopher Hutt founded a business venture, CAMRA Investments Ltd., to buy up endangered pubs. The nostalgic appeal of traditional ales cut across the Tory-Labour political divides that shook the United Kingdom in the 1970s.

Britain also had a lively homebrewing movement, having legalized the activity a decade earlier. In the 1960s, the drugstore chain Boots began marketing kits giving amateurs easy access to materials that dramatically improved the quality of their brewing. Boots' success attracted the attention of competitors, first rival chains such as Woolworths and then long-established malting firms, including Edme of Mistley (founded in 1880) and Munton & Fison of Suffolk (1921), which began packaging their products for retail. Homebrewers naturally gathered to share their hobby. In 1969, for example, John Harrison helped found a brewing club in the town of Maidenhead, Berkshire, and in 1976 he printed a booklet called "An Introduction to Old British Beers and How to Make Them." British homebrewing was something of a sideline to winemaking, which had gained popularity after wartime sugar rationing ended in 1953. Cyril J. J. Berry of Andover, Hampshire, publisher of the *Amateur Winemaker* magazine, produced a volume on *Home Brewed Beers and Stouts* in 1963. Likewise, the Winemakers National Guild of Judges, formed in 1964, added a beer section in 1978. According to one estimate, homebrew accounted for 10 percent of all British beer by the late 1970s.[11]

Consumer demand inspired a renaissance of craft beer, as many family and local breweries that had fallen on hard times were revived by the next generation. In 1972, Martin Sykes relaunched the Selby Brewery of Middleborough, North Yorkshire, established in 1894 and closed in 1954. Others started anew with skills acquired in the industry. David Bruce, a former brewer for Courage, built the Firkin chain of brewpubs starting in London in 1979 with the Elephant and Castle. A few amateurs also made the transition from homebrewing to opening pubs, such as John Payne, whose Smiles Bitter of Bristol "began as a plastic bucket effort."[12] All told, about seventy new real ale breweries opened in the United Kingdom during the 1970s.

Similar efforts were underway in Belgium. In Oudenaard, Rose Blancquaert began as a secretary at Liefmans after World War II and learned to brew as the company struggled with falling demand in the 1950s. She convinced her boss, Paul van Geluwe, to adjust the recipes to meet changing tastes. When he died unexpectedly in 1972, she took over the operation. Meanwhile, in Hoegaarden, a milkman named Pierre Celis started homebrewing a distinctive local white beer (*witbier*) when the town's last brewery closed in 1957. He began selling to the public in 1965 and over two decades built a thriving regional market. In 1970, in the town of Breendonk, a family maker of Scottish ales named Moortgat consulted brewing scientist Jean de Clerck to help develop a strong golden ale using Pilsner malts, which they marketed as Duvel, meaning the Devil in Flemish.[13]

Homebrewing played an even more important role in launching the US craft movement than it had across the Atlantic. Technically illegal since Prohibition, homebrew's bootlegging and back-to-the-land image suffered from the awful taste of the beer, often fermented in garbage cans with Fleischmann's yeast, Pabst Blue Ribbon malt, and granulated sugar. Quality only began to improve in the late 1960s when homebrewers got access to British brewing kits through mail-order catalogs and wine supply stores in immigrant neighborhoods. Homebrewing clubs formed in countercultural enclaves from Los Angeles, California (Maltose Falcons), to Burlington, Vermont (Vermont Homebrewers Association). Free spirits elsewhere included a "swinging Choctaw [who] makes homebrew," profiled in *Nanih Waiya* magazine in 1973.[14] The movement also had connections to the tech industry. The "Homebrew Computer Club" was started in Menlo Park,

California, where Steve Jobs and Steve Wozniak demonstrated the first Apple computer in 1976. The term "microbrewery" deliberately borrowed from Silicon Valley's new microcomputers. Charlie Papazian, the charismatic impresario who drew these disparate groups together, began homebrewing around 1970 when he was a University of Virginia student, and later taught night classes on brewing in Boulder, Colorado. He founded the American Homebrewers Association and published its first newsletter, *Zymurgy*, in 1978, a year before this activity was legalized. Papazian self-published his class notes, which he expanded into *The Complete Joy of Homebrewing* (1984), the movement's bible. In 1981, CAMRA invited him to serve as a guest judge at the Great British Beer Festival. Upon meeting Michael Jackson, Papazian suggested an American festival. Jackson replied: "Yes of course, it would be a great start, but where would you find interesting beer?"[15]

The answer lay with the nascent American microbrewing industry, which was animated by the eccentric, outlaw spirit of homebrewing. Fritz Maytag, heir to the washing machine fortune, purchased the failing Anchor Brewing Company of San Francisco in 1965. The recent college graduate brought to the business an appreciation for strong flavors inherited from his father's Amish-style cheese-making hobby. After a decade spent learning to brew and modernizing the factory, he broke into the nascent market for premium, imported beers such as Heineken. Meanwhile, Jack McAuliffe showed it was possible to open a small brewery without a family fortune. He had learned to homebrew while stationed as a navy technician in Scotland, and continued after returning to California, where he earned an engineering degree. Unable to afford San Francisco real estate or even proper machinery, he moved to Sonoma and scavenged junkyards for dairy tanks. Despite his gruff manner, McAuliffe acquired a business partner—Suzanne Stern, a widowed Vassar graduate who had moved to California for a new start—and an intern—Don Barkley, who was willing to work for beer to learn the business. In 1976, they opened the New Albion Brewery and gained a cult following in the Bay Area. Nevertheless, the owners ran into trouble with distribution and could not finance needed expansion. With the brewery's failure, McAuliffe became an icon of American craft beer, a rugged individualist and mad scientist who brewed flavorful beer using junkyard scrap before being laid low by evil distributors and bankers. His founding father narrative also set an industry pattern of erasing the female business partner and unpaid intern whose labor and financial support underwrote the business.[16]

A more communitarian branch of the craft movement spread across the British Commonwealth through CAMRA's growing network of real ale aficionados. In 1982, John Mitchell founded North America's first brewpub in Horseshoe Bay, British Columbia, after a tour of English pubs. Another early CAMRA outpost opened at the Wellington County Brewery in Guelph, Ontario. Canadians preferred the term "cottage brewer," to differentiate themselves from the tech-inspired microbreweries of the United States. Meanwhile, Lex Mitchell left his position at South African Breweries to make all-malt draught lager and cask-conditioned seasonal ales at an eponymous brewpub near Durban in 1983. Phil Sexton, an employee at Swan, in Western Australia, converted to the Real Ale religion while pursuing an advanced degree in Malting and Brewing at the University of Birmingham. He returned home in 1984 from a pilgrimage to Burton-on-Trent with a small-scale, custom brew kit and founded Brewtech, later renamed Matilda Bay. Real ale even acquired a following in India among those whose affiliations lay more with the Commonwealth than with Hinduism and Islam, which prohibited alcohol.[17]

Craft beer also began to spread from Anglo-Belgian locales into countries once dominated by lager beers. In Germany, where small breweries remained a strong commercial presence, the brewpub atmosphere characterized by beautiful copper kettles was adopted by firms such as Thiers of Dortmund and Hovels Hausbrauerei of Essen. In the Netherlands, pioneering pub owners in university towns began importing ale from the United Kingdom and Belgium in the 1970s. Leaders of the movement included a young couple, Piet de Jongh and Els Jonkers, who took over her family's Breda cafe, renaming it De Breyard. By 1980, CAMRA had attracted enough Dutch members to form a national craft beer society, PINT. A year later, former employees of a shuttered Allied Breweries plant in Arcens reopened under the name De Arcense Stoombierbrouwerij and began producing the Hertog Jan brand of Belgian- and British-style ales. Italian youth likewise opened craft beer bars as gender-mixed alternatives to the wine cafes habituated by older men. The country's first microbrewers, Gianfranco Oradini of Trentino and Peppiniello Esposito of Sorrento, took their inspiration from Bavaria instead of Belgium. Japan's first craft beer bar was opened in Sapporo in 1980 by Phred Kaufman, a US Vietnam War draft evader who had worked in a Hokkaido beer hall. Inspired by Michael Jackson, he introduced Belgian ales and American craft beers. In 1988, an Iwami sake brewer, Shintaro Konishi, began importing beers he had discovered on vacation in Belgium before opening a European-style craft brewery of his own.[18]

The American craft brewing industry grew up in collaboration with these international networks. Inspired by the example of CAMRA, Charlie

Papazian launched the Great American Beer Festival in 1982 with twenty varieties of beer, some of them from Boulder-area homebrewers. He also founded a trade organization for professional microbrewers alongside the Homebrewers Association. Within two years, the beer festival had outgrown its Boulder origins and moved to the larger convention space in Denver, while expanding the number of categories from the original four—beer, ale, stout, and "unusual brews." Papazian traveled widely and invited international experts to lecture to American brewers. For example, Rose Blancquaert spoke in 1986 at the Sixth Annual Microbrewers Conference in Portland, Oregon. The organization's trade journal, *The New Brewer*, was edited part time by foreign correspondent Virginia Thomas and her photojournalist husband, David Bjorkman, who served as art director. They filed stories on Central American breweries while covering the region's civil wars in the 1980s. Thomas also ensured that the journal included the work of female craft brewers such as Carol Stoudt of Stoudt Brewery in Pennsylvania and Mellie Pullman of the Schirf Brewing Company in Utah.[19]

The social and knowledge networks of the nascent Brewers Association were complemented by transnational business connections. Fritz Maytag first built a sustainable business by carving out a niche in the premium import market, and importers continued to drive an interest in Anglo-Belgian beers. Charles and Rose Ann Finkel, of Merchant du Vin in Seattle, began distributing Samuel Smith and other specialty beers in 1978 after reading Jackson's *World Guide to Beer*. Liefmans likewise entered the US market in the 1980s as Belgian wholesalers expanded their portfolio of exports. European factories also proved an important source for modern equipment, critical to the growth of microbreweries. Jack McAuliffe had failed when he could not expand beyond his makeshift setup. Ken Grossman of Sierra Nevada Brewing Co. in Chico, California, and Mark Stutrud of Summit Brewery in St. Paul, Minnesota, purchased secondhand German equipment in the 1980s to replace their original homebrew kit. American manufacturers and consultants also began to appreciate this new market for small-scale producers. Surveying the exhibition hall of the National Microbrewers Association in 1987, one observer joked: "There's so much equipment on display here, all we need is water and a little more plumbing and we can brew, ferment, and bottle a complete batch of beer."[20] Harvard MBA and management consultant Jim Koch leveraged the industry most effectively with the Boston Beer Company. By hiring facilities from a regional brewer and marketing Samuel Adams lager himself, Koch bypassed the growing pains of earlier craft breweries to sell a sector-topping 700,000 barrels of beer a year by 1995.

Defining beer styles and creating a language of taste was another transnational undertaking. Industry scientists had long sought to define precise sensory terms for quality control purposes, culminating in 1979 with Morton Meilgaard's introduction of a beer flavor wheel. Craft beer competition judges depended at first on this industry approach to evaluation, focusing on flavors that deviated from accepted standards rather than appreciating beer's diverse sensory qualities. In reaction to this clinical approach, journalists and brewers association leaders began to lay the groundwork for defining the flavor profiles of regional beer styles. Michael Jackson led the way with his *World Guide to Beer*, which sought to categorize the variegated beers of Belgium by color, ranging from white to red and brown, as well as wild beers, abbey beers, and strong ales. Jackson also observed the divergence between Old and New World brewers. In 1982, he described New Albion beer, shortly before the brewery closed, as "what might be regarded as the English style."[21] His hesitation lay in the beer's use of American hops, particularly the Cascade, which had been released in 1972 and was promptly rejected by mass-market brewers such as Coors because of its strong flavor. Fritz Maytag and Ken Grossman also used Cascade in their Anchor Liberty Ale and Sierra Nevada Pale Ale.[22]

From the 1960s to the 1980s, craft brewers throughout the Anglo-Belgian world envisioned a new approach to brewing focused not on stripping out any possible imperfection but rather, as Michael Jackson put it, "getting flavor into the beer."[23] Yet sensory taste was only part of a craft ideal that opposed corporate control and sought to build community around local pubs. Already in the 1980s, some craft brewers felt that revolutionary spirit was threatened by Jim Koch's contract brewing model as well as by giant brewers' encroachment on the sector. Coors and Miller introduced craft-lookalike brands Killian Red and Blue Moon, while movement pioneers lost control of their breweries. A 1985 fire forced Pierre Celis to sell his underinsured Hoegaarden brewery to the Belgian giant, Interbrew, which also purchased the Belle Vue lambic brewery, Leffe abbey beers, and the Dutch craft brand Hertog Jan. Meanwhile, the Australian firm CUB, maker of Foster's Lager, bought out Matilda Bay.[24]

This early convergence between craft and mass-market brewing raised significant questions about the viability of the former's business model. Renowned industry consultant Robert S. Weinberg observed: "Craft brewers have a wonderful thing because they're having their inefficiencies subsidized by a public that regards the higher price as a valid testimony of the superiority of the product."[25] It remained to be seen if consumers would demand social commitment or if superior flavor alone would justify the premium as the craft sector grew beyond a small but globalized niche into a significant industry in its own right.

The Bitter

Bert Grant, a flamboyant Scottish Canadian who opened the first post-Prohibition brewpub in the United States, is often credited with the contemporary revival of India Pale Ale. The bracingly bitter beer resulted from a near tragedy in 1983, when Grant lost a large part of his olfactory nerve during brain surgery. "I can still sense a lot of the flavor of beer, but the more subtle tastes and smells, especially in the hops, escape me now," he explained in his autobiography, *The Ale Master*. "Some say that's why my beers are 'over-the-top' hoppy—I add hops to the level where I can smell them!"[26] With his deep knowledge of brewing history, he named the beer after the British colonial trade in heavily hopped ale to India. Grant himself qualified his claim for reviving the style by recalling that the Ballantine Brewery of New Jersey had long marketed an IPA, and both Maytag and McAuliffe had experimented with the Cascade hops that gave American IPAs their distinctive citrus aroma, if not with the same intensity as Grant's IPA. "It was full of both the resiny flavour and bitterness of the hops." Michael Jackson declared: "nothing could match the shock of that first encounter."[27] IPAs grew ever stronger as a new generation of brewers, including Greg Koch of Stone, pushed the boundaries of taste.

Bitterness extended beyond the taste of beer when, after promising early growth in its largest markets, craft brewing hit a wall in the mid-1990s and stagnated for a full decade. Microbreweries and brewpubs in the United States peaked at 1,625 in 1998, fell to 1,469 in 2000, and recovered to their earlier peak only by 2009. Craft brewers complained with some justice that giant brewers ordered distributors not to carry their products, although the real competition for the high-end market came from imports like Heineken. Perhaps the biggest problem was simply undercapitalization in a difficult business environment. Meanwhile, the British government sought to promote competition with the Beer Orders of 1989, which required large breweries to divest their tied houses and to offer "guest ale" in each establishment. Rather than providing outlets for independent brewers, the newly freed pubs were bought up by hospitality conglomerates called Pubcos, which allocated their guest taps to mass-market beers. In the three decades after 1980, the overall number of pubs in the United Kingdom fell from 70,000 to 55,000.[28]

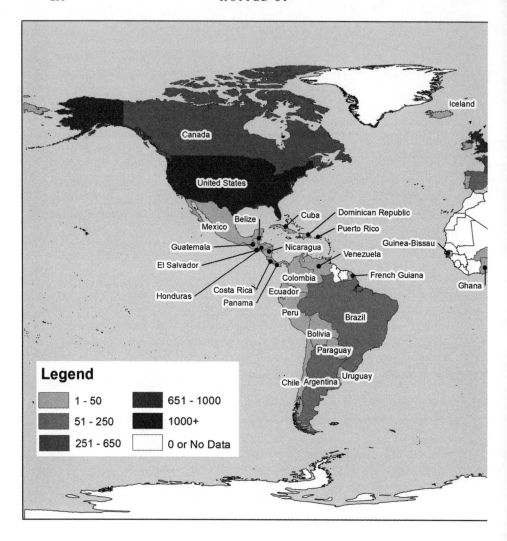

FIGURE 7.2 World Map of Microbreweries, 2010. Sources: Brewers Association, "Craft Breweries by Category," accessed June 21, 2019, www.brewersassociation.org/statistics/number-of-breweries/; Beer Canada, "2018 Industry Trends," accessed June 21, 2019, https://industry.beercanada.com/statistics; Brewers of Europe, "Beer Statistics, 2018 Edition," December 2018, www.beveragedaily.com/Article/2018/12/06/EU-beer-statistics-Microbreweries-and-craft-beer-provide-big-boost; Masayuki Otsuka, "Cracking Open Japan's Craft Beer Market," USDA Foreign Agricultural Service, August 31, 2018, https://gain.fas.usda.gov/Recent%20GAIN%20Publications/Cracking%20Open%20Japan%E2%80%99s%20Craft%20Beer%20Market_Tokyo%20ATO_Japan_8-31-2018.pdf; data elsewhere was summarized in mid-2019 from www.ratebeer.com/breweries. Drawn by William Sturm.

Peak Hops

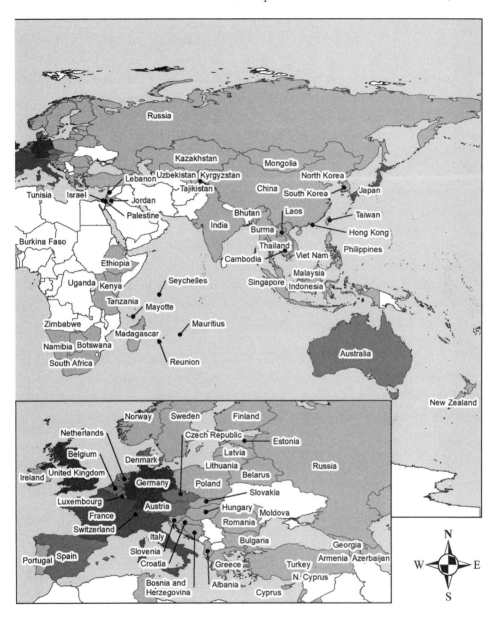

Not strictly an Anglo-American phenomenon, craft brewing found adherents in both traditional and new beer markets as part of a wider artisanal reaction against the spread of mass consumer culture. Figure 7.2 provides a map of craft breweries around 2010 showing the extent of their growth in these formative decades. The fluid definition of terms such as "microbrewery" and "brewpub" make international comparisons difficult, even in North America and those parts of Europe where professional associations and government statisticians maintained accurate counts. Elsewhere, the map is based on crowd-sourced data of questionable provenance, but despite these limitations, the patterns seem plausible.[29] The United States alone had more than a quarter of all the world's craft breweries in 2010, while the British Commonwealth accounted for another 20 percent, and the rest of Europe had 40 percent. Latin America accounted for under 5 percent, and in Asia, only Japan had a significant number of craft breweries. Nevertheless, when measured per capita, the distribution looked quite different, with Switzerland far and away the world's leading craft brewer, while the United States ranked below the traditionally wine-drinking countries of France and Italy (see Table 7.1).

In Europe, small breweries serving local markets had maintained a presence despite the consolidation elsewhere, and in many cases their renewed growth reflected a return to tradition rather than the adoption of new, American-influenced beer culture. After the fall of the Iron Curtain, Czechs replaced antiquated, Soviet-era machinery with small-scale production, opening 220 new breweries in two decades. Czech brewers displayed a flair for creativity, moving away from standardized pale lager by reviving or inventing local styles. Vienna's Ottakringer Brewery, founded in the mid-nineteenth century in a working-class neighborhood by Jewish brewers Ignaz and Jacob Kuffner, opened a brewpub alongside its traditional factory to sell innovative brands such as the Avalanche Double IPA and Crown Princess Imperial Vienna Lager. In France and Italy, craft beer offered an outlet for youthful rebellion; Teo Musso played rock 'n' roll music to the vats of fermenting beer at the Baladin Brewery, which he founded in 1996 in the Langhe region of Italy, home to the Slow Food movement. Meanwhile, Latin American craft brewing began as a hobby of wealthy "juniors" such as the aptly named Eduardo Bier, who opened Brazil's first brewpub in Porto Alegre in 1996, and Benny Silberwasser, the king of Bogotá brewpubs.[30]

The boom-and-bust cycle of craft beer was particularly intense in Japan, the only Asian country to make the top-twenty rankings. Japanese traditions of craftsmanship encouraged an interest in fine beers, and Belgian exporters

Table 7.1 Microbreweries Ranked by Population, 2010. Although the United States had by far the greatest number of craft breweries, when measured per capita, it fell far behind many European rivals. Source: See Figure 7.2.

Microbreweries	Number	Per 100,000 inhabitants
Switzerland	313	402
Denmark	86	156
United Kingdom	898	145
Belgium	134	124
Austria	97	116
New Zealand	42	96
Lithuania	27	86
Czech Republic	90	86
Canada	280	82
Germany	659	81
France	373	59
Italy	336	56
United States	1700	55
Australia	119	54
Norway	26	54
Sweden	49	52
Netherlands	71	43
Argentina	113	28
Chile	44	26
Japan	260	20

found a receptive audience there; kriek was a particular favorite during the annual cherry blossom festival. The Oregon craft brewer Rogue also developed a wide following in the country by rebranding their line with local references—changing Shakespeare stout to Brown Bear and Rogue Red to Red Fox—while also brewing beers specifically for the Japanese market, such as one with the tart Hokkaido haskap berry. Japanese craft brewing took off in 1994, with the repeal of minimum production requirements and the legalization of homebrewing. The giant firms Sapporo and Asahi were supportive, and some 310 microbreweries opened in just four years. Many brewpubs appealed to the tourist market, such as the Gotenba Kogen Resort, a Disneyesque take on Alpine architecture with a view of Mount Fuji. The Sanda Ya local brewery

FIGURE 7.3 Vienna's Ottakringer Brewery, with a modern, glass-enclosed craft brewpub built onto the nineteenth-century factory. Photo by the author, 2018.

was founded by a steakhouse owner named Kihachiro, who fired his original Austrian brewmaster and personally took over the brewing. But rapid growth outstripped demand, leading to a decade of stagnation in the Japanese craft industry.[31] Nevertheless, by 2010, craft beer had gained a world-wide foothold among cosmopolitan elites. It offered an alternative to the formerly proletarian image of beer, although small producers still posed little threat to mass-market lagers.

Both in the North Atlantic and around the world, the growth of craft beer depended on a transnational infrastructure of finance, education, and engineering. The success of Boston Beer and Sierra Nevada convinced bankers to lend money to entrepreneurs whose only experience was homebrewing. When these novices ran into trouble, they consulted experts such as Keith Thomas at London Polytechnic and Michael Lewis at the University of California, Davis, who provided technical support to craft brewers through university extension services. Berlin's venerable Brewing Institute (VLB) and the Siebel Institute in Chicago, formerly corporate training programs and consultants, began to enroll aspiring craft brewers. Specialist labs such as Wyeast of Mount Hood, Oregon, assembled portfolios of high-quality, top-fermenting varieties beyond the basic "beer yeast" for mass-market lager. Technological innovation meanwhile allowed engineering firms such as DME Solutions, established in 1991 in Prince Edward Island, Canada, to provide complete kits for opening craft breweries. The storied Kiuchi sake brewery of Japan purchased an early model in 1994 when it began making a western beer called Hitachino Nest. Even so-called turnkey breweries required installation support from local engineers. Another DME customer, Mazen Hajjar, who founded Lebanon's first microbrewery in the chaos of the 2006 war, recalled: "The brewery arrived in these big containers. I opened them and searched in vain for an instruction book."[32]

Professional organizations also sought to transform a rather anarchic social movement into a coherent industry. Both CAMRA and the Brewers Association replaced volunteers with professional staff, while comparable organizations formed elsewhere, including the Dutch Small Brewery Collective (KBC) and the Japanese Craft Brewers Association. The proliferation of festivals, from Britain and the United States to the Osaka International Beer Summit, served to educate consumers but also required common standards for judging. In 1985, the United States Brewers Association created the Beer Judge Certification Program to facilitate the evaluation of beer styles, and three years later, CAMRA began conducting a series of tasting trials under the direction of Mark Dorber at the White Horse Pub in London. Attempts to define beer styles generated confrontations between traditionalists seeking to preserve historic beers and innovators keen to personalize their products. Already in a 1994 seminar, Michael Jackson complained that India Pale Ale was "widely used, but beers no longer fit [the] description."[33] Meanwhile, some CAMRA members bemoaned the gentrification of their leisure space through "flowery language" that had the "hallmarks of Southern [England] middle-class beer snobs."[34]

Nevertheless, it was a working-class lad from the north who had helped to forge a global community of beer connoisseurs through his lifestyle journalism. Beginning in 1982, Jackson had published regular editions of the *Pocket Guide to Beer* to keep readers informed about the best new microbreweries opening around the world. He updated his *World Guide* with a comprehensive volume titled *Michael Jackson's Beer Companion* (1993). His most popular work was a six-part television series filmed in 1989 with Britain's Channel 4 titled "The Beer Hunter." The series attracted a devoted following of viewers such as Andrew Lennox, who wrote from Australia to describe his father's plans to take him for his twenty-first birthday on a "Beer Hunter" trip to the Pilsener Urquell brewery. Jackson also received regular updates from correspondents. "As a result of my work with the Ministry of Agriculture, Fisheries and Food," wrote Keith Mitchell, "I can indulge my real interest as a Beer Hunter."[35] Jackson lectured widely and published tasting notes and brewery updates in a series of volumes, countless articles, and eventually a popular website,

Beerhunter.com. Brewers around the world sought the imprimatur his favorable reviews would garner. Importer Deh-Ta Hsiung, for example, offered to organize a tasting of Chinese beers at a popular London restaurant. Jackson could not fit the dinner into his hectic travel and writing schedule but did accept samples, which he tasted with his partner, Paddy Gunningham, perhaps over Chinese takeout. He recorded on a paper towel: "Five Star Beijing. At home 92. Clean taste, says Paddy, sherberty finish. I thought sweet, corn taste. Yes, definitely sweet, slight 'brown paper—gum arabic' tastes."[36] Working with industry required delicate negotiations. Jackson sought to remain impartial while still promoting underdogs, including small Belgian and Czech breweries, as well as craft beer more generally. He insisted that advertisements list tasting notes as such, always attributed to "Michael Jackson—The Beer Hunter ™."[37]

Because of his influence, Jackson's publications provide an ideal historical source for tracing the development of beer connoisseurship from dry industry terminology used to identify defects toward a more colorful language for celebrating the unique flavor characteristics of individual beers. The *World Guide* of 1977, researched largely through an industry survey, provided more quantitative data on original gravities and alcohol by volume, with only general descriptions of the actual taste of these beers. Just five years later, in the first *Pocket Guide*, Jackson began to employ a bold new vocabulary for reviewing beers, which had become still more nuanced and poetic a decade later in the *Beer Companion*. The 1982 *Guide* used 83 separate descriptive terms, while the 1993 *Companion* expanded to 128 terms. While the latter volume is about twice as long as the former, much of the additional material focused on production methods and beer culture, so the larger number of reviews in 1993 mostly reflected the decade's growth of microbreweries.[38]

Figure 7.4 visualizes Jackson's terminology up through the 1982 *Guide* in the form of a flavor wheel. In these early works, he still depended largely on beer industry professionals' descriptions of common beer faults such as "pasteurized," "skunky," "cardboard," "damp paper," the more "sulphury" smells of "cabbage" and "corn," and "carbonic," a British term used to distinguish unnaturally gassed beer from the milder sparkle of hand-pumped "real ale." But unlike the brewing engineer Meilgaard, whose original flavor wheel offered only a single term for "fruity," Jackson distinguished "apple," "orange," "peach," "pear," and "plummy." Expanding the vocabulary of beer criticism was clearly on his mind when he wrote that an Irish dry stout "even deserves the same adjectives used by Hugh Johnson to describe a genuine amontillado

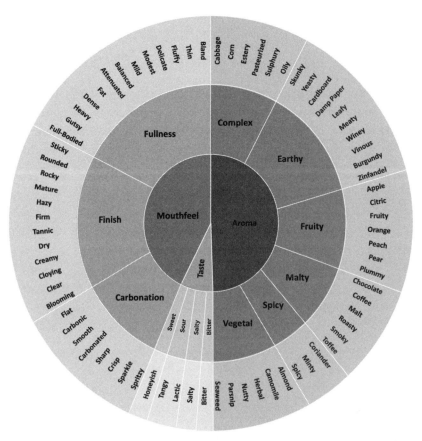

FIGURE 7.4 This flavor wheel visualizes the terminology used by Michael Jackson to describe beer in the 1970s and early 1980s. The predominance of terms for mouthfeel reflect the origins of connoisseurship in the language of industrial quality control. Sources: Michael Jackson, *The World Guide to Beer* (Philadelphia: Running Press, 1977); Michael Jackson, *Pocket Guide to Beer* (New York: Putnam, 1982). Drawn by Ngai Ying Cheung.

in his *World Atlas of Wine:* 'Dry and almost stingingly powerful of flavour, with a dark, fat, rich tang.'"[39]

By 1993, Jackson had deployed a rich metaphoric language to describe beers. For example, his description of the Belgian brewery Liefmans's Gouden Band Special from the *World Guide* in the 1970s had emphasized its stylistic character as "a medium-strength brown ale, with a dry palate and a slightly sweet aftertaste." Reevaluating it for the *Companion* in the 1990s he detected a "Montilla palate and champagne spritziness." In drawing comparisons with sherry proper, he distinguished between "cream," "dry," "olorosa," and "Pedro Ximenez." He constantly pushed himself to extend his palate, olfactory range, and literary style. The "coffee" and "smoky" flavors he detected in 1982 had become "strong coffee on a winter's night" and "fire from logs of fruitwood." Likewise, he disaggregated sourness into "lactic," "citric," "vinegary," and "acidity worthy of Dorothy Parker."[40]

This new vocabulary of beer criticism also led to a greater emphasis on aroma and taste instead of mouthfeel, which had arguably been Jackson's richest category in the early years. In 1982, he used almost as many terms for texture as for aroma, but by 1993 terms for smell had expanded to two-thirds of the total and those for mouthfeel had fallen to one-fifth. Although the 1993

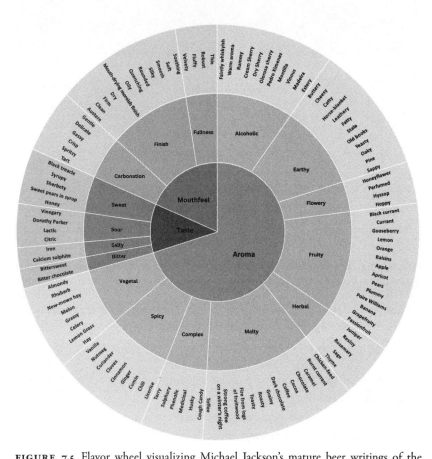

FIGURE 7.5 Flavor wheel visualizing Michael Jackson's mature beer writings of the 1990s, revealing the proliferation of terms for taste and especially aroma as well as the nuanced, poetic language of connoisseurship. The category of sourness, for example, ranged from "lactic" and "citric" to "vinegary" and "acidity worthy of Dorothy Parker." Sources: Michael Jackson, *Michael Jackson's Beer Companion* (Philadelphia: Running Press, 1993); Michael Jackson, *Pocket Guide to Beer* (various editions). Drawn by Ngai Ying Cheung.

Companion still employed such descriptive terms as "velvety," "fluffy," and "mouth-drying moreish finish," earlier descriptions such as "gutsy," "rocky," "creamy," and "sticky" had disappeared. Terms for taste more than doubled over the decade; in 1982, he used a very basic listing of "sweet," "bitter," and "salty," separating only the "sour" into "lactic" and "tangy," whereas in 1993, he offered multiple nuances of "sweet," "sour," "bitter," and even mineral "saltiness."

Jackson's transition from industrial critique to poetic evocation contributed to a larger promotional agenda that sought to raise the status of beer and acknowledge its world historical significance. This is not to say that Jackson no longer had unfavorable reactions when tasting. His personal archive contains numerous unpublished notes such as this one for a mass-market Pilsner: "Flat as a fart, greeny, cloudy, cough-mixture aroma."[41] But he generally kept such observations to himself and friends, preferring in his public writing to encourage brewers rather than engage in partisan attacks. Moreover, he endowed the beverage with a suitably illustrious history, in the process demonstrating his role as a working-class "organic intellectual." To situate his narratives in cultural context, Jackson kept working files such as: "Notes for Belgian paintings (with Marxist analysis)."[42] His historical narratives nevertheless focused on great men and founding fathers, such as the "Sedlmayr Project," which sought to reconstruct the genealogy of lager brewing with special attention to Gabriel Sedlmayr. For research, Jackson relied largely on interviews, although he also commissioned translations of vital texts. If his historical contributions did not equal his influence as a journalist and tastemaker, his writings still offer astute observations.[43]

Over time, the imagined community of beer connoisseurship, tourism, and history reached far beyond professional critics. Homebrewing clubs circulated newsletters as early as the 1970s, and their content often underscores their audience's cosmopolitan perspective. A Kentucky club celebrated the 1995 defeat of Anheuser Busch's attempted takeover of the Budweiser brewery in the Czech Republic. Members also reported on exotic beers as well as familiar styles available while touring far-flung destinations. Chris Pietruski of London described a microbrewery in El Bolsón, Patagonia, Argentina, where he sampled a blackcurrant beer, "nothing like any of the Belgian fruit beers I have tried." John Westlake of Nottingham enjoyed equally dramatic landscapes at Machu Picchu, Arequipa, and Lima, but refreshed himself with local lagers such as a "Pilsen lager that bears little relation to a true Pilsner beer but is nonetheless a good flavorsome drink well suited to a hot, dry climate."[44] In 1985, Patrick Smith and a multinational group of African and European colleagues undertook a "Great Beer Safari," a three-week pub crawl from the Ivory Coast to Nigeria, sampling global imports such as Heineken and Guinness as well as local startups like Cross River Brewery's Champion beer and Premier Brewery's eponymous brand. That same year, Joseph Weeres, a professor of education at Claremont College in California, won a fellowship to study Chinese beer culture, based on his expertise as a homebrewer. He reported on his trip to fellow readers of *Zymurgy* magazine, encouraging potential beer tourists but warning them not to expect easy access to breweries. "We got into most of them because we had a friend from Hong Kong with us who sold liquor in China."[45]

With its strong connections to the computer industry, the beer community went online in the early days of email and the internet. In the 1980s, Rob Gardner offered a "Brewsletter" over the first commercial service provider, CompuServe, while Steve Conklin created an email newsletter called "The Hophead." Tom Fryer founded the Oxford Bottled Beer Database in 1992 as an aggregate of supermarket listings, but with the site generating no income and a flood of spam, the database withered. A more permanent online home emerged with the establishment of the BeerAdvocate website in 1996. Its cofounders, Todd and Jason Alström, started posting their own reviews and later opened it as a public forum. Sensory metaphors predominated from the first posting, for Berkshire Brewing Company's Steel Rail Extra Pale Ale, "a very light ale with an extremely refreshing amount of carbonation. Lovely honey, lemon, and nut overtones followed by light sweet malt afters."[46] A rival website, RateBeer.com, went online in 2000, at the peak of the dot-com bubble. Unlike so many failed tech companies, these beer sites attracted devoted followings. More than 6,000 reviewers published nearly 300,000 reviews in RateBeer's first four years.[47]

Like users of other social media platforms, aspiring beer advocates and raters navigated a flood of information. On their homepages, the two websites offered a similar range of options to review beers, find events, and join discussion forums. To encourage more activity, the websites awarded levels of status. On BeerAdvocate, "Beer Karma" points accumulated to different levels of expertise, including "Crusader" and "Poobah." RateBeer was regarded as a more cosmopolitan community, allowing non-English-language reviews, while BeerAdvocate became the site of choice for beer traders in the United States. Users debated the relative merits of their rating algorithms, especially after AB InBev took a minority stake in RateBeer. Regardless, there was a striking convergence in the highest rated beers on both sites—imperial stouts, double IPAs, Belgian Quadrupels—full-bodied, heavily hopped, and high in alcohol.

In addition to a numerical score, reviews on both websites often included narratives that both expressed an individual's encounter with the beer and also affirmed their connections to the larger community of connoisseurs. The numerical ratings, and for many, the reviews as well, followed the Beer Judge Certification Program criteria of aroma, appearance, taste, mouthfeel, and overall experience. Beginning in 2005, the American Homebrewers Association sought to professionalize this community with a feature in *Zymurgy* magazine called "Commercial Calibration," in which a panel of four master judges ranked widely available commercial beers to model the scoring system.[48] Those who told a story often began by setting the scene, with a description of where the beer was purchased or an acknowledgment of who provided it, especially in the case of highly coveted, limited-edition brews. The narrative then proceeded to the pour, including discussions of the glassware used as well as the foamy head. Accounts of aroma, taste, and mouthfeel often drew comparisons with other beers in the same category, and they engaged explicitly with community members' experiences of the same beer. Reviewers were often self-reflective about their expectations, albeit with formulaic references to whether they found highly rated beers to be "worth the hype."

This community of taste expressed its identity through both figurative descriptions and concrete terms. Reviewers showed their affinity for the group with terms such as "quintessentially beery" while sneering at the "blissful ignorance" of outsiders. Although at least one reviewer declared that Budweiser "tastes like America," the patriotism of the national community was more often outweighed by the loyalty to the beer community and its disdain for Bud. Common descriptors of pale lagers included "watery," "thin," and "grassy," as well as "corn" and "rice" (references to the adjunct grains used in place of malted barley), and, in a surprising number of cases, simply "nothing." Perhaps the most common term of all, "skunky," comprised an entire spectrum, including "slight skunk," "mild skunky," "subtle skunkyness," "just a hint of skunkiness," "a mesh of skunk," "buttery, skunky," and "weird skunkiness." On occasion, reviewers felt obliged to acknowledge "no skunkiness."[49] Whether regular consumers of these beers would taste "skunk" is another question.

Even with its global reach, the community of homebrewers was dominated by males who identified white. In the United States, the Brewers Association estimated in the mid-1990s that 97 percent of homebrewers were men, the majority of them college educated. To its credit, the organization sought to expand the movement to include more women, and the first "Commercial Calibration" feature included master judge Beth Zangari among its tasters. Nevertheless, the editors of *Zymurgy* magazine catered to the masculinity of existing members, for example, illustrating a story on medieval brewing experiments not with a historically accurate brewster but rather with a fantasy-inspired broadsword and armor. Advertisers likewise reinforced this militant culture; the Northern Brewer supply company of St. Paul, Minnesota, advertised its advanced brewing kit as a "Fully Operational Battle Station."[50] Bottle labels such as the heavily muscled gargoyle on Stone Brewery's Arrogant Bastard Ale further buttressed this masculinity. Anecdotal evidence suggests that the international homebrewing community was likewise heavily male and identified with Europe and North America. This culture of masculine social distinction in turn shaped the bitter flavor profile of craft beers.

The IPA exerted a gravitational pull on craft beers around the turn of the millennium. California produced some of the best-known IPAs, and West Coast brewers launched a "hop arms race," a predictably military metaphor for the escalation of rankings on the International Bitterness Unit (IBU) scale. The Lagunitas Brewery, founded by Tony Magee in 1993, released an IPA with 51 IBUs, far above the 38 of Sierra Nevada Pale Ale. An old hippie, Magee embraced the northern California pot culture, while to the south, in Escondido, former recording studio entrepreneur Greg Koch's Stone IPA cranked up the IBUs to 71. Koch and his partner Steve Wagner claimed to have stumbled on the original, punk-inspired Arrogant Bastard Ale with a recipe miscalculation that doubled the intended hop load. Surfer Sam Calagione, who established an East Coast outpost at Dogfish Head Brewery in Delaware, created a continuous hopping system for its 90-Minute IPA, which clocked in at 90 IBUs.[51]

The unbridled pursuit of hop megatonnage inevitably led to a backlash. Vinnie Cilurzo, brewer of Russian River's renowned Pliny the Elder Imperial IPA, commented on the unbalanced profile of imitators. Without a "sturdy malt base," he observed, "it's a hop tea, and it's pretty undrinkable."[52] Nevertheless, one RateBeer commentator wrote of Pliny, "this beer was made to try and hurt your mouth."[53] Other critics decried the misogyny inherent in brand names such as the Buffalo Bill Brewery's triple-hopped Alimony Ale, which claimed to be the "bitterest beer in America."[54] In contrast to West Coast hop bombs, a New England–style of hazy IPAs aimed to bring out hop taste and mouthfeel in place of sheer bitterness. Meanwhile, English brewers alluded to the beer's historical origins by adding Earl Grey tea to the brew kettle. Brewers Down Under used Tasmanian Cascade and other aromatic local hops to infuse a terroir character to their International Style Pale Ale.[55]

The Australasian Pale Ale reflected the growing diversification as craft spread globally. Brewers began to look beyond British and Belgian models to explore regional German top-fermented beers such as Kolsch, Alt, and Hefeweisse. Of the latter, Michael Jackson wrote: "Younger people, who are the greatest devotees, seem to regard a wheat beer with a sediment in much the same light as a bread with visible grains or seeds. These are the beer world's answer to 'wholefood.'"[56] The search for local terroir extended beyond hops to include Fal Allen's brown ale with galangal and gula melaka at Archipelago Brewery in Singapore and Àlex Padró's Catalan winter ale with honey and rosemary at Llúpols i Llevats in Barcelona. Historical revivalism continued with the Dead Brewers Society, which collected pre–World War I regional British ales, while Samuel Smith recreated an Oatmeal Stout at the request of Charles Finkle, the Seattle-based importer at Marchant du Vin. Meanwhile, Hannover's Lindener Gild-Bräu Brewery developed a line of Broyhan beers, and a Haarlem brewery made a historic Jopen beer to commemorate the town's 750th anniversary in 1995.[57]

Despite craft's global success, many of its social ideals had turned bitter with industrial consolidation. The movement also lost a voice for moderation in 2007 when Michael Jackson succumbed to Parkinson's disease. Many early pioneers resented the growing corporatization, particularly among contract brewers, dismissed by Bert Grant as "just a bunch of promoters who are jumping on the bandwagon."[58] Nevertheless, other aspiring craft brewers such as Dave Bonighton and Cam Hines used contracts with existing facilities as a step to opening their acclaimed Mountain Goat Brewery in Melbourne, Australia. Oregon homebrewers even joined Anheuser Busch in a lawsuit intended to force contract brewers to disclose their methods; the St. Louis giant was seeking to head off microbrewing ventures by Coors and Miller, although AB hedged its bets by buying stakes in the Redhook and Widmer breweries. More ominously, the Belgian giant InBev continued to buy up breweries large and small to fulfill its self-proclaimed destiny as the "World's Local Brewer," even as the global craft market matured and flavor profiles shifted once again after 2010.[59]

The Sour

Before the introduction of pure yeast in the 1880s, all beers were more or less sour due to the widespread presence of acetic and lactic acid bacteria as well as wild yeast strains like Brettanomyces. By the 1950s, biological control systems had essentially eliminated the problem from industrial breweries, and within another fifty years the availability of professional yeast and sanitizers ensured that with careful practice homebrewers could avoid contamination. Once the age-old fear of foxing had been conquered, a world of sourness opened up for investigation and connoisseurship. As with the bitter flavors of IPA, many consumers found sour beers distasteful at first. When Boston-area brewer Dann Paquette served a Brett-flavored beer at the Great American Beer Festival in 1998, volunteers moved a trashcan over to the booth because so many visitors were spitting out the beer.[60] But once past the initial revulsion, sour beers held great appeal within the craft beer movement. With no simple recipe for reproducing Belgian methods of barrel aging and spontaneous fermentation, those who invested the time and money in acquiring knowledge and equipment faced little competition. Meanwhile, craft aficionados satisfied their paradoxical desire for both novelty and antiquity in a single glass of sour beer, as historic beer styles—or at least old-sounding beer names—were reinvented by modern brewers. But even as the craft beer movement continued to expand and become localized around the world, the persistence of white, male exclusivity continued to limit the appeal of craft beer to many potential consumers.

The revival of sour beer coincided with the return of stable growth in the craft brewing market. In the United States, the sector exploded in the 2010s, expanding from 1,756 to more than 8,000 breweries selling 13 percent of the nation's beer by volume. Belgium achieved an even more remarkable revival of regional beers, as Pilsner's market share collapsed from 80 percent in the 1970s to 30 percent by the 2010s. Although pale lager retained its overall dominance globally, microbreweries opened in remote locations of sub-Saharan Africa, Central Asia, and South America. Small firms benefited from continued innovation that lowered the minimum efficient volume of production. The Calgary firm Cask Brewery Systems designed canning equipment for limited runs with improved lining to preserve flavor. Distribution remained a problem for many micros, but global consolidation actually increased outlets in countries such as Mexico, where local entrepreneurs could effectively protest unfair practices by foreign-owned goliaths.[61]

The fashion for sour proved to be a bonanza for European small-scale brewers, who had faced ruin a generation earlier. Beer tourism became a growing phenomenon, as visitors flocked to Jean-Pierre Van Roy's Museum of Gueuze in Brussels and toured the Trappist breweries in the Belgian countryside. While many firms preserved their traditional methods, others invested their growing income by updating equipment. Rodenbach, the Roeselare-based brewer of Flemish red beers, retired its open-air coolship and installed modern centrifuge and heat exchange equipment in 1992. Likewise in Germany, top fermentation began to challenge the hegemony of lager. The sour Berliner Weisse, once a favorite of the bourgeoisie, survived in socialist East Germany. Craft brewers later replaced the traditional red and green shots of raspberry syrup and woodruff essence with tropical fruits. In the 1980s, even before the Wall fell, a Leipzig publican named Lothar Goldhahn contracted Berliner Weisse breweries to revive the salt-flavored local sour beer Gose.[62]

The knowledge transfers that carried sour beers around the world at the turn of the twenty-first century mirrored the nineteenth-century spread of lager beer. Migrant brewers carried their technical know-how with them. For example, in 1996, Rodenbach's brewmaster, Peter Bouckaert, established a local version of Flemish barrel aging at the New Belgium Brewery of Fort Collins, Colorado. After the fire at Hoegaarden, Pierre Celis moved to Austin, Texas, in the early 1990s and recreated his fabled beer there under the name Celis White. In addition, craft brewers made pilgrimages to traditional firms such as Cantillon, Rodenbach, and Liefmans to learn their techniques. Indeed, Kim Jordan and Jeff Lebesch founded New Belgium in 1988 after such a tour. Homebrewers also experimented with wild yeast. One US military officer returned to New York from a NATO posting in Brussels eager to make his own Belgian beers. After spritzing a diluted lambic sediment, he made an "exquisite" beer but in the process disrupted the yeast ecology of his wife's award-winning sourdough bread; clearly their home was only big enough for one microbiota.[63]

The Old World ideal of terroir infused many attempts to develop sour beer cultures. The New Glarus Brewery created a Wisconsin version of a Belgian red beer using local sour cherries. Businesswoman Deborah Carey had founded the brewery in 1993 with her husband Dan, a former manager at Anheuser Busch, with the goal of imagining an American wild sour beer rather than imitating a lambic. Midwestern beer terroir developed further in the 2010s when Chicago breweries began to buy secondhand Kentucky bourbon barrels to age their imperial stouts and Belgian reds. Even as Rodenbach moved away from the traditional open-air cooling tank, the Allagash Brewing Co. of Portland, Maine, installed one in 2007 after brewmaster Jason Perkins's Belgian tour. Despite the romance of alfresco brewing, quality control remained a problem, and Perkins admitted that "roughly 10 percent of Allagash's wild beer gets dumped because it's undrinkable."[64]

Precisely because of this variability, sour beers became an object of almost religious devotion. Henry Nguyen of the Monkish Brewing Company of Torrance, California, found more than 300 people camping out in his parking lot at 3 a.m. to line up for the release of a new variety. Cult behavior became particularly intense around extreme beers. Some radical brewers sought to stand out from the crowd by pursuing ever higher numerical ratings, with Double Imperial IPAs reportedly weighing in at 1,000 or even 2,000 IBUs. Meanwhile, the Scottish firm Brewdog made news in 2010 with a 32 percent alcohol beer called Tactical Nuclear Penguin. The trade journal *Modern Brewery Age* reported: "The amazing thing is that it actually tastes like a beer."[65] When a German rival brewed an even higher alcohol beer, Brewdog escalated further by producing a dozen bottles of 55 percent alcohol End of History beer, wrapped in taxidermied squirrels and stoats. Garrett Oliver, the influential brewmaster at the Brooklyn Brewery, dismissed such gimmicks: "The whole idea of extreme beer is bad for craft brewing. It doesn't expand the tent—it shrinks it."[66]

Beyond the headlines showcasing extreme products, a growing rank of global brewers applied their own taste sensibilities to expand the range of beers. Brazilian brewers commanded a sophisticated repertoire of sweet and sour tropical flavors such as *jabuticaba* (Brazilian grapetree), *pimenta rosa* (Brazilian peppertree), and *erva mate* (mate tea). The Perro Libre (Free Dog) collective of São Paulo brewed a Gose with cashew apples and salt from the Bolivian Uyuni Salt Flats, while the 2 Cabeças (Two Heads) Brewery of Porto Alegre created an IPA with passion fruit and jelly palm. South African brewers also innovated with local ingredients such as *buchu*, a medicinal herb with peppermint and orange aromas, in Triggerfish's Belgian blonde ale, baobab fruit in Zwakala Brewery's weissbier, and Ukhamba Beerworx's sorghum saison. The Mexican brewery Minerva of Jalisco brewed with another local product, agave, to create an Imperial Tequila Ale, while across the border in California, Stone Brewery sought inspiration from Mexico's complex, dark-chile-and-chocolate dish *mole* to brew Xocoveza. Brewers globally were likewise drawn by the siren song of extreme beer, often intended to appeal to the tourists. The Baja Brewery of Mexico produced a Peyote Pale Ale, while in Sucre, Bolivia, Victor Escobar brewed Ch'ama ("force," in Aymara), a coca-infused beer that, according to Malina E., an exchange student from Hamburg, tasted like Hefeweizen.[67]

Global craft pioneers preserved connections to Northern Europe and North America through travel, education, and diaspora. Homebrewing hobbyists remained the essential wellspring of the movement as both consumers and entrepreneurs. The counterculture was another hotbed of craft brewing; old hippies established breweries from the beaches of El

Salvador to the highlands of Bolivia, even as young Latin Americans learned to drink and brew craft beer while studying abroad. Diasporic connections led Toronto-born Jonathan So to establish Beertopia, a Hong Kong craft beer festival. The IT industry likewise maintained an affinity with microbrewing. Software engineers Bryan Do and Mark Hamon founded breweries in Korea after leaving Microsoft and Apple, respectively. Many so-called cyber desis and IT wallahs of Bangalore, India, acquired a taste for American-style craft beer on business trips to Seattle or Silicon Valley. Elsewhere in the British Commonwealth, connections back to England and CAMRA inspired a taste for real ale.[68]

These international networks brought new opportunities for collaborations, fostering communities both imagined and real. An early exponent of collaborative brewing, Garrett Oliver traveled widely, from traditional brewing capitals of England and Belgium to emerging craft hubs of Japan and Brazil, to conduct seminars and experiment with local ingredients. By the 2000s, Danish brothers Mikkel and Jeppe Bjergso led a new tribe of so-called gypsy brewers who created recipes expressly for production by far-flung contract brewers. International collaboration was not limited to globe-trotting celebrities. Jim and Jason Ebel of Two Brothers Brewing in Warrenville, Illinois, contacted Hildegard van Ostaden, brewmaster of the Urthel Brewery in Belgium, for assistance in brewing a Flemish red ale. They created the recipe by email, and then van Ostaden traveled for the actual brew and again for the release. The Iberian world produced its own brewing networks, as when Perro Libre collaborated with the Basque Laugar Brewery to make Braskadi, an imperial stout with cacao and palo santo, a fragrant wood used in Inka ritual. These joint ventures were not always long distance. Development scholar Ignazio Cabras observed a "collaborative competition" among neighboring microbrewers in Britain who shared equipment and expertise and even exchanged kegs to increase the novelty for customers.[69]

Nevertheless, this collaborative spirit did not always extend to women. Pioneers such as Mellie Pullman and Carol Stoudt showed that the most direct path for a woman to gain employment in the masculine space of the microbrewery was as boss. Inspired by Pullman, Teri Fahrendorf left her career as a systems analyst in the late 1980s to attend the Siebel Brewing School, but she remained unemployed until 1991, when a restaurateur in Eugene, Oregon, provided the backing for her to open the Steelhead Brewpub. On a 2007 road trip, she met many other women brewers who had experienced discrimination, and together they formed a support group called the Pink Boots Society. It has grown to include more than 2,000 members in sixteen countries.

Borrowing a cue from disability activists, progressive brewers introduced mechanical systems to eliminate the need for some of the industry's physically demanding jobs, which took a toll on male as well as female workers. Women of color faced additional challenges entering the industry. Even in South Africa, where Shebeen Queens were celebrated as anti-Apartheid fighters, Happy Sekanka faced skepticism at the Oakes Brew House in Modderfontein, east of Johannesburg. "They ask me, 'Where is the brewer?' Then I tell them, 'I'm the brewer.' Then they go like, 'No ways!' The fact also—I'm just going to say this—is because I'm black, and brewing this craft beer, they just don't understand why a black lady is brewing the beer."[70]

The resistance to women as brewers also extended to their status as consumers of craft beer. Many men within the movement adopted essentialist notions of a woman's taste for beer, embodied in offerings such as "Cherry Lambic (for the girls to drink)."[71] Craft beer labels often featured scantily clad women and misogynistic names such as Wailing Wench and Raging Bitch. To fight such sexism, female brewmasters organized groups such as the Brazilian Colectivo ELA (Portuguese for SHE, the acronym stands for Empower, Liberate, Act) and the Canadian Queen of Craft. Even the grungy environment of brewpubs that conveyed authenticity to male patrons turned off women. In a trade article on attracting more female customers, journalist Alexia Chianis offered the seemingly obvious but often ignored advice of cleaning the women's washroom. Male behavior thus served to remind women that they were outsiders in a masculine world of craft beer.[72]

This atmosphere of exclusivity has also ensured that, as the trade journal *The New Brewer* admitted, the "craft beer community tends to be very, very white."[73] Prominent brewers such as Sam Calagione and Greg Koch pointed out the need for greater diversity within the movement. Indeed, a survey commissioned by the United States Brewers Association about 2015 found that less than 4 percent of craft beer consumers were black, while 80 percent were white. "It seems like craft beer has been closely tied to an experience that a lot of people of color either don't want to be a part of or don't feel welcome engaging with," explained one young urban professional.[74] Garrett Oliver declined to blame the industry for the lack of diversity and pointed instead to racism within the wider society. J. Jackson-Beckham, the Brewers Association's first diversity ambassador, helped to organize an African American craft beer festival, Fresh Fest, in Pittsburgh in 2018. As with white businesses, minority-owned craft breweries have been most successful when selling to their own communities. "We like to be able to share our passion with other folks like us," said Shyla Sheppard, a member of the Mandan, Hidatsa, and Arikara Nation, who co-owns the Bow and Arrow Brewing Company of Albuquerque, New Mexico, with her Navajo partner, Missy Begay. "Our buddies are Native professionals: doctors and lawyers or even farmers and ranchers."[75] A Latino-owned brewery in Chicago, 5 Rabbit, cancelled a lucrative contract to supply a blond ale to the Trump Hotel in 2015 when Donald Trump launched his presidential candidacy with a racist attack on Mexicans. The brewery sold the remaining stock with a caricature of Trump's hair on a label reading: "¡Chinga tu pelo!" (Fuck your hair).[76]

Indigenous beverages have also experienced a global revival, although often within the contexts of culinary tourism and urban gentrification. Mexican pulque had maintained a loyal but aging clientele of rural and urban workers until the 1990s, when agave acreage dedicated to pulque (rather than tequila) hit new lows and most of Mexico City's 1,500 working-class pulquerías had closed their doors. No sooner had this market vanished than tourist demand for authenticity led to a pulque revival in the upscale neighborhoods of Roma and Coyoacán, reaching as far afield as Los Angeles and New York City. Meanwhile, Mexican hipsters experimented with new ingredients such as coffee, mint, and oats in place of more traditional *curados* made with coconut, mango, and pineapple. Bolivian chicha, Japanese sake, and African sorghum beers likewise became trendy tourist attractions and markers of nationalism. Anthropologist Ute Röschenthaler found that while African elders may drink bottled lagers as a status symbol within villages, young urban professionals often preferred indigenous brews to demonstrate their authenticity.[77]

Although craft beer advocates dreamed of an alternative to corporate pale lager, the movement grew through a middle-class connoisseurship that claimed moral authority through values such as artisanal autonomy, small scale, local materials, variable outputs, and environmental sustainability. While this pattern was perhaps most obvious in the individualistic consumer culture of the United States, it similarly marked Britain's more communal craft movement, as the connoisseurship of real ale became a status marker that excluded many working-class consumers.[78]

For many, the appeal of the craft beer movement lay in the survival of community. In aging small towns from England to Germany, craft supported local pubs and beer halls. As their aging owners retired and passed away, cooperatives formed to continue running these local social venues. Communalism could also coexist with cosmopolitan experiences of global culture. In 2001, Daniel Goh fled a corporate technology job to sell craft beer in a Singapore hawker stall, allowing customers to pair novel beers with laksa (spicy noodle soup) and chicken rice. Two more stands opened nearby, transforming the space into a thriving craft beer community. Nevertheless, minorities often came to associate breweries with gentrification, a standby of the artistic pioneers of urban colonization that ultimately leads to the displacement of traditional residents. This trend occurred not just in urban areas of North America and Europe, but also among the Hutongs, a warren of traditional housing in the heart of old Beijing. There two Americans opened the Great Leap Brewery making beers such as Iron Buddle Blonde, incorporating tea from Fujian.[79]

The craft brewing community has also sought to claim moral authority through environmentally sustainable production. Already in the early 2000s, the climate crisis had begun to affect brewers, who had to navigate production through erratic swings in the prices of barley and hops resulting from extreme weather patterns. Environmental activists also called attention to the industry's heavy demands for water, especially for cleaning equipment, although breweries' usage remained lower than for rival drinks such as coffee. In response to calls for sustainability, some craft brewers developed local barley supplies, although reducing the commodity chain for hops has been more difficult. Organic brewing began in Germany in the 1980s, and model brewers in North America such as New Belgium and New Glarus sought to increase the efficiency of water and energy usage. The Seven Brothers Brewery of Manchester, England, even made beer out of waste from a Kellogg's

FIGURE 7.6 Daniel Goh, a refugee from corporate IT, finds community selling craft beer in a Singapore hawker stall. Photo by Rick Halpern, 2014.

breakfast cereal factory. Carlsberg and other large-scale brewers have likewise seen the economic and reputational advantages of reducing their footprints. In the Global South, microbrewing became recognized as a form of appropriate technology sought out by development experts. To take one example, Clement Djameh, of the Inland Brewery near Accra, Ghana, brewed with malted local sorghum rather than imported barley malt and powered a kegerator by burning palm kernel shells to avoid spoiled beer during frequent power outages.[80]

Nevertheless, the growth of craft beer has frequently been driven by less than honorable practices, especially in labor relations. Workers generally remained poorly paid and enjoyed few benefits under a business model that relied on temporary interns who hoped to acquire the skills to open their own breweries. In a 2014 search, journalist Don McIntosh found precisely one unionized microbrewery in the entire United States.[81] Discrimination against women and minorities also remained pervasive. Studies showed that consumers continued to devalue the products of female brewers. Indeed, some of the most prominent women in craft beer, including Mellie Pullman and Teri Fahrendorf, gave up day-to-day brewing jobs for better working conditions and healthcare benefits in education and allied industries.[82]

Although selling to different market segments, craft brewers still competed with corporate giants, especially at the chokepoint of distribution. In 2015, the US Justice Department launched an investigation into AB InBev for requiring distributors to sign exclusive contracts. Meanwhile in Kenya, former librarian Tabitha Karanja, founder of Keroche Breweries, struggled against East African Breweries' control of distribution to bring her high-quality Summit lager to low-income consumers. To compete in the marketplace, craft brewers often collaborated with the giants in their own pursuit of scale. In 2017, Tony Magee sold a half interest in his stoner brewery Lagunitas to Heineken for a reported $500 million, while the self-styled punk founders of Brewdog, James Watt and Martin Dickie, accepted a £213 million private equity investment from venture capitalists TSG Consumer. Craft beer and high tech continued to converge as blockbuster deals inspired the creation of beer brands, like apps, with the goal of selling out. But this strategy was a risky one, as the premium of craft beer remained dependent on a sense of purpose and community.[83]

For a craft movement born of an age of globalization, the global pandemic of Covid-19 posed a mortal threat to small breweries in the spring of 2020.

Between border closures and nationwide lockdowns, countless kegs of fine beer swirled down the drain for want of pubs to serve them. Nevertheless, a sense of community came to the rescue of many micros. The Attic Brewing Company of Philadelphia delivered their Be Free or Die Pilsner with its Harriet Tubman label to customers isolated at home, as did the Bellwoods Brewery of Toronto, maker of sour beers like Jelly King. At the height of the pandemic, small groups of socially distanced people lingered by the make-shift takeout window of my downtown Toronto local, Bar Volo. Brewers took hope knowing that craft had revived from its decade of millennial stagnation after the Great Recession of 2008, when fine beer provided an affordable luxury in hard times, like lipstick during the Great Depression of the 1930s.

Yet this optimism must be tempered by knowledge of even longer historical continuities. Just as Gabriel Sedlmayr and Anton Dreher crafted their distinctive Munich and Vienna lagers through a conscious strategy of market segmentation, contemporary brewers seek to attract consumers with exciting new tastes. The tools that have enabled the craft movement—efficient, small-scale brewing technology and reliable supply chains for malt, hops, and yeast—are themselves products of the mass production that many craft partisans denounce. The experience of early industrial brewers, particularly the wave of concentration at the end of the nineteenth century, holds lessons for today's microbrewers, who worry that their own business model may become unsustainable. While touting ties to local communities, and even some locally sourced ingredients, most breweries purchase malt and hops from transnational firms. Marketing often depends on distributors beholden to AB InBev and other industry giants, who have muscled their way into the craft market. Although owners may draw a living wage, workers often scrape by on poorly paid internships in the hopes one day of opening a microbrewery of their own.

Consumers have been willing so far to pay a premium for the quality and community of craft beer, and their continued dedication will ultimately determine whether today's microbreweries, like their counterparts a century ago, are forced to "get big or get out." Indeed, when small breweries go out of business, or appear to sell out, this is often blamed on the power of nefarious corporations, when in fact consumers helped to inflate a craft beer bubble with their incessant demands for novelty and exclusivity. Patrons' insistence on finding a new beer to sample on each visit requires brewpubs to maintain unsustainably long lines of taps. Brewers have likewise contributed to this exclusivity with tales of founding fathers and a snobbish masculinity exemplified by the muscular gargoyle mascot of Stone Brewery's Arrogant

Bastard Ale. Adding context to beer culture, then, means undoing one of its founding premises: the craft movement's cultural associations with white men. There are successful minority and female brewers, despite the discrimination that makes them less likely to participate in craft beer culture. As long as craft beer remains limited to white males, it will never challenge the makers of mass-produced pale lagers on a global scale. Changing that culture can help to ensure the survival of a contemporary golden age of brewing.

Conclusion

IN 2009, ANNICK De Splenter opened the Gruut City Brewery in Ghent, Belgium, with a plan to turn back the clock on brewing with hops not just two decades, to pre-IPA levels, but more than five centuries, to the unhopped, gruit beers of medieval brewsters. This was no amateur hobby project. She came from a long line of brewers, whose family firm, Riva, was founded in 1896 and had purchased Liefmans in the 1990s after Rose Blancquaert retired. Having been told by her professors at the Ghent School of Brewing that it was impossible to make beer without hops, De Splenter set out to prove them wrong. Experimenting with botanicals, herbs, fruits, and spices, she created her own unique interpretations of Belgian classics, including a gingery white, peppery blond, anise amber, and peanut brown. Customers could even personalize their beers, ordering custom brews with their own selection of flavorings. She explained: "It's soft beer, not aggressive as some hopped beers can be. My beers are not sweet—they're drinkable."[1] De Splenter won a devoted following, and other small breweries around the world were likewise inspired to make beer without hops. While gruit, like the wider craft movement, is still a boutique taste, it represents a viable alternative to the hegemony of mass-produced pale lager.

Hopped Up has presented a history of how humans have made beer and how they have made meaning with these beers. It has followed the invention of beer styles as they served to commodify the beverage, creating status symbols with the cachet of local origins, even after production had become thoroughly globalized. Variations existed in techniques and ingredients since the earliest experiments with brewing in paleolithic times, but these differences did not constitute styles in the modern sense of a codified system or taxonomy classifying beers by brewing method, color, aroma, flavor, and carbonation, among other factors.[2] Indeed, a taxonomy requires a global perspective rather than local knowledge. The ancients assigned labels to distinguish specialties such as the Egyptian iron beer and the Babylonian one-year beer. They even recognized a notion of terroir in the value assigned to beers from the Syrian city of Qode. The literati of medieval China ranked beers by virtue, comparing mellow, golden beers to the worthies and sour, dark beers to fools. European brewers likewise adjusted their recipes to fit the rank of the consumer, from the nobility and clergy to commoners. Varieties proliferated in both northern Europe and China during the sixteenth century, as the nouveaux riches began to demand special beers as a claim to gentility. Thus, the connection between status and style became aspirational, a commodity that could be purchased rather than an inherent personal quality.

Only with advances in industrial capitalism did beer styles achieve their modern, standardized form, beginning with pale ales and porters in Britain and lighter and darker lagers on the continent. Scientific beer analysis provided the technological basis for the standardization of styles, while intellectual property law and commercial treaties defined their institutional framework, in opposition to geographical designations. Although historical memory has assigned great weight to moments of invention, styles changed over time with technology and consumer preferences.[3] As pale lager displaced other styles, particularly in North America, brewers invented new categories to differentiate popular, premium, super-premium, light, and dry beers. Some firms sought to define styles around individual brands, as in the case of Anheuser Busch's Budweiser, although arguably Guinness accomplished this objective most successfully with stout. Beer styles positively exploded from the innovation-driven world of craft, for example, Annick De Splenter's reinvention of medieval gruit as a modern style. The imagined geography of beer styles also continued to evolve, as Munich came to be associated with helles lager rather than the nineteenth-century dunkel, while craft brewers created new varieties of West Coast, New England, and even German IPAs.[4]

Technology contributed to the development of beer styles, defining the possibilities for transforming starches into alcoholic beverages, but the adoption of new brewing methods responded to market demands and changing tastes. Prehistoric hunters and gatherers learned to malt grains and ferment beverages through their observation of plant life cycles, a knowledge that ultimately led to the domestication of crops. Brewing was therefore an integral part of the agricultural revolution and the rise of social complexity. Moreover, archaeologists now believe that a desire for sociability rather than sheer hunger drove the cultivation of new foods, which were consumed on festive occasions. Fueling celebrations for more than 10,000 years, beer has reinforced communal solidarity and mobilized labor for collective projects.

Over the centuries, the exchange of technological advances in brewing contributed to regional divergences and convergences in beer varieties, but always in tandem with social and cultural developments. Brewers in particular regions adopted ingredients and devised methods, from West Asian barley and East Asian bacterial ferments to Central European hops and lager yeasts, and then carried them more or less widely. These innovations and transfers were by turns gradual and abrupt; commercial hopped beers burst onto the scene in thirteenth-century Germany, but brewers in the Low Countries took a century or more to master the technique and displace imports. In the case of London porter, the first industrial beer, technological change followed from market demand rather than driving it. The progressive lightening of beer across the nineteenth and twentieth centuries depended on advances in malting, fermentation, adjunct grains, and biological control. Nevertheless, the standardization and proliferation of beer styles responded to industrial imperatives to constrain organic variation among plants, enzymes, and yeast, which in turn responded to consumers' demands for both novelty and predictability, which provided the impetus for market segmentation. This consumer-led differentiation in pursuit of flavor and social distinction reached new heights as the craft beer industry adapted large-scale technologies to small-batch production.

The connections between taste and social and technological change are notoriously difficult to disentangle. Neuroscientific research has confirmed Marcel Proust's observation that sensory perception is filtered through the "remembrance of things past," especially taste memories. Sociologists meanwhile have examined the ways that communities of taste take shape through the development of languages to describe foods and to rank them within social hierarchies. The historical record provides numerous examples of the formation of taste communities around beers, from the early modern proliferation of varieties in Germany and China to the early twentieth-century reception of lager in Japan and Mexico and the present-day invention of craft beer connoisseurship on the internet.

In all of these cases, tastes for novel drinks were situated within existing social contexts while responding to their unique sensory characteristics. Early modern experiments with hops and spices were guided by notions of balance and vitality in European humoral theory and Chinese traditional medicine. The nineteenth-century shift from dark to light beers, both the English preference for pale ales over porters and the German shift from Munich to Pilsner lagers, likewise reflected the place of beer within the larger diet.

As industrialization increased the affordability of food supplies, including sugar, wheat flour, and preserved meat from around the world, the middle classes and factory workers no longer needed heavy, dark beers to fill them up. Instead, they came to prefer lighter, more drinkable beers to accompany such modern leisure activities as sports and dancing. Beer essentially shifted categories, from meal to entertainment.

At the same time, the pursuit of purity through industrial food processing helped to recast strong flavors like Brettanomyces as a source of contamination. Pale lager's clean taste had different sensory appeals in Mexico, where it contrasted with the sourness of pulque, and Japan, where purity was a long-standing culinary and cultural ideal. The enduring global demand for Guinness stout as a source of strength for nursing mothers and manly men likewise confirms the way tastes are situated in wider cultural beliefs and practices.

Twentieth-century advances in food technology spurred the progressive lightening of pale lagers while also inspiring and facilitating the taste revolution of craft beer. The marketing of novel processed foods, from baby foods to soft drinks, inculcated a taste for bland, sweet flavors among the young, contributing to a preference for lighter beers as people aged. This trend may help to explain an observation by Bob Weinberg, the most respected authority on the US beer industry in the second half of the twentieth century: "I honestly believe that 90 percent plus of the American people do not like the taste of beer, and that the only reason they drink beer is because it's a lubricant of social intercourse."[5] When Michael Jackson complained that mass-market brewers were taking the taste out of beer, he was reacting to a widespread consumer preference. Jackson's lament, in turn, reflected a backlash against the food industry by those seeking more authentic, wholesome products. The international counterculture of the 1960s rejected not only the artificiality of TV dinners and pale lager but also the hegemony of French haute cuisine. As many former hippies matured and joined the ruling class, they founded a new dining culture around the figure of the omnivore, a globe-trotting gourmet typified by Anthony Bourdain, who was equally at home in Hanoi street markets and Parisian restaurants. An advertising campaign captured the omnivore's sensibility with the Most Interesting Man in the World's slogan: "I don't always drink beer, but when I do, I prefer Dos Equis." For those who do always drink beer, the omnivore found a choice of beers for every occasion. As brewing scientist Charles Bamforth has said, "in a 300-year-old thatched West Sussex pub . . . a pint of flat, generously hopped ale is a delight. However," on a scorching day at the ballpark, "an ice-cold Bud is to die for."[6]

Beer manufacturers added another dimension to the experience of taste by associating their brands and styles with colorful stories. The ancient Egyptian quaffing a cup of Qode beer may have imagined an exotic Syrian city, just as modern-day beer hunters prized even an ordinary pale lager consumed in a far-off land. Tales of founding fathers gave personality to beer styles, from the early modern beers attributed to Broihan and Mumme to legendary eighteenth-century English industrial brewers Harwood and Hodgson and their nineteenth-century Central European counterparts, Groll and Sedlmayr. Lacking the giant brewers' advertising budgets, the craft movement created legends around figures like Fritz Maytag and Jack McAuliffe, although the largest craft firm, the Boston Beer Company, used television commercials to claim underdog status for its CEO, Jim Koch. Advertising executives likewise understood the importance of creating a personality around mass-market brands, and promotions since the postwar era have increasingly been targeted toward distinct market segments. Whether displayed on slick television spots or homespun craft beer labels, these branding narratives often adopted the tone of stand-up comedy, including the frequent use of sexist and racist messaging to create market appeal.

Looking at global history through beer sheds light on changing human experiences across time and space. One might suppose that the chronology of beer followed a progressive expansion of European domination, from local to regional markets during the early modern era, to national and imperial brands in the nineteenth and twentieth centuries, culminating in cross-border mergers with the global lager in the twenty-first century. But such a trajectory ignores long-term continuities as well as periods of retrenchment. Long-distance trade of course was limited in earlier times by preservation and transportation technologies, while today's global beer brands are generally brewed under contract. Nevertheless, international shipping was profitable for brewers such as Bass, Guinness, and Beck's, albeit on a relatively small scale. The travels of skilled brewers as migrants and empire builders were just as important in globalizing incipient European beer styles. Beer also faced moments of declining demand. Hanseatic beer markets were pummeled in the seventeenth century by climate change and the competition from drinks such as gin and coffee. The nineteenth-century international trade in beer was reversed in the first half of the twentieth century by war, depression, and import substitution.

Global perspective can also help reveal the importance of borrowing and exchange in the development of brewing traditions that have often been attributed to isolated nations or civilizations. Recurring patterns of trickle trade depended on the movement of goods, people, and ideas. From medieval European hopped beers to nineteenth-century pale ales and lagers, and twenty-first-century craft beers, new styles were first traded to satisfy elite demands for exotic goods. But as the migrations of brewers and technology transfers allowed those styles to be reproduced locally and became accessible to all ranks of society, those earlier trade routes were closed off. The circuits of mobility of beer, brewers, and breweries also varied over time. Britain and Bavaria imported skilled workers from other regions to learn the methods of medieval hopped beer, but they later pioneered industrial brewing techniques. The sending regions of brewers were dispersed and variable; Scottish migrants played an outsized role in populating the British empire and overseas breweries, while Bavarians composed only a minority of expatriate lager brewers.[7] As lager beer gained an international following in the late nineteenth century, aspiring brewers from the Americas, Asia, Australia, and Africa traveled to Europe to study bottom fermentation, just as craft brewers a hundred years later made pilgrimages to Belgium to learn spontaneous fermentation. But these migrations and knowledge transfers also traveled in other directions. Heinrich Beck, Freddy Heineken, and Eddie Taylor all contributed to the introduction of North American production methods, marketing strategies, and organizational patterns to Europe.

The history of pale lager also helps to rethink the meaning of beer style, as ongoing, global innovations continued to transform the style long after Joseph Groll's original brewing of Pilsner in 1842. Combining industrial brewing techniques from the United Kingdom with Bavarian advances in bottom fermentation, pale lager later achieved its sparkling clarity through the incorporation of adjunct grains including sorghum, rice, and maize indigenous to Africa, Asia, and the Americas. The recipe evolved further in the twentieth century with new equipment and techniques such as Japanese advances in microfiltration and Mexican malting techniques. The introduction of flavored malt beverages facilitated still more localization in the twenty-first century, with such regional creations as Chinese clam-juice beer. Although beer lovers may cringe at the thought, the technological path of pale lager leads from Pilsner to Bud Light Lime.

The global geographies of beer emerged not only from mobilities but also from what remained behind in places of origin. Foods with a sense of place, or terroir, such as Itami sake or Belgian lambics, have commanded premium prices, even as the legal definitions of beer style established in commercial courts and trade treaties of the early twentieth century detached Munich and Pilsner lagers from their towns of origin. This detachment of beer styles was in part a result of localization, as people adapted exotic goods to suit their own taste preferences and cultural patterns. Japanese brewers best illustrate these adjustments in style and flavor, although such changes happened every time an individual brewer thought beer might sell better with a little tweak of the recipe. At the same time, imports were incorporated into local drinking cultures, where they acquired their own meaning. For example, Chinese traditional medicine in Malaysia considered lager beer to be "cooling," while Guinness was "heating" and invigorating.[8] Moreover, the spread of pale lager, far from completely displacing indigenous drinks, has arguably contributed to a revival of many local brewing traditions. To take two examples from Bolivia, Quechua-speaking herders in the highlands drank pale lager brands like Cusqueño on an everyday basis, but for ceremonial events, they brewed chicha and drank it from reproductions of two-handled pots found at Machu Picchu. A similar pattern emerged in the Amazonian lowlands, on the other side of the Andes, where Tsimané people fermented a manioc brew called *Shocdye'* as a way of maintaining communal identities.[9]

Global vision also reveals the power relationships that have shaped the production and consumption of beer, particularly the politics of prohibition and empire. Brewers devoted considerable energy to fighting prohibitionist regimes and preserving their legal right to work, from North American brewing magnates to South African shebeen operators. They did so through global networks that ran parallel to campaigns of temperance advocates such as the Women's Christian Temperance Union.[10] Imperial officials paradoxically sought to restrict drinking among indigenous populations even as they facilitated the supply of alcohol to European settlers. When complete prohibition threatened their ability to mobilize labor, as in Durban, South Africa, officials created elaborate restrictions that made native workers feel as if they were "drinking in a cage." In situations like this, illicit alcohol offered laborers a form of resistance, as they sometimes covertly and other times openly flaunted the rules. As recently as 2013, secular Turkish opponents of the authoritarian Islamist regime of President Recep Tayyip Erdogan gathered in Taksim Square, where beer gardens had flourished a century earlier, and in conservative rural towns alike, holding up bottles of Efes beer and shouting defiantly, "Cheers Tayyip."[11]

Long associated with communal drinking, beer has nevertheless reinforced hierarchies and inequalities of the societies in which it is embedded. Kinship-based societies that imposed a rough equality on members nevertheless often maintained distinctions between the Big Men who had ready access to beer and lesser members who had to work for their drinks. With the rise of tributary states in ancient Egypt and Mesopotamia, beer came to be considered inferior in status to wine, a stereotype that continued through the ages from Greece and Rome to the medieval Church, nineteenth-century pubs, and present-day wine connoisseurs. Beer varieties have also expressed status and exclusivity, as the imported hopped beers of Hamburg and Einbeck displaced local, unhopped ales in the late Middle Ages. While industrial brewers sought to segment markets between social classes, through the quality of ingredients or simply different advertising messages, Victorian pub culture enforced a working-class solidarity with the demands of the round, even on those who could not afford to participate. The craft beer movement replaced the shared tables of the nineteenth-century beer garden with long rows of taps, which allowed individual consumers to display their social distinction.

Beer culture has a long history of excluding women, although for thousands of years brewing was considered to be women's work. As production became commercialized and profitable, men took control, even if the beers sold at market were not necessarily superior to homebrew, especially when the latter was prepared on ceremonial occasions to enhance the household's prestige. The introduction of new technologies, such as brewing with hops in medieval Europe, often facilitated the marginalization of women. The old-fashioned taste of unhopped ales became associated with negative gender stereotypes in John Skelton's poem of the witchlike alewife Elinor Rumming and the Kräuterfrauen outlawed by Bavarian brewing regulations. Nevertheless, women remained essential to the family-centered organization of early modern breweries, even after they were tacitly or formally excluded from guild membership. The industrialization of brewing and the scientific training of brewing schools further marginalized women to the tasks of bottling and quality control. Meanwhile, women were excluded from Victorian pubs, or at best allowed into separate ladies' rooms. Wartime mobilizations drafted women back into breweries, but once the crises had passed, men reasserted their positions in the industry and filled well-paying jobs. Even the decentralization of the craft beer movement did not appreciably change the opportunities available to women as employees, although it did make it easier for female entrepreneurs to open their own businesses, which they have done in increasing numbers.

Even as they offered sites of collective sociability, pubs have simultaneously excluded people based on race and ethnicity as well as gender and class. Ancient Babylonian stereotypes differentiated civilized, beer-drinking people from the nomadic barbarians who fermented horse milk. In a similar fashion, European colonists scorned the brewing traditions of subject peoples as primitive and unhygienic. At times, introducing lager beer to the natives became associated with the civilizing mission of empire, but just as often, imperial officials sought to forbid drinking among subject peoples. In the United States, Prohibition was fueled in large part by racialized and nativist fears that former slaves and recent immigrants would challenge white supremacy. Access to beer and brewery jobs remained a subject of struggle during the civil rights movements, in North America as in South Africa. Likewise, British and Australian pubs became sites of contention, the former around Caribbean and Asian immigrants and the later focused on aboriginal peoples. Whiteness has persisted within the contemporary craft beer movement, particularly through the culture's embrace of medieval origins, which have been imagined as a time of European racial purity.[12]

Mass-produced and craft beers alike are essentially capitalist commodities with mutually intwined destinies, although they are marketed with vastly different messages. Attempts by large brewers to muscle their way into the craft sector caused outrage among many who believed that these firms failed to respect the movement's traditions and ideals. In much the same way, ethnic-style fast-food restaurants and industrial producers of organic microgreens coopted the counterculture food movement of the 1960s.[13] But craft beer was capitalist from the very beginning, as is evident in the work of entrepreneurs such as Fritz Maytag and Jim Koch as well as industry-trained brewers Bert Grant, Lex Mitchell, and Phil Sexton. Indeed, some have argued that contemporary capitalism has been defined by an anti-capitalist ethos of the 1960s counterculture, which replaced the security and stability of bureaucratic corporatism with a desire for creativity expressed—in its most extreme form—by the mantra to "move fast and break things." This spirit animated not only the craft movement but also the investment bankers behind AB InBev. Journalists Kevin McCoy and Nathan Bomey observed that Carlos Brito's "approach to business is less global beverage titan and more tech start-up CEO."[14]

Not all craft brewers dream of building a brand that they can sell out for millions. Many seek to support a local community, much like immigrant family restaurants. The viability of small-scale production has made craft brewing an accessible form of entrepreneurship, but to justify the premium price it depends on maintaining a moral high ground through associations with desirable qualities such as local, artisanal, communal, sustainable, and nostalgic beers. Small breweries have proved more adaptable than the giants. For example, as kegs of fine beer poured down the drain at the outbreak of the Covid-19 pandemic, these companies switched first to making disinfectant and, when that market became saturated, found alternative distribution methods to reach locked-down customers. In another example of small brewers' innovation, when Russia invaded Ukraine in 2022, a Lviv microbrewery began producing a craft Molotov cocktail that was "soupy, sticky, and burn[ed] like crazy," the better to disable Russian military vehicles.[15] Ultimately, the convergence of craft and mass-market comes down to small brewers' dependence on the wider industry's technology and raw ingredients, while in return their innovation and enthusiasm have reinvigorated beer cultures at a time when giant conglomerates' sales have stagnated in the Global North.

In a world of commodities, true value lies in our shared humanity, and fermented grain beverages have been communal drinks par excellence. Since ancient times, people have drunk beer in all of its diverse forms to relax after a day's work and to celebrate festive occasions. In seeking to recover that sense of human connection and escape the alienation of industrial capitalism, many have turned to craft beer. Nevertheless, the local IPA is embedded in the same industrial relationships as the global lager. We should look for comfort not in the distinction of our beer but from a more open and inclusive sociability in our pub, Kneipe, taberna, izakaya, or shebeen.

Acknowledgments

THIS BOOK IS dedicated to all the friends who have helped me to research and write it over the years. Academics can be a generous group, and countless colleagues have offered their services as research assistants. Inspiration for the project came from a conversation with two renowned world historians, Donna Gabaccia and Dirk Hoerder. Donna has always been willing to join me in "scientific experiments," even when she would rather have been drinking wine.

Oxford University Press facilitated my first research trip for this project, to the New York Public Library, while doing the book launch for my last book, *Planet Taco*. Fortuitously, it coincided with Garrett Oliver's presentation of the *Oxford Companion to Beer*. Beer and tacos, a perfect combination. I thank my editor Susan Ferber and publisher Niko Pfund for their support from the very beginning. I also appreciate the careful attention of Jacqueline Pavlovic and Sheila Oakley in the final stages of the book's preparation.

Subsequent research trips have taken me around the world, and I am particularly grateful to archivists and librarians Eibhlin Colgan and Aoife Walshe at Guinness, Dublin; Robert Curry of the Special Collections at Oxford Brookes University, Oxford; Axel Borg and Audrey Russek at the University of California, Davis; Michaela Knör at the Versuchs- und Lehranstalt für Brauerei, Berlin; and Anna Krutsch at the Deutsches Museum, Munich.

Yet I could never have completed the archival work or managed the linguistic challenges of such a global project alone. I offer thanks for the research assistance of Stephanie Borkowsky, Kathy Burke, Florian Danecke, Sanchia DeSouza, Joel Dickau, Ed Dunsworth, Chi-Hoon Kim, the late Jay Kim, Ariadna Pauliuc, Michael Roellinghoff, William Sturm, and Cherrie Wang. Three colleagues in particular, Jackson Yuebin Guo, Valeria Mantilla-Morales, and Yu Wang, provided such valuable assistance that they became co-authors on articles that appear in the bibliography.

In Toronto, I have always appreciated the insightful suggestions and unwavering support of colleagues at the Culinaria Research Centre: Noah Allison, Nino Bariola, Shyon Baumann, Camille Bégin, Dan Bender, Michaël Bruckert, Sarah Cappeliez, Bryan Dale, Bob Davidson, Greg de St. Maurice, Sarah Elton, Rick Halpern, Colleen Hammelman, Lisa Haushofer, Cindy Hu, Marney Isaac, Ryan Isakson, Josée Johnston, Kelsey Kilgore, Catherine Koonar, Ken MacDonald, Irina Mihalache, Lena Mortensen, Merin Oleschuk, Steve Penfold, Kristin Plys, Jackie Rohel, Jo Sharma, Alison Smith, Nick Tosaj, and Liz Zanoni. Also in Toronto, I have enjoyed the intellectual community of the Latin American Research Group, especially Anne Rubenstein, Lucho Van Isschot, Kevin Coleman, Gillian McGillivray, and Tamara Walker. Finally, my colleagues Takashi Fujitani, Franca Iacovetta, Jennifer Jenkins, and Ian Radforth provided valuable assistance.

Other colleagues have helped me advance the project as article editors. I thank Carol Helstosky, Krishnendu Ray and Cecilia Leong Salobir, Simone Cinotto, Steffan Igor Ayora Díaz, Marina Camargo de Heck, Benjamin R. Cohen, Michael S. Kideckel, and Anna Zeide, Erika Rappaport, Elizabeth Schmidt, and Lisa Jacobson, and Jana Weis and Nancy Bodden. Numerous anonymous readers also helped out, and I would happily buy each of them a beer. Portions of this book have been adapted from the following publications:

Pilcher, Jeffrey M. "Does Your Beer Have Style? The Nineteenth-Century Invention of European Beer Styles." In *Acquired Tastes: Stories about the Origins of Modern Food*, edited by Benjamin R. Cohen, Michael S. Kideckel, and Anna Zeide, 65–80. Cambridge: The MIT Press, 2021.

Pilcher, Jeffrey M. "The Globalization of Guinness: Marketing Taste, Transferring Technology." *Jahrbuch für Wirtschaftsgeschichte* 65, no. 1 (2024): 17–35.

Pilcher, Jeffrey M. "Imperial Hops: Beer in the Age of Empire." *Global Food History* 10, no. 1 (March 2024): 52–67.

Pilcher, Jeffrey M. "'Beer with Chinese Characteristics': Marketing Beer Under Mao." Coauthored with Yu Wang and Yuebin Jackson Guo. *Revista de Administração de Empresas: Journal of Business Management* (São Paulo) 58, no. 3 (May–June 2018): 303–315.

Pilcher, Jeffrey M. "National Beer in a Global Age: Technology, Taste, and Mobility, 1880–1914." *Quaderni storici* 151, no. 1 (April 2016): 51–70.

Pilcher, Jeffrey M. "'Tastes Like Horse Piss': Asian Encounters with European Beer." *Gastronomica* 16, no. 1 (Spring 2016): 28–40.

Pilcher, Jeffrey M. "Hop Movements: The Global Invention of Craft Beer." In *Food Mobilities: Making World Cuisines*, edited by Daniel E. Bender and Simone Cinotto, 325–44. Toronto: University of Toronto Press, 2023.

Pilcher, Jeffrey M. "Dos Equis and Five Rabbit: Beer and Taste in Greater Mexico." In *Taste, Politics, and Identities in Mexican Food*, edited by Steffan Igor Ayora Díaz, 161–74. London: Bloomsbury, 2018.

Scholarly workshops and public lectures have been just as important as published essays in refining my ideas about beer. For invitations to present my work I thank Marcelo Borges, Chris Boyer, Rebecca Earle and Beat Kümin, Paul Freedman, Jorge González and Tommaso Gravante, Glen Goodman, Viridiana Hernández Fernández, Roger Horowitz, Alice Julier, Julie McIntyre, Robert Nelson, Tore Olsson, David Parker and Aditi Sen, Rod Phillips, Rick Wilk, and Victoria Wolff and Melitta Adamson.

Beer historians have been a particularly generous group, and I thank Martyn Cornell, Susan Gauss, Mareen Heying, Franz Hofer, Marc Jacobs, Jennifer Jordan, Theresa McCulla, Max Nelson, Zachary Nowak, Ron Pattinson, Eline Poelmans, Malcolm Purinton, Pavla Simkova, Robert Terrell, and Richard Unger for their many suggestions over the years. I have benefited equally from the suggestions of non-specialists, including Miranda Brown, Andrew Hoyt, Claudia Kreklau, Jake Lahne, Lisong Liu, M. J. Maynes, Rebekah Pite, Claudia Rapp, Eric Rath, Peter Scholliers, and Annemarie Steidl. The gang at 42 North joined in my first explorations of the world of beer.

Finally, I have depended on the support of my family. My mother, father, and stepmother are all teetotalers but never moralized about my adventures. While Tim and Michelle don't drink beer, they are party hosts par excellence. Liss and Kyle, my Kansas cousins, and the Cousins' Balcony all provided amiable companionship. Last but not least, I thank the next generation of research assistants, Sean and Joseline, Nikki and Mike, and Dianna and Mike. Cheers.

Notes

INTRODUCTION

1. "Around the World in 80 Beers," September 8, 2009, http://www.puretravel.com/blog/2009/09/08/around-the-world-in-80-beers/.

2. "Letters," *The Economist*, August 31, 2013.

3. J. E. Browly, "The Consulting Brewer, His Dangers and His Uses, with Some Practical Brewing Notes," *Journal of the Institute of Brewing* (hereafter *JIB*) 2, no. 2 (March–April 1896): 88.

4. "Deutsche Exportbiere," *Allgemeine Brauer- und Hopfen Zeitung* (hereafter *ABHZ*) 22, no. 5 (January 15, 1882): 36; John E. Siebel, *One Hundred Years of Brewing* (1903; repr., New York: Arno Press, 1974), 681.

5. "Van Laer on Belgian Beers," *American Brewer's Review* (hereafter *ABR*) 10, no. 1 (July 20, 1896): 1–2.

6. Quotes from Frances Hayashida, "*Chicha* Histories: Pre-Hispanic Brewing in the Andes and the Use of Ethnographic and Historical Analogues," in *Drink, Power, and Society in the Andes*, ed. Justin Jennings and Brenda J. Bowser (Gainesville: University Press of Florida, 2009), 243.

7. Audrey I. Richards, *Land, Labour and Diet in Northern Rhodesia: An Economic Study of the Bemba Tribe* (London: Oxford University Press, 1939), 77.

8. Henry J. Bruman, *Alcohol in Ancient Mexico* (Salt Lake City: University of Utah Press, 2000), 77.

9. Fanny Calderón de la Barca, *Life in Mexico: The Letters of Fanny Calderón de la Barca*, ed. Howard T. Fisher and Marion Hall Fisher (Garden City, NY: Doubleday, 1966), 79.

10. W. Puck Brecher, "Brewing Spirits, Brewing Songs: Saké, *Haikai*, and the Aestheticization of Suburban Space in Edo Period Itami," *Japan Studies Review* 14 (2010): 30.

256   *Notes to pages 4–13*

11. Karin Hackel-Stehr, "Das Brauwesen in Bayern vom 14. bis 16. Jahrhundert, insbesondere die Entstehung und Entwicklung des Reinheitsgebotes (1516)" (Ph.D. diss, Technische Universität Berlin, 1987).

12. "Der Charakter des Bieres," *Deutsche Brauer-Nachrichten* (hereafter *DBN*) 36, no. 45 (November 9, 1928): 529.

13. Barbara Smit, *The Heineken Story: The Remarkably Refreshing Tale of the Beer that Conquered the World* (London: Profile Books, 2014), 112.

14. Philip H. Howard, "Too Big to Ale: Globalization and Consolidation in the Beer Industry," in *The Geography of Beer: Regions, Environment, and Societies*, ed. Mark Patterson and Nancy Hoalst Pullen (Dordrecht: Springer, 2014), 155–65; A. M. McGahan, "The Emergence of the National Brewing Oligopoly: Competition in the American Market, 1933–1958," *Business History Review* 65, no. 2 (Summer 1991): 262.

15. Garrett Oliver, "Beer Style," in *The Oxford Companion to Beer*, ed. Garrett Oliver (New York: Oxford University Press, 2012), 115. See also Holger Starke, *Von brauerhandwerk zur Brauindustrie: Die Geschichte der Bierbrauerei in Dresden und Sachsen, 1800–1914* (Cologne: Böhlau Verlag, 2005), 81.

16. J.-Th. De Raadt, "La bière de Bruxelles au vieux temps," *Le Petit Journal du Brasseur* (hereafter *PJB*) 7, no. 271 (June 9, 1899): 201.

17. "La réclame de la Brasserie de Lembecq," *PJB* 18, no. 825 (July 8, 1910): 789; "La gueuse-lambic de Bruxelles," *PJB* 11, no. 494 (November 20, 1903): 1212; "La densité et l'atténuation du lambic," *PJB* 7, no. 266 (May 5, 1899): 162; "Le sucrage du faro," *PJB* 12, no. 530 (August 10, 1904): 859–60.

18. William Cronon, *Nature's Metropolis: Chicago and the Great West* (New York: W. W. Norton, 1991), 207–47; Erika Rappaport, *A Thirst for Empire: How Tea Shaped the Modern World* (Princeton, NJ: Princeton University Press, 2017); William Roseberry, "The Rise of Yuppie Coffees and the Reimagination of Class in the United States," *American Anthropologist* 98:4 (1996) 762–75.

19. Richards, *Land, Labour and Diet*, 78.

20. Michael Jursa, "Babylonia in the First Millennium BCE: Economic Growth in Times of Empire," in *The Cambridge History of Capitalism*, ed. Larry Neal and Jeffrey G. Williamson, 2 vols. (Cambridge: Cambridge University Press, 2014), 1:24–42.

21. Wolfgang Schivelbusch, *Tastes of Paradise: A Social History of Spices, Stimulants, and Intoxicants* (New York: Vintage Books, 1993), 203.

22. J. Nikol Beckham, "Entrepreneurial Leisure and the Microbrew Revolution: The Neoliberal Origins of the Craft Beer Movement," in *Untapped: Exploring the Cultural Dimensions of Craft Beer*, ed. Nathaniel G. Chapman, J. Slade Lellock, and Cameron D. Lippard (Morgantown: West Virginia University Press, 2017), 99–100.

23. Classic works include Thomas C. Cochrane, *The Pabst Brewing Company: The History of an American Business* (New York: New York University Press, 1948); Peter

Mathias, *The Brewing Industry in England, 1700–1830* (Cambridge: Cambridge University Press, 1959); Wolfgang Behringer, *Löwenbräu: Von den Anfängen des Münchner Brauwesens bis zur Gegenwart* (Munich: Süddeutscher Verlag, 1991); T. R. Gourvish and R. G. Wilson, *The British Brewing Industry, 1830–1980* (Cambridge: Cambridge University Press, 1994); Anne Kelk Mager, *Beer, Sociability, and Masculinity in South Africa* (Bloomington: Indiana University Press, 2010).

24. Richard W. Unger, *Beer in the Middle Ages and the Renaissance* (Philadelphia: University of Pennsylvania Press, 2004), 133.

25. Maureen Ogle, *Ambitious Brew: The Story of American Beer* (Orlando, FL: Harcourt, 2006), viii, ix.

26. Carl Rach, "Have We Ever Properly Tried to Brew Bavarian Beer?," *Transactions of the American Brewing Institute* (hereafter *TABI*) 2 (1902): 177.

27. Francis Wyatt, "The Proper Brewing of the Best Beers," *TABI* 2 (1902): 188.

28. Rach, "Have We Ever Properly Tried," 178.

29. Donna R. Gabaccia, "Inventing 'Little Italy,'" *The Journal of the Gilded Age and the Progressive Era* 6, no. 1 (January 2007): 7–41.

30. Sidney W. Mintz, *Sweetness and Power: The Place of Sugar in Modern History* (New York: Viking, 1985).

CHAPTER I

1. "The Brewing of Beer," *The Kalevala*, trans. John Martin Crawford, 1888, accessed October 1, 2018, http://www.sacred-texts.com/neu/kveng/kvrune20.htm.

2. Thomas A. DuBois, *Finnish Folk Poetry and the* Kalevala (New York: Garland Publishing, 1995); Patricia E. Sawin, "Lönnrot's Brainchildren: The Representation of Women in Finland's *Kalevala*," *Journal of Folklore Research* 25, no. 3 (1988): 187–217; Matti Kuusi, Keith Bosley, and Michael Branch, eds., *Finnish Folk Poetry: Epic* (Helsinki: Finnish Literature Society, 1977), 205–11.

3. DuBois, *Finnish Folk Poetry*, 101; D. Y. DeLyser and W. J. Kasper, "Hopped Beer: The Case for Cultivation," *Economic Botany* 48, no. 2 (1994): 167–68.

4. DuBois, *Finnish Folk Poetry*, 285–90; Sawin, "Lönnrot's Brainchildren," 203–4.

5. "Ilmarinen's Wedding Feast," *The Kalevala*, http://www.sacred-texts.com/neu/kveng/kvrune21.htm.

6. Robert J. Braidwood et al., "Symposium: Did Many Once Live by Beer Alone?" *American Anthropologist* 55, no. 4 (October 1953): 515–26; Solomon H. Katz and Mary M. Vogt, "Bread and Beer: The Early Uses of Cereals in the Human Diet," *Expedition* 28, no. 2 (1986): 23–34; Li Liu, Jiajing Wang, Danny Rosenberg, Hao Zhao, Györgi Lengyel, and Dani Nadel, "Fermented Beverage and Food Storage in 13,000 y-old Stone Mortars at Raqefet Cave, Israel: Investigating Natufian Ritual Feasting," *Journal of Archaeological Science: Reports* 21 (2018): 783–93; Amaya Arranz-Otaegui, Lara Gonzalez Carretero, Monica N. Ramsey, Dorian Q. Fuller,

and Tobias Richter, "Archaeobotanical Evidence Reveals the Origins of Bread 14,400 Years Ago in Northeastern Jordan," *Proceedings of the National Academy of Sciences* 115, no. 31 (July 31, 2018): 7925–30.

7. Patrick McGovern, *Uncorking the Past: The Quest for Wine, Beer, and Other Alcoholic Beverages* (Berkeley: University of California Press, 2009), 31–39, 122–23, 235.

8. Liu, Wang, Rosenberg, Zhao, Lengyel, and Nadel, "Fermented Beverage at Raqefet Cave"; Li Liu, Jiajing Wang, Danny Rosenberg, Hao Zhao, Györgi Lengyel, and Dani Nadel, "Response to Comments on Archaeological Reconstruction of 13,000-y old Natufian Beer Making at Raqefet Cave, Israel," *Journal of Archaeological Science: Reports* 28 (2019): 101914.

9. Jeremy Geller, "Bread and Beer in Fourth Millennium Egypt," *Food and Foodways* 5, no. 3 (1993): 265.

10. Robert L. Curtis, *Ancient Food Technology* (Leiden: Brill, 2001), 134.

11. Delwen Samuel, "Archaeology of Ancient Egyptian Beer," *Journal of the American Society of Brewing Chemists* 54, no. 1 (1996): 3–12; Curtis, *Ancient Food Technology*, 132–33; Geller, "Bread and Beer," 259.

12. "Hymn to Ninkasi," translated by Miguel Civil, accessed May 29, 2024, https://people.umass.edu/mrenaud/kas/poem.htm . See also Virginia R. Badler, Patrick E. McGovern, and Rudolph H. Michel, "Drink and Be Merry! Infrared Spectroscopy and Ancient Near Eastern Wine," *MASCA Research Papers in Science and Archaeology* 7 (1990): 25–36; McGovern, *Uncorking the Past*, 66–68, 97; Jean Bottéro, *The Oldest Cuisine in the World: Cooking in Mesopotamia*, trans. Teresa Lavender Fagan (Chicago: University of Chicago Press, 2004), 89.

13. Elsa Perruchini, Claudia Glatz, M. M. Hald, J. Casana, and J. L. Toney, "Revealing Invisible Brews: A New Approach to the Chemical Identification of Ancient Beer," *Journal of Archaeological Science* 100 (2018): 176–90; McGovern, *Uncorking the Past*, 97.

14. McGovern, *Uncorking the Past*, 66; Curtis, *Ancient Food Technology*, 137; H. F. Lutz, *Viticulture and Brewing in the Ancient Orient* (New York: G. E. Stechert, 1922), 76–77, 83.

15. David N. Edwards, "Sorghum, Beer, and Kushite Society," *Norwegian Archaeological Review* 29, no. 2 (1996): 65–77; McGovern, *Uncorking the Past*, 234–59; Lutz, *Viticulture and Brewing*, 72.

16. Jiajing Wang, Li Liu, Terry Ball, Linjie Yu, Yuanqing Li, and Fulai Xing, "Revealing a 5000-y-old Beer Recipe in China," *Proceedings of the National Academy of Sciences* 113, no. 23 (June 7, 2016): 6444–48; H. T. Huang, *Fermentations and Food Science*, part 5 of *Biology and Biological Technology*, volume 6 of *Science and Civilisation in China*, ed. Joseph Needham (Cambridge: Cambridge University Press, 2000), 151–68.

17. Quote from Huang, *Fermentations and Food Science*, 161.

Notes to pages 25–30

18. Ibid., 169–88, 279; Jiri Jakl, unpublished manuscript, 73; James McHugh, *An Unholy Brew: Alcohol in Indian History and Religions* (New York: Oxford University Press, 2021), 32–37.

19. Huang, *Fermentations and Food Science*, 154; McGovern, *Uncorking the Past*, 255.

20. Quotes from Justin Jennings, Kathleen L. Antrobus, Sam J. Atencio, Erin Glavich, Rebecca Johnson, German Loffler, and Christine Luu, "'Drinking Beer in a Blissful Mood': Alcohol Production, Operational Chains, and Feasting in the Ancient World," *Current Anthropology* 46, no. 2 (April 2005): 279. See also Tamara L. Bray, "Inka Pottery as Culinary Equipment: Food, Feasting, and Gender in Imperial State Design," *Latin American Antiquity* 14, no. 1 (2003): 3–28.

21. Bruman, *Alcohol in Ancient Mexico*, 68–73, 86; William B. Taylor, *Drinking, Homicide, and Rebellion in Colonial Mexican Villages* (Stanford, CA: Stanford University Press, 1979); Raúl Guerrero Guerrero, *El pulque: Religión, cultura, folklore* (Mexico City: INAH, 1980); Marisol Correa-Ascencio, Ian G. Robertson, Oralia Cabrera-Cortés, Rubén Cabrera-Castro, and Richard P. Evershed, "Pulque Production from Fermented Agave Sap as a Dietary Supplement in Prehispanic Mesoamerica," *Proceedings of the National Academy of Sciences* 111, no. 39 (2014): 14223–28.

22. Max Nelson, *The Barbarian's Beverage: A History of Beer in Ancient Europe* (London: Routledge, 2005), 13–21, 49, 60, 80; Unger, *Beer in the Middle Ages*, 21; Ingrid Tamerl, *Das Holzfass in der römischen Antike* (Innsbruck: Studienverlag, 2010).

23. Judith M. Bennett, *Ale, Beer, and Brewsters in England: Women's Work in a Changing World, 1300–1600* (New York: Oxford University Press, 1996), 17–18; Unger, *Beer in the Middle Ages*, 28–29.

24. McGovern, *Uncorking the Past*, 258–59; Nelson, *The Barbarian's Beverage*, 45.

25. Michael Dietler, "Driven by Drink: The Role of Drinking in the Political Economy and the Case of Early Iron Age France," *Journal of Anthropological Archaeology* 9 (1990): 367; McGovern, *Uncorking the Past*, 257.

26. Sarah Milledge Nelson, "Feasting the Ancestors in Early China," in *The Archaeology and Politics of Food and Feasting in Early States and Empires*, ed. Tamara L. Bray (New York: Kluwer Academic, 2003), 65–89. See also Anne P. Underhill, "An Analysis of Mortuary Ritual at the Dawenkou Site, Shandong China," *Journal of East Asian Archaeology* 2, no. 1–2 (2000): 93–127; Anne P. Underhill, "Urbanization and New Social Contexts for Consumption of Food and Drinks in Northern China," *Archaeological Research in Asia* 14 (2018): 7–19; Perruchini, Glatz, Hald, Casana, and Toney, "Revealing Invisible Beers," 179; Nelson, *The Barbarian's Beverage*, 17; Lutz, *Viticulture and Brewing*, 99, 105.

27. Curtis, *Ancient Food Technology*, 211; Jeffrey H. Tigay, *The Evolution of the Gilgamesh Epic* (Philadelphia: University of Pennsylvania Press, 1982), 206–8.

28. McHugh, *An Unholy Brew*, 88–92, quote from 81; Unger, *Beer in the Middle Ages*, 26, 27, 39.

29. Huang, *Fermentations and Food Science*, 161, 173, 180, 257, quotes from 170–71.

260   *Notes to pages 31–35*

30. Lutz, *Viticulture and Brewing*, 73, 107, 110, 128; Bottéro, *Oldest Cuisine in the World*, 77.

31. Taylor, *Drinking, Homicide, and Rebellion*, 61–62; Bruman, *Alcohol in Ancient Mexico*, 63.

32. Roel Sterckx, "Alcohol and Historiography in Early China," *Global Food History* 1, no. 1 (2015): 16, 17.

33. McHugh, *An Unholy Brew*, 11, 21, 79, 83–85.

34. Nelson, *The Barbarian's Beverage*, 25–39, quote from 46.

35. Ibid., 48, 162 note 42.

36. Ibid., 76; Bennett, *Ale, Beer, and Brewsters*, 18–24; Judith M. Bennett, "Conviviality and Charity in Medieval and Early Modern England," *Past and Present* 134 (February 1992): 19–41.

37. Bennett, *Ale, Beer, and Brewsters*, 106; Unger, *Beer in the Middle Ages*, 31–33, 41, 207–13.

38. Zahi Hawass, "The Discovery of the Tombs of the Pyramid Builders at Giza," accessed September 3, 2021, https://www.guardians.net/hawass/buildtomb.htm; Lutz, *Viticulture and Brewing*, 116; Geller, "Bread and Beer in Egypt," 265.

39. Paul S. Goldstein, "From Stew-Eaters to Maize-Drinker: The *Chicha* Economy and the Tiwanaku Expansion," in *The Archaeology and Politics of Food and Feasting in Early States and Empires*, ed. Tamara L. Bray (New York: Kluwer Academic, 2003), 143–72, quotes from 144, 166; John E. Clark and Michael Blake, "The Power of Prestige: Competitive Generosity and the Emergence of Rank Societies in Lowland Mesoamerica," in *Factional Competition and Political Development in the New World*, ed. Elizabeth M. Brumfiel and John W. Fox (Cambridge: Cambridge University Press, 1994), 17–30.

40. Michael E. Moseley et al., "Burning Down the Brewery: Establishing and Evacuating an Imperial Colony at Cerro Baúl, Peru," *Proceedings of the National Academy of Sciences* 102, no. 48 (November 29, 2005): 17264–71; Matthew Sayre, David Goldstein, William Whitehead, and Patrick Ryan Williams, "A Marked Preference: *Chicha de molle* and Huari State Consumption Practices," *Ñawpa Pacha: Journal of Andean Archaeology* 32, no. 2 (2012): 231–82; William H. Isbell and Amy Groleau, "The Wari Brewer Woman: Feasting, Gender, Offerings, and Memory," in *Inside Ancient Kitchens: New Directions in the Study of Ancient Meals and Feasts*, ed. Elizabeth A. Klarich (Boulder: University Press of Colorado, 2010), 191–219.

41. Peter Gose, "The State as a Chosen Woman: Brideservice and the Feeding of Tributaries in the Inka Empire," *American Anthropologist* 102, no. 1 (March 2000): 86; Bray, "Inka Pottery as Culinary Equipment"; Christine Hastorf, "Gender, Space, and Food in Prehistory," in *Engendering Archaeology: Women and Prehistory*, ed. Joan M. Gero and Margaret W. Conkey (Oxford: Basil Blackwell, 1991), 150–51.

42. Huang, *Fermentations and Food Science*, 1117; Lutz, *Viticulture and Brewing*, 72, 76.

43. Quoted in Jackson Yue Bin Guo, "Tastes in the Jade Flagons: Alcohol Tasting and the Reconstruction of Late Imperial Chinese Literati Identity, 15th–18th Centuries," *Global Food History* 7, no. 3 (2021): 189.

44. Cobo, *History of the Inca Empire*, 28; Lutz, *Viticulture and Brewing*, 76; Bennett, *Ale, Beer, and Brewsters*, 22.

45. Unger, *Beer in the Middle Ages*, 25.

46. Guo, "Tastes in the Jade Flagons," 185, 186.

47. Quoted in Erik Aerts, "Le Houblon ou les Prix des Céréales? Expliquer la Hausse de la Consommation de Bière en Brabant et en Flandre (1300–1500)," *Food and History* 20, no. 2 (2022): 31–57; Unger, *Beer in the Middle Ages*, 26, 31–32; Nelson, *The Barbarian's Beverage*, 110–11; Ian S. Hornsey, *A History of Beer and Brewing* (London: RSC Publishing, 2003), 534.

48. Anna Scinska, Eliza Koros, Boguslaw Habrat, Andrzej Kukwa, Wojciech Kostowski, and Przemyslaw Bienkowski, "Bitter and Sweet Components of Ethanol Taste in Humans," *Drug and Alcohol Dependence* 60, no. 2 (August 1, 2000): 199–296; Lutz, *Viticulture and Brewing*, 91; Unger, *Beer in the Middle Ages*, 24; Huang, *Fermentations and Food Science*, 164.

49. George Philliskirk, "Esters," in *The Oxford Companion to Beer*, ed. Garrett Oliver (New York: Oxford University Press, 2012), 329.

50. William Ellis, *The London and Country Brewer*, 3d ed. (London: J & J Fox, 1737), 22; Bennett, *Ale, Beer, and Brewsters*, 85.

51. Quoted in Bruman, *Alcohol in Ancient Mexico*, 70. See also Hornsey, *History of Beer and Brewing*, 71.

52. Quotes from Huang, *Fermentations and Food Science*, 181. See also Perruchini, Glatz, Hald, Casana, and Toney, "Revealing Invisible Brews," 188; Bruman, *Alcohol in Ancient Mexico*, 78; Kuusi, Bosley, and Branch, *Finnish Folk Poetry*, 210.

53. Brian Stross, "Food, Foam and Fermentation in Mesoamerica," *Food, Culture, and Society* 14, no. 4 (December 2011): 477–501; Michael E. Smith, Jennifer B. Wharton, and Jan Marie Olson, "Aztec Feasts, Rituals, and Markets: Political Uses of Ceramic Vessels in a Commercial Economy," in *The Archaeology and Politics of Food and Feasting in Early States and Empires*, ed. Tamara L. Bray (New York: Kluwer Academic/Plenum Publishers, 2003), 247–49.

54. Sterckx, "Alcohol and Historiography," 16; Jeffrey M. Pilcher, "Conclusion: In Maya Food Studies, Who Is Maya? What Is Food?," in *Her Cup for Sweet Cacao: Food in Ancient Maya Society*, ed. Traci Ardren (Austin: University of Texas Press, 2020), 366–79.

55. Guo, "Tastes in the Jade Flagons," 185, 189; Lutz, *Viticulture and Brewing*, 72.

56. Jack Goody, *Cooking, Cuisine, and Class: A Study in Comparative Sociology* (Cambridge: Cambridge University Press, 1982); Rachel MacLean and Timothy Insoll, "Archaeology, Luxury and the Exotic: The Examples of Islamic Gao (Mali) and Bahrain," *World Archaeology* 34, no. 3 (February 2003): 558–70.

57. McGovern, *Uncorking the Past*, 267.

CHAPTER 2

1. Quoted in Nelson, *The Barbarian's Beverage*, 110.
2. Unger, *Beer in the Middle Ages*, 53–59.
3. See, for example, Sven Beckert, *Empire of Cotton: A Global History* (New York: Alfred A. Knopf, 2014); John Tutino, *Mexican Heartland: How Communities Shaped Capitalism, a Nation, and World History, 1500–2000* (Princeton, NJ: Princeton University Press, 2018).
4. Unger, *Beer in the Middle Ages*.
5. Ibid., 38–42.
6. Ibid., 53–59.
7. Ibid., 55–56, 79; Bennett, *Ale, Beer, and Brewsters*, 85–87.
8. Unger, *Beer in the Middle Ages*, 59, 66–67, 77–79, 86.
9. Valeria Hansen, *The Year 1000: When Explorers Connected the World—and Globalization Began* (New York: Scribner, 2020), 42.
10. Unger, *Beer in the Middle Ages*, 66–67, 93–96, 113–15.
11. Beat Kümin, *Drinking Matters: Public Houses and Social Exchange in Early Modern Central Europe* (Basingstoke: Palgrave Macmillan, 2007), quotes from 67, 97; James A. Galloway, "Driven by Drink? Ale Consumption and the Agrarian Economy of the London Region, c. 1300–1400," in *Food and Drink in Medieval Europe*, ed. Martha Carlin and Joel T. Rosenthal (London: Hambledon Press, 1998), 99; Unger, *Beer in the Middle Ages*, 52, 57, 59.
12. Unger, *Beer in the Middle Ages*, 6, 146–54; Hubert Verachtert and Guy Derdelinckx, "Belgian Acidic Beers: Daily Reminiscences of the Past," *Cerevisia* 38 (2014): 128.
13. Richard W. Unger, *A History of Brewing in Holland, 900–1900: Economy, Technology and the State* (Leiden: Brill, 2001), 213; Unger, *Beer in the Middle Ages,* 48, 59, 71, 112, 173, 180–83, 212.
14. Unger, *Beer in the Middle Ages*, 220–23.
15. Bennett, *Ale, Beer, and Brewsters*, 82–83, 88–92; Unger, *Beer in the Middle Ages*, 225–27; Unger, *Brewing in Holland*, 160–61; Kümin, *Drinking Matters*, 61, 70–71.
16. Unger, *Beer in the Middle Ages*, 185.
17. Ibid., 59, 114, 185.
18. Hornsey, *History of Beer and Brewing*, 387–88; Unger, *Brewing in Holland*, 132. On the premium of German beer in Denmark, see Gerthe Jacobsen, "Women's Work and Women's Role: Ideology and Reality in Danish Urban Society, 1300–1550," *Scandinavian Economic History Review* 31, no. 1 (1983): 17. For the Broihan legend, see Max Delbrück, *Illustriertes Brauerei-Lexicon* (Berlin: Parey, 1925), 182; Siebel, *One Hundred Years of Brewing*, 676.
19. Johann von Justi, *Oeconomische Schriften über die wichtigsten Gegenstände der Stadt- und Landwirthschaft*, 2 vols. (Berlin: Real-Schule, 1760), 2:32. See also Unger, *Brewing in Holland*, 184–88.

Notes to pages 50–55   263

20. Unger, *Beer in the Middle Ages*, 101.

21. Ibid., 231–46.

22. Tutino, *Mexican Heartland*, 66, 91.

23. Taylor, *Drinking, Homicide, and Rebellion*, 35–50, quote from 43.

24. Ibid., 47–62, quote from 57.

25. On the seventeenth-century crisis and the silver trade, see Tutino, *Mexican Heartland*; Geoffrey Parker, *Global Crisis: War, Climate Change, and the Seventeenth Century* (New Haven, CT: Yale University Press, 2013); Arturo Giráldez, *The Age of Trade: The Manila Galleons and the Dawn of the Global Economy* (Lanham, MD: Rowman and Littlefield, 2015). On alcohol consumption and social unrest, Daniel Nemser, "'To Avoid This Mixture': Rethinking Pulque in Colonial Mexico City," *Food and Foodways* 19, nos. 1–2 (2011): 98–121; John E. Kicza, "The Pulque Trade of Late Colonial Mexico City," *The Americas* 37, no. 2 (1980): 196.

26. Herman W. Konrad, *A Jesuit Hacienda in Colonial Mexico: Santa Lucía, 1756–1767* (Stanford, CA: Stanford University Press, 1980); Doris Ladd, *The Mexican Nobility at Independence, 1780–1826* (Austin: University of Texas Press, 1976); Kicza, "The Pulque Trade," 203; Tutino, *Mexican Heartland*, 102, 109; Taylor, *Drinking, Homicide, and Rebellion*, 38; Juan Pedro Viqueira Albán, *Propriety and Permissiveness in Bourbon Mexico*, trans. Sonya Lipsett-Rivera and Sergio Rivera Ayala (Wilmington, DE: SR Books, 1999), 139–41.

27. John Kicza, *Colonial Entrepreneurs, Families, and Business in Bourbon Mexico City* (Albuquerque: University of New Mexico Press, 1983), 123–29; Manuel Payno, *Memoria sobre el maguey mexicano y sus diversos productos* (Mexico City: Imprenta de A. Boix, 1864).

28. Alexander von Humboldt, *Examen político sobre la Isla de Cuba*, translated by Vicente González Arnao, 2 vols. (Gerona: A. Oliva, 1836), 2:338.

29. Payno, *Memoria sobre el maguey*, 438.

30. Manuel Orozco y Berra, *Apendice al diccionario universal de historia y geografía* (Mexico City: J. M. Andrade y F. Escalante, 1855), 361.

31. Guerrero, *El pulque*, 143. For recipes, see *El cocinero mexicano*, 3 vols. (Mexico City: Imprenta de Galvan, 1831), 3:426–48.

32. Calderón de la Barca, *Life in Mexico*, 227, 562; Guerrero, *El pulque*, 103, 112.

33. Áurea Toxqui, "Taverns and Their Influence on the Suburban Culture of Late-Nineteenth-Century Mexico City," in *The Growth of Non-Western Cities: Primary and Secondary Urban Networking, c. 900–1900*, ed. Kenneth R. Hall (Lanham, MD: Lexington Books, 2011), 241–69; Áurea Toxqui, "Breadwinners or Entrepreneurs? Women's Involvement in the *Pulquería* World of Mexico City, 1850–1910," in *Alcohol in Latin America: A Social and Cultural History*, ed. Gretchen Pierce and Áurea Toxqui (Tucson: University of Arizona Press, 2014), 104–30; Mario Ramírez Rancaño, *Ignacio Torres Adalid y la industria pulquera* (Mexico City: Plaza y Valdes, 2000); Rodolfo Ramírez Rodríguez, "La formación de un mercado regional en el noreste del valle de México. De minas, ferrocarril y

264   *Notes to pages 55–60*

haciendas pulqueras (1850–1870)," *Anuario de Historia Regional y de las Fronteras* 22, no. 1 (2017): 17–48.

34. Penelope Francks, "Inconspicuous Consumption: Sake, Beer, and the Birth of the Consumer in Japan," *Journal of Asian Studies* 68, no. 1 (February 2009): 146. On the distinctiveness of early Japanese capitalism, see David L. Howell, *Capitalism from Within: Economy, Society, and the State in a Japanese Fishery* (Berkeley: University of California Press, 1995).

35. Eric C. Rath, "Sake's Lost Women: Gender and Brewing in Pre-Modern Japan," paper presented at the Cambridge Centre for Research in the Arts, Social Sciences, and Humanities Seminar, "Beyond Cooking: Global Histories of Food Making and Gender Across the Early Modern World," April 29, 2022; Suzanne Gay, *The Moneylenders of Late Medieval Kyoto* (Honolulu: University of Hawai'i Press, 2001), 41–45; Nicolas Baumert, *Le Saké: Une exception japonaise* (Tours and Rennes: Presses universitaires François-Rabelais and Presses universitaires de Rennes, 2011), 138–42; Eric C. Rath, *Japan's Cuisines: Food, Place and Identity* (London: Reaktion, 2016), 235, n. 52.

36. Matao Miyamoto, "Quantitative Aspects of Tokugawa Economy," in *Emergence of Economic Society in Japan, 1600–1859*, vol. 1 of *The Economic History of Japan: 1600–1990*, ed. Akira Hayami, Osamu Saitô, and Ronald P. Toby (Oxford: Oxford University Press, 1999), 41–45.

37. Edward E. Pratt, *Japan's Protoindustrial Elite: The Economic Foundations of the Gōnō* (Cambridge, MA: Harvard University Press, 1999), 18, 29–30, 51, 71–79; Thomas C. Smith, "Premodern Economic Growth: Japan and the West," *Past & Present* 60 (1973): 140–41; Rath, *Japan's Cuisines*, 213.

38. Quoted in Eric C. Rath, *Food and Fantasy in Early Modern Japan* (Berkeley: University of California Press, 2006), 66.

39. Ibid.; Eric C. Rath, "The Tastiest Dish in Edo: Print, Performance, and Culinary Entertainment in Early-Modern Japan," *East Asian Publishing and Society* 3 (2013): 202; Eric C. Rath, "Known Unknowns in Japanese Food History," *Asia Pacific Perspectives* 16, no. 2 (2020), https://jayna.usfca.edu/asia-pacific-perspecti ves/journal/asia-pacific-perspectives/v16n2/rath.html; Francks, "Inconspicuous Consumption," 155–56.

40. Tessa Morris-Suzuki, *The Technological Transformation of Japan: From the Seventeenth to the Twenty-First Century* (Cambridge: Cambridge University Press, 1994), 49–52; Baumert, *Le Saké*, 144–46, 162–64; Rath, *Japan's Cuisines*, 73, 235.

41. Eric C. Rath, "The Invention of Local Food," in *Globalization and Asian Cuisine: Transnational Networks and Contact Zones*, ed. James Farrer (London: Palgrave Macmillan, 2015), 145–64; Morris Suzuki, *The Technological Transformation of Japan*, 50; Rath, *Japan's Cuisines*, 174–75; Pratt, *Japan's Protoindustrial Elite*, 52, 60.

42. Pratt, *Japan's Protoindustrial Elite*, 6, 22, 29, 59–60, 71; Smith, "Premodern Economic Growth," 140.

Notes to pages 61–67

43. Brian W. Platt, "Elegance, Prosperity, Crisis: Three Generations of Tokugawa Village Elites," *Monumenta Nipponica* 55, no. 1 (Spring 2000): 60; Eric C. Rath, "Sex and Sea Bream: Food and Prostitution in Hishikawa Moronobu's A Visit to the Yoshiwara," in *Seduction: Japan's Floating World: The John C. Weber Collection*, ed. Laura W. Allen (San Francisco: Asian Art Museum, 2015), 32; Franckes, "Inconspicuous Consumption," 142, 145.

44. Mathias, *The Brewing Industry in England*, xxvi.

45. Quoted in Unger, *Beer in the Middle Ages*, 99. There is a vast literature on the introduction of beer to Britain. See Milan Pajec, "'Ale for the Englishman Is a Natural Drink': The Dutch and the Origins of Beer Brewing in Late Medieval England," *Journal of Medieval History* 45, no. 3 (2019): 285–300.

46. Henry Buttes (1599) quoted in George Evans Light, "All Hopped Up: Beer, Cultivated National Identity, and Anglo-Dutch Relations, 1524–1625," *Jx* 2, no. 2 (Spring 1998): 164.

47. John Gerard, *The Herball or Generall Historie of Plants* (London: John Norton, 1597), 737–38; Lien Bich Luu, *Immigrants and the Industries of London, 1500–1700* (Aldershot: Ashgate, 2005), 270, 279; Light, "All Hopped Up," 164.

48. Bennett, *Ale, Beer, and Brewsters*, 61–63, 95–97; Joan Thirsk, *Foods in Early Modern England: Phases, Fads, Fashions, 1500–1760* (Hambledon: Continuum, 2007), 305–6.

49. Mathias, *The Brewing Industry*, 6; Luu, *Immigrants and Industries*, 276–78, 189, 201, 287; Unger, *Beer in the Middle Ages*, 129–30.

50. Martyn Cornell, "Porter for the Geography of Beer," in *The Geography of Beer: Culture and Economics*, ed. Nancy Hoalst-Pullen and Mark W. Patterson (Cham: SpringerLink, 2020), 8. See also John Robert Krenzke, "Resistance by the Pint: How London Brewers Shaped the Excise and Created London's Favorite Beer," *Journal of Early Modern History* 23 (2019): 507.

51. Mathias, *The Brewing Industry*, 14–15, 23, 25, 58, 413, quote from 62; James Sumner, "Status, Scale, and Secret Ingredients: The Retrospective Invention of London Porter," *History and Technology* 24, no. 3 (September 2008): 292, 299.

52. Mathias, *The Brewing Industry*, 66, 74, 83, 94; James Sumner, "John Richardson, Saccharometry and the Pounds-per-Barrel Extract: The Construction of a Quantity," *British Journal for the History of Science* 34 (2001): 255–73.

53. Mathias, *The Brewing Industry*, 26, 107–8, 132, 146, 231. Note that "twopenny" pale ale was priced by the pint.

54. W. L. Tizard, *The Theory and Practice of Brewing*, 2d ed. (London: Gilbert and Rivington, 1846), 116.

55. Mathias, *The Brewing Industry*, 12, 15–16, 171–91.

56. Ibid., 151–61, 167; Patrick Lynch and John Vaizey, *Guinness's Brewery in the Irish Economy, 1759–1876* (Cambridge: Cambridge University Press, 1960), 3–6.

57. Sumner, "Status, Scale, and Secret Ingredients," 299–301; Mathias, *The Brewing Industry*, 72, 77, 94, 419–23.

Notes to pages 68–71

58. B. Ann Tlusty, "Full Cups, Full Coffers: Tax Strategies and Consumer Culture in the Early Modern German Cities," *German History* 32, no. 1 (2014): 10; Unger, *Brewing in the Middle Ages*, 109, 114.

59. Brian Gibson and Giani Litti, "*Saccharomyces pastorianus*: Genomic Insights Inspiring Innovation for Industry," *Yeast* 32, no. 1 (January 2015): 17–27.

60. Horst Dornbusch, Michael Zepf, and Garrett Oliver, "Lager," in *The Oxford Companion to Beer*, ed. Garrett Oliver (New York: Oxford University Press, 2012), 532; Starke, *Von Brauerhandwerk zur Brauindustrie*, 47.

61. Hackel-Stehr, "Das Brauwesen in Bayern," 81–82, 88–89.

62. Fritz Sedlmayr, *Die "prewen" Munchens seit 1363 bis zu aufhebung der Lehensverleihung durch den Landesfursten (1814)* (Nuremberg: Hans Carl, 1969), 246. See also Unger, *Beer in the Middle Ages*, 149.

63. Benno Scharl, *Beschreibung der Braunbier-Brauerei im Königreich Bayern* (Munich: Joseph Lindbauer, 1826), 34; Unger, *Beer in the Middle Ages*, 149–50, 153; Unger, *Brewing in Holland*, 353; Bertrand Hell, *Bière et Alchimie* (Paris: L'Oeil d'Or, 2015), 28.

64. Hackel Stehr, "Das Brauwesen in Bayern," 33, 61–62, 349–50; Unger, *Beer in the Middle Ages*, 57, 109, 158.

65. Sheilagh C. Ogilvie, *A Bitter Living: Women, Markets, and Social Capital in Early Modern Germany* (Oxford: Oxford University Press, 2003); Sheilagh C. Ogilvie, "Consumption, Social Capital, and the 'Industrious Revolution' in Early Modern Germany," *Journal of Economic History* 70, no. 2 (June 2010): 287–325.

66. Karl Gattinger, *Bier und Landesherrschaft: Das Weißbiermonopol der Wittelsbacher unter Maximilian I. von Bayern* (Munich: Karl M. Lipp, 2007), 47, 71–74, 192; Hackel Stehr, "Das Brauwesen in Bayern," 163, 167, 224; Unger, *Beer in the Middle Ages*, 109, 114, 191; Scharl, *Beschreibung der Braunbier-Brauerei*, 77.

67. Qutoed in Tlusty, "Full Cups, Full Coffers," 17. See also B. Ann Tlusty, *Bacchus and Civic Order: The Culture of Drink in Early Modern Germany* (Charlottesville: University Press of Virginia, 2001), 204–5; Kümin, *Drinking Matters*, 18, 30; Kim Carpenter, "'We Demand Good and Healthy Beer': The Nutritional and Social Significance of Beer for the Lower Classes in Mid-Nineteenth-Century Munich," in *The City and the Senses*, ed. Alexander Cowan and Jill Steward (New York: Routledge, 2016), 136.

68. Scharl, *Beschreibung der Braunbier-Brauerei*, 81, quote from 33. See also Justi, *Oeconomische Schriften*, 2:36; Unger, *Beer in the Middle Ages*, 153–54; Hackel Stehr, "Das Brauwesen im Bayern," 343; Wolfgang Behringer, *Die Spaten-Brauerei, 1397–1997: Die Geschichte eines Münchner Unternehmens vom Mittelalter bis zur Gegenwart* (Munich: Piper, 1997), 135–36.

69. Lisa Bauer and Sonja Meinelt, "Munich from Below," in *Ecopolis München: Environmental Histories of a City*, ed. L. Sasha Gora, Environment & Society Portal, *Virtual Exhibitions* 2 (2017), Rachel Carson Center for Environment and Society, http://www.environmentandsociety.org/node/8052; Unger, *Brewing in Holland*, 354.

Notes to pages 71–78   267

70. Scharl, *Beschreibung der Braunbier-Brauerei*, 62–65; Mikuláš Teich, *Bier, Wissenschaft und Wirtschaft in Deutschland, 1800–1914: Ein Beitrag zur deutschen Industrialisierungsgeschichte* (Vienna: Böhlau, 2000), 266; Elaine Leong, "Brewing Ale and Boiling Water in 1651," in *The Structures of Practical Knowledge*, ed. Mateo Valeriani (Cham: Springer, 2017), 69.

71. Kümin, *Drinking Matters*, 58; Unger, *Brewing in Holland*, 354.

72. Carpenter, "'We Demand Good Beer,'" 136–37; Behringer, *Die Spaten-Brauerei*, 123–35.

73. Scharl, *Beschreibung der Braunbier-Brauerei*, 76.

74. Eric Rath, "Sake's Lost Women."

CHAPTER 3

1. Quoted in Michael Jackson, "The Birth of Lager," March 1, 1996, http://www.beerhunter.com/documents/19133-000255.html. See also Behringer, *Die Spaten-Brauerei*, 162.

2. J. John, "Bier und Malzfabrikation in Oesterreich vom Standpunkte des Exportes," *Der Bayerische Bierbrauer* (hereafter *BaB*) 2, no. 2 (February 1867): 22.

3. Christian Schäder, *Münchner Brauindustrie, 1871–1945: Die Wirtschaftsgeschichtliche Entwicklung eines Industriezweiges* (Marburg: Tectum Verlag, 1999), 97; Behringer, *Die Spaten-Brauerei*, 166–67.

4. Siebel, *One Hundred Years of Brewing*, 61–62. See also Behringer, *Die Spaten-Brauerei*, 166–67; Gerda Möhler, *Das Münchner Oktoberfest: Vom bayerischen Landwitschaftsfest zum größten Volkfest der Welt* (Munich: BLV Verlagsgesellschaft, 1981).

5. Quoted in Behringer, *Die Spaten-Brauerei*, 166.

6. "Gabriel Sedlmayr," *BaB* 9, no. 9 (September 1874): 129–31; Behringer, *Die Spaten-Brauerei*, 173, 182–95. Production levels were recorded by volume of malt consumed; conversion from malt to beer is based on Behringer, *Löwenbräu*, 133, 161.

7. Behringer, *Die Spaten-Brauerei*, 133–34, 152–53, 179; Behringer, *Löwenbräu*, 129–46; Evelin Heckhorn and Hartmut Wiehr, *München und sein Bier: Vom Brauhandwerk zur Bierindustrie* (Munich: Hugendubel, 1989), 24–27.

8. Ernst Rüffer, "Ein Wort über das Entstehen und die Fernhaltung des Pechgeschmackes im Biere," *ABHZ* 44, no. 188 (August 12, 1904): 2221. See also Carpenter, "'We Demand Good Beer,'" 141, 144, 148; Behringer, *Die Spaten-Brauerei*, 177; Behringer, *Löwenbräu*, 128.

9. Starke, *Von Brauerhandwerk zur Brauindustrie*, 169.

10. Politisches Archiv für Auswärtiges Amt (hereafter PAAA), Berlin, R88308, C. Müller-Munz, "Verband der Bierimporteure in der Schweiz," October 5, 1923.

11. Rüffer, "Ein Wort über das Enstehen." See also Schäder, *Münchner Brauindustrie*, 164–65; Siebel, *One Hundred Years of Brewing*, 680; Starke, *Von Brauerhandwerk zur Brauindustrie*, 118, 134–35; Behringer, *Die Spaten-Brauerei*, 169, 180; Henry

268   *Notes to pages 78–83*

Godim, *Berlin und seine Brauereien: Gesamtverzeichnis der Braustandorte von 1800 bis 1925* (Berlin: Edition Berliner Unterwelten, 2016), 44, 155.

12. *Statistik des Deutschen Reiches für das Jahre 1882* (Berlin: Verlag von Puttkammer & Mühlbrecht, 1882), 220; "Bierbrauerei in Oberbayern," *ABHZ* 26, no. 61 (May 23, 1886): 706; Behringer, *Die Spaten-Brauerei,* 135, 167–69.

13. "Allgemeine Landes-Jubiläums-Ausstellung in Prag," *Der Böhmische Bierbrauer* (hereafter *BoB*) 18, no. 13 (July 1, 1891): 293–300; Starke, *Von Brauerhandwerk zur Brauindustrie,* 87.

14. Quote from "Etwas Cultur-historisches und Statistisches vom Bier," *BaB* 3, no. 8 (August 1868): 118. See also "Allgemeine Landes-Jubiläums-Ausstellung," 294–96; "Bierbrauerei in Budweis," *ABHZ* 35, no. 78 (June 30, 1895): 1202–3; Michael Jackson Collection, Special Collections, Oxford Brookes University, Oxford, UK (hereafter MJ), 4/25/34, Michael Jackson, "The History of the Original Golden Beer," typescript July 2003.

15. "Entwicklung und Stand der Dreher'schen Brauereien," *Allgemeine Hopfen Zeitung* (hereafter *AHZ*) 12 (February 13, 18, 1868): 46, 50.

16. "8. ordentliche Generalversammlung," *Wochenschrift für Brauerei* (hereafter *WfB*) 7, no. 26 (June 27, 1890): 637.

17. Quoted in Siebel, *One Hundred Years of Brewing,* 227, see also 293, 332. My thanks to Martyn Cornell.

18. Ranjit S. Dinghe, "A Taste for Temperance: How American Beer Got to Be So Bland," *Business History* 58, no. 5 (2011): 758; Eliza Leslie, *Pencil Sketches, or Outlines of Character and Manners* (Philadelphia: Carey, Lea and Blanchard, 1837), 147; Juan Ricardo Couyoumdjian, "Una bebida moderna: La cerveza en Chile en el siglo XIX," *Historia* 2, no. 37 (2004): 313.

19. Department of Homeland Security, *Yearbook of Immigration Statistics: 2008* (Washington, DC: Office of Immigration Statistics, 2009), 6; George F. W. Young, *The Germans in Chile: Immigration and Colonization, 1849–1914* (New York: Center for Migration Studies, 1974), 8.

20. Quoted in R. Körner, "Die Bierbrauei in Südamerika," *BaB* 9, no. 1 (January 1874): 10; Mimi Cowan, "Immigrants, Nativists, and the Making of Chicago, 1835–1893" (Ph.D. dissertation, Boston College, 2015); Brian Alberts, "Beer to Stay: Brewed Culture, Ethnicity, and the Market Revolution" (Ph.D. dissertation, Purdue University, 2018), 78–79, 175; Young, *The Germans in Chile,* 155–56.

21. Siebel, *One Hundred Years of Brewing;* Perry R. Duis, *The Saloon: Public Drinking in Chicago and Boston, 1880–1920* (Urbana: University of Illinois Press, 1983), 17–18; Couyoumdjian, "Una bebida moderna," 311–36; Patricio Bernedo Pinto, "Los industriales alemanes de Valdivia, 1850–1914," *Historia* 32 (1999): 5–42.

22. Susan Appel, "Refrigeration and the Architecture of Nineteenth-Century American Breweries," *IA: The Journal for the Society of Industrial Archaeology* 16, no. 1 (1990): 21–38; Cochrane, *The Pabst Brewing Company,* 112–19; Couyoumdjian,

Notes to pages 83–88 269

"Una bebida moderna," 322, 328; Körner, "Die Bierbrauerei in Südamerika," 10–13; Siebel, *One Hundred Years of Brewing*, 644.

23. *Cincinnati Commercial*, March 6, 1875; *Morning Oregonian*, September 8, 1879.

24. Quoted in Cochrane, *The Pabst Brewing Company*, 116.

25. Ogle, *Ambitious Brew*, 80–83.

26. Bernedo Pinto, "Los industriales alemanes de Valdivia," 17; Couyoumdjian, "Una bebida moderna," 323–24; Bureau of Foreign and Domestic Commerce, *Trade Directory of South America* (Washington, DC: Government Printing Office, 1914), 97, 98.

27. John Simmons Ceccatti, "Science in the Brewery: Pure Yeast Culture and the Transformation of Brewing Practices in Germany at the End of the Nineteenth Century" (Ph.D. dissertation, University of Chicago, 2001); Siebel, *One Hundred Years of Brewing*, 61–75, 92, 121–34; Mikael Hard, "In the Icy Waters of Calculation: The Scientification of Refrigeration Technology and the Rationalization of the Brewing Industry in the 19th Century" (Ph.D. dissertation, University of Gothenburg, 1988).

28. "Mittheilungen aus der Staatsbrauerei und Versuchsbrauerei in Weihenstephan," *BaB* 2, no. 3 (March 1867): 43–45; "Etwas Cultur-historisches vom Bier," 123; Behringer, *Die Spaten-Brauerei*, 152; Ceccatti, "Science in the Brewery," 43; Karl Kretschmer, "Ein Beitrag zur Geschichte und Technologie der Untergärung," in *Jahrbuch der Gesellschaft für die Geschichte und Bibliographie des Brauwesens* (Berlin: VLB, 1983), 123–93; Cochrane, *The Pabst Brewing Company*, 112–13; Francis Wyatt, "Presidential Address," *TABI* 1 (1901): 3, 15; E. M. Sigsworth, "Science and the Brewing Industry, 1850–1900," *Economic History Review* 17, no. 3 (1965): 538, 540.

29. John Ceccatti, "Science in the Brewery," 6, 32, 50; Cochrane, *The Pabst Brewing Company*, 112–13.

30. For a list of trade publications, see *Documentary History of the United States Brewers' Association*, 2 vols. (New York: United States Brewers' Association, 1896), 1:79–82. See also "Abstracts of Papers Published in Other Journals," *JIB* 2, no 7 (December 1896): 558–63; "Empiricism and Science in the Brewing Industry," *ABR* 10, no. 1 (July 1896): 6–9; Ceccatti, "Science in the Brewery," 44; Ogle, *Ambitious Brew*, 75; "Etwas Cultur-historisches vom Bier," 123.

31. Ogle, *Ambitious Brew*, 44–45; Cecatti, "Science in the Brewery," 36–37; *Institute of Brewing Centenary* (London: Institute of Brewing, 1986), 12–29; Sigsworth, "Science and the Brewing Industry," 539; "Über die amerikanische Brauindustrie," *Zeitschrift für das gesammte Brauwesen* (hereafter *ZgB*) 17, no. 11 (1894): 88–89; Jules Vuylsteke, "Die Bierbereitung in der Vereinigten Staaten," *WfB* 10, no. 21 (May 26, 1893): 536–38; "Model European Brewhouse of the Tuborg Brewery," *ABR* 18, no. 8 (August 1904): 341–42.

32. Versuchs und Lehranstalt für Brauerei (hereafter VLB), Berlin, special collections, student ledger; "Verzeichnis der Theilnehmer der Brauerschule," 1897–1913.

Students were listed at the start of each course, beginning with "Der erste braukursus," *WfB* 5, no. 29 (July 20, 1888): 589–90. Weihenstephan enrollments were likewise published regularly in *Der bayerische Klein und Mittel-Brauer* (hereafter *BKMB*); *ZgB*.

33. Quoted in "Arguments on the Beer Standards," *Western Brewer* (hereafter *WB*) 31, no. 7 (July 1906): 346; see also R. E. Evans, "On the Colouring Matter Employed in the Brewery," *JIB* 1, no. 1 (January–February 1895): 33.

34. Quoted in Alfred C. Chapman, "The Production of Light Bottled Beer," *JIB* 2, no. 4 (August 1896): 277–78; Siebel, *One Hundred Years of Brewing*, 54–55.

35. Gregory Paul Casey, "Germany's Extensive History of Brewing with Malt Substitutes: Birthplace of America's Adjunct Lager Beer," *Master Brewers Association of the Americas Technical Quarterly* 57, no. 3 (2020): 152–60; Starke, *Von Brauerhandwerk zur Brauindustrie*, 415–17; Birgit Speckle, *Streit ums Bier in Bayern: Wertvorstellungen um Reinheit, Gemeinschaft und Tradition* (Münster: Waxmann, 2001); Frank von Tongeren, "Standards and International Trade Integration: A Historical Review of the German 'Reinheitsgebot,'" in *The Economics of Beer*, ed. Johan Swinnen (Oxford: Oxford University Press, 2011), 51–61.

36. Julius Liebmann, "Pure Yeast Culture in Practical Brewing," *TABI* 1 (1901): 21. See also Cecatti, "Science in the Brewery," 12–14, 52–53, 64; "Ueber den Ruhn'scheu Pasteurisirapparat," *WfB* 7, no. 4 (Jarnuary 24, 1890): 81.

37. G. Harris Morris, "Some Experiences in the Use of Pure Cultivated Yeast," *JIB* 6, no. 5 (September–October 1900): 351–52.

38. Max Wallerstein, "The Relation of the Proteids of Barley to Its Malting Qualities," *TABI* 3 (1905): 25. See also E. S. Beaven, "Barley for Brewing since 1886," *JIB* 42, no. 6 (November 1936): 489; "Canada's Malz und Gersteexport nach den Vereinigen Staaten," *ABHZ* 22, no. 80 (October 5, 1882): 716; Starke, *Von Brauerhandwerk zur Brauindustrie*, 484.

39. Max Levy, "Untersuchungen der Hopfen des Jahrganges 1891," *Bayerische Brauer-Journal* (hereafter *BBJ*) 2, no. 37 (September 17, 1892): 437; F. Schönfeld, "Judging the Aroma of Hops," *The Brewers' Journal* 40, no. 4 (February 1916): 146.

40. Emanuel Gross, *Hops in Their Botanical, Agricultural and Technical Aspect and as an Article of Commerce*, trans. Charles Salter (London: Scott, Greenwood, and Co, 1900), 309. See also David Fairchild, *The World Was My Garden: Travels of a Plant Explorer* (New York: Charles Scribner's Sons, 1939), 167–69.

41. Heinrich Joh. Barth, Christiane Klinke, and Clause Schmidt, *The Hop Atlas: The History and Geography of the Cultivated Plant* (Nuremberg: Joh. Barth & Sohn, 1994), 30–38; *Report from the Select Committee on the Hop Industry* (London: Henry Hansard and Son, 1890), 2–3; "Imports of German Hops in the United States," *ABR* 10, no. 6 (December 1896): 210.

42. Horace Brown and Harris Morris, "Analyse eines Bieres aus dem letzen Jahrhundert," *ABHZ* 30, no. 41 (March 23, 1890): 515; E. Leyfer, "Colorimetrie des Bieres," *BaB* 4, no. 3 (March 1869): 49–60.

Notes to pages 90–97

43. Georg Holzner, "Dr. Elsner's Ansichten über Bieranalysen," *ZgB* 13 (1878): 487.

44. E. Donath, "Die Zusammensetzung der Biere des Jahres 1899," *WfB* 28, no. 24 (June 15, 1900): 343–45; Robert Wahl and Max Henius, *American Handy Book of the Brewing, Malting, and Auxiliary Trades*, 2d ed. (Chicago: Wahl & Henius, 1902), 823–30.

45. Michaela Knör, "Christel Goslich," in *125 Jahre Versuchs- und Lehranstalt für Brauerei in Berlin e.V.* (Berlin: VLB, 2008), 53; "Bericht uber den Buchhaltungskurs," *BKMB* 30, no. 12 (September 1919); "Maschinenfabrik Germania," *WfB* 3, no. 8 (February 19, 1886): 112; *La Bière et les Boissons Fermentées* 19, no. 1 (January 1911); G. Graf, "Der Hopfen und seine Kultur in Bayern," *ZgB* 31, no. 20 (May 15, 1908): 212; *Tenth Anniversary Reunion. Alumni and Former Students American Brewing Academy of Chicago* (Chicago: Blakely Printing Company, 1901), unpaginated directory of auxiliary trades.

46. Starke, *Von Brauerhandwerk zur Brauindustrie*, 478, 480; Richard Wilson, "The British Brewing Industry since 1750," in *The Brewing Industry: A Guide to Historical Records*, ed. Lesley Richmond and Alison Turton (Manchester: Manchester University Press, 1990), 1.

47. Siebel, *One Hundred Years of Brewing*, 608, 697, 702, 712, 716–17; Teuteberg, "Die Nahrung der socialen Unterschichten," cited by Carpenter, "'We Demand Good Beer,'" 144.

48. Carpenter, "'We Demand Good Beer,'" 153.

49. Behringer, *Löwenbräu*, 119; "Warum Bier nicht aus Gläsern getrunken warden soll," *ABHZ* 30, no 43 (March 28, 1890): 539–40.

50. James S. Roberts, *Drink, Temperance and the Working Class in Nineteenth-Century Germany* (Boston: George Allen & Unwin 1984), 46–47, 116; Mikuláš Teich, "The Mass Production of Draught and Bottled Beer in Germany, 1880–1914: A Note," in *Dynamics of the International Brewing Industry since 1800*, ed. R. G. Wilson and T. R. Gourvish (London: Routledge, 1998), 78–79.

51. Henry Vizetelly, *Berlin under the New Empire*, 2 vols. (London: Tinsley Brothers, 1879), 2:328; Carpenter, "'We Demand Good Beer,'" 154.

52. T. J. Clark, *The Painting of Modern Life: Paris in the Art of Manet and His Followers* (London: Thames and Hudson, 1985), 234, 241. See also Fiona Fisher, "Presenting the Perfect Pint: Drink and Visual Pleasure in Late Nineteenth-Century London," *Visual Resources* 28, no. 4 (2012): 324–39; Ogle, *Ambitious Brew*, 86–92; Mark Girouard, *Victorian Pubs* (New Haven: Yale University Press, 1984), 110; David W. Gutzke, "Gender, Class, and Public Drinking during the First World War," *Histoire sociale/Social History* 27, no. 54 (November 1994): 367–91; Gourvish and Wilson, *The British Brewing Industry*, 267–73, 296, 435.

53. Colin C. Owen, *"The Greatest Brewery in the World": A History of Bass, Ratcliff, & Gretton* (Chesterfield: Derbyshire Record Society, 1992), 65; Starke, *Von Brauerhandwerk zur Brauindustrie*, 334; Max Nelson, "The History of the Wood-Pulp Beer Coaster," *American Breweriana Journal, Museum Commemorative*

Edition (2008): 82–83; Behringer, *Die Spaten-brauerei*, 97; Cochrane, *The Pabst Brewing Company*, 130; Duis, *The Saloon*, 22–23. José Falce, *La Bière: Une histoire de femmes* (Paris: L'Harmattan, 2015).

54. "Deutsche Exportbiere," *ABHZ* 22, no. 5 (January 15, 1882): 36.

55. "Pseudo-Medaillen von St Louis in Sicht," *Tageszeitung für Brauerei* 2, no. 231 (October 1, 1904): 1059.

56. Cochrane, *The Pabst Brewing Company*, 137–38.

57. August Dehme, "Beschreibung von Eiswagen zum Biertransport im Sommer," *BaB* 3, no. 5 (May 1868): 88–89; Gourvish and Wilson, *The British Brewing Industry*, 151–65; Duis, *The Saloon*, 23–24.

58. "Die Brauindustrie Deutschlands in den letzten zwei Decennien," *BBJ* 2, no. 29 (July 23, 1892): 338; "Bierbrauerei in Oberbayern," 706; W. May, "Statistisches," *ZgB* 17, no. 8 (1894): 64, 209; John, "Bier und Malzfabrikation in Oesterreich," 22.

59. "Ueber den Bierconsum in Frankreich," *WfB* 3, no. 38 (September 17, 1886): 595; "Die Konkurrenz der Biere in Paris," *WfB* 3, no. 49 (December 3, 1886): 757; M. Döring, "Die Bier-Sorten in Russland," *ABHZ* 26, no. 26 (February 28, 1886): 298; Georg Henne, "Ueber die Bierbrauerei-Verhältnisse in Sibirien," *WfB* 14, no. 19 (May 7, 1897): 220; "Ungarn's Brauindustrie," *ABHZ* 23, no. 93 (November 22, 1883): 971; "Bierverkehr in Serbien," *ABHZ* 30, no. 65 (May 9, 1890): 814.

60. "Saazer Hopfen in Philadelphia," *Der Schwäbische Bierbrauer* (hereafter *SB*) 10, no. 37 (September 11, 1881): 304. Unger, *Brewing in Holland*, 355–56.

61. John, "Bier und Malzfabrikation in Oesterreich," 23, 24.

62. "Die Fortschritte im Brauwesen auf den hochfürstl," *BaB* 8, no 7 (July 1873): 104.

63. Starke, *Von Brauerhandwerk zur Brauindustrie*, 82, 85, 334.

64. "Bières belges et bières étrangères," *Gazette De Charleroi*, March 13, 1930.

65. Rach, "Discussion of Dr. Wyatt's Paper," *TABI* 3 (1906): 234; "Frankreichs Biereinfuhr in Deutschland," *SB* 11, no. 16 (April 16, 1882): 123–24.

66. John, "Bier und Malzfabrikation in Oesterreich," 25.

67. Schäder, *Münchner Brauindustrie*, 97.

68. "Bierbrauerei in Preussisch-Schlesien," *ABHZ* 22, no. 32 (April 20, 1882): 255; Siebel, *One Hundred Years of Brewing*, 681.

69. Ernst Thomas, "Ueber die herstellung von Dortmunder Bier," *ABHZ* 35, no. 75 (June 23, 1895): 1151; "Bierbrauerei in Berlin," *ABHZ* 22, no. 90 (November 9, 1882): 821; Godim, *Berlin und seine Brauereien*, 100; Wilhelm Windisch, "Pilsener Bier—norddeutsches helles Bier," *WfB* 14, no. 30 (July 23, 1897): 377.

70. John, "Bier und Malzfabrikation in Oesterreich," 24; "Das Darren des Malzes," *BoB* 26, no. 1 (January 1, 1899): 1–5.

71. Windisch, "Pilsener Bier," 378. G. Kohlrausch, "Analysen einiger österreichischen Biere," *SB* 28, no. 4 (July 11, 1875): 161.

72. Alexander Bain and Julius Liebmann, "Discussion," *TABI* 1 (1902): 29–30.

73. Bode, "Pilsener Bier," *Tageszeitung für Brauerei* 2, no. 74 (March 27, 1904): 338.

Notes to pages 101–105

74. Windisch, "Pilsener Bier," 380. On Delbrück, see Ceccatti, "Science in the Brewery," 132.

75. Carl Rach, "Have We Ever Properly Tried to Brew Bavarian Beer," *TABI* 2 (1902): 177; Francis Wyatt, "The Proper Brewing of the Best Beers," *TABI* 2 (1902): 188.

76. Alfred C. Chapman, "The Production of Light Bottled Beer," *JIB* 2, no. 4 (August 1896): 274; Sigsworth, "Science and the Brewing Industry," 545–46; Gourvish and Wilson, *The British Brewing Industry*, 40–47, 78–101; R. G. Wilson, "The Changing Taste for Beer in Victorian Britain," in *Dynamics of the International Brewing Industry since 1800*, ed. R. G. Wilson and T. R. Gourvish (London: Routledge, 1998), 93–104.

77. W. L. Hiepe, "Pure Beer," *JIB* 2, no. 6 (November–December 1896): 497.

78. "Californisches Steam Bier," *ABHZ* 35, no. 20 (March 8, 1895): 437; Henry O. Sturm, "The Brewing of Ale in America and Canada," *Brewers Technical Review* 10, no. 12 (November 1935): 380; Zachary Nowak, "Something Brewing in Boston: A Study of Forward Integration in American Breweries at the Turn of the Twentieth Century," *Enterprise & Society* 18, no. 2 (June 2017): 332; Rach, "Discussion," *TABI* 1 (1901): 111.

79. "Fragenkaften," *WfB* 7, no. 42 (October 17, 1890): 1089; Starke, *Von Brauerhandwerk zur Brauindustrie*, 359; Rach, "Discussion," *TABI* 1 (1901): 119–20.

80. Johannes Krudewig, "Trinkt Kölner BoerL Quer durch Kölner Hrauhäuser (1929)," accessed April 5, 2019, https://www.koelner-brauerei-verband.de/historie/historis che-koelnische-brauhaeuser/trinkt-koelner-bier-quer-durch-koelner-brauhaeuser-1929.html.

81. "Personal Mention," *ABR* 18, no. 9 (September 1, 1904): 393. Paul Mumme, "Obergärige Biereim allgemeinen und Danziger Topenbier im besonderen," *WfB* 23, no. 2 (January 13, 1906): 12–16; "Etwas Cultur-historisches vom Bier"; Starke, *Von Brauerhandwerk zur Brauindustrie*, 119; F. Schönfeld "Wird der Character des Berliner Weissbieres durch die Herstellung des blanken Weissbieres und durch kurzes Kochen der Würze geändert?" *WfB* 17, no. 19 (May 11, 1900): 267–68; Eduard Maria Schranka, "Culturhistorisch-literarisches Lexikon der Biere und Biernamen," *BoB* 18, no. 21 (November 1, 1891): 492–93; Godim, *Berlin und seine Brauereien*, 32–33, 158–60.

82. "Ueber die Gründung neuer Aktienbrauereien," *WfB* 5, no. 25 (June 22, 1888): 497. See also Paul Sturges, "Beer and Books: Michael Thomas Bass, Derby Public Library, and the Philanthropy of the Beerage," *Libraries and Culture* 31, no. 2 (Spring 1996): 251–53; Mary O'Sullivan, "Yankee Doodle Went to London: Anglo-American Breweries and the London Securities Market, 1888–92," *Economic History Review* 68, no. 4 (2015): 1365–87; Richard G. Wilson and Terry R. Gourvish, "The Foreign Dimensions of British Brewing (1880–1980)," in *Production, Marketing and Consumption of Alcoholic Beverages since the Late Middle Ages*, ed. Erik Aerts, Louis M. Cullen, and Richard G. Wilson (Leuven: Leuven University Press, 1990),

274   *Notes to pages 105–109*

122–37; Cochrane, *The Pabst Brewing Company*, 180; Couyoumdjian, "Una bebida moderna," 321–22; *Trade Directory of South America*, 262, 277; Schader, *Münchner Brauindustrie*, 322–28; Cecatti, "Science in the Brewery," 33–34.

83. "Die Dampfkessel-Explosionen im Deutschen Reiche während des Jahres 1892," *WfB* 10, no. 38 (September 22, 1893): 1018; "Explosions in Breweries," *American Brewers' Review* 17, no. 1 (July 1903): 4. For examples of female brewery owners, see "Bezeichnis von den Bierbrauern in Schwabach," *ABHZ* 3, no. 63 (August 6, 1863): 253; "Die Bierbrauereien Münchens," *AHZ* 16, no. 69 (June 10, 1876): 275; "Brauereistatistik Prags," *AHZ* 16, no. 173 (December 19, 1876): 690.

84. "Zur Wahrung des 'echt Pilsener' Bieres," *BoB* 26, no. 7 (April 1, 1899): 195.

85. Starke, *Von Brauerhandwerk zur Brauindustrie*, 334–39; "Ist der Ausdruck 'Pilsener Bier' nur Zeit noch Herkunstangabe oder Bereits der Name ein Biertypus?" *WfB* 14, no. 15 (April 9, 1897): 173–74; PAAA, R89805/20, Bohlund and Reuter to Foreign Office, June 7, 1922 (3724–37); PAAA, R89807/26, "Die Pilsener Prozess vor der Reichsgericht," 1933.

86. "Rückgang des Konsums des Wiener Bieres," *ZGB* 22, no. 1 (1900): 15; Schräder, *Münchner Brauindustrie*, 92–100.

87. Karl Dubský, "Uiber Geschmacksreinheit der Biere," *BoB* 26, no. 19 (October 1, 1899): 565.

88. Martin Stack, "Was Big Beautiful? The Rise of National Breweries in America's Pre-Prohibition Brewing Industry," *Journal of Macromarketing* 30, no. 1 (2010): 50–60.

89. Jeffrey M. Pilcher, "National Beer in a Global Age: Technology, Taste, and Mobility, 1880–1914," *Quaderni storici* 151, no. 1 (April 2016): 51–70; Wilson, "Changing Taste in Victorian Britain," 99–102; Dinghe, "A Taste for Temperance," 1–32.

90. Karl Dubský, "Ernste und heitere Betrachtungen eines Bierphilosophen," *BoB* 26, no. 16 (August 15, 1899): 475.

91. Wallerstein, "Transactions," *TABI* 2 (1902): 35.

CHAPTER 4

1. Quoted in Francie Chassen-López, "The Traje de Tehuana as National Icon: Gender, Ethnicity, and Fashion in Mexico," *The Americas* 71, no. 2 (October 2014): 301.

2. Quoted in Bill Yenne, *Guinness: The 250-Year Quest for the Perfect Pint* (Hoboken, NJ: John Wiley, 2007), 76.

3. Edgar Boulangier, *Un Hiver au Cambodge: Chasses au tigre, à l'éléphant et au buffle sauvage, souvenirs d'une mission officielle remplie en 1880–1881*, 2d ed. (Tours: Alfred Mame et Fils, 1888), 311.

4. "Der Brauer und sein Vaterland," *SB* 10, no. 26 (June 26, 1881): 205.

5. Malcolm Purinton, "Empire in a Bottle: Commerce, Culture and the Consumption of the Pilsner Beer in the British Empire, 1870–1914" (Ph.D. dissertation, Northeastern University, 2016).

Notes to pages 110–113   275

6. Biographical information for "Arthur Trevelyan Shand, New York City, 1853–1920," from Ancestry.com, accessed March 8, 2021. See also David Hughes, *"A Bottle of Guinness Please": The Colourful History of Guinness* (Wokingham, UK: Phimboy, 2006), 179–86; Yenne, *Guinness*, 66.

7. India Office Records, British Library, London (hereafter IOR), E/4/763/708, illegible, January 7, 1840; E/1/9/484, Thomas Frankland, December 31, 1718; IOR, E/1/9/456, Peter Godfrey, December 16, 1718; Unger, *Beer in the Middle Ages*, 129–30; Unger, *Brewing in Holland*, 130, 328; Rebecca Earle, *The Body of the Conquistador: Food, Race, and the Colonial Experience in Latin America, 1492–1700* (Cambridge: Cambridge University Press, 2012); E. M. Collingham, *Imperial Bodies: The Physical Experience of the Raj, c. 1800–1947* (Cambridge: Polity Press, 2001).

8. G. I. Wolseley, "The Native Army of India," *The North American Review* 127, no. 263 (July–August 1878): 136.

9. Quoted in Alan Pryor, "Indian Pale Ale: An Icon of Empire," in *Global Histories, Imperial Commodities, Local Interactions*, ed. Jonathan Curry-Machado (London: Palgrave Macmillan, 2013), 46; Gourvish and Wilson, *The British Brewing Industry*, 169–75; Malcolm Purinton, "India Pale Ale" (unpublished manuscript).

10. Hughes, *A Bottle of Guinness*, 110.

11. PAAA, R901-246260, Pretoria Consular Report, March 10, 1926; Bundesarchiv, Berlin Lichterfeld (hereafter BABL), R2-24333-a, "Export Brauereien," March 5, 1942; Hermann Kellenbenz, "Shipping and Trade between Hamburg-Bremen and the Indian Ocean, 1870–1914," *Journal of Southeast Asian Studies* 13, no. 2 (September 1982): 355, 358; J. E. O'Conor, *Review of the Accounts of the Sea-Borne Foreign Trade of British India* (Simla: Government Central Branch Press, 1883), 51; "Mittheilungen über auswärtigen Handel," *WfB*, 3, no. 10 (March 5, 1886): 139.

12. "Der Handel mit Bier in Nordafrika," *WfB* 5, no. 37 (September 14, 1888): 750. See also "Die Bierbrauerei auf der Triester Austellung 1882," *ABHZ* 22, no. 89 (November 5, 1882): 811; "Egyptens Bier-Einfuhr 1885," *WfB* 3, no. 43 (October 22, 1886): 662; "Zur Einfuhr von Bier in Jerusalem und Jaffa 1886," *WfB* 4, no. 28 (July 16, 1887): 557; "Der Brauereibetrieb in wärmeren Zonen und der Bier-Export," *WfB* 5, no. 36 (September 7, 1888): 725; Guinness Dublin Brewery, Guinness Archive, Diageo Ireland, Dublin (hereafter GDB), GDB/BR15/0729.04, J. C. Haines, "Report of Mr. Haines' Journey Through Egypt, etc.," 1907, 8; Cochrane, *The Pabst Brewing Company*, 246; Perry, "The Brewer's Trademark," *TABI* 1 (May 17, 1902): 301.

13. GDB, GDB/BR15/0729.12, J. C. Haines, "Report of the Visit of Mr. J. C. Haines to Japan, China, Straits Settlements, Ceylon, India, (North Western Provinces, Karachi, Bombay and Bengal) in Connection with Our Business There," 1900, 13, quote from 14.

14. GDB, GDB/BR15/0729.13, Arthur T. Shand, "Report of Mr. Shand's Through Journey South Africa, Egypt, etc.," 1906, 33.

276 *Notes to pages 114–117*

15. Ibid., 97.

16. Gilberto Freyre, *The English in Brazil: Aspects of British Influence on the Life, Landscape and Culture of Brazil*, trans. Christopher J. Tribe (Oxford: Boulevard, 2011), 160.

17. Karen Racine, "'This England and This Now': British Cultural and Intellectual Influence in the Spanish American Independence Era," *Hispanic American Historical Review* 90, no. 3 (2010): 423–54; *El Siglo XIX*, May 15, 1844.

18. Quoted in Sajal Nag, "Modernity and Its Adversaries: Michael Madhusudan, Formation of the 'Self' and the Politics of Othering in 19th Century India," *Economic and Political Weekly* 42, no. 5 (February 3, 2007): 431. Indra Munshi Saldanha, "On Drinking and 'Drunkenness': History of Liquor in Colonial India," *Economic and Political Weekly* 30, no. 37 (September 16, 1995): 2323–31.

19. Haines, "Report of Japan, China, Straits," 19.

20. Ibid., 19–21; Courtenay Ilbert, "British India," *Journal of the Society of Comparative Legislation*, New Series, 10, no. 2 (1910): 307.

21. Haines, "Report of Egypt," 11. Omar D. Foda, "The Pyramid and the Crown: The Egyptian Beer Industry from 1897 to 1963," *International Journal of Middle Eastern Studies* 46 (2014): 139–58. See also Shand, "Report of South Africa, Egypt," 47.

22. Shand, "Report of South Africa, Egypt," 47; Foda, "The Pyramid and the Crown," 145; Stephanie Boyle, "The Salty and the Sweet: The Role of Chickpeas at the Festival (*Mulid*) of Ahmad al-Badawi in the Egyptian Delta, 1850s to 1890s," *Global Food History* 7, no. 1 (2021): 58–70.

23. GDB, BR15/0729.01, J. C. Haines, "Report of the Visit of Mr. J. C. Haines to Australia in Connection with Our Business There," 1900, 15, 26; Haines, "Report of Japan, China, Straits," 19; GDB, BR15/0729.06, Arthur T. Shand, "Report of Mr Shand's Journey Through Australasia," 1908, 8.

24. Shand, "Report of South Africa, Egypt," 109. See also Shand, "Report of Australasia," 170–71; GDB, BR15/0729.03, Arthur T. Shand, "Report of Mr. Shand's Journey Through Australia and New Zealand," 1904, 32; Haines, "Report of Australia," 9.

25. Shand, "Report of South Africa, Egypt," 10; Shand, "Report of Australasia," 112.

26. Quote from GDB, CO05.02/05.0004.25.1, extract from letter of Goddard to Secretary, September 22, 1927. See also Owen, *"The Greatest Brewery,"* 65; GDB, BR15/0729.07, Arthur T. Shand, "Report of Mr. A. T. Shand's Journeys Through the Maritime Provinces of Canada and the West Indies," 1910, 30–31, 35; Shand, "Report of Australasia," 1908, 72–73, 108.

27. GDB, CO05.02/05.0004.36, Board Memo, December 5, 1928

28. Quoted in Simon Heap, "Beer in Nigeria: A Social Brew with an Economic Head," in *Beer in Africa: Drinking Spaces, States and Selves*, ed. Steven Van Wolputte and Mattia Fumanti (Münster: Lit Verlag, 2010), 116; Ute Röschenthaler, "The Social Life of White Man Mimbo, and the Ancestral Consumption of Bottled Beer in South-West Cameroon," in *Beer in Africa: Drinking Spaces, States and Selves*, ed. Steven Van Wolputte and Mattia Fumanti (Münster: Lit Verlag, 2010), 131–65;

GDB, CO05.02/05.0004.32, Bhen Bark to A. Guinness, Son & Co, February 11, 1930.

29. Quote from GDB, CO05.02/0004.35.2, Goddard to G. S. Green, May 27, 1927; GDB, CO05.02/05.0004.34, Goddard, "Report on Conditions Obtaining in British West Africa," June 28, 1928; GDB, CO05.02/05.0004.25.1, extract of letter from Goddard to Secretary, September 22, 1927.

30. Rajat Kanta Ray, "The Bazaar: Changing Structural Characteristics of the Indigenous Section of the Indian Economy before and after the Great Depression," *The Indian Economic and Social History Review* 25 (1988): 271; Anthony Webster, *Gentlemanly Capitalists: British Imperialism in Southeast Asia, 1770–1890* (London: I. B. Taurus, 1998).

31. Malte Fuhrmann, "Beer, the Drink of a Changing World: Beer Production and Consumption on the Shores of the Aegean in the 19th Century," *Turcica* 45 (2014): 93–94, quote from 102.

32. Susan M. Gauss and Edward Beatty, "The World's Beer: The Historical Geography of Brewing in Mexico," in *The Geography of Beer: Regions, Environment, and Societies*, ed. Mark Patterson and Nancy Hoalst Pullen (Dordrecht: Springer, 2014), 58; Malcolm F. Purinton, "Good Hope for the Pilsner: Commerce, Culture, and the Consumption of the Pilsner Beer in British Southern Africa, c. 1870–1914," in *Alcohol Flows Across Cultures: Drinking Cultures in Transnational and Comparative Perspective*, ed. Waltraud Ernst (London: Routledge, 2020), 124–25; Gerald Groenewald, "Tavern of Two Oceans: Alcohol, Taxes, and Leases in the Seventeenth-Century Dutch World," *New Contree* 73 (November 2015): 1–15; Siebel, *One Hundred Years of Brewing*, 158, 622, 627, 669; Sleeman Collection, University of Guelph (hereafter SC), Box 1, File 6, M. A. Abbey to G. Sleeman, December 4, 1871.

33. IOR, E/4/72913/25, Lt. Col. Bratton to Captain Burlton, June 24, 1836.

34. Haines, "Report of Japan, China, Straits," 15, 16; IOR, E/4/72913/84, Col. W. Cullen to Secretary of Government at Madras, October 31, 1838; IOR, E/4/950/741, Fort St. George, October 24, 1837; Prachi Raturi Misra, "The Mussoorie Brew Which Had Ghalib Hooked," *Times of India*, Oct 3, 2015, http://timesofindia.indiatimes.com/city/dehradun/The-Mussoorie-brew-which-had-Ghalib-hooked/articleshow/49210000.cms; O'Conor, *Review of the Accounts*, 51; IOR, L/MIL/7/9936/509, Commisariat Department Contract, October 18, 1884; "Brauerei in Ostindien," *ABHZ* 26, no. 51 (April 30, 1886): 595.

35. Fuhrmann, "Beer on the Aegean," 86–101; Foda, "The Pyramid and the Crown," 140, 142.

36. René Hutois, "Souvenirs de l'Ethiopie d'avant-guerrre et de sa premiere brasserie-malterie," *PJB* 69, no. 2855 (August 4, 1961): 516; PAAA, Addis Abeba/369/1, Pierre Guillaumin and Josef Pfeffer, "Geschäftsbericht der St. Georg-Brauerei," November 10, 1931; PAAA, Addis Abeba/369/15, Guillaumin to German Minister, February 2, 1933; PAAA, Addis Abeba/370/16, "Anwesenheitsliste," July

278   *Notes to pages 120–125*

28, 1935; PAAA, Addis Abeba/371/35, "Une visite à la Brasserie St. Georges," *Le Courriere d'Éthiopie*, June 20, 1930; PAAA, Addis Abeba/371/44, Manuscript Handelsregister, August 2, 1930; PAAA, Addis Abeba/372/10, Vertrag J. Pfeffer and H. Maschke, December 2, 1928; PAAA, Addis Abeba/372/57, Guillaumin to German Minister, January 16, 1933; PAAA, Addis Abeba/372/72, Tribunal Consulaire, February 9, 1933.

37. Mager, *Beer, Sociability, and Masculinity*; Purinton, "Good Hope for the Pilsner," 126–34; Shand, "Report of South Africa, Egypt," 6–9, 35.

38. B. Schirmer, "Australasian Notes," *WB* 31, no. 2 (February 1906): 79, no. 3 (March 1906): 149. "Zur Bier-Einfuhr in Neusüdwales," *WfB* 3, no. 47 (1886): 725; "Australian Brewing Industry," *Australian Brewing and Wine Journal* 58, no. 9 (June 20, 1940): 6; Shand, "Report of Australia," 60–63, 72–75; Haines, "Report of Australia," 22.

39. Haines, "Report of Australia," 7.

40. Quoted in Siebel, *One Hundred Years of Brewing*, 671.

41. GDB, BR15/0729.05, Arthur T. Shand, "Report of Mr. Shand's Journey Through South America," 1907, 53.

42. *Tenth Anniversary Reunion. Alumni and Former Students American Brewing Academy of Chicago* (Chicago: Blakely Printing Company, 1901) 146; Gabriela Recio, "El nacimiento de la industria cervecera en México, 1880–1910," in *Cruda realidad: Producción, consumo y fiscalidad de las bebidas alcohólicas en México y América Latina, siglos xvii–xx*, ed. Ernesto Sánchez Santiró (Mexico City: Instituto Mora, 2007), 155–85; "The Brewing Industry in Mexico," *The American Bottler* 27, no. 8 (August 15, 1907): 76.

43. *Revista de Yucatán*, October 14, 1918. For Dos Equis clara and oscura, see Augusto Genin, *La cerveza entre los antiguos mexicanos y en la actualidad* (Mexico City: Tip Corral Hnos, 1924), 31.

44. Quote from Mariano R. Suárez, "Una gran industria que es orgullo de México," *Excelsior*, March 11, 1959.

45. Siebel, *One Hundred Years of Brewing*, 646; A. Köllenberger, "Die Brauerei in Bolivia," *ABHZ* 26, no. 61 (May 31, 1886): 708–9.

46. Manuel Forgues, *Sinopsis químico-filosófica de la chicha boliviana y fabricación industrial del alcohol* (Cochabamba: Editorial del Universo, 1909), quotes from 14–16. On Bignon, see Paul Gootenberg, *Andean Cocaine: The Making of a Global Drug* (Chapel Hill: University of North Carolina Press, 2008), 37–43, 66.

47. *Who's Who in Japan* (Tokyo: Who's Who, 1915), 314; "Japan's Beer King Passes Away," *Japan Magazine* 23 (1933): 188.

48. Quoted by Jeffrey W. Alexander, *Brewed in Japan: The Evolution of the Japanese Beer Industry* (Vancouver: University of British Columbia Press, 2013), 8–9. Dutch sailors had earlier presented beer to the Shogun's court but left no tasting notes.

49. Clarence Ludlow Brownell, *The Heart of Japan*, 3d ed. (London: Methuen, 1904), 169. Alexander, *Brewed in Japan*, 11–14.

Notes to pages 125–128   279

50. Harold S. Williams, ed. *Tales of the Foreign Settlements in Japan* (Rutland, VT: Charles E. Tuttle, 1958), 195.

51. Alexander, *Brewed in Japan*, 56–64, quote from 33; Harald Fuess, "Der Aufbau der Bierindustrie in Japan während der Meiji-Zeit (1868–1912): Konsum, Kapital und Kompetenz," *Bochumer Jahrbuch für Ostasienforschung* 27 (2003): 238–39, 245–58. Hokkaido University Northern Studies Collection, Sapporo, Japan, Capron, Horace 014, Horace Capron, *Bīru Jōzōyō Hoppu Saibai no Yōten / Kepuron* [Important Points About the Cultivation of Hops for Beer Brewing], 1874; Pratt, *Japan's Proto-Industrial Elite*, 77; "Bierbrauerei und Bierconsum in Japan," *ABHZ* 23, no. 6 (January 21, 1883): 53; "Deutsche Brauereimaschinen für Japan," *WfB* 5, no. 22 (June 1, 1888): 438–39.

52. Alexander, *Brewed in Japan*, 59–61, 72–76; Ernest Small, "The Relationships of Hop Cultivars and Wild Variants of *Humulus lupulus*," *Canadian Journal of Botany* 58 (1980): 676–86; Jeff Haas, "'They Have No Idea What It Is to Run a Malthouse': A Wisconsin Beer Maker in Japan," *The Wisconsin Magazine of History* 87, no. 2 (December 1, 2003): 14–29.

53. Cartoon reproduced in *Biru to Nihonjin: Meiji Taisho Showa Biru Fukkyushi* [Beer and the Japanese: The History of the Spread of Beer in the Meiji, Taisho, and Showa Periods] (Tokyo: Sanseidō, 1984), 118. All translations from Japanese by Michael Roellinghoff unless otherwise indicated. See also Francks, "Inconspicuous Consumption," 158.

54. Richard Barry, *A Monster Heroism* (New York, Moffat, Yard & Co., 1905), 108; Katarzyna Cwiertka, *Modern Japanese Cuisine: Food, Power and National Identity* (London: Reaktion, 2006), 56–86; *Biru to Nihonjin*, 129, 139, 185, 217.

55. "Jōzō shiken daisankai kōshūsha no chabanashikai" [The Third Meeting of Students at the Brewing Examination Centre], *Journal of the Brewing Society of Japan* (hereafter *JBSJ*) 2, no. 2 (1907): 175.

56. Nakano Makiko, *Makiko's Diary: A Merchant Wife in 1910 Kyoto*, trans. Kazuko Smith (Stanford, CA: Stanford University Press, 1995), 149; Francks, "Inconspicuous Consumption," 158; Alexander, *Brewed in Japan*, 185.

57. Ikeda Keisui, "Seishu no Kaigai Yushutu ni Okite" [On the Export of Sake], *JBSJ* 1, no. 4 (1906): 1.

58. Quoted in Alexander, *Brewed in Japan*, 72.

59. Takenami Shō, "Jōgakusan no Kyōsei" [Acoustic Mirror of Jogakusan Mountain], *JBSJ* 3, no. 12 (1908): 70.

60. Charles Bamforth, *Beer: Tap into the Art and Science of Brewing*, 3d ed. (New York: Oxford University Press, 2009), 65.

61. Quote from Wilson, "The Changing Taste for Beer," 100.

62. Quoted in *Biru to Nihonjin*, 102.

63. "Bierbrauerei und Bierexport Japans," *Globus* 90, no. 21 (December 6, 1906): 339.

64. Theodore Jun Yoo, "Shaken or Stirred? Recreating *Makgeolli* for the Twenty-First Century," in *Encounters Old and New in World History: Essays Inspired by Jerry*

280   *Notes to pages 128–133*

         H. Bentley, ed. Alan Karras and Laura J. Mitchell (Honolulu: University of Hawai'i Press, 2017), 108.

65. Ibid., 109; Alexander, *Brewed in Japan*, 131–34.

66. Norman Smith, *Intoxicating Manchuria: Alcohol, Opium, and Culture in China's Northeast* (Vancouver: University of British Columbia Press, 2012), 74–77; "Beer Brewing," in *Industrial Expansion of Japan and Manchoukuo* (Tokyo: Chugai shogyo shimpa-sha, 1935), 39; "Taiwan Tobacco and Liquor Corporation: Historical Sketch," accessed June 18, 2013, http://en.ttl.com.tw/; Zhiguo Yang, "'This Beer Tastes Really Good': Nationalism, Consumer Culture and Development of the Beer Industry in Qingdao, 1903–1993," *Chinese Historical Review* 14, no. 1 (Spring 2007): 34.

67. Alexander, *Brewed in Japan*, 143–45.

68. Ellen Hellmann, *Rooiyard: A Sociological Survey of an Urban Native Slum Yard* (Cape Town: Oxford University Press for the Rhodes-Livingstone Institute, 1948), 45, 48.

69. Quoted in Paul la Hausse, *Brewers, Beerhalls, and Boycotts: A History of Liquor in South Africa* (Johannesburg: Ravan Press, 1988), 7.

70. George French Angas, *The Kaffirs Illustrated* (London: J. Hogarth, 1849), plate 26.

71. Patrick A. McAllister, *Xhosa Beer Drinking Rituals: Power, Practice and Performance in the South African Rural Periphery* (Durham, NC: Carolina Academic Press, 2006), 25, 309–13; Patrick A. McAllister, *Building the Homestead: Agriculture, Labour and Beer in South Africa's Transkei* (Aldershot, UK: Ashgate, 2001), 122–23; Jonathan Crush, "The Construction of Compound Authority: Drinking at Havelock, 1938–1944," in *Liquor and Labor in Southern Africa*, ed. Crush and Charles Ambler (Athens: Ohio University Press, 1992), 369.

72. Richards, *Land, Labour and Diet*, 78, quote from 80; McAllister, *Xhosa Beer Drinking Rituals*, 21.

73. Crush, "The Construction of Compound Authority," 369; McAllister, *Xhosa Beer Drinking Rituals*, 22, 201–23; Sabine Luning, "To Drink or Not to Drink: Beer Brewing, Rituals, and Religious Conversion in Maane, Burkina Faso," in *Alcohol in Africa: Mixing Business, Pleasure and Politics*, ed. Deborah Fahy Bryceson (Portsmouth, NH: Heineman, 2002) 234–41.

74. Jonathan Crush and Charles Ambler, eds., *Liquor and Labor in Southern Africa* (Athens: Ohio University Press, 1992); quote from Julie Baker, "Prohibition and Illicit Liquor on the Witwatersrand, 1902–1932," in *Liquor and Labor in Southern Africa*, ed. Jonathan Crush and Charles Ambler (Athens: Ohio University Press, 1992), 142.

75. Quotes from Paul la Hausse, "Drink and Cultural Innovation in Durban: The Origins of the Beerhall in South Africa, 1902–1916," in *Liquor and Labor in Southern Africa*, ed. Jonathan Crush and Charles Ambler (Athens: Ohio University Press, 1992), 89, 92; Charles Ambler and Jonathan Crush, "Alcohol in Southern African

Notes to pages 133–138

Labor History," in *Liquor and Labor in Southern Africa*, ed. Jonathan Crush and Charles Ambler (Athens: Ohio University Press, 1992), 29; Baker, "Prohibition and Illicit Liquor," 141–43.

76. Quotes from la Hausse, *Brewers, Beerhalls and Boycotts*, 22, italics in original; la Hausse, "Drink and Cultural Innovation," 78–114.

77. La Hausse, "Drink and Cultural Innovation," 101–2; Ambler and Crush, "Alcohol in Southern African History," 26; Richard Parry, "The 'Durban System' and the Limits of Colonial Power in Salisbury, 1890–1935," in *Liquor and Labor in Southern Africa*, ed. Jonathan Crush and Charles Ambler (Athens: Ohio University Press, 1992), 125; Ruth Edgecombe, "The Role of Alcohol in Labor Acquisition and Control on the Natal Coal Mines, 1911–1938," in *Liquor and Labor in Southern Africa*, ed. Jonathan Crush and Charles Ambler (Athens: Ohio University Press, 1992), 194.

78. Justin Willis, *Potent Brews: A Social History of Alcohol in Africa, 1850–1999* (Athens: Ohio University Press, 2002), 123; McAllister, *Xhosa Beer Drinking Rituals*, 29; la Hausse, *Brewers, Beerhalls and Boycotts*, 20; la Hausse, "Drink and Cultural Innovation," 102.

79. Helen Bradford, "'We Women Will Show Them': Beer Protests in the Natal Countryside, 1929," in *Liquor and Labor in Southern Africa*, ed. Jonathan Crush and Charles Ambler (Athens: Ohio University Press, 1992), 208–34, quote from 225; la Hausse, *Brewers, Beerhalls and Boycotts*, 30–38, 42.

80. Crush, "The Construction of Compound Authority," 379–80; Parry, "The 'Durban System' in Salisbury," 127; Ambler and Crush, "Alcohol in Southern African History," 3.

81. Dunbar Moodie, "Alcohol and Resistance on the South African Gold Mines, 1903–1962," in *Liquor and Labor in Southern Africa*, ed. Jonathan Crush and Charles Ambler (Athens: Ohio University Press, 1992), 168; la Hausse, *Brewers, Beerhalls and Boycotts*, 43–44, 54; Parry, "The 'Durban System' in Salisbury," 132.

82. la Hausse, "Drink and Cultural Innovation," 93–94; Parry, "The 'Durban System' in Salisbury," 125, 129; Moodie, "Alcohol and Resistance," 165, 171; Willis, *Potent Brews*, 37.

83. Quoted in Bradford, "'We Women Will Show Them,'" 218, see also 227; Sigrun Helmfrid, "Thirsty Men and Thrifty Women: Gender, Power, and Agency in the Rural Beer Trade in Burkina Faso," in *Beer in Africa: Drinking Spaces, States, and Selves*, ed. Steven Van Wolputte and Mattia Fumanti (Berlin: Lit Verlag, 2010), 203; Willis, *Potent Brews*, 111; la Hausse, *Brewers, Beerhalls, and Boycotts*, 47.

84. Willis, *Potent Brews*, 100; Parry, "The 'Durban System' in Salisbury," 133; Moodie, "Alcohol and Resistance," 175–77.

85. Willis, *Potent Brews*, 99; Bradford, "'We Women Will Show Them,'" 211.

86. McAllister, *Xhosa Beer Drinking Rituals*, 152–61, 281.

87. Mager, *Beer, Sociability, and Masculinity*, 27.

CHAPTER 5

1. "Van Laer on Belgian Beers," *ABR* 10, no. 1 (July 1896): 1, 2; "Concours de Bière Nationale," *PJB* 12, no. 499 (January 8, 1904): 9–10.

2. William Elliot Griffis, *Belgium: The Land of Art* (Boston: Houghton Mifflin, 1912), 146; "Maison Louis Cornélis," *Gazette de Charleroi*, June 9, 1902; "Bières en bouteilles," *Le Courrier de L'Escaut*, March 20, 1910.

3. Michael Jackson, *The Great Beers of Belgium* (Antwerp: Coda, 1994), 209.

4. M. Van Laer, "Recherches sur les bières à double face," *PJB* 8, no. 302 (January 26, 1900): 76–77; "Krieken-lambic," *Le XXe Siècle*, August 21, 1904; "Le lambic d'honneur," *Le Soir*, July 26, 1901; "Manneken Pis va donner du faro," *Journal de Bruxelles*, July 4, 1914.

5. "L'inventeur de la bière," *La Réforme*, November 17, 1903; "Le règne du lambic," *PJB* 7, no. 260 (March 24, 1899): 112.

6. "Notes d'un flaneur," *Journal de Bruxelles*, January 29, 1900; "Chronique Bruxellois," *Le Soir*, January 22, 1903. See also "La gueuze lambic au Transvaal," *Le XXe Siècle*, August 31, 1905; "Vol à l'américaine," *Le XXe Siècle*, April 5, 1903.

7. H. Van der Harten, "Le concours national," *PJB* 12, no. 501 (January 22, 1904): 86; "Concours de Bière Nationale," *PJB* 12, no. 499 (January 8, 1904): 9–10; Jef Van den Steen, *Ale Spéciale Belge: Bière Traditionelle de Chez Nous* (Tielt: Lannoo, 2016).

8. Van den Steen, *Ale Spéciale Belge*, 21–23.

9. Verachtert and Derdelinckx, "Belgian Acidic Beers," 121–28; "Perdu," *Le Soir*, July 8, 1902; "Exposition de Milan," *Le Soir*, November 15, 1906; "Au Café Central," *Le Soir*, October 11, 1923; "A notre clientele," *Le Soir*, May 31, 1926.

10. The family history was reconstructed through digital searches in the liberal-leaning and lambic-loving Brussels newspaper *Le Soir*, available from the BelgicaPress database at the Bibliothèque Royale de Belgique, as well as "Nécrologie," *PJB* 11, no. 455 (February 13, 1903): 165. "En vente," *Gazette de Charleroi*, July 15, 1900.

11. "Allo! Allo!" *Le Soir*, January 26, 1928; G. M. J., "Une visite aux Brasseries Artois," *PJB* 33, no. 1328 (May 8, 1925): 569–74.

12. The poster was reprinted on the front cover of *Le Journal du Brasseur* 106 (December 1999).

13. "Petite Gazette," *Le Soir*, September 5, 1933.

14. "Trappisten Bier," *Le Soir*, August 15, 1893.

15. "Les Trappistes et leur bière," *Le Soir*, December 31, 1934. On the relationship between Verlinden and Westmalle, see Jackson, *Great Beers of Belgium*, 292. On fraudulent Trappist claims, see Jef Van den Steen, *Trappist: The Seven Magnificent Beers* (Leuven: Davidsfonds, 2010), 14.

16. Jeremy King, *Budweisers into Czechs and Germans: A Local History of Bohemian Politics, 1848–1948* (Princeton, NJ: Princeton University Press, 2002); PAAA, R89806/22, Fischer to Trade Department, January 30, 1924; PAAA, R89806/24, illegible to von Stockhammern, April 17, 1924.

Notes to pages 147–149   283

17. PAAA, R89805/20, Bohlund and Reuter to Foreign Office, June 7, 1922; PAAA, R89805/35, Verband Deutsche Ausfuhrbrauereien to Reichsminister, April 24, 1922; Präsidium Deutschen Brauer Bundes to Minister Ernahrung Landwirtschaft Agriculture, June 21, 1922; Verband Munich Brauereien to MEL, April 6, 1922; PAAA, R89806/37, Verband Deutsche Ausfuhrbrauereien, November 30, 1928; PAAA, R105527/37, Wallburg to Nelson, December 31, 1927; "Austellung von Brauerei, 1925/26," March 18, 1927; Jaroslav Koutnik, March 7, 1929.

18. Erich Ludendorff and Adolf Hitler were convicted of treason for their role in the Beer Hall Putsch.

19. PAAA, R89807, newspaper clipping "Trinkt Paneuropa-Bier!," January 23, 1931; "Gegen die Einführung Pilsner Bieres," *Tageszeitung für Braeurei* 23, no. 163 (July 15, 1925): 799.

20. PAAA, R89807, beer coaster, October 10, 1933; Czechoslovak legation to Foreign Ministry, July 8, 1933; "Boycott gegen Pilsner Bier," September 13, 1933; Garn to Hüffer, January 16, 1934.

21. PAAA, R87462/47, Paris Embassy to Foreign Office, January 17, 1928; Döhle, "Vorwurf des Dumping," March 16, 1928; PAAA/R901-111528, Landesgruppe Sachsen, August 1, 1938; Verbalnote from Czech legation, September 16, 1938.

22. Leopold Chmela, *The Economic Aspect of the German Occupation of Czechoslovakia* (Prague: Orbus, 1948), 34; Jaromír Balcar and Jaroslav Kučera, "System Transformation as Consequence of the German Occupation?" in *Paying for Hitler's War: The Consequences of Nazi Hegemony for Europe*, ed. Jonas Scherner and Eugene N. White (New York: Cambridge University Press, 2016), 343–63. Chad Carl Bryant, *Prague in Black: Nazi Rule and Czech Nationalism* (Cambridge, MA: Harvard University Press, 2009), 71; Tycho van der Hoog, *Breweries, Politics, and Identities: The History behind Namibian Beer* (Basel: Basler Afrika Bibliographien, 2019), 57.

23. MJ, 4/25/2, extract from Pivní Kuryr, translated by Dave Cunningham, 2000.

24. John Gillespie, "The People's Drink: The Politics of Beer in East Germany (1945–1971)" (M.A. thesis, Middle Tennessee State University, 2017), 40, 86, 96, 127–28; George P. Wrench, "Russia Turns to Beer," *Brewers Digest* 14, no. 1 (December 1938): 17–18; personal communication from VLB librarian Michaela Knör.

25. "La révolte du lambic," *Le Soir*, July 3, 1940; "Promenade dans nos brasseries," *Le Soir*, July 12, 1940.

26. Henry Lemaire, "Feu le faro," *Le Soir*, September 9, 1959; "Félix Van Roost," *Le Soir*, September 26, 1956; "Monsieur Jean-Henri Dewolfs," *Le Soir*, June 1, 1960.

27. William James Adams, "Determinants of Concentration in Beer Markets in Germany and the United States: 1950–2005," in *The Economics of Beer*, ed. Johan F. M. Swinnen (New York: Oxford University Press, 2011), 227–44.

28. Carlos Herrera, *Pablo Díez Fernández: Empresario modelo* (Mexico City: Universidad Autónoma Metropolitana Iztapalapa, 2001), 42.

29. Gourvish and Wilson, *British Brewing Industry*, 536–47; A. M. McGahan, "The Emergence of the National Brewing Oligopoly: Competition in the American Market, 1933–1958," *Business History Review* 65, no. 2 (Summer 1991): 269–70; Oliver, *Oxford Companion to Beer*, 261–62, 349–50, 434; J. Hoogan, "Aspects of Fermentation in Conical Vessels," *JIB* 83 (May–June 1977): 133–38.

30. Gourvish and Wilson, *British Brewing Industry*, 548–52; McGahan, "National Brewing Oligopoly," 246–48; Herman W. Ronnenberg, "The American Brewing Industry since 1920," in *The Dynamics of the International Brewing Industry since 1800*, ed. R. G. Wilson and T. R. Gourvish (London: Routledge, 1998), 200–201.

31. F. P. Siebel, Jr., "Determination of the Flavor and Aroma of Beer," *Brewers Technical Review* (hereafter *BTR*) 13, no. 1 (December 1937): 23–25.

32. Heinrich Leurs, "Organoleptic Characteristics of Beer," *BTR* 22, no. 7 (July 1947): 43–45; Heinrich Leurs, "The Formation of Flavor Substances in Fermentation," *BTR* 23, no. 9 (September 1948): 45–49, 53. On the Copenhagen system, see Jean de Clerck, *A Textbook of Brewing*, trans. Kathleen Barton Wright, 2 vols. (London: Chapman and Hall, 1957 [1948]), 1:529; Kjell Bengtsson and Erik Helm, "Principles of Taste Testing," *Wallerstein Laboratories Communications* 9 (1946): 171–80; Elsie Siguen, "Formation of Coloring and Aromatic Substances in Malt," *BTR* 9, no. 11 (October 1934): 293–94; "Iron City Brewery Remodels Labs," *Brewers' Digest* (hereafter *BD*) 45, no. 9 (September 1960): 109.

33. Kurt Becker, "Tomorrow's Beers Are Not Yesterday's," *BD* 26, no. 8 (August 1951): 40–41.

34. Kurt Becker, "Beer Foam," *BD* 24, no. 1 (January 1949): 37. See also James S. Wallerstein, "The Nature and Origin of Beer Foam," *Communications on the Science and Practice of Brewing* 1 (December 1937): 31–38.

35. Gauss and Beatty, "The World's Beer," 62.

36. Bamforth, *Beer*, 87. Barbara Hibino, "Cervecería Cuauhtémoc: A Case Study of Technological and Industrial Development in Mexico," *Mexican Studies/Estudios Mexicanos* 8, no. 1 (1992): 23–43.

37. Steffan Igor Ayora Díaz and Gabriela Vargas Cetina, "Romantic Moods: Food, Beer, Music, and the Yucatecan Soul," in *Drinking Cultures: Alcohol and Identity*, ed. Thomas M. Wilson (Oxford: Berg, 2005), 162.

38. José Martínez Rey, *Historia de la industria cervecera en Colombia* (Bucaramanga: Sic Editorial, 2006); Raúl Sanabria Tirado, *Bavaria S.A. y Valores Bavaria S.A.* (Bogotá: Monografías de Administración, Universidad de los Andes, 2003).

39. Craig Heron, *Booze: A Distilled History* (Toronto: Between the Lines, 2003), 302–7; Matthew J. Bellamy, *Brewed in the North: A History of Labatt's* (Montreal: McGill-Queens University Press, 2019), 160, 214–19.

40. McGahan, "National Brewing Oligopoly," 236; Ronnenberg, "The American Brewing Industry," 200–201.

Notes to pages 156–160   285

41. McGahan, "National Brewing Oligopoly," 243, 278–80; Ogle, *Ambitious Brew*, 211–16, 231–32; Ronnenberg, "The American Brewing Industry," 203; Philip Van Munching, *Beer Blast: The Inside Story of the Brewing Industry's Bizarre Battles for Your Money* (New York: Random House, 1997), 72–73.

42. Daniel Okrent, *Last Call: The Rise and Fall of Prohibition* (New York: Scribner, 2010), 42–46; Marni Davis, *Jews and Booze: Becoming American in the Age of Prohibition* (New York: New York University Press, 2012), 120–30.

43. John R. Edwardson, "Hops: The Botany, History, Production and Utilization," *Economic Botany* 6, no. 2 (April–June 1952): 174.

44. Allyson P. Brantley, *Brewing a Boycott: How a Grassroots Coalition Fought Coors and Remade American Consumer Activism* (Chapel Hill: University of North Carolina Press, 2021); Eric Fure-Slocum, *Contesting the Postwar City: Working-Class and Growth Politics in 1940s Milwaukee* (New York: Cambridge University Press, 2013), 187.

45. Kiran Mazumdar-Shaw, *Ale and Arty: The Story of Beer* (New Delhi: Penguin Books India, 2000), xii–xiii.

46. Gourvish and Wilson, *The British Brewing Industry*, 447–74; Tony Millns, "The British Brewing Industry, 1945–95," in *The Dynamics of the International Brewing Industry since 1800*, ed. R. G. Wilson and T. R. Gourvish (London: Routledge, 1998), 142–59.

47. Gourvish and Wilson, *The British Brewing Industry*, 456–58; Ray Bailey, "The Rise of the Lager in the UK," *Boak & Bailey*, September 19, 2007, https://boakandbai ley.com/2007/09/the-rise-of-lager-in-the-uk/.

48. Brian Keith Axel, *The Nation's Tortured Body: Violence, Representation, and the Formation of a Sikh "Diaspora"* (Durham, NC: Duke University Press, 2001), 169–78; David W. Gutzke, *Pubs and Progressive: Reinventing the Public House in England, 1896–1960* (DeKalb: Northern Illinois University Press, 2006).

49. "Australian Brewing Industry," *Australian Brewing and Wine Journal* 58, no. 9 (June 20, 1940): 6; David T. Merrett, "Stability and Change in the Australian Brewing Industry, 1920–94," in *The Dynamics of the International Brewing Industry since 1800*, ed. R. G. Wilson and T. R. Gourvish (London: Routledge, 1998), 229–46; André Sammartino, "Craft Brewing in Australia: 1979–2015," in *Economic Perspectives on Craft Beer: A Revolution in the Global Beer Industry*, ed. Christian Garavaglia and Johan Swinnen (New York: Palgrave Macmillan, 2018), 397–423.

50. Diane Kirkby, "'Beer, Glorious Beer': Gender Politics and Australian Popular Culture," *The Journal of Popular Culture* 37, no. 2 (2003): 244–56. *Sydney Morning Herald*, June 20, 1975; December 28, 1977. My thanks to Julie McIntyre.

51. Norbert Dannhaeuser, "From the Metropolis into the Up-Country: The Stockist System in India's Developing Mass Consumer Market," *The Journal of Developing Areas* 21, no. 3 (April 1987): 259–76; "Where Spirits Command," *Economic and Political Weekly* 10, no. 22 (May 31, 1975): 854; Mazumdar-Shaw, *Ale and Arty*, 52–56.

52. Jonathan Foreman, "Ale under the Veil: The Only Brewery in Pakistan," *The Telegraph*, March 24, 2012; Beverly Ann D'Cruz, "How Mumbai's Masalawaalis Make a Single Spice from 30 Ingredients," *Atlasobscura.com*, September 20, 2019, https://www.atlasobscura.com/articles/bottle-masala?fbclid=IwAR24 UFZ-c7Y4rJdIDYRMPmWYvaerxNya7CxOzu5DhLsMHndGshPCJgFt9pA; Krishnendu Ray, personal communication, July 24, 2013; Raghu Karnad, "City in a Bottle," *Caravan Magazine*, July 1, 2012, http://www.caravanmagazine.in/reportage/city-bottle.

53. Mazumdar-Shaw, *Ale and Arty*, xiii.

54. Willis, *Potent Brews*, 172–73, 183–90, quote from 189; Röschenthaler, "The Social Life of White Man Mimbo," 137; Heap, "Beer in Nigeria," 109–29; MJ, 4/40/1/2, "Tusker" typescript, 1986.

55. Mager, *Beer, Sociability, and Masculinity*, 23, 27–31, 52–54; Willis, *Potent Brews*, 175, 182.

56. Steven Haggblade, "The Shebeen Queen and the Evolution of Botswana's Sorghum Beer Industry," in *Liquor and Labor in Southern Africa*, ed. Jonathan Crush and Charles Ambler (Athens: Ohio University Press, 1992), 395–412; Deborah Fahy Bruceson, "Changing Modalities of Alcohol Usage," in *Alcohol in Africa: Mixing Business, Pleasure, and Politics*, ed. Fahy (Portsmouth, NH: Heinemann, 2002), 43.

57. GDB, BR02.05/0001, "Visit to Accra Brewery," March 15, 1949; Hughes, *A Bottle of Guinness*, 194, 210–12; Yenne, *Guinness*, 97.

58. GDB, BR02.14.0001, L. McMullin to S. R. Duff, August 2, 1966. See also GDB, BR02.05.0024.2, D. O. Williams to A. H. Hughes, September 19, 1963; Hughes, *A Bottle of Guinness*, 211–12; Yenne, *Guinness*, 156–60.

59. GDB, BR02.05.0024.2, D. Harper to G. E. Dewey, November 14, 1968; Hughes, *A Bottle of Guinness*, 211–18.

60. GDB, BR02.06.0002, East Africa tasting reports, 1968; GDB, BR02.14.0004, Malaysia tasting reports, 1967.

61. GDB, BR02.14.0017, J. H. D. Hughes to Managing Director, March 18, 1969; Hughes, *A Bottle of Guinness*, 211.

62. Willis, *Potent Brews*, 176.

63. For a fuller discussion of early brewing in China, see Jeffrey M. Pilcher, Yu Wang, and Yuebin Jackson Guo, "'Beer with Chinese Characteristics': Marketing Beer under Mao," *Revista de Administração de Empresas: Journal of Business Management* (São Paulo) 58, no. 3 (May–June 2018): 303–15. On the Great Leap Forward, see Frank Dikotter, *Mao's Great Famine: The History of China's Most Devastating Famine* (New York: Walker & Co., 2010). For Maoist priorities, see Charles Hoffmann, "The Maoist Economic Model," *Journal of Economic Issues* 5, no. 3 (September 1971): 14. Production figures from Zhu Mei and Qi Zhidao, *Pijiu jiangzuo yi* [Lectures on Beer], in *Heilongjiang fajiao* [Heilongjiang Fermentation] (Harbin: Helongjiang sheng qingongye yanjiusuo, 1981). All translations from the Chinese by Yu Wang and Yuebin Jackson Guo unless otherwise indicated.

64. Yang, "'This Beer Tastes Really Good,'" 29–58; Smith, *Intoxicating Manchuria*; Xiao Zu, "Pijiu zai beiping" [Beer in Beijing], *Shibao banquekan* [Shibao Biweekly] 2, no. 16 (1937): 74–75; Zheng Yimei, "He pijiu ji" [Drinking Beer], *Lianyi zhiyou xunbao* [Friends of Lianyi] 68 (1928): 1.

65. Cao Zhongye, *Zhong guo ming jiu zhi* [Famous Alcoholic Beverages from China] (Beijing: Zhong guo lu you chu ban she, 1982), 133; Hanchao Lu, *Beyond the Neon Lights: Everyday Shanghai in the Early Twentieth Century* (Berkeley: University of California Press, 1999), 259–62; Xu Ke, *Qing bai lei chao* [Collection of Anecdotes and Romances of the Qing Period] (Shanghai: Shanghai Shang wu yin shu guan, 1917).

66. Xu Wangzhi, "Fakanci" [Opening Remarks], *Niangzao zazhi* 1, no. 1 (1939); Zhu Mei, "Nanwang de suiyue" [Unforgettable Years], *Niang Jiu* [Liquor Making] 2 (1991): 49–51; Zhu Mei, "Pijiu de lishi" [The History of Beer], *Niangzao zazhi* [Journal of the Chinese Society of Fermentation] 2 (1939), 17–18; Zhang Zheng, "Ershi shiji chu habu minzu gongshangye de kaituozhe zhiyi ji shuanghesheng chuangshiren zhang tinge" [One of the Economic Explorers in Early Twentieth Century Harbin—On the Founder of Shuanghesheng, Zhangtingge], *Heilongjiang Shizhi* [Heilongjiang History and Gazetteer] 5 (2015): 49–50; Michael R. Godley, "Bacchus in the East: The Chinese Grape Wine Industry, 1892–1938," *Business History Review* 60, no. 3 (1986): 383–409.

67. Yin Xiucen, "Twenty bottles of beer, let's empty them!" *Zhonghua dianying lianhe gufen youxian gongsi yizhounian jinian tekan* [Special issue for the one-year anniversary of China Film Company, Shanghai] (May 1, 1944): 1.

68. "Pijiu gongchang zhi nugong" [Female Workers in a Beer Factory], *Funu Zazhi* [The Ladies' Journal] 2, no. 11 (1941): 36.

69. Xiao, "Pijiu zai beiping," 74–75; Xu, *Qing bai lei chao*.

70. Yang Sao, "Pijiu song" [Ode to Beer], *Taibai* [The Morning Star] 2, no. 11 (1035): 483–84.

71. Zhu and Qi, *Pijiu jiangzuo yi*.

72. Quote from Zhu Mei, "Nanwang de suiyue" [Unforgettable Years], *Niang Jiu* [Liquor Making] 2 (1991): 49–51. "Nanwang de suiyue," 51. See also, Yang, "'This Beer Tastes Really Good,'" 42–45; Zhu Mei, Qi Zhidao, and Wu Gengyong, "Zhongguo niangzao gongye sanshinian de jishu chengjiu" [Thirty Years' Achievements of Chinese Brewing Industry], *Helongjiang niangzao* [Helongjiang Brewing] 2 (1980): 39–43.

73. Dorothy J. Solinger, *Chinese Business under Socialism: The Politics of Domestic Commerce, 1949–1980* (Berkeley: University of California Press, 1984), 215–29; Cao, *Zhong guo ming jiu zhi*.

74. Zhu Mei, *Zenyang ban xiaoxing pijiu chang* [How to Run a Small-Scale Brewery] (Beijing: Light Industry Press, 1958). See also Charles Kraus, "A Microbrewery Revolution in Socialist China," October 2, 2015, https://crkraus.com/2015/10/02/a-microbrewery-revolution-in-socialist-china/.

288   *Notes to pages 170–177*

75. "1964 quanguo xuexi Qingdao pijiu caozuofa," accessed June 11, 2017, http://money.163.com/09/0815/14/5GP1R9NP00253JOU.html; Robert Ash, "Squeezing the Peasants: Grain Extraction, Food Consumption, and Rural Living Standards in Mao's China," *The China Quarterly* 188 (2006): 972; Jeremy Brown, *City versus Countryside in Mao's China: Negotiating the Divide* (Cambridge: Cambridge University Press 2012), 69–73.

76. "Qingdao pijiu bainian xuanyan" [One Hundred Year Statement of Qingdao Beer], N.d., accessed June 11, 2017, http://www.china.com.cn/market/394643.htm.

77. "1964 quanguo xuexi Qingdao."

78. Quote from *Qingdao shizhishangyejuan* [Qingdao Municipal Gazetteers: Commerce volume] (Beijing: Wu zhou chuan bo chu ban she, 2000), 242. See also Deborah S. Davis, "Introduction: A Revolution in Consumption," in *The Consumer Revolution in Urban China*, ed. Deborah S. Davis (Berkeley: University of California Press, 2000), 6–7; *Nongcun shiyong shouce* [Practical Handbook for Countryside Users] (Shanghai: Shanghai Culture Press, 1964), 144; Cao, *Zhong guo ming jiu zhi*.

79. Zhu Mei, "Pijiu de lishi," 17–18; Guo Yuantao, *Global Big Business and the Chinese Brewing Industry* (London: Routledge, 2006), 66.

80. Jos. Vloeberghs (Jean van Noordhoven), "La Brasseries Belge au XXe siècle," *PJB* 74, no. 3089 (April 8, 1966): 221.

81. M. Andriessens, "Perspective pour la petite et moyenne brasserie en Belgique," *PJB* 74, no 3087 (March 25, 1966): 190–95.

CHAPTER 6

1. "Yuppy Drinkers Suffer Corona-ry," *Denver Post*, May 31, 1986.

2. José Manuel López, "Bebe EU cerveza mexicana," *Reforma* (Mexico City), April 19, 2007.

3. MJ, 4/40/14/1, Wolfgang Stark press release, February 1995.

4. Martin Stack, Myles Gartland, and Tim Keane, "Path Dependency, Behavioral Lock-in and the International Market for Beer," in *Brewing, Beer and Pubs: A Global Perspective*, ed. Ignazio Cabras, David Higgins, and David Preece (London: Palgrave Macmillan, 2016), 61–62.

5. Jeffrey D. Karrenbrock, "The Internationalization of the Beer Brewing Industry," *Federal Reserve Bank of St. Louis* 72, no. 6 (November–December 1990): 3–19.

6. Unger, *Brewing in Holland*, 360–69; Smit, *The Heineken Story*, 19–23.

7. Smit, *The Heineken Story*, 40–46, 54–60, 64–67; James J. Nagle, "Imports of Beer Climbing Sharply," *New York Times*, November 27, 1955.

8. Smit, *The Heineken Story*, 76–80, 127–28, 135–37, 140–42, quote from 141.

9. Robert Shea Terrell, "'Lurvenbrow': Bavarian Beer Culture and Barstool Diplomacy in the Global Market, 1945–1964," in *Alcohol Flows Across Cultures: Drinking Cultures in Transnational and Comparative Perspective*, ed. Waltraud Ernst (London: Routledge, 2020), 217.

Notes to pages 177–181

10. David H. Jernigan and Isidore S. Obot, "Thirsting for the African Market," *African Journal of Drug and Alcohol Studies* 5, no. 1 (2006): 57–70; Sammartino, "Craft Brewing in Australia," 400.

11. Quoted in Bryan Miller, "American Beer: How Changing Tastes Have Changed It," *New York Times*, May 12, 1982. See also "Visionary Brewer Joe Owades Dies at 87," *Modern Brewery Age*, December 26, 2005.

12. Ogle, *Ambitious Brew*, 286–87; "Lowenbrau Promotion Under Investigation by Trade Commission," *Washington Post*, July 23, 1978; Smit, *The Heineken Story*, 194–98.

13. Quote from Teresa da Silva Lopes and Mark Casson, "Entrepreneurship and the Development of Global Brands," *Business History Review* 81, no. 4 (Winter 2007): 662; Alexander, *Brewed in Japan*, 180–85, 227–29, 240; Adam Pasion, "What's So 'Nama' about Nama Beer," *Japan Daily*, July 26, 2015.

14. Florence Fabricant, "'Dry' Beers Flood the Market: A Wave or a Mirage?" *New York Times*, August 16, 1989; Leo Lewis, "The Beer That Conquered Japan with a Dry Bite," *The Times*, August 9, 2003.

15. "Interview with Prof. Charlie Bamforth," *Modern Brewery Age*, September 10, 2010.

16. Ogle, *Ambitious Brew*, 288–90; Van Munching, *Beer Blast*, 41–45.

17. Van Munching, *Beer Blast*, 120–30.

18. Tonya Garcia, "Lots of people will buy into your message of kicking back with a cold one, even if the beer is mediocre," *Adweek*, June 22, 2015. See also Deshpande Rohit, Gustavo Herrero, and Kirsten O'Neil Massaro, "Corona Beer," Harvard Business School Case 502-023, November 2001, https://www.hbs.edu/faculty/Pages/item.aspx?num=28639; Ashok Som, "Corona Beer: From a Local Mexican Player to a Global Brand," *Case Centre*, 2008, https://www.thecasecentre.org/educators/products/view?id=79876.

19. Mike Zellner, "Mexican Jumping Beers," *Beverage World* 112, no. 1539 (April 1993): 60; Dianne Klein, "Mexico's Poor-Man's Brew Makes Big Splash in U.S.," *Houston Chronicle*, August 3, 1986.

20. Bruce Horovitz, "Corona Beer a Big Success: Import's Popularity Baffles the Analysts," *Los Angeles Times*, March 30, 1986; Bob Greene, "Solving the Mystery of a Beer with Lime," *Chicago Tribune*, September 3, 1986.

21. Jonathan Peterson, "Brewer Will Battle False Rumor about Its Product," *Los Angeles Times*, July 28, 1987; Jonathan Peterson, "Weird Rumor No Joke When It's about Your Firm's Product," *Minneapolis Star and Tribune*, August 24, 1987; Van Munching, *Beer Blast*, 134–36.

22. "Impresionante, la demanda que tiene la cerveza Corona en EU," *El Universal*, September 11, 1986; "Corona se coloca como la cerveza Mexicana de mayor venta en EU," *Excelsior*, September 8, 1986.

23. Van Munching, *Beer Blast*, 135–36.

24. Quote from Andrea Adelson, "A Workers' Beer Gains Status," *New York Times*, July 11, 1987; Smit, *The Heineken Story*, 206.

25. Hillary Chura, "Brands: In Trouble—In Demand," *Advertising Age* 72, no. 2 (January 8, 2001): 4; Zellner, "Mexican Jumping Beers," 60; Michael Jackson, *The Running Press Pocket Guide to Beer*, 7th ed. (Philadelphia: Running Press, 2000), 87; Suein L. Hwang, "Beer: Corona, of the Lime Wedge, Makes an Unlikely Comeback," *Wall Street Journal*, November 20, 1997.

26. Protz quoted in "Sales Say Mexican Beer Is No Lemon," *The Guardian*, July 4, 1992; Richard Ali, "U.S. Lager Invades British Beer Market," *AgExporter* 8, no. 9 (December 1996): 17. On the supposed invention of lime, see Rob McKibbon, "Sunset on a Golden Dream," *The Independent*, July 29, 1991; Robert Michaels, "Who Put the First Lime in a Corona?" accessed May 5, 2021, https://www.quora.com/Who-put-the-first-lime-in-a-Corona.

27. MJ, 4/40/6, Alan J. Pugsley to R. E. Campbell, August 20, 1987; Keith Villa, "Flavored Malt Beverage," in *The Oxford Companion to Beer*, ed. Garrett Oliver (New York: Oxford University Press, 2012), 362; Dave Infante, "Tequiza Sunset," *VinePair*, May 28, 2021, https://vinepair.com/articles/tequiza-agave-infused-ber/; Doreen Hemlock, "Latin, Caribbean Beers Gain Popularity at the Expense of U.S. Microbrews," *Sun-Sentinel*, August 16, 1999.

28. Timothy Wise, "How Beer Explains 20 Years of Nafta's Devastating Effects on Mexico," accessed May 14, 2014, http://triplecrisis.com/how-beer-explains-20-years-of-naftas-devastating-effects-on-mexico/; Dan Botz, *Mask of Democracy: Labor Suppression in Mexico Today* (Boston: South End Press, 1992), 131–43; Carlos Galguera Roiz, "Una oportunidad de definición," *Uno Más Uno* (Mexico City), April 4, 1990.

29. Jack Kenny, "The Challenge of Specialty Imports," *Modern Brewery Age*, July 10, 1995; Martin Stack, "The Internationalization of Craft Beer," in *New Developments in the Brewing Industry*, ed. Eric Støjer Madsen, Jens Gammelgaard, and Bersant Hobdari (Oxford: Oxford University Press, 2020), 265; Heather Wood, *The Beer Directory: An International Guide* (Pownal, VT: Storey Publishing, 1995), 3–7, 206–11.

30. "The Real Face of Iran," *The Guardian*, April 8, 2007; Pamela G. Hollie, "Asia's Growing Taste for Beer," *International Herald Tribune*, February 15, 1983; "Efes Beer Sales in Russia Down 5.3% in Q2," *Interfax: Russia & CIS Food & Agriculture Weekly*, July 15, 2009.

31. Quoted in Rob Crilly, "Pakistan Brewery's Beer Battle with India," *The Telegraph*, January 6, 2011; "Pakistan's Only Brewery Thrives within Islamic State," *Modern Brewery Age*, June 13, 2005.

32. Kenneth G. Elzinga, Carol Horton Tremblay, and Victor J. Tremblay. "Craft Beer in the USA: Strategic Connections to Macro- and European Brewers," in *Economic Perspectives on Craft Beer: A Revolution in the Global Beer Industry*, ed. Christian Garavaglia and Johan Swinnen (New York: Palgrave Macmillan, 2018), 62–63; Alfons Weersink, Kevin Probyn-Smith, and Mike Von Massow, "The Canadian

Notes to pages 184–189

Craft Beer Sector," in *Economic Perspectives on Craft Beer: A Revolution in the Global Beer Industry*, ed. Christian Garavaglia and Johan Swinnen (New York: Palgrave Macmillan, 2018), 92.

33. Kate Taylor, "Bud Light Just Revived Its Most Controversial Mascot of All Time," *Insider.com*, February 5, 2017, https://www.businessinsider.com/who-is-bud-light-dog-spuds-mackenzie; Van Munching, *Beer Blast*, 64–66; William Knoedelseder, *Bitter Brew: The Rise and Fall of Anheuser-Busch and America's King of Beer* (New York: Harper Collins, 2012), 135–37, 164–68; Julie Macintosh, *Dethroning the King: The Hostile Takeover of Anheuser-Busch, an American Icon* (Hoboken, NJ: John Wiley & Sons, 2011), 59–62.

34. GDB/BR/02.05.0001, "West African Tour Market Survey," 1949.

35. Brenda Murphy, "'Power' and 'Greatness'—Superheroes and Masculinities: Guinness as a Social and Cultural Signifier in Southern Africa," *Southern African-Irish Studies* 4, 2, no. 1 (2012): 52. GDB/CO05.02/05.0003.15, G. S. Green, "Overseas Advertising and Propaganda, 1928–1929," September 13, 1927; Yenne, *Guinness*, 94, 98.

36. GDB/SA03.03/0005.04, Eric F. Keartland to District Manager, September 4, 1962, R. W. S. Greene to Keartland, September 13, 1962.

37. Murphy, "'Power' and 'Greatness,'" 55.

38. Anne Mager, "'One Beer, One Goal, One Nation, One Soul': South African Breweries, Heritage, Masculinity and Nationalism, 1960–1999," *Past and Present* 188, no. 1 (2005): 170; Mager, *Beer, Sociability, and Masculinity*, 47–48. See also Nathan Michael Corzine, "Right at Home: Freedom and Domesticity in the Language of Imagery of Beer Advertising, 1933–1960," *Journal of Social History* 43, no. 4 (Summer 2010): 843–66; Ronnenberg, "The American Brewing Industry," 205; Victor J. Tremblay and Carol Horton Tremblay, *Industry and Firm Studies*, 4th ed. (New York: Routledge, 2007), 69–70; Victor J. Tremblay and Carol Horton Tremblay, *The U.S. Brewing Industry: Data and Economic Analysis* (Cambridge: MIT Press, 2005); McGahan, "National Brewing Oligopoly," 236; Ogle, *Ambitious Brew*, 282–87.

39. Smit, *The Heineken Story*, 112–13. On industry practices, see Elizabeth Rose McFall, *Advertising: A Cultural Economy* (London: Sage, 2004).

40. Hagley Library, Dichter Papers, BX007.144C, Ernest Dichter, "A Psychological Research Study on the Sales and Advertising Problems of Berghoff and Gettelman Beers," October 1952; GDB, BR02.05/0024/1, Public Attitude Surveys, Ltd., "A Research Plan for Maiden," November 1971; Millns, "The British Brewing Industry," 143; "A-B Loses the Top Ad Meter Spot," *Modern Brewery Age*, February 2, 2009.

41. Personal communication from Gabriel Earle, March 2019; Lawrence A. Wenner and Steven J. Jackson, eds., *Sport, Beer, and Gender: Promotional Culture and Contemporary Social Life* (New York: Peter Lang, 2009); Mager, *Beer, Sociability, and Masculinity*, 50, 59; Heap, "Beer in Nigeria," 111.

42. Tom Reichert, *The Erotic History of Advertising* (New York: Prometheus Books, 2003), 294–99; Dominic Walsh, "Taste for Big-Stage Battle Stirs Beer Chief," *The Times* (London), May 23, 2003.

43. Jonathan Roberts, "Michael Power and Guinness Masculinity in Africa," in *Beer in Africa: Drinking Spaces, States and Selves*, ed. Steven Van Wolputte and Mattia Fumanti (Münster: Lit Verlag, 2010), 29–52; Murphy, "'Power' and 'Greatness,'" 49–50; Smit, *The Heineken Story*, 272.

44. James R. Walker, Nelson Hathcock, and Robert V. Bellamy, Jr., "Domesticating the Brew: Gender and Sport in Postwar Magazine Advertising for Beer," in *Sport, Beer, and Gender: Promotional Culture and Contemporary Social Life*, ed. Lawrence A. Wenner and Steven J. Jackson (New York: Peter Lang, 2009), 35–54; Corzine, "Right at Home," 846; Mager, *Beer, Sociability, and Masculinity*, 51; Ira Teinowitz, "Looking for Women: Miller Ads Pay More Attention to Females," *Advertising Age*, March 16, 1992.

45. Robert M. Seiler, "Selling Patriotism/Selling Beer: The Case of the 'I AM CANADIAN!' Commercial," *The American Review of Canadian Studies* (Spring 2002): 45–66.

46. I thank Roger Horowitz for sharing the transcript of his interview with Gale Robinson and Marshall Goldberg, April 1, 2013. See also Mager, *Beer, Sociability, and Masculinity*, 61.

47. E. J. Schultz, "How This Man Made Dos Equis a Most Interesting Marketing Story," *Advertising Age* 83, no. 10 (2012); Behringer, *Löwenbräu*, 217; Terrell, "'Lurvenbrow,'" 211, 217; Yenne, *Guinness*, 198; MJ, 4/40/17/1, Owen Barstow to Craig Williamson, December 12, 1995; Duncan Macleod, "Sapporo Legendary Biru," June 7, 2010, http://theinspirationroom.com/daily/2010/sapporo-legend ary-biru/.

48. Leo Lewis, "The Beer That Conquered Japan with a Dry Bite," *The Times*, August 9, 2003.

49. Paul Manning and Ann Uplisashvili, "'Our Beer': Ethnographic Brands in Postsocialist Georgia," *American Anthropologist* 109, no. 4 (2007): 634.

50. Terrell, "'Lurvenbrow,'" 206–9; Robert Terrell, "The Reinheitsgebot: Between German Consumer Culture and the European Market," *The Taproom*, February 14, 2018, https://seeingthewoods.org/2018/02/14/the-taproom-robert-terrell/.

51. Morton C. Meilgaard, C. E. Dalgliesh, and J. L. Clapperton, "Beer Flavour Terminology," *JIB* 85 (January–February 1979): 38–42; Richard Severo, "Hints of Apple and Banana Found Playing a Role in Beer," *New York Times*, September 22, 1981; Ann C. Noble, R. A. Arnold, B. M. Masuda, S. D. Pecore, J. O. Schmidt, and P. M. Stern, "Progress towards a Standardized System of Wine Aroma Terminology," *American Journal of Enology and Viticulture* 35, no. 2 (1984): 107–9.

52. "Perfect Draught Bass," *The Guardian* (Manchester), December 13, 1989.

53. Terrell, "'Lurvenbrow,'" 210–11; "Octoberfest Plagued by Growing Elitism," *Modern Brewery Age*, October 9, 2000; Mike Cronin and Daryl Adair, *The Wearing*

of the Green: A History of St. Patrick's Day (London: Routledge, 2002), 218; Jeffrey M. Pilcher, "Cinco de Mayo: From the Battlefield to the Beer Bottle," *History News Network*, May 4, 2010, https://historynewsnetwork.org/article/126189.

54. Interview with Vanessa Winstone, National Brewery Centre, Burton Upon Trent, February 27, 2019; Nick Nissley and Andrea Casey, "The Politics of the Exhibition: Viewing Corporate Museums through the Paradigmatic Lens of Organizational Memory," *British Journal of Management* 13 (2002): S35–S45; Patricia Wells, "The Favorite Brew of Singapore," *New York Times*, June 12, 1983.

55. Breandán Kearney, "Are You Experienced: How Brussels Got a New Beer Museum," June 11, 2021, https://www.beercity.brussels/home/beurs-bourse-belg ian-beer-world.

56. Olivier van Beeman, *Heineken in Africa: A Multinational Unleashed* (London: Hurst & Company, 2019), 49–54, 58–59; "SABMiller in Africa: The Beer Frontier," *The Economist*, May 31, 2014; Nathalie Thomas, "Brewers Launch Battle for African Market," *Sunday Telegraph* (London), June 3, 2012.

57. See, for example, Walsh, "Taste for Big-Stage."

58. "Graham Mackay, ex-SABMiller Chair, Dies at Age 64," *Modern Brewery Age*, December 18, 2013; Walsh, "Taste for Big-Stage."

59. Stack, Gartland, and Keane, "Path Dependency, Behavioral Lock-in," 67, 69.

60. Karrenbrock, "Internationalization of Beer Brewing," 8; Charles Batchelor and Lisa Wood, "Ebulient Australian Who Aims to Tap World Market," *Financial Times* (London), September 19, 1986; Smit, *The Heineken Story*, 183–84.

61. "Carlos Brito: el amo del mundo cervecero," *Noticias Financieras* (Miami), August 28, 2013; Rivera Mena, Villafán Vidales, and García García, "South of the Border," 164–67; John Barham, "Brazilian Beer Giant Plays the Politics," *Financial Times*, December 7, 1999; "Beer Monster: A Giant Drinks Merger," *The Economist*, September 19, 2015.

62. Mzwandile Faniso, "Africa Needs Regulation Similar to EU," *The Star* (South Africa), June 9, 2009; "S. African Beer Giant Chugs Across Continent," *Rocky Mountain News* (Denver), January 28, 1996; Jamie Doward, "South African Challenge," *The Observer*, January 27, 2002; "SABMiller in Africa."

63. "The SABMiller's Tale under Graham Mackay," *The Sunday Telegraph* (London), May 14, 2006; Kerry J. Byrne, "European Budweiser Immigrates with an Alias," *Boston Herald*, April 8, 2001; Simon Loretz and Harald Oberhofer, "'When Helping the Small Hurts the Middle': Beer Excise Duties and Market Concentration," in *Brewing, Beer and Pubs: A Global Perspective*, ed. Ignazio Cabras, David Higgins, and David Preece (London: Palgrave Macmillan, 2016), 106.

64. Kristian Jakobsen, "Market Leadership, Firm Performance, and Consolidation in the Central and Eastern European Brewing Sector," in *The Global Brewery Industry: Markets, Strategies, and Rivalries*, ed. Jens Gammelgaard and Christoph Dörrenbächer (Cheltenham, UK: Edward Elgar, 2013), 47–76; "SABMiller Plans to Steal Share from Rivals in Europe," *Reuters News*, September 28, 2006; Stephanie

Strom, "Pabst Raids Dad's Beer Fridge as It Looks to the Future," *New York Times*, April 1, 2016.

65. Junfei Bai, Jikun Huang, Scott Rozelle, and Matt Boswell, "Beer Battles in China: The Struggle over the World's Largest Beer Market," in *The Economics of Beer*, ed. Johan Swinnen (Oxford: Oxford University Press, 2011), 268.

66. Tim Clissold, *Mr. China: A Memoir* (New York: HarperBusiness, 2006); "Chinese Beer Production," *Globe & Mail* (Toronto), January 4, 1988; "Beer Too Strong for Bottles," *The Advertiser* (Adelaide), March 31, 1999; John W. Slocum, Jr., et al., "Fermentation in the China Beer Industry," *Organizational Dynamics* 35 (2006): 32–48.

67. "Brewers Turn on the Taps for Share of Chinese Market," *Australian*, January 3, 1996. See also Loizos Heracleous, "When Local Beat Global: The Chinese Beer Industry," *Business Strategy Review* 12, no. 3 (2001): 37–45; "Noble Eyes Chinese Beer Gusher," *Globe & Mail*, July 3, 1993; Carl Mortished, "Brewer Regards Market in China as No Small Beer," *The Times*, May 17, 1996.

68. Heracleous, "When Local Beat Global," 41; Gregory Cancelada, "A-B Raises Its Stake in Chinese Brewer Tsingtao," *St. Louis Post-Dispatch*, October 22, 2002.

69. Heracleous, "When Local Beat Global," 37.

70. Kenneth Bertrams, Julien Del Marmol, Sander Geerts, and Eline Poelmans, *Becoming the World's Biggest Brewer: Artois, Piedboeuf, and Interbrew (1880–2000)* (Oxford: Oxford University Press, 2020), 258, 262–63, 288–98, 324–30.

71. "Powell's Ludicrous Merger Deserved to Be Leaked," *The Independent*, November 29, 2001.

72. "Stella's English International," *Financial Mail*, July 2, 2000; John Heinz, "Powell Steps Down as CEO of Interbrew," *Globe & Mail*, December 21, 2002.

73. Mager, *Beer, Sociability, and Masculinity*, 146–48; "Kahn Takes a Bow from the World of Beer," *Star* (South Africa), July 27, 2012; "SAB Entry into US Is Sign of Perceived A-B Vulnerability," *Modern Brewery Age*, June 17, 2002; Kerry J. Byrne, "European Budweiser Immigrates with an Alias," *Boston Herald*, April 8, 2001; "Se asocio la Modelo con la Anheuser Busch," *La Jornada* (Mexico City), March 23, 1993.

74. "Jorge Paulo Lemann," *Bloomberg.com*, accessed July 9, 2019, https://www.bloomb erg.com/billionaires/profiles/jorge-p-lemann/.

75. Johan Swinnen and Devin Briski, *Beeronomics: How Beer Explains the World* (New York: Oxford University Press, 2017), 81; "At Labatt, They Miss the Belgians," *Globe & Mail*, September 14, 2006; "Belgian Regulators Poised to Probe Brewer InBev," *Agence France Presse*, April 19, 2006; "Belgian Press: Brazilians, Belgians in InBev Power Struggle," *Dow Jones International News*, September 14, 2006; "InBev Dismisses Brazilian Bias Claim," *Just-Drinks*, November 15, 2006.

76. Macintosh, *Dethroning the King*, 337–38; Ian M. Taplin, Jens Gammelgaard, Christoph Dörrenbächer, and Mike Geppert, "The Demise of Anheuser-Busch: Arrogance, Hubris, and Strategic Weakness in the Face of Intense

Internationalization," in *The Global Brewery Industry: Markets, Strategies, and Rivalries*, ed. Jens Gammelgaard and Christoph Dörrenbächer (Cheltenham, UK: Edward Elgar, 2013), 269–87; Jeremiah McWilliams, "Will A-B, InBev Brew Up a Deal? Analysts Think So," *St. Louis Post-Dispatch*, July 24, 2007.

77. "Brito Tells ABI Shareholders That the Company Is on Track," *Modern Brewery Age*, April 30, 2009.

78. "Comment: The Evisceration of A-B," *Modern Brewery Age*, December 22, 2008; "Analyst Notes 'Clock Is Ticking' for AB-InBev," *Modern Brewery Age*, November 24, 2008.

79. Stephanie Strom, "Anheuser-Busch Inbev's Growth Playbook Starts with Its Checkbook," *New York Times*, October 10, 2015; John Conlin, "Bitch Slapped in Dallas," *Modern Brewery Age*, November 25, 2011; "ABI UK Recalls Second Batch Due to Glass Shards," *Modern Brewery Age*, December 6, 2010.

80. "Comment: The Evisceration of A-B."

81. "Graham Mackay Looks at the Global Beer Market," *Modern Brewery Age*, February 19, 2010; "Bankers Continue Drumbeat for InBev Purchase of SAB," *Modern Brewery Age*, September 26, 2011.

82. Chad Bray, "Anheuser-Busch InBev and SABMiller Reach Tentative Agreement on Merger," *New York Times*, October 13, 2015.

83. Quoted by Strom, "Anheuser-Busch InBev's Growth Playbook."

84. "Bud Far from Stella," *The Economist*, May 11, 2019; Peter Eavis, "Kraft's Taste for Thrift Turns into a Costly Stake," *New York Times*, February 22, 2019.

CHAPTER 7

1. Alix Faßmann, "In Mariendorf braut sich was zusammen: Der Bier-Jesus aus Amerika," *Berliner Kurier*, July 24, 2014.

2. J. Nikol Beckham, "Entrepreneurial Leisure and Microbrew," 81–82.

3. Benedict Anderson, *Imagined Communities: Reflections on the Origins and Spread of Nationalism*, rev. ed (London: Verso, 1991). On IPA market share, see Michael A. Elliott, "The Rationalization of Craft Beer from Medieval Monks to Modern Microbrewers: A Weberian Analysis," in *Untapped: Exploring the Cultural Dimensions of Craft Beer*, ed. Nathaniel G. Chapman, J. Slade Lellock, and Cameron D. Lippard (Morgantown: West Virginia University Press, 2017), 62.

4. MJ, 4/21/81, Jackson to Rose Blanquaert, February 24, 1976.

5. Michael Jackson, *The World Guide to Beer* (Philadelphia: Running Press, 1977), 123.

6. Quote from MJ, 4/40/7, Jackson to Nicky Careem, September 24, 1976; 4/25/3, Jaroslav Kořán to Jackson, August 5, 1976; 4/40/17/2, M. E. Robertson to Susan Van Tijn, June 28, 1976. See also Carolyn Smagalski, "Quintessentially Michael," in *Beer Hunter, Whiskey Chaser*, ed. Ian Buxton (London: Neil Wilson Publishing, 2009), 6–7.

7. Jackson, *World Guide to Beer*, 4.

8. "Ale Debate Uncapped in Britain," *Atlanta Constitution*, May 3, 1979.

9. Quoted in C. M. Mason, and K. N. McNally, "Market Change, Distribution, and New Firm Formation and Growth: The Case of Real-Ale Breweries in the United Kingdom," *Environment and Planning A* 29, no. 2 (1997): 408.

10. Roger Protz, ed., *Good Beer Guide* (St. Albans, UK: CAMRA, 1980), 15; Richard Boston, "A Bitter Rebuke for Beer Guide," *The Guardian*, March 11, 1974.

11. Roger Protz and Tony Millns, eds., *Called to the Bar: An Account of the First 21 Years of the Campaign for Real Ale* (St. Albans, UK: CAMRA, 1992); William Mares, *Making Beer* (New York: Alfred A. Knopf, 1984), 21, 105; Michael Jackson, "Peering into Porter's Dark Past," *Zymurgy* 11, no. 4 (Winter 1988): 21–23; "Guild History," *National Guild of Wine and Judges*, December 27, 2018, http://www. ngwbj.org.uk/guild_history.html.

12. "Ale Debate Uncapped"; Brian Glover, "The Growth of the Microbreweries," in *Called to the Bar: An Account of the First 21 Years of the Campaign for Real Ale*, ed. Roger Protz and Tony Millns (St. Albans, UK: CAMRA, 1992) 101–7.

13. Kimberly Craven, "Brewery Calls Boss 'Madame,'" *The Oregonian*, September 1986; Raymond Billen, *Pierre Celis: My Life* (Antwerp: Media Market Communications, 2005); Jackson, *Great Beers of Belgium*, 336–41.

14. "A Swinging Choctaw Makes Homebrew," *Nanih Waiya* (1973): 17–18; Stephen Morris, *The Great Beer Trek* (New York: Penguin, 1984), 206.

15. Charlie Papazian, *Microbrewed Adventures: A Lupulin-Filled Journey to the Heart and Flavor of the World's Great Craft Beers* (New York: Harper Collins, 2005), 17, see also 3.

16. There are many accounts of craft beer's American founding fathers; a convenient starting place is Steve Hindy, *The Craft Beer Revolution: How a Band of Microbrewers Is Transforming the World's Favorite Drink* (New York: Palgrave Macmillan, 2014). On the forgotten founding mother, see Frank Prial, "In California Wine Country, a Rare Beer," *New York Times*, June 12, 1979.

17. Vincent Cottone, "Craft Brewing Comes of Age," *The New Brewer* (hereafter *NB*) 1, no. 5 (September–October 1984): 3; Michael Jackson, *Pocket Guide to Beer* (New York: Simon and Schuster, 1991), 166–71.

18. Michael Jackson, "A Microcosm of Micros," *NB* 3, no. 1 (January–February 1986): 21; Leon Krijnen, "Hoe Piet de Jongh De Breyard een huiskameragevoel gaf," January 25, 2019, https://www.bredavandaag.nl/nieuws/algemeen/277548/ hoe-piet-de-jongh-de-beyerd-een-huiskamergevoel-gaf-; Michiel van Dijk, Jochem Kroezen, and Bart Slob, "From Pilsner Desert to Craft Beer Oasis: The Rise of Craft Brewing in the Netherlands," in *Economic Perspectives on Craft Beer: A Revolution in the Global Beer Industry*, ed. Christian Garavaglia and Johan Swinnen (New York: Palgrave Macmillan, 2018), 259–93; Christian Garavaglia, "The Birth and Diffusion of Craft Breweries in Italy," in *Economic Perspectives on Craft Beer: A Revolution in the Global Beer Industry*, ed. Christian Garavaglia and Johan Swinnen (New York: Palgrave Macmillan, 2018), 229–58; Eric Johnston, "Craft

Beer Connoisseur Knows His Suds," *The Japan Times*, February 4, 2012; Michael Jackson, "Japan's Beer Turns Turtle, Even in the Land of Ninja," September 2, 1998, http://www.beerhunter.com/documents/19133-000003.html.

19. Papazian, *Microbrewed Adventures*; Paul Gatza, "National Homebrew Competition," *Zymurgy* 23, no. 2 (March–April 2000): 5; Craven, "Brewery Calls Boss 'Madame'"; Meg Roland, "The Feminine Face of Brewing," *NB* 6, no. 3 (July–August 1989): 24–29. David Bjorkman and Virginia Thomas, "The Very Last Word," *NB* 13, no. 4 (September–October 1996): 130.

20. Charlie Papazian, "1987: The Best Yet," *NB* 4, no. 6 (November–December 1987): 7; MJ, 4/40/11, Hans Gunther Schultze-Berndt, "Old Beers Revitalized," VLB lecture, March 25, 1987; Stuart Harris, "Expanding at the Seams," *NB*, unnumbered (November 1983): 4; Ogle, *Ambitious Brew*, 313.

21. Michael Jackson, *Pocket Guide to Beer* (New York: Putnam, 1982), 110; Jackson, *World Guide to Beer*, 115–27; Oliver, "Beer Style," 115.

22. Peter A. Kopp, *Hoptopia: A World of Agriculture and Beer in Oregon's Willamette Valley* (Oakland: University of California Press, 2016), 166.

23. Michael Jackson, "Harmonic Convergence," *NB* 4, no. 6 (November–December 1987): 33.

24. Ogle, *Ambitious Brew*.

25. Virginia Thomas, "Here's Looking at You," *NB* 13, no. 1 (January–February 1996): 21.

26. Bert Grant, *The Ale Master* (Seattle: Sasquatch Books, 1998), 97.

27. Michael Jackson, *Michael Jackson's Beer Companion* (Philadelphia: Running Press, 1993), 85.

28. Kenneth G. Elzinga, Carol Horton Tremblay, and Victor J. Tremblay, "Craft Beer in the USA: Strategic Connections to Macro- and European Brewers," in *Economic Perspectives on Craft Beer: A Revolution in the Global Beer Industry*, ed. Christian Garavaglia and Johan Swinnen (New York: Palgrave Macmillan, 2018), 55–88; Ignazio Cabras, "Beer On! The Evolution of Micro- and Craft Brewing in the UK," in *Economic Perspectives on Craft Beer: A Revolution in the Global Beer Industry*, ed. Christian Garavaglia and Johan Swinnen (New York: Palgrave Macmillan, 2018), 373–96; David Andrews and Simon Turner, "Is the Pub Still the Hub?" *International Journal of Contemporary Hospitality Management* 24, no. 4 (2012): 542–52.

29. Whereas a craft brewery in Europe is defined by production of up to 1,000 hectoliters (hl), the largest "craft" brewery in the United States, the Boston Brewing Co., produced more than 5,000,000 hl in 2018.

30. Charles W. Bamforth and Ignazio Cabras, "Interesting Times: Changes for Brewing," in *Brewing, Beer and Pubs: A Global Perspective*, ed. Ignazio Cabras, David Higgins, and David Preece (London: Palgrave Macmillan, 2016), 18; MJ, 4/40/12/1, Charlie Papazian to Jackson, March 31, 1997; "Bogota's Brewpub Boom," *Zymurgy* 28, no. 2 (March–April 2005): 5.

31. MJ, 4/37/2/2, Michael Jackson to Roger Prost, May 13, 1996; Ryoji Oda, "List of Microbreweries," 1996; Wayne Gabel, "On the Trail of American Ales," "Iwate Brewer Takes to the Road," undated clippings; "Craft Beer Market in Japan," accessed April 17, 2013, http://beertaster.org/index-e.html.

32. Quoted in Steve Hindy, "Building a Beer Culture in Lebanon," *NB* 29, no. 4 (July–August 2012): 86.

33. MJ, 4/17/104/2, Jackson to Henrietta [?], February 14, 1994. See also MJ, 4/37/2/2, Ilse Shelton to Jackson, February 20, 1996; Charlie Papazian, "Introducing: Beer Style Guidelines," *NB* 9, no. 1 (January–February 1992): 10–16.

34. Quoted in Thomas Thurnell-Read, "The Embourgeoisement of Beer: Changing Practices of 'Real Ale' Consumption," *Journal of Consumer Culture* 18, no. 4 (2018): 552.

35. MJ, 4/40/8, Mitchell to Jackson, October 22, 1991; 4/25/3, Andrew Lennox to Jackson, July 9, 1992.

36. MJ, 4/40/8, Deh-Ta Hsiung to Jackson, September 30, 1992; tasting notes, 1992; 4/25/3, Andrew Lennox to Jackson, July 9, 1992.

37. MJ, 4/25/20, David Porteous to Frances Kelly, September 20, 2006.

38. Jeffrey M. Pilcher and Valeria Mantilla-Morales, "Is That Grapefruit in My Beer? The Rise of a Global Taste Community for Craft Beer," *Foodmobilites.net*, 2020, https://foodmobilities.net/exhibits/show/craft_ingredients_and_commodit/grapefruit_in_my_beer.

39. Michael Jackson, *Pocket Guide to Beer* (New York: Putnam, 1982), 88.

40. Jackson, *Michael Jackson's Beer Companion*, 50, 97, 119, 189.

41. MJ, 4/40/3, tasting note dated 1987.

42. MJ, 4/21/3/1, "Notes for Belgian paintings (with Marxist analysis)," May 14, 1999.

43. MJ, 4/17/46, Sedlmayr Project manuscript, April 21, 1995.

44. MJ, 4/40/12/1, Chris Pietruski to Jackson, December 31, 1995; John Westlake, "From Our Own Correspondent," *CAMRA Nottingham Branch Newsletter*, September 1986.

45. Joseph Weeres, "Beer Trek through China," *Zymurgy* 10, no. 3 (Fall 1987): 25; Patrick Smith, "The Great Beer Safari," *New African Survey* (August 1985): 53–66.

46. Quoted in Ben Keene, "The Year in Beer: Breaking Down 2018's Ratings and Reviews," *Beer Advocate*, December 31, 2018, https://www.beeradvocate.com/articles/17813/the-year-in-beer-breaking-down-2018s-ratings-and-reviews/. See also Steve Conklin, "Computerbrew," *Zymurgy* 11, no. 4 (Winter 1988): 29–31; Jessica Boak and Ray Bailey, "A Lost Decade of Beer Writing," *Boak and Bailey*, October 19, 2015, https://boakandbailey.com/2015/10/a-lost-decade-of-beer-writing/.

47. Eric K. Clemons, Guodong "Gordon" Gao, and Lorin M. Hitt, "When Online Reviews Meet Hyperdifferentiation: A Study of the Craft Beer Industry," *Journal of Management Information Systems* 23, no. 2 (Fall 2006): 158.

48. "Commercial Calibration," *Zymurgy* 28, no. 1 (January–February 2005): 45–47.

49. Quotes from Pilcher and Mantilla-Morales, "Is That Grapefruit in My Beer?"

50. "Fully Operational Battle Station," *Zymurgy* 32, no. 4 (July–August 2000): 6; "Commercial Calibration"; Carlton K. Larsen, "Relax and Have a Homebrew: Beer, the Public Sphere, and (Re)Invented Traditions," *Food and Foodways* 7, no. 4 (1997): 282; Matt Jarvis, "A Medieval Brewing Experiment," *Zymurgy* 29, no. 1 (January–February 2006): 25–26.

51. IBU ratings were taken from brewery websites.

52. Jim Parker, "Double IPAs," *NB* 22, no. 1 (January–February 2004): 30.

53. Joshua M. Bernstein, *Brewed Awakening: Behind the Beers and Brewers Leading the World's Craft Brewing Revolution* (New York: Sterling Epicure, 2011), 18.

54. Matthew Zimmermann and Chad B. Stice, *Microbrews: A Guide to America's Best New Beers and Breweries* (Kansas City, MO: Andrews and McMeel, 1996), 6.

55. Neil Fisher, "Embracing the Haze: The Rise of New England IPAs," *NB* 35, no. 4 (July–August 2018): 56; Roger Protz, *IPA: A Legend in Our Time* (London: Pavilion, 2017), 7; Brad Rogers, "Australian Pale Ale," *NB* 25, no. 1 (January–February 2008): 21.

56. Jackson, *Michael Jackson's Beer Companion*, 57.

57. Cara Parks, "Brewed Free in Catalonia," November 15, 2013, http://roadsandkingd oms.com/2013/free-beer/; Greg Giorgio, "Oatmeal Stout," *NB* 9, no 6 (November– December 1992): 33–34; MJ, 4/40/11, Lindener Gild-Bräu to Jackson, June 28, 1981; van Dijk, Kroezen, and Slob, "From Pilsner Desert," 288.

58. Grant, *The Ale Master*, 140.

59. Ogle, *Ambitious Brew*, 328–33; André Sammartino, "Craft Brewing in Australia," 397–423.

60. Bernstein, *Brewed Awakening*, 46.

61. "Brewers Association Releases Annual Growth Report for 2019," April 14, 2020, https://www.brewersassociation.org/press-releases/brewers-association- releases-annual-growth-report-for-2019/; Eline Poelmans and Johan Swinnen, "Belgium: Craft Beer Nation?," in *Economic Perspectives on Craft Beer: A Revolution in the Global Beer Industry*, ed. Christian Garavaglia and Johan Swinnen (New York: Palgrave Macmillan, 2018), 137–60; Greg Kitsock, "The Beer Can's Rebirth," *NB* 22, no. 4 (July–August 2005): 35–37; Joshua Partlow, "Mexican Microbrewers Step Out of the Shadow of the Country's Beer Giants," *Washington Post*, July 13, 2015.

62. MJ, 4/21/43; NB (May–June 1996); Fal Allen, *Gose: Brewing a Classic German Beer for the Modern Era* (Boulder, CO: Brewers Publications, 2018), 25–26.

63. MJ, 4/21/76, Hasung "Sara" Lee to Jackson, April 4, 1991; Andrea Shea, "Brewers Gone Wild: Taming Unpredictable Yeast for Flavorful Beer," *The Salt*, January 23, 2015, http://www.npr.org/blogs/thesalt/2015/01/23/379326150/brewers-gone-wild- taming-unpredictable-yeast-for-flavorful-beer; Jeff Sparrow, "Wild Brews," *Zymurgy* 29, no. 2 (March–April 2006): 28–31.

64. Kyle Nabilcy, "Savor the Sour: Enjoying the Wild and Funky Beers of Wisconsin," *The Daily Page*, January 16, 2014, http://www.thedailypage.com/daily/article.

300   *Notes to pages 231–234*

php?article=41846; Gustave Axelson, "In Chicago, a Tasting Tour of Barrel-Aged Beer," *New York Times*, October 5, 2014.

65. "Tactical Nuclear Penguin Brewdog," *Modern Brewery Age*, January 3, 2011; Joshua M. Bernstein, "Brewers' Newest Craft: Crowd Control," *New York Times*, February 6, 2017.

66. Quoted in Burkhard Bilger, "A Better Brew: The Rise of Extreme Brewing," *The New Yorker*, November 24, 2008.

67. Alessandro de Sá Mello de Costa, Rafael Cuba Mancebo, and Luís Alexandre Grubits De Paola Pessoa, "Museus Corporativos Estratégicos: Uma Analise do Espaço de Memória de Cervejaria Bohemia," *Sociedade, Contabilidade e Gestão* 11, no. 2 (May–August 2016): 111; Felipe Sgorla, "Cervejeiros artseanais: Recursos, precursos e empresarialização de si," *Política & Trabalho* 48 (January–June 2018): 22; "Manifesto," Perro Libre, Sao Paulo, accessed August 3, 2018, http://www.perrolibre.com.br/manifesto/; "Meet the Brewer: Bernardo Cuoto, 2 Cabeças," October 1, 2014, https://theholbornmag.com/2014/10/01/meet-the-brewer-bernardo-couto-2-cabecas/; Lucy Corne, "In Search of South African Beers," *BLEFA: The Keg*, accessed June 22, 2020, https://www.blefakegs-blog.de/en/in-search-of-south-african-beer/; Ruben Hernández, "Fusionan cerveza y tequila," *Reforma*, January 21, 2011; "Cerveza de coca, un atractivo turístico," *Cervezas de Bolivia*, May 19, 2013, http://cerveza.ind.com.bo/search/label/Cerveza%20Ch%27ama.

68. Andy Newbom, "Brewing a California IPA in El Salvador," March 13, 2012, http://www.brewrevolution.com/2012/03/cerveza-artesanal-brewing-a-california-ipa-in-el-salvador/; Kyle Navis, "Bolivian Beer," August 31, 2015, http://allaboutbeer.com/bolivian-beer/; Noah Lederman, "Suds Korea," September 13, 2015, http://roadsandkingdoms.com/2015/suds-korea/; Sudesh Mishra, "News from the Crypt: India, Modernity, and the West," *New Literary History* 40, no. 2 (Spring 2009): 315–44; Meagan Fitzpatrick, "Hong Kong's Craft Beer Lovers Brewing Success," April 7, 2013, http://www.cbc.ca/news/world/story/2013/04/07/fitzpatrick-hong-kong-craft-beer.html.

69. Ignazio Cabras, "A Pint of Success: How Beer Is Revitalizing Cities and Local Economies in the United Kingdom," in *Untapped: Exploring the Cultural Dimensions of Craft Beer*, ed. Nathaniel G. Chapman, J. Slade Lellock, and Cameron D. Lippard (Morgantown: West Virginia University Press, 2017), 46; Jim Clarke, "Beer Collaborations," February 10, 2010, http://imbibemagazine.com/beer-collaborations/; "Manifesto."

70. Quoted in Mildred Europa Taylor, "Cheers to the All-Female South African Brewery Shaking Up the Beer Industry," *Face2FaceAfrica.com*, October 17, 2018, https://face2faceafrica.com/article/cheers-to-the-all-female-south-african-brewery-shaking-up-the-beer-industry. See also Courtney Iseman, "According to History, We Can Thank Women for Beer," *Huffington Post*, September 14, 2018, https://www.huffingtonpost.ca/entry/women-making-beer_us_5b914f13e4b0c

f7b003d8263; Bill Simpson, "Driving for Diversity," *NB* 13, no. 6 (November–December 1996): 69–71; Greg Kitsock, "Women in Craft Brewing," *NB* 14, no. 1 (January–February 1997): 24–30.

71. MJ, 4/40/12/1/30, Max Catani to Jackson, December 4, 1997.

72. Nathaniel G. Chapman, Megan Nanney, J. Slade Lellock, and Julie Mikles-Schulterman, "Bottling Gender: Accomplishing Gender through Craft Beer Consumption," *Food, Culture & Society* 21, no. 3 (2018): 308; Noëlle Phillips, *Craft Beer Culture and Modern Medievalism: Brewing Dissent* (Leeds, UK: Arc Humanities Press, 2019), 63–65; Dave Infante, "The 13 Most Sexist Names & Labels in Craft Beer," June 26, 2015, https://www.thrillist.com/drink/nation/sexist-beer-labels-and-names-in-craft-beer; Sgorla, "Cervejeiros artseanais," 28; Alexia Chianis, "It's Not All About the Beer: 4 Steps to Get More Women into Your Brewpub," *NB* 25, no. 1 (January–February 2008): 35–38.

73. Mike Kallenberger, "Crafting Diversity," *NB* 27, no. 1 (January–February 2010): 40.

74. Dave Infante, "There Are Almost No Black People Brewing Craft Beer. Here's Why," December 3, 2015, https://www.thrillist.com/drink/nation/there-are-almost-no-black-people-brewing-craft-beer-heres-why.

75. Quoted in Dave Infante, "Cultivating Customers as Diverse as the Beers," *New York Times*, January 16, 2019.

76. Andrés Araya, "Chinga-Tu-Pelo," accessed June 15, 2017, http://www.5rabbitbrewery.com/chinga-tu-pelo/.

77. Adolfo Escalante et al., "*Pulque*, a Traditional Mexican Alcoholic Fermented Beverage: Historical, Microbiological, and Technical Aspects," *Frontiers in Microbiology* 7 (June 2016): 1–18; Marisa J. Valadez Montes, "'Pulque limpio'/ 'Pulque sucio': Disputas en torno a la legitimidad y la producción social del valor," *Revista Colombiana de Antropología* 50, no. 2 (July–December 2014): 41–63; Chris O'Brien, "Mongonzo Beers: To Your Health," *NB* 22, no 5 (July August 2005): 21–22; Röschenthaler, "White Man Mimbo," 159.

78. Thurnell-Read, "The Embourgeoisement of Beer," 539.

79. Melissa Eddy, "The Endangered Village Beer Hall Adds to Germany's Cultural Debate," *New York Times*, October 7, 2018. Brian Spencer, "In Singapore, Craft Beer Where You'd Least Expect It," *New York Times*, March 1, 2016; Justin Bergman, "What to Do in Beijing," *New York Times*, February 22, 2015.

80. Jenn Orgolini, "The Sustainable Craft Brewery," *NB* 28, no. 2 (March–April 2011): 50–56; Charles W. Bamforth and Ignazio Cabras, "Interesting Times: Changes for Brewing," in *Brewing, Beer and Pubs: A Global Perspective*, ed. Ignazio Cabras, David Higgins, and David Preece (New York: Palgrave Macmillan, 2016), 22; Horst Dornbusch and Walter König, "2009 European Harvest: Dramatic Reversal for Hops, Good Year for Barley," *NB* (November–December 2009): 38–45; Tom Philpott, "Craft Beer Uses 4 Times as Much Barley as Corporate Brew," *Mother Jones*, January 20, 2015; David Yaffe-Bellany, "Stale Corn Flakes? No, a Fine I.P.A.," *New York Times*, July 6, 2019; Louise Matsakis, "Ghana's First Microbrewery Is

Changing the Way Beer Is Made in Africa," December 30, 2016, https://munchies.vice.com/en_us/article/53qkgk/ghanas-first-microbrewery-is-changing-the-way-beer-is-made-in-africa.

81. Don McIntosh, "A Quest to Find Union Beer," *Northwest Labor Press*, July 29, 2014, https://nwlaborpress.org/2014/07/union-beer/. See also Dave Infante, "Craft Beer's Moral High Ground Doesn't Apply to Its Workers," accessed May 17, 2018, https://splinternews.com/craft-beer-s-moral-high-ground-doesnt-apply-to-its-work-1826080180.

82. Elise Tak, Shelley J. Correll, and Sarah A. Soule, "Gender Inequality in Product Markets: When and How Status Beliefs Transfer to Products," *Social Forces* (2019), https://doi.org/10.1093/sf/soy125.

83. Diane Bartz, "Exclusive: U.S. Probes Allegations AB InBev Seeking to Curb Craft Beer Distribution," October 12, 2015, http://www.thefiscaltimes.com/latestnews/2015/10/12/Exclusive-US-probes-allegations-AB-InBev-seeking-curb-craft-beer-distribution; Marina Waruru, "The Female Kenyan Brewer Taking on a Global Drinks Giant," May 4, 2015, http://www.bbc.com/news/business-32495853; Josh Noel, "Lagunitas Selling Remaining Stake to Heineken as Founder Magee Seeks Growth for Brand," *The Chicago Tribune*, May 4, 2017; Rob Davies, "Indie Brewers Fight Back in Bitter Row over Beer Brands' Craft Credentials," *The Guardian*, July 11, 2017; Hilary Osborne, "Punk Beermaker Brewdog Sells 22% of Firm to Private Equity House," *The Guardian*, April 9, 2017.

CONCLUSION

1. Quoted in Roger Protz, "Annick's Gruut Beer Is the Spice of Life," *Protz on Beer*, January 31, 2016, https://protzonbeer.co.uk/features/2016/01/31/annick-s-gruut-beer-is-the-spice-of-life.

2. Oliver, "Beer Style," 115.

3. Sumner, "Status, Scale and Secret Ingredients," 289–90.

4. Josh Weikert, "German IPA: It Should Be More of a Thing," *Craft Beer and Brewing*, November 22, 2021, https://beerandbrewing.com/german-ipa-it-should-be-more-of-a-thing/.

5. Virginia Thomas, "Here's Looking at You," *NB* 13, no. 1(January–February 1996): 14–15.

6. Bamforth, *Beer*, xiii.

7. Ian Donnachie, "Following the Flag: Scottish Brewers and Beers in Imperial and International Markets, 1850–1939," in *The Dynamics of the International Brewing Industry since 1800*, ed. R. G. Wilson and T. R. Gourvish (New York: Routledge, 1998), 124.

8. MJ, 4/40/3/56, Kai Plaugmann to Jackson, September 28, 1976; MJ, 4/40/3/60, Phang An Hing to Jackson, October 21, 1976.

Notes to pages 246–249 303

9. Tamara L. Bray, "To Dine Splendidly: Imperial Pottery, Commensal Politics, and the Inka State," in *The Archaeology and Politics of Food and Feasting in Early States and Empires*, ed. Tamara L. Bray (New York: Kluwer Academic, 2003), 117; Ariela Zycherman, "*Shocdye'* as World: Localizing Modernity through Beer in the Bolivian Amazon," *Food, Culture & Society* 18, no. 1 (March 2015): 51.

10. Jeffrey M. Pilcher, "The Globalization of Alcohol and Temperance from the Gin Craze to Prohibition," in *The Routledge History of Food*, ed. Carol Helstosky (New York: Routledge, 2015), 156–78.

11. Tim Arango, "Resisting by Raising a Glass," *The New York Times*, June 9, 2013.

12. Nathaniel G. Chapman and David L. Brunsma, *Beer and Racism. How Beer Became White, Why It Matters, and the Movements to Change It* (Bristol: Bristol University Press, 2020).

13. Warren Belasco, *Appetite for Change: How the Counterculture Took On the Food Industry*, 2d ed. (Ithaca, NY: Cornell University Press, 2007).

14. Kevin McCoy and Nathan Bomey, "The New King of Beer," *USA Today*, November 12, 2015. See also Leo Boltanski and Eve Chiapello, *The New Spirit of Capitalism* (London: Verso, 2005).

15. "Makeshift Arms Are Pouring Out of Ukraine's Ateliers," *The Economist*, March 12, 2022.

Select Bibliography

ARCHIVAL SOURCES

Bibliothèque Royale de Belgique, Brussels, Belgium.

Bundesarchiv, Berlin Lichterfeld, Germany (BABL).

Guinness Dublin Brewery, Guinness Archive, Diageo Ireland, Dublin, Ireland (GDB).

Hagley Library, Dichter Papers, Wilmington, Delaware, USA.

Hokkaido University Northern Studies Collection, Sapporo, Japan.

India Office Records, British Library, London, UK (IOR).

Michael Jackson Collection, Special Collections, Oxford Brookes University, Oxford, UK (MJ).

Politisches Archiv für Auswärtiges Amt, Berlin, Germany (PAAA).

Sleeman Collection, University of Guelph, Guelph, Ontario, Canada (SC).

Versuchs und Lehranstalt für Brauerei, Special Collections, Berlin, Germany (VLB).

ARTICLES, BOOKS, AND THESES

Adams, William James. "Determinants of Concentration in Beer Markets in Germany and the United States: 1950–2005." In *The Economics of Beer*, edited by Johan Swinnen, 227–44. New York: Oxford University Press, 2011.

Aerts, Erik. "Le Houblon ou les Prix des Céréales? Expliquer la Hausse de la Consommation de Bière en Brabant et en Flandre (1300–1500)." *Food and History* 20, no. 2 (2022): 31–57.

Alexander, Jeffrey W. *Brewed in Japan: The Evolution of the Japanese Beer Industry.* Vancouver: University of British Columbia Press, 2013.

Ambler, Charles, and Jonathan Crush. "Alcohol in Southern African Labor History." In *Liquor and Labor in Southern Africa*, edited by Jonathan Crush and Charles Ambler, 1–55. Athens: Ohio University Press, 1992.

Appel, Susan. "Refrigeration and the Architecture of Nineteenth-Century American Breweries." *IA: The Journal for the Society of Industrial Archaeology* 16, no. 1 (1990): 21–38.

Badler, Virginia R., Patrick E. McGovern, and Rudolph H. Michel. "Drink and Be Merry! Infrared Spectroscopy and Ancient Near Eastern Wine." *MASCA Research Papers in Science and Archaeology* 7 (1990): 25–36.

Bai, Junfei, Jikun Huang, Scott Rozelle, and Matt Boswell. "Beer Battles in China: The Struggle over the World's Largest Beer Market." In *The Economics of Beer*, edited by Johan Swinnen, 267–87. Oxford: Oxford University Press, 2011.

Baker, Julie. "Prohibition and Illicit Liquor on the Witwatersrand, 1902–1932." In *Liquor and Labor in Southern Africa*, edited by Jonathan Crush and Charles Ambler, 139–61. Athens: Ohio University Press, 1992.

Bamforth, Charles W., and Ignazio Cabras. "Interesting Times: Changes for Brewing." In *Brewing, Beer and Pubs: A Global Perspective*, edited by Ignazio Cabras, David Higgins, and David Preece, 15–33. London: Palgrave Macmillan, 2016.

Bamforth, Charles. *Beer: Tap into the Art and Science of Brewing.* 3d. ed. New York: Oxford University Press, 2009.

Barth, Heinrich Joh., Christiane Klinke, and Clause Schmidt. *The Hop Atlas: The History and Geography of the Cultivated Plant.* Nuremberg: Joh. Barth & Sohn, 1994.

Baumert, Nicolas. *Le Saké: Une exception japonaise.* Tours and Rennes: Presses universitaires François-Rabelais and Presses universitaires de Rennes, 2011.

Beckham, J. Nikol. "Entrepreneurial Leisure and the Microbrew Revolution: The Neoliberal Origins of the Craft Beer Movement." In *Untapped: Exploring the Cultural Dimensions of Craft Beer*, edited by Nathaniel G. Chapman, J. Slade Lellock, and Cameron D. Lippard, 80–101. Morgantown: West Virginia University Press, 2017.

Behringer, Wolfgang. *Die Spaten-Brauerei, 1397–1997: Die Geschichte eines Münchner Unternehmens vom Mittelalter bis zur Gegenwart.* Munich: Piper, 1997.

Behringer, Wolfgang. *Löwenbräu: Von den Anfängen des Münchner Brauwesens bis zur Gegenwart.* Munich: Süddeutscher Verlag, 1991.

Bellamy, Matthew J. *Brewed in the North: A History of Labatt's.* Montreal: McGill-Queens University Press, 2019.

Bennett, Judith M. "Conviviality and Charity in Medieval and Early Modern England." *Past and Present* 134 (February 1992): 19–41.

Bennett, Judith M. *Ale, Beer, and Brewsters in England: Women's Work in a Changing World, 1300–1600.* New York: Oxford University Press, 1996.

Bernstein, Joshua M. *Brewed Awakening: Behind the Beers and Brewers Leading the World's Craft Brewing Revolution.* New York: Sterling Epicure, 2011.

Bertrams, Kenneth, Julien Del Marmol, Sander Geerts, and Eline Poelmans. *Becoming the World's Biggest Brewer: Artois, Piedbouef, and Interbrew (1880–2000).* Oxford: Oxford University Press, 2020.

Billen, Raymond. *Pierre Celis: My Life.* Antwerp: Media Market Communications, 2005.

Biru to Nihonjin: Meiji Taisho Showa Biru Fukkyushi [Beer and the Japanese: The History of the Spread of Beer in the Meiji, Taisho, and Showa Periods]. Tokyo: Sanseidō, 1984.

Bradford, Helen. "'We Women Will Show Them': Beer Protests in the Natal Countryside, 1929." In *Liquor and Labor in Southern Africa*, edited by Jonathan Crush and Charles Ambler, 208–34. Athens: Ohio University Press, 1992.

Braidwood, Robert J., et al. "Symposium: Did Man Once Live by Beer Alone?" *American Anthropologist* 55, no. 4 (October 1953): 515–26.

Brantley, Allyson P. *Brewing a Boycott: How a Grassroots Coalition Fought Coors and Remade American Consumer Activism*. Chapel Hill: University of North Carolina Press, 2021.

Bray, Tamara L. "Inka Pottery as Culinary Equipment: Food, Feasting, and Gender in Imperial State Design." *Latin American Antiquity* 14, no. 1 (2003): 3–28.

Bray, Tamara L. "To Dine Splendidly: Imperial Pottery, Commensal Politics, and the Inka State." In *The Archaeology and Politics of Food and Feasting in Early States and Empires*, edited by Tamara L. Bray, 143–72. New York: Kluwer Academic, 2003.

Brecher, W. Puck. "Brewing Spirits, Brewing Songs: Saké, *Haikai*, and the Aestheticization of Suburban Space in Edo Period Itami." *Japan Studies Review* 14 (2010): 17–44.

Bruman, Henry J. *Alcohol in Ancient Mexico*. Salt Lake City: University of Utah Press, 2000.

Cabras, Ignazio. "A Pint of Success: How Beer Is Revitalizing Cities and Local Economies in the United Kingdom." In *Untapped: Exploring the Cultural Dimensions of Craft Beer*, edited by Nathaniel G. Chapman, J. Slade Lellock, and Cameron D. Lippard, 39–58. Morgantown: West Virginia University Press, 2017.

Cabras, Ignazio. "Beer On! The Evolution of Micro- and Craft Brewing in the UK." In *Economic Perspectives on Craft Beer: A Revolution in the Global Beer Industry*, edited by Christian Garavaglia and Johan Swinnen, 373–96. New York: Palgrave Macmillan, 2018.

Cabras, Ignazio, David Higgins, and David Preece, eds. *Brewing, Beer and Pubs: A Global Perspective*. London: Palgrave Macmillan, 2016.

Cao, Zhongye. *Zhong guo ming jiu zhi* [Famous Alcoholic Beverages from China]. Beijing: Zhong guo lu you chu ban she, 1982

Carpenter, Kim. "'We Demand Good and Healthy Beer': The Nutritional and Social Significance of Beer for the Lower Classes in Mid-Nineteenth-Century Munich." In *The City and the Senses*, edited by Alexander Cowan and Jill Steward, 131–55. New York: Routledge, 2016.

Casey, Gregory Paul. "Germany's Extensive History of Brewing with Malt Substitutes: Birthplace of America's Adjunct Lager Beer." *Master Brewers Association of the Americas Technical Quarterly* 57, no. 3 (2020): 152–60.

Ceccatti, John Simmons. "Science in the Brewery: Pure Yeast Culture and the Transformation of Brewing Practices in Germany at the End of the Nineteenth Century." Ph.D. dissertation, University of Chicago, 2001.

Chapman, Nathaniel G., and David L. Brunsma. *Beer and Racism. How Beer Became White, Why It Matters, and the Movements to Change It.* Bristol: Bristol University Press, 2020.

Chapman, Nathaniel G., J. Slade Lellock, and Cameron D. Lippard, eds. *Untapped: Exploring the Cultural Dimensions of Craft Beer.* Morgantown: West Virginia University Press, 2017.

Chapman, Nathaniel G., Megan Nanney, J. Slade Lellock, and Julie Mikles-Schulterman. "Bottling Gender: Accomplishing Gender through Craft Beer Consumption." *Food, Culture & Society* 21, no. 3 (2018): 296–313.

Clemons, Eric K., Guodong "Gordon" Gao, and Lorin M. Hitt. "When Online Reviews Meet Hyperdifferentiation: A Study of the Craft Beer Industry." *Journal of Management Information Systems* 23, no. 2 (Fall 2006): 149–71.

Cochrane, Thomas. *The Pabst Brewing Company: The History of an American Business.* New York: New York University Press, 1948.

Cornell, Martyn. "Porter for the Geography of Beer." In *The Geography of Beer: Culture and Economics*, edited by Nancy Hoalst-Pullen and Mark W. Patterson, 7–22. Cham, Switzerland: SpringerLink, 2020.

Correa-Ascencio, Marisol, Ian G. Robertson, Oralia Cabrera-Cortés, Rubén Cabrera-Castro, and Richard P. Evershed. "Pulque Production from Fermented Agave Sap as a Dietary Supplement in Prehispanic Mesoamerica." *Proceedings of the National Academy of Sciences* 111, no. 39 (2014): 14223–28.

Corzine, Nathan Michael. "Right at Home: Freedom and Domesticity in the Language of Imagery of Beer Advertising, 1933–1960." *Journal of Social History* 43, no. 4 (Summer 2010): 843–66.

Costa, Alessandro de Sá Mello de, Rafael Cuba Mancebo, and Luís Alexandre Grubits De Paola Pessoa. "Museus Corporativos Estratégicos: Uma Analise do Espaço de Memória de Cervejaria Bohemia." *Sociedade, Contabilidade e Gestão* 11, no. 2 (May–August 2016): 100–17. https://revistas.ufrj.br/index.php/scg/article/view/13381.

Couyoumdjian, Juan Ricardo. "Una bebida moderna: La cerveza en Chile en el siglo XIX." *Historia* 2, no. 37 (2004): 311–36.

Crush, Jonathan. "The Construction of Compound Authority: Drinking at Havelock, 1938–1944." In *Liquor and Labor in Southern Africa*, edited by Jonathan Crush and Charles Ambler, 367–94. Athens: Ohio University Press, 1992.

Crush, Jonathan, and Charles Ambler, eds. *Liquor and Labor in Southern Africa.* Athens: Ohio University Press, 1992.

Curtis, Robert L. *Ancient Food Technology.* Leiden: Brill, 2001.

da Silva Lopes, Teresa, and Mark Casson. "Entrepreneurship and the Development of Global Brands." *Business History Review* 81, no. 4 (Winter 2007): 651–80.

de Clerck, Jean. *A Textbook of Brewing.* Translated by Kathleen Barton Wright. 2 vols. London: Chapman and Hall, 1957 [1948].

Delbrück, Max. *Illustriertes Brauerei-Lexicon.* Berlin: Parey, 1925

Select Bibliography

DeLyser, D. Y., and W. J. Kasper. "Hopped Beer: The Case for Cultivation." *Economic Botany* 48, no. 2 (1994): 166–70.

Díaz, Ayora, Steffan Igor, and Gabriela Vargas Cetina. "Romantic Moods: Food, Beer, Music, and the Yucatecan Soul." In *Drinking Cultures: Alcohol and Identity*, edited by Thomas M. Wilson, 155–78. Oxford: Berg, 2005.

Dietler, Michael. "Driven by Drink: The Role of Drinking in the Political Economy and the Case of Early Iron Age France." *Journal of Anthropological Archaeology* 9 (1990): 352–406.

Dinghe, Ranjit S. "A Taste for Temperance: How American Beer Got to Be So Bland." *Business History* 58, no. 5 (2011): 1–32.

Documentary History of the United States Brewers' Association. 2 vols. New York: United States Brewers' Association, 1896.

Donnachie, Ian. "Following the Flag: Scottish Brewers and Beers in Imperial and International Markets, 1850–1939." In *The Dynamics of the International Brewing Industry since 1800*, edited by R. G. Wilson and T. R. Gourvish, 123–41. New York: Routledge, 1998.

Duis, Perry R. *The Saloon: Public Drinking in Chicago and Boston, 1880–1920.* Urbana: University of Illinois Press, 1983.

Edgecombe, Ruth. "The Role of Alcohol in Labor Acquisition and Control on the Natal Coal Mines, 1911–1938." In *Liquor and Labor in Southern Africa*, edited by Jonathan Crush and Charles Ambler, 187–207. Athens: Ohio University Press, 1992.

Edwards, David N. "Sorghum, Beer, and Kushite Society." *Norwegian Archaeological Review* 29, no. 2 (1996): 65–77.

Edwardson, John R. "Hops: The Botany, History, Production and Utilization." *Economic Botany* 6, no. 2 (April–June 1952): 160–75.

Elliott, Michael A. "The Rationalization of Craft Beer from Medieval Monks to Modern Microbrewers: A Weberian Analysis." In *Untapped: Exploring the Cultural Dimensions of Craft Beer*, edited by Nathaniel G. Chapman, J. Slade Lellock, and Cameron D. Lippard, 59–79. Morgantown: West Virginia University Press, 2017.

Elzinga, Kenneth G., Carol Horton Tremblay, and Victor J. Tremblay. "Craft Beer in the USA: Strategic Connections to Macro- and European Brewers." In *Economic Perspectives on Craft Beer: A Revolution in the Global Beer Industry*, edited by Christian Garavaglia and Johan Swinnen, 55–88. New York: Palgrave Macmillan, 2018.

Escalante, Adolfo, et al. "*Pulque*, a Traditional Mexican Alcoholic Fermented Beverage: Historical, Microbiological, and Technical Aspects." *Frontiers in Microbiology* 7 (June 2016): 1–18.

Falce, José. *La Bière: Une histoire de femmes.* Paris: L'Harmattan, 2015.

Fisher, Fiona. "Presenting the Perfect Pint: Drink and Visual Pleasure in Late Nineteenth-Century London." *Visual Resources* 28, no. 4 (2012): 324–39.

Foda, Omar D. "The Pyramid and the Crown: The Egyptian Beer Industry from 1897 to 1963," *International Journal of Middle Eastern Studies* 46 (2014): 139–58.

Forgues, Manuel. *Sinopsis químico-filosófica de la chicha boliviana y fabricación industrial del alcohol.* Cochabamba: Editorial del Universo, 1909.

Francks, Penelope. "Inconspicuous Consumption: Sake, Beer, and the Birth of the Consumer in Japan." *Journal of Asian Studies* 68, no. 1 (February 2009): 135–64.

Fuess, Harald. "Der Aufbau der Bierindustrie in Japan während der Meiji-Zeit (1868–1912): Konsum, Kapital und Kompetenz." *Bochumer Jahrbuch für Ostasienforschung* 27 (2003): 231–67.

Fuhrmann, Malte. "Beer, the Drink of a Changing World: Beer Production and Consumption on the Shores of the Aegean in the 19th Century." *Turcica* 45 (2014): 79–123.

Galloway, James A. "Driven by Drink? Ale Consumption and the Agrarian Economy of the London Region, c. 1300–1400." In *Food and Drink in Medieval Europe*, edited by Martha Carlin and Joel T. Rosenthal, 87–100. London: Hambledon Press, 1998.

Gammelgaard, Jens, and Christoph Dörrenbächer, eds. *The Global Brewery Industry: Markets, Strategies, and Rivalries.* Cheltenham, UK: Edward Elgar, 2013.

Garavaglia, Christian. "The Birth and Diffusion of Craft Breweries in Italy." In *Economic Perspectives on Craft Beer: A Revolution in the Global Beer Industry*, edited by Christian Garavaglia and Johan Swinnen, 229–58. New York: Palgrave Macmillan, 2018.

Garavaglia, Christian, and Johan Swinnen, eds. *Economic Perspectives on Craft Beer: A Revolution in the Global Beer Industry.* New York: Palgrave Macmillan, 2018.

Gattinger, Karl. *Bier und Landesherrschaft: Das Weißbiermonopol der Wittelsbacher unter Maximilian I. von Bayern.* Munich: Karl M. Lipp, 2007.

Gauss, Susan M., and Edward Beatty. "The World's Beer: The Historical Geography of Brewing in Mexico." In *The Geography of Beer: Regions, Environment, and Societies*, edited by Mark Patterson and Nancy Hoalst Pullen, 57–65. Dordrecht: Springer, 2014.

Gay, Suzanne. *The Moneylenders of Late Medieval Kyoto.* Honolulu: University of Hawai'i Press, 2001.

Geller, Jeremy. "Bread and Beer in Fourth Millennium Egypt." *Food and Foodways* 5, no. 3 (1993): 255–67.

Gibson, Brian, and Giani Litti. "*Saccharomyces pastorianus*: Genomic Insights Inspiring Innovation for Industry." *Yeast* 32, no. 1 (January 2015): 17–27.

Gillespie, John. "The People's Drink: The Politics of Beer in East Germany (1945–1971)." M.A. thesis, Middle Tennessee State University, 2017.

Girouard, Mark. *Victorian Pubs.* New Haven: Yale University Press, 1984.

Glover, Brian. *Brewing for Victory: Brewers, Beer and Pubs in World War II.* Cambridge: Lutterworth Press, 1995.

Godim, Henry. *Berlin und seine Brauereien: Gesamtverzeichnis der Braustandorte von 1800 bis 1925.* Berlin: Edition Berliner Unterwelten, 2016.

Goldstein, Paul S. "From Stew-Eaters to Maize-Drinker: The *Chicha* Economy and the Tiwanaku Expansion." In *The Archaeology and Politics of Food and Feasting in*

Early States and Empires, edited by Tamara L. Bray, 143–72. New York: Kluwer Academic, 2003.

Gourvish, T. R., and R. G. Wilson. *The British Brewing Industry, 1830–1980*. Cambridge: Cambridge University Press, 1994.

Grant, Bert. *The Ale Master*. Seattle: Sasquatch Books, 1998.

Gross, Emanuel. *Hops in Their Botanical, Agricultural and Technical Aspect and as an Article of Commerce*. Translated by Charles Salter. London: Scott, Greenwood, and Co., 1900.

Guerrero Guerrero, Raúl. *El pulque: Religión, cultura, folklore*. Mexico City: INAH, 1980.

Guo, Jackson Yue Bin. "Tastes in the Jade Flagons: Alcohol Tasting and the Reconstruction of Late Imperial Chinese Literati Identity, 15th–18th Centuries." *Global Food History* 7, no. 3 (2021): 181–201.

Guo, Yuantao. *Global Big Business and the Chinese Brewing Industry*. London: Routledge, 2006.

Gutzke, David W. "Gender, Class, and Public Drinking during the First World War." *Histoire sociale/Social History* 27, no. 54 (November 1994): 367–91.

Gutzke, David W. *Pubs and Progressive: Reinventing the Public House in England, 1896–1960*. DeKalb: Northern Illinois University Press, 2006.

Haas, Jeff. "'They Have No Idea What It Is to Run a Malthouse': A Wisconsin Beer Maker in Japan." *The Wisconsin Magazine of History* 87, no. 2 (December 1, 2003): 14–29.

Hackel-Stehr, Karin. "Das Brauwesen in Bayern vom 14. bis 16. Jahrhundert, insbesondere die Entstehung und Entwicklung des Reinheitsgebotes (1516)." Ph.D. diss, Technische Universität Berlin, 1987.

Haggblade, Steven. "The Shebeen Queen and the Evolution of Botswana's Sorghum Beer Industry." In *Liquor and Labor in Southern Africa*, edited by Jonathan Crush and Charles Ambler, 395–412. Athens: Ohio University Press, 1992.

Hard, Mikael. "In the Icy Waters of Calculation: The Scientification of Refrigeration Technology and the Rationalization of the Brewing Industry in the 19th Century." Ph.D. dissertation, University of Gothenburg, 1988.

Hayashida, Frances. "*Chicha* Histories: Pre-Hispanic Brewing in the Andes and the Use of Ethnographic and Historical Analogues." In *Drink, Power, and Society in the Andes*, edited by Justin Jennings and Brenda J. Bowser, 232–56. Gainesville: University Press of Florida, 2009.

Heap, Simon. "Beer in Nigeria: A Social Brew with an Economic Head." In *Beer in Africa: Drinking Spaces, States and Selves*, edited by Steven Van Wolputte and Mattia Fumanti, 109–29. Münster: Lit Verlag, 2010.

Heckhorn, Evelin, and Hartmut Wiehr. *München und sein Bier: Vom Brauhandwerk zur Bierindustrie*. Munich: Hugendubel, 1989.

Hell, Bertrand. *Bière et Alchimie*. Paris: L'Oeil d'Or, 2015.

Hellmann, Ellen. *Rooiyard: A Sociological Survey of an Urban Native Slum Yard*. Cape Town: Oxford University Press for the Rhodes-Livingstone Institute, 1948.

Helmfrid, Sigrun. "Thirsty Men and Thrifty Women: Gender, Power, and Agency in the Rural Beer Trade in Burkina Faso." In *Beer in Africa: Drinking Spaces, States, and Selves*, edited by Steven Van Wolputte and Mattia Fumanti, 195–222. Berlin: Lit Verlag, 2010.

Heron, Craig. *Booze: A Distilled History*. Toronto: Between the Lines, 2003.

Herrera, Carlos. *Pablo Díez Fernández: Empresario modelo*. Mexico City: Universidad Autónoma Metropolitana Iztapalapa, 2001.

Hibino, Barbara. "Cervecería Cuauhtémoc: A Case Study of Technological and Industrial Development in Mexico." *Mexican Studies/Estudios Mexicanos* 8, no. 1 (1992): 23–43.

Hindy, Steve. *The Craft Beer Revolution: How a Band of Microbrewers Is Transforming the World's Favorite Drink*. New York: Palgrave Macmillan, 2014.

Hoalst-Pullen, Nancy, and Mark W. Patterson, eds. *The Geography of Beer: Culture and Economics*. Cham, Switzerland: SpringerLink, 2020.

Hornsey, Ian S. *A History of Beer and Brewing*. London: RSC Publishing, 2003.

Howard, Philip H. "Too Big to Ale: Globalization and Consolidation in the Beer Industry." In *The Geography of Beer: Regions, Environment, and Societies*, edited by Mark Patterson and Nancy Hoalst-Pullen, 155–65. Dordrecht: Springer, 2014.

Huang, H. T. *Fermentations and Food Science*. Part 5 of *Biology and Biological Technology*. Volume 6 of *Science and Civilisation in China*, edited by Joseph Needham. Cambridge: Cambridge University Press, 2000.

Hughes, David. *"A Bottle of Guinness Please": The Colourful History of Guinness*. Wokingham, UK: Phimboy, 2006.

Ikäheimo, J. "Exclusive Craft Beer Events: Limnoid Spaces of Performative Craft Consumption." *Food, Culture & Society* 23, no. 3 (2020): 296–314.

Isbell, William H., and Amy Groleau, "The Wari Brewer Woman: Feasting, Gender, Offerings, and Memory." In *Inside Ancient Kitchens: New Directions in the Study of Ancient Meals and Feasts*, edited by Elizabeth A. Klarich, 191–219. Boulder: University Press of Colorado, 2010.

Jackson, Michael. *Michael Jackson's Beer Companion*. Philadelphia: Running Press, 1993.

Jackson, Michael. *The World Guide to Beer*. Philadelphia: Running Press, 1977.

Jakobsen, Kristian. "Market Leadership, Firm Performance, and Consolidation in the Central and Eastern European Brewing Sector." In *The Global Brewery Industry: Markets, Strategies, and Rivalries*, edited by Jens Gammelgaard and Christoph Dörrenbächer, 47–76. Cheltenham, UK: Edward Elgar, 2013.

Jennings, Justin, Kathleen L. Antrobus, Sam J. Atencio, Erin Glavich, Rebecca Johnson, German Loffler, and Christine Luu. "'Drinking Beer in a Blissful Mood': Alcohol Production, Operational Chains, and Feasting in the Ancient World." *Current Anthropology* 46, no. 2 (April 2005): 275–303.

Karrenbrock, Jeffrey D. "The Internationalization of the Beer Brewing Industry." *Federal Reserve Bank of St. Louis* 72, no. 6 (November–December 1990): 3–19.

Katz, Solomon H., and Mary M. Vogt. "Bread and Beer: The Early Uses of Cereals in the Human Diet." *Expedition* 28, no. 2 (1986): 23–34.

Katz, Solomon H., Fritz Maytag, and Miguel Civil. "Brewing an Ancient Beer." *Archaeology* 44, no. 4 (July/August 1991): 24–33.

Kicza, John E., "The Pulque Trade of Late Colonial Mexico City." *The Americas* 37, no. 2 (1980): 193–221.

Knoedelseder, William. *Bitter Brew: The Rise and Fall of Anheuser-Busch and America's King of Beer*. New York: Harper Collins, 2012.

Knör, Michaela. "Christel Goslich." In *125 Jahre Versuchs- und Lehranstalt für Brauerei in Berlin e.V.*, 53. Berlin: VLB, 2008.

Konrad, Herman W. *A Jesuit Hacienda in Colonial Mexico: Santa Lucía, 1756–1767*. Stanford, CA: Stanford University Press, 1980.

Kopp, Peter A. *Hoptopia: A World of Agriculture and Beer in Oregon's Willamette Valley*. Oakland: University of California Press, 2016.

Krenzke, John Robert. "Resistance by the Pint: How London Brewers Shaped the Excise and Created London's Favorite Beer." *Journal of Early Modern History* 23 (2019): 499–518.

Kretschmer, Karl. "Ein Beitrag zur Geschichte und Technologie der Untergärung." In *Jahrbuch der Gesellschaft für die Geschichte und Bibliographie des Brauwesens*, 123–93. Berlin: VLB, 1983.

Kümin, Beat. *Drinking Matters: Public Houses and Social Exchange in Early Modern Central Europe*. Basingstoke: Palgrave Macmillan, 2007.

la Hausse, Paul. "Drink and Cultural Innovation in Durban: The Origins of the Beerhall in South Africa, 1902–1916." In *Liquor and Labor in Southern Africa*, edited by Jonathan Crush and Charles Ambler, 78–114. Athens: Ohio University Press, 1992.

la Hausse, Paul. *Brewers, Beerhalls, and Boycotts: A History of Liquor in South Africa*. Johannesburg: Ravan Press, 1988.

Larsen, Carlton K. "Relax and Have a Homebrew: Beer, the Public Sphere, and (Re) Invented Traditions." *Food and Foodways* 7, no. 4 (1997): 265–88.

Leong, Elaine. "Brewing Ale and Boiling Water in 1651." In *The Structures of Practical Knowledge*, edited by Mateo Valeriani, 55–75. Cham, Switzerland: Springer, 2017.

Light, George Evans. "All Hopped Up: Beer, Cultivated National Identity, and Anglo-Dutch Relations, 1524–1625." *Jx* 2, no. 2 (Spring 1998): 159–78.

Liu, Li, Jiajing Wang, Danny Rosenberg, Hao Zhao, Györgi Lengyel, and Dani Nadel. "Fermented Beverage and Food Storage in 13,000 y-old Stone Mortars at Raqefet Cave, Israel: Investigating Natufian Ritual Feasting." *Journal of Archaeological Science: Reports* 21 (2018): 783–93.

Liu, Li, Jiajing Wang, Danny Rosenberg, Hao Zhao, Györgi Lengyel, and Dani Nadel. "Response to Comments on Archaeological Reconstruction of 13,000-y old Natufian Beer Making at Raqefet Cave, Israel." *Journal of Archaeological Science: Reports* 28 (2019): 101914.

Loretz, Simon, and Harald Oberhofer. "'When Helping the Small Hurts the Middle': Beer Excise Duties and Market Concentration." In *Brewing, Beer and Pubs: A Global Perspective*, edited by Ignazio Cabras, David Higgins, and David Preece, 97–119. London: Palgrave Macmillan, 2016.

Luning, Sabine. "To Drink or Not to Drink: Beer Brewing, Rituals, and Religious Conversion in Maane, Burkina Faso." In *Alcohol in Africa: Mixing Business, Pleasure and Politics*, edited by Deborah Fahy Bryceson, 234–41. Portsmouth, NH: Heineman, 2002.

Lutz, H. F. *Viniculture and Brewing in the Ancient Orient*. New York: G. E. Stechert, 1922.

Lynch, Patrick, and John Vaizey, *Guinness's Brewery in the Irish Economy, 1759–1876*. Cambridge: Cambridge University Press, 1960.

Macintosh, Julie. *Dethroning the King: The Hostile Takeover of Anheuser-Busch, an American Icon*. Hoboken, NJ: John Wiley & Sons, 2011.

Mager, Anne Kelk. *Beer, Sociability, and Masculinity in South Africa*. Bloomington: Indiana University Press, 2010.

Mager, Anne. "'One Beer, One Goal, One Nation, One Soul': South African Breweries, Heritage, Masculinity and Nationalism, 1960–1999." *Past and Present* 188, no. 1 (2005): 163–94.

Manning, Paul, and Ann Uplisashvili. "'Our Beer': Ethnographic Brands in Postsocialist Georgia." *American Anthropologist* 109, no. 4 (2007): 626–41.

Martínez Rey, José. *Historia de la industría cervecera en Colombia*. Bucaramanga: Sic Editorial, 2006.

Mason, C. M., and K. N. McNally. "Market Change, Distribution, and New Firm Formation and Growth: The Case of Real-Ale Breweries in the United Kingdom." *Environment and Planning A* 29, no. 2 (1997): 405–17.

Mathias, Peter. *The Brewing Industry in England, 1700–1830*. Cambridge: Cambridge University Press, 1959.

Mazumdar-Shaw, Kiran. *Ale and Arty: The Story of Beer*. New Delhi: Penguin Books India, 2000.

McAllister, Patrick A. *Building the Homestead: Agriculture, Labour and Beer in South Africa's Transkei*. Aldershot, UK: Ashgate, 2001.

McAllister, Patrick A. *Xhosa Beer Drinking Rituals. Power, Practice and Performance in the South African Rural Periphery*. Durham, NC: Carolina Academic Press, 2006.

McGahan, A. M. "The Emergence of the National Brewing Oligopoly: Competition in the American Market, 1933–1958." *Business History Review* 65, no. 2 (Summer 1991): 229–84.

McGovern, Patrick. *Ancient Brews: Rediscovered and Re-created*. New York: W. W. Norton & Company, 2017.

McGovern, Patrick. *Uncorking the Past: The Quest for Wine, Beer, and Other Alcoholic Beverages*. Berkeley: University of California Press, 2009.

Meilgaard, Morton C., C. E. Dalgliesh, and J. L. Clapperton. "Beer Flavour Terminology." *Journal of the Institute of Brewing* 85 (January–February 1979): 38–42.

Merrett, David T. "Stability and Change in the Australian Brewing Industry, 1920–94." In *The Dynamics of the International Brewing Industry since 1800*, edited by R. G. Wilson and T. R. Gourvish, 229–46. London: Routledge, 1998.

Millns, Tony. "The British Brewing Industry, 1945–95." In *The Dynamics of the International Brewing Industry since 1800*, edited by R. G. Wilson and T. R. Gourvish, 142–59. London: Routledge, 1998.

Möhler, Gerda. *Das Münchner Oktoberfest: Vom bayerischen Landwitschaftsfest zum größten Volksfest der Welt*. Munich: BLV Verlagsgesellschaft, 1981.

Moodie, Dunbar. "Alcohol and Resistance on the South African Gold Mines, 1903–1962." In *Liquor and Labor in Southern Africa*, edited by Jonathan Crush and Charles Ambler, 162–86. Athens: Ohio University Press, 1992.

Moseley, Michael E., et al. "Burning Down the Brewery: Establishing and Evacuating an Imperial Colony at Cerro Baúl, Peru." *Proceedings of the National Academy of Sciences* 102, no. 48 (November 29, 2005): 17264–71.

Murphy, Brenda. "'Power' and 'Greatness'—Superheroes and Masculinities: Guinness as a Social and Cultural Signifier in Southern Africa." *Southern African-Irish Studies* 4, 2, no. 1 (2012): 45–68.

Mutch, Alistair. *Strategic and Organizational Change: From Production to Retailing in UK Brewing 1950–1990*. London: Routledge, 2006.

Nelson, Max. *The Barbarian's Beverage: A History of Beer in Ancient Europe*. London: Routledge, 2005.

Nelson, Sarah Milledge. "Feasting the Ancestors in Early China." In *The Archaeology and Politics of Food and Feasting in Early States and Empires*, edited by Tamara L. Bray, 65–89. New York: Kluwer Academic, 2003.

Nemser, Daniel. "'To Avoid This Mixture': Rethinking Pulque in Colonial Mexico City." *Food and Foodways* 19, nos. 1–2 (2011): 98–121.

Nowak, Zachary. "Something Brewing in Boston: A Study of Forward Integration in American Breweries at the Turn of the Twentieth Century." *Enterprise & Society* 18, no. 2 (June 2017): 324–59.

O'Sullivan, Mary. "Yankee Doodle Went to London: Anglo-American Breweries and the London Securities Market, 1888–92." *Economic History Review* 68, no. 4 (2015): 1365–87.

Ogle, Maureen. *Ambitious Brew: The Story of American Beer*. Orlando, FL: Harcourt, 2006.

Oliver, Garrett, ed. *The Oxford Companion to Beer*. New York: Oxford University Press, 2012.

Owen, Colin C. *"The Greatest Brewery in the World": A History of Bass, Ratcliff, & Gretton*. Chesterfield: Derbyshire Record Society, 1992.

Pajec, Milan. "'Ale for the Englishman Is a Natural Drink': The Dutch and the Origins of Beer Brewing in Late Medieval England." *Journal of Medieval History* 45, no. 3 (2019): 285–300.

Papazian, Charlie. *Microbrewed Adventures: A Lupulin-Filled Journey to the Heart and Flavor of the World's Great Craft Beers*. New York: Harper Collins, 2005.

Parry, Richard. "The 'Durban System' and the Limits of Colonial Power in Salisbury, 1890–1935." In *Liquor and Labor in Southern Africa*, edited by Jonathan Crush and Charles Ambler, 115–38. Athens: Ohio University Press, 1992.

Patterson, Mark, and Nancy Hoalst-Pullen, eds. *The Geography of Beer: Regions, Environment, and Societies*. Dordrecht: Springer, 2014.

Payno, Manuel. *Memoria sobre el maguey mexicano y sus diversos productos*. Mexico City: Imprenta de A. Boix, 1864.

Perruchini, Elsa, Claudia Glatz, M. M. Hald, J. Casana, and J. L. Toney. "Revealing Invisible Brews: A New Approach to the Chemical Identification of Ancient Beer." *Journal of Archaeological Science* 100 (2018): 176–90.

Phillips, Noëlle. *Craft Beer Culture and Modern Medievalism: Brewing Dissent*. Leeds, UK: Arc Humanities Press, 2019.

Pilcher, Jeffrey M. "Does Your Beer Have Style? The Nineteenth-Century Invention of European Beer Styles." In *Acquired Tastes: Stories about the Origins of Modern Food*, edited by Benjamin R. Cohen, Michael S. Kideckel, and Anna Zeide, 65–80. Cambridge, MA: MIT Press, 2021.

Pilcher, Jeffrey M. "Dos Equis and Five Rabbit: Beer and Taste in Greater Mexico." In *Taste, Politics, and Identities in Mexican Food*, edited by Steffan Igor Ayora Díaz, 161–74. London: Bloomsbury, 2018.

Pilcher, Jeffrey M. "The Globalization of Alcohol and Temperance from the Gin Craze to Prohibition." In *The Routledge History of Food*, edited by Carol Helstosky, 156–78. New York: Routledge, 2015.

Pilcher, Jeffrey M. "National Beer in a Global Age: Technology, Taste, and Mobility, 1880–1914." *Quaderni storici* 151, no. 1 (April 2016): 51–70.

Pilcher, Jeffrey M. "'Tastes Like Horse Piss': Asian Encounters with European Beer." *Gastronomica* 16, no. 1 (Spring 2016): 28–40.

Pilcher, Jeffrey M., and Valeria Mantilla-Morales. "Is That Grapefruit in My Beer? The Rise of a Global Taste Community for Craft Beer." *Foodmobilites.net*, 2020. https://foodmobilities.net/exhibits/show/craft_ingredients_and_commodit/grapefruit_in_my_beer.

Pilcher, Jeffrey M., Yu Wang, and Yuebin Jackson Guo. "'Beer with Chinese Characteristics': Marketing Beer under Mao." *Revista de Administração de Empresas: Journal of Business Management* (São Paulo) 58, no. 3 (May–June 2018): 303–15.

Poelmans, Eline, and Johan Swinnen. "Belgium: Craft Beer Nation?" In *Economic Perspectives on Craft Beer: A Revolution in the Global Beer Industry*, edited by Christian Garavaglia and Johan Swinnen, 137–60. New York: Palgrave Macmillan, 2018.

Protz, Roger. *IPA: A Legend in Our Time*. London: Pavilion, 2017.

Protz, Roger, and Tony Millns, eds. *Called to the Bar: An Account of the First 21 Years of the Campaign for Real Ale*. St. Albans, UK: CAMRA, 1992.

Pryor, Alan. "Indian Pale Ale: An Icon of Empire." In *Global Histories, Imperial Commodities, Local Interactions*, edited by Jonathan Curry-Machado, 38–57. London: Palgrave Macmillan, 2013.

Purinton, Malcolm F. "Good Hope for the Pilsner: Commerce, Culture, and the Consumption of the Pilsner Beer in British Southern Africa, c. 1870–1914." In *Alcohol Flows Across Cultures: Drinking Cultures in Transnational and Comparative Perspective*, edited by Waltraud Ernst, 123–38. London: Routledge, 2020.

Purinton, Malcolm. "Empire in a Bottle: Commerce, Culture and the Consumption of the Pilsner Beer in the British Empire, 1870–1914." Ph.D. dissertation, Northeastern University, 2016.

Ramírez Rancaño, Mario. *Ignacio Torres Adalid y la industria pulquera*. Mexico City: Plaza y Valdes, 2000.

Rath, Eric C. "Known Unknowns in Japanese Food History." *Asia Pacific Perspectives* 16, no. 2 (2020): 34–47. https://jayna.usfca.edu/asia-pacific-perspectives/journal/asia-pacific-perspectives/v16n2/rath.html.

Recio, Gabriela. "El nacimiento de la industria cervecera en México, 1880–1910." In *Cruda realidad: Producción, consumo y fiscalidad de las bebidas alcohólicas en México y América Latina, siglos xvii–xx*, edited by Ernesto Sánchez Santiró, 155–85. Mexico City: Instituto Mora, 2007.

Richards, Audrey I. *Land, Labour and Diet in Northern Rhodesia: An Economic Study of the Bemba Tribe*. London: Oxford University Press, 1939.

Roberts, James S. *Drink, Temperance and the Working Class in Nineteenth-Century Germany*. Boston: George Allen & Unwin 1984.

Roberts, Jonathan. "Michael Power and Guinness Masculinity in Africa." In *Beer in Africa: Drinking Spaces, States and Selves*, edited by Steven Van Wolputte and Mattia Fumanti, 29–52. Münster: Lit Verlag, 2010.

Ronnenberg, Herman W. "The American Brewing Industry since 1920." In *The Dynamics of the International Brewing Industry since 1800*, edited by R. G. Wilson and T. R. Gourvish, 193–212. London: Routledge, 1998.

Röschenthaler, Ute. "The Social Life of White Man Mimbo, and the Ancestral Consumption of Bottled Beer in South-West Cameroon." In *Beer in Africa: Drinking Spaces, States and Selves*, edited by Steven Van Wolputte and Mattia Fumanti, 131–65. Münster: Lit Verlag, 2010.

Sammartino, André. "Craft Brewing in Australia: 1979–2015." In *Economic Perspectives on Craft Beer: A Revolution in the Global Beer Industry*, edited by Christian Garavaglia and Johan Swinnen, 397–423. New York: Palgrave Macmillan, 2018.

Samuel, Delwen. "Archaeology of Ancient Egyptian Beer." *Journal of the American Society of Brewing Chemists* 54, no. 1 (1996): 3–12.

Sanabria Tirado, Raúl. *Bavaria S.A. y Valores Bavaria S.A.* Bogotá: Monografías de Administración, Universidad de los Andes, 2003.

Sayre, Matthew, David Goldstein, William Whitehead, and Patrick Ryan Williams. "A Marked Preference: *Chicha de molle* and Huari State Consumption Practices." *Ñawpa Pacha: Journal of Andean Archaeology* 32, no. 2 (2012): 231–82.

Schäder, Christian. *Münchner Brauindustrie, 1871–1945: Die Wirtschaftsgeschichtliche Entwicklung eines Industriezweiges*. Marburg: Tectum Verlag, 1999.

Select Bibliography

Scharl, Benno. *Beschreibung der Braunbier-Brauerei im Königreich Bayern*. Munich: Joseph Lindbauer, 1826.

Schivelbusch, Wolfgang. *Tastes of Paradise: A Social History of Spices, Stimulants, and Intoxicants*. New York: Vintage Books, 1993.

Sedlmayr, Fritz. *Die "prewen" Munchens seit 1363 bis zu aufhebung der Lehensverleihung durch den Landesfursten (1814)*. Nuremberg: Hans Carl, 1969.

Seiler, Robert M. "Selling Patriotism/Selling Beer: The Case of the 'I AM CANADIAN!' Commercial." *The American Review of Canadian Studies* (Spring 2002): 45–66.

Sgorla, Andrey Felipe. "Cervejeiros artseanais: Recursos, precursos e empresarialização de si." *Política & Trabalho* 48 (January–June 2018): 21–37.

Siebel, John E. *One Hundred Years of Brewing*. 1903; repr., New York: Arno Press, 1974.

Sigsworth, E. M. "Science and the Brewing Industry, 1850–1900." *Economic History Review* 17, no. 3 (1965): 536–50.

Slocum, John W., Jr., et al. "Fermentation in the China Beer Industry." *Organizational Dynamics* 35 (2006): 32–48.

Smit, Barbara. *The Heineken Story: The Remarkably Refreshing Tale of the Beer that Conquered the World*. London: Profile Books, 2014.

Smith, Norman. *Intoxicating Manchuria: Alcohol, Opium, and Culture in China's Northeast*. Vancouver: University of British Columbia Press, 2012.

Speckle, Birgit. *Streit ums Bier in Bayern: Wertvorstellungen um Reinheit, Gemeinschaft und Tradition*. Münster: Waxmann, 2001.

Stack, Martin, Myles Gartland, and Tim Keane. "Path Dependency, Behavioral Lock-in and the International Market for Beer." In *Brewing, Beer and Pubs: A Global Perspective*, edited by Ignazio Cabras, David Higgins, and David Preece, 54–73. London: Palgrave Macmillan, 2016.

Stack, Martin. "The Internationalization of Craft Beer." In *New Developments in the Brewing Industry*, edited by Eric Støjer Madsen, Jens Gammelgaard, and Bersant Hobdari, 255–72. Oxford: Oxford University Press, 2020.

Stack, Martin. "Was Big Beautiful? The Rise of National Breweries in America's Pre-Prohibition Brewing Industry." *Journal of Macromarketing* 30, no. 1 (2010): 50–60.

Starke, Holger. *Von brauerhandwerk zur Brauindustrie: Die Geschichte der Bierbrauerei in Dresden und Sachsen, 1800–1914*. Cologne: Böhlau Verlag, 2005.

Sterckx, Roel. "Alcohol and Historiography in Early China." *Global Food History* 1, no. 1 (2015): 13–32.

Sumner, James. "John Richardson, Saccharometry and the Pounds-per-Barrel Extract: The Construction of a Quantity." *British Journal for the History of Science* 34 (2001): 255–73.

Sumner, James. "Status, Scale, and Secret Ingredients: The Retrospective Invention of London Porter." *History and Technology* 24, no. 3 (September 2008): 289–306.

Swinnen, Johan, ed. *The Economics of Beer*. Oxford: Oxford University Press, 2011.

Swinnen, Johan, and Devin Briski. *Beeronomics: How Beer Explains the World*. Oxford: Oxford University Press, 2017.

Select Bibliography

Tamerl, Ingrid. *Das Holzfass in der römischen Antike.* Innsbruck: Studienverlag, 2010.

Taplin, Ian M., Jens Gammelgaard, Christoph Dörrenbächer, and Mike Geppert. "The Demise of Anheuser-Busch: Arrogance, Hubris, and Strategic Weakness in the Face of Intense Internationalization." In *The Global Brewery Industry: Markets, Strategies, and Rivalries,* edited by Jens Gammelgaard and Christoph Dörrenbächer, 269–87. Cheltenham, UK: Edward Elgar, 2013.

Taylor, William B. *Drinking, Homicide, and Rebellion in Colonial Mexican Villages.* Stanford, CA: Stanford University Press, 1979.

Teich, Mikuláš. *Bier, Wissenschaft und Wirtschaft in Deutschland, 1800–1914: Ein Beitrag zur deutschen Industrialisierungsgeschichte.* Vienna: Böhlau, 2000.

Teich, Mikuláš. "The Mass Production of Draught and Bottled Beer in Germany, 1880–1914: A Note." In *The Dynamics of the International Brewing Industry since 1800,* edited by R. G. Wilson and T. R. Gourvish, 75–79. London: Routledge, 1998.

Terrell, Robert. "The Reinheitsgebot: Between German Consumer Culture and the European Market." *The Taproom,* February 14, 2018. https://seeingthewoods.org/2018/02/14/the-taproom-robert-terrell/.

Terrell, Robert Shea. "'Lurvenbrow': Bavarian Beer Culture and Barstool Diplomacy in the Global Market, 1945–1964." In *Alcohol Flows Across Cultures: Drinking Cultures in Transnational and Comparative Perspective,* edited by Waltraud Ernst, 204–20. London: Routledge, 2020.

Thurnell-Read, Thomas. "The Embourgeoisement of Beer: Changing Practices of 'Real Ale' Consumption." *Journal of Consumer Culture* 18, no. 4 (2018): 435–57.

Tizard, W. L. *The Theory and Practice of Brewing.* 2d ed. London: Gilbert and Rivington, 1846.

Tlusty, B. Ann. *Bacchus and Civic Order: The Culture of Drink in Early Modern Germany.* Charlottesville: University Press of Virginia, 2001.

Tlusty, B. Ann. "Full Cups, Full Coffers: Tax Strategies and Consumer Culture in the Early Modern German Cities." *German History* 32, no. 1 (2014): 1–28.

Toxqui, Áurea. "Breadwinners or Entrepreneurs? Women's Involvement in the *Pulquería* World of Mexico City, 1850–1910." In *Alcohol in Latin America: A Social and Cultural History,* edited by Gretchen Pierce and Áurea Toxqui, 104–30. Tucson: University of Arizona Press, 2014.

Toxqui, Áurea. "Taverns and Their Influence on the Suburban Culture of Late-Nineteenth-Century Mexico City." In *The Growth of Non-Western Cities: Primary and Secondary Urban Networking, c. 900–1900,* edited by Kenneth R. Hall, 241–69. Lanham, MD: Lexington Books, 2011.

Tremblay, Victor J., and Carol Horton Tremblay. *The U.S. Brewing Industry: Data and Economic Analysis.* Cambridge, MA: MIT Press, 2005.

Unger, Richard W. *Beer in the Middle Ages and the Renaissance.* Philadelphia: University of Pennsylvania Press, 2004.

Unger, Richard W. *A History of Brewing in Holland, 900–1900: Economy, Technology and the State.* Leiden: Brill, 2001.

van Beeman, Olivier. *Heineken in Africa: A Multinational Unleashed*. London: Hurst & Company, 2019.

Van den Steen, Jef. *Ale Spéciale Belge: Bière Traditionelle de Chez Nous*. Tielt: Lannoo, 2016.

Van den Steen, Jef. *Trappist: The Seven Magnificent Beers*. Leuven: Davidsfonds, 2010.

van der Hoog, Tycho. *Breweries, Politics, and Identities: The History behind Namibian Beer*. Basel: Basler Afrika Bibliographien, 2019.

van Dijk, Michiel, Jochem Kroezen, and Bart Slob. "From Pilsner Desert to Craft Beer Oasis: The Rise of Craft Brewing in the Netherlands." In *Economic Perspectives on Craft Beer: A Revolution in the Global Beer Industry*, edited by Christian Garavaglia and Johan Swinnen, 259–93. New York: Palgrave Macmillan, 2018.

Van Munching, Philip. *Beer Blast: The Inside Story of the Brewing Industry's Bizarre Battles for Your Money*. New York: Random House, 1997.

Verachtert, Hubert, and Guy Derdelinckx. "Belgian Acidic Beer: Daily Reminiscences of the Past." *Cerevisia* 38 (2014): 121–28.

von Justi, Johann. *Oeconomische Schriften über die wichtigsten Gegenstände der Stadt- und Landwirthschaft*. 2 vols. Berlin: Real-Schule, 1760.

von Tongeren, Frank. "Standards and International Trade Integration: A Historical Review of the German 'Reinheitsgebot.'" In *The Economics of Beer*, edited by Johan Swinnen, 51–61. Oxford: Oxford University Press, 2011.

Wahl, Robert, and Max Henius. *American Handy Book of the Brewing, Malting, and Auxiliary Trades*. 2d ed. Chicago: Wahl & Henius, 1902

Wang, Jiajing, Li Liu, Terry Ball, Linjie Yu, Yuanqing Li, and Fulai Xing. "Revealing a 5000-y-old Beer Recipe in China." *Proceedings of the National Academy of Sciences* 113, no. 23 (June 7, 2016): 6444–48.

Wenner, Lawrence A., and Steven J. Jackson, eds. *Sport, Beer, and Gender: Promotional Culture and Contemporary Social Life*. New York: Peter Lang, 2009.

Willis, Justin. *Potent Brews: A Social History of Alcohol in Africa, 1850–1999*. Athens: Ohio University Press, 2002.

Wilson, R. G. "The Changing Taste for Beer in Victorian Britain." In *The Dynamics of the International Brewing Industry since 1800*, edited by R. G. Wilson and T. R. Gourvish, 93–104. London: Routledge, 1998.

Wilson, R. G., and T. R. Gourvish, eds. *The Dynamics of the International Brewing Industry since 1800*. London: Routledge, 1998.

Wilson, Richard. "The British Brewing Industry since 1750." In *The Brewing Industry: A Guide to Historical Records*, edited by Lesley Richmond and Alison Turton, 1–22. Manchester: Manchester University Press, 1990.

Wilson, Richard G., and Terry R. Gourvish. "The Foreign Dimensions of British Brewing (1880–1980)." In *Production, Marketing and Consumption of Alcoholic Beverages since the Late Middle Ages*, edited by Erik Aerts, Louis M. Cullen, and Richard G. Wilson, 122–37. Leuven: Leuven University Press, 1990.

Wood, Heather. *The Beer Directory: An International Guide*. Pownal, VT: Storey Publishing, 1995.

Yang, Zhiguo. "'This Beer Tastes Really Good': Nationalism, Consumer Culture and Development of the Beer Industry in Qingdao, 1903–1993." *Chinese Historical Review* 14, no. 1 (Spring 2007): 29–58.

Yenne, Bill. *Guinness: The 250-Year Quest for the Perfect Pint.* Hoboken, NJ: John Wiley, 2007.

Yoo, Theodore Jun. "Shaken or Stirred? Recreating *Makgeolli* for the Twenty-First Century." In *Encounters Old and New in World History: Essays Inspired by Jerry H. Bentley,* edited by Alan Karras and Laura J. Mitchell, 107–18. Honolulu: University of Hawai'i Press, 2017.

Zhu, Mei. *Zenyang ban xiaoxing pijiu chang* [How to Run a Small-Scale Brewery]. Beijing: Light Industry Press, 1958.

Zimmermann, Matthew, and Chad B. Stice, *Microbrews: A Guide to America's Best New Beers and Breweries.* Kansas City, MO: Andrews and McMeel, 1996.

Zycherman, Ariela. "*Shocdye'* as World: Localizing Modernity through Beer in the Bolivian Amazon." *Food, Culture & Society* 18, no. 1 (March 2015): 51–69.

JOURNALS AND NEWSPAPERS

Allgemeine Brauer- und Hopfen Zeitung (ABHZ).
Allgemeine Hopfen Zeitung (AHZ).
American Brewer's Review (ABR).
Der Bayerische Bierbrauer (BaB).
Bayerische Brauer-Journal (BBJ).
Der bayerische Klein und Mittel-Brauer (BKMB).
La Bière et les Boissons Fermentées.
Der Böhmische Bierbrauer (BoB).
Brauwelt.
The Brewers' Journal.
Brewers Technical Review (BTR).
Deutsche Brauer-Nachrichten (DBN).
Journal of the Brewing Society of Japan (JBSJ).
Journal of the Institute of Brewing (JIB).
The New Brewer (NB).
Niangzao zazhi [Journal of the Chinese Society of Fermentation].
Le Petit Journal du Brasseur (PJB).
Der Schwäbische Bierbrauer (SB).
Tageszeitung für Brauerei (TfB).
Transactions of the American Brewing Institute (TABI).
Wallerstein Laboratories Communications.
Western Brewer (WB).
Wochenschrift für Brauerei (WfB).
Zeitschrift für das gesammte Brauwesen (ZgB).
Zymurgy.

Index

For the benefit of digital users, indexed terms that span two pages (e.g., 52–53) may, on occasion, appear on only one of those pages.

AB InBev
    acquisitions, 4, 201, 202, 226
    antitrust investigations of, 200–1, 237
    corporate culture, 197, 248
    cost cutting, 197, 200–1, 202–3
    global dominance, 203, 229, 238
    origins, 196–97, 200–1
    price increases, 200–3
    see also Ambev; Anheuser Busch;
        Interbrew
Addis Ababa, 119–20
additives, 69, 134, 136
    see also brewing: adjuncts
Adorno, Theodor, 14–15
advertising
    agencies, 4, 174, 188
    celebrities and, 180
    craft beer, 206, 244
    focus groups, 180–81, 188
    mass media, 141, 188
    Molson "Rant," 190
    "Most Interesting Man in the World,"
        190–91, 243
    posters, 96–97, 185–86, 191, 194
    sex and, 189

    sponsorship, 184–85, 188–89
    Super Bowl, 184–85, 188, 201–2
    see also Anheuser Busch; beer:
        coasters; Guinness; Heineken;
        labels; mascots
affordable luxury, 62–63, 140–41, 149–
    50, 237–38
African Americans, 156–57, 234–35
agave, 2–3, 19–20, 25–26, 51–52, 54–55,
    72–73, 232, 235
alchemy, 71
alcohol
    content, 8, 23, 25, 49, 59, 90, 106–7,
      161
    see also festivals; labor: mobilizing
Allied Breweries, 158, 160, 212
Allsopp, 111
Altbier, 102–3
Alvarez, Carlos, 179–80, 181
Ambev (Drinks Company of the
    Americas), 196–97, 199–201
Amstel Brewery, 176, 177
Amsterdam, 4, 45–46, 48–49, 99, 176
Anchor Brewing Company, 211, 214
Andwanter, Carl, 83, 98

324   *Index*

Anheuser Busch
  advertising, 96–97, 184–85, 188–89,
    190, 191, 201
  buyout, 4, 13, 200
  Clysdale horses, 191
  competition, 97–98, 155–56, 181–83
  expansion, 156, 195–96, 197,
    198, 225–26
  exports, 183
  legal battles, 178, 197, 200, 229
  market share, 195–96, 199–201
  see also AB InBev; Bud Light;
    Budweiser
Apartheid, 130–31, 138, 161–62,
    195, 233–34
Arrogant Bastard Ale, 205, 227–
    28, 238–39
Artois Brewery, 145, 177, 199
Asahi Brewery, 56, 124, 178–79, 191, 198,
    200–1, 202, 203, 218–20
attemperators, 63–65, 66–67, 138
Augustiner Brewery, 77, 78
Australia
  brewing industry, 115–16, 118, 163, 196
  craft beer, 211–12, 214, 229
  taste for beer, 121, 141, 157–58, 159–60
Austria, 3, 88, 89–90, 98, 142, 147
authenticity, 18, 38, 146, 191, 194, 234, 235
Aztec Empire, 31, 51–52, 55

Babylon, 8, 22–23, 28–31, 37, 240–41,
    247–48
bacteria, 19–20, 49–50, 163, 223–24,
    229–30
bacterial contamination, 18–19, 68–69,
    88–89, 150, 152–53, 229–30
Bacterium Club, 87
Baden, 26, 82, 87–88
Balkans, 98–99
Ballantine Brewery, 155–56, 215
Balling, Carl, 85–87
Baltic Sea, 8–9, 43, 45–46, 66, 197

Bamforth, Charles, 127–28, 243
Bangalore, 118–19, 160, 232–33
Bangkok, 116–17
Bantu beer, 133, 162
barley
  advantages for brewing, 36, 40
  beer, 8, 17, 18, 21–22, 24, 26–27, 49,
    125, 168
  colonial planting of, 118, 128–29
  markets, 46–47, 70, 89, 236–37
  varieties, 89, 168
  see also Bavaria: brewing regulations;
    brewing: adjuncts; malt
Bass Brewery
  advertising, 96–97, 191–92
  agents, 110, 111–12, 144–45
  buyout, 158, 195, 199
  exports, 66, 111, 112–13, 114, 198, 244
  laboratory, 87
  museum, 193
  trademark, 116, 124–25
Batavia, 110–11, 118
Bavaria
  brewing industry, 46, 67–69,
    70, 244–45
  brewing regulations, 3–4, 69, 88
  brewing schools, 83, 86, 87–88
  bottling, 77, 81–82
  exports, 79–80, 112
  government of, 72, 88, 147–48
  see also fermentation: bottom
Bavaria Brewery (Colombia), 153–55, 202
Baverstock, James, 85–86
Beck, Heinrich, 112, 244–45
Beck's Brewery
  buyout, 199–200
  expansion, 120, 198
  exports, 112, 177, 201, 244
  non-alcoholic lager, 1
beer
  antibacterial properties, 13–14, 37, 44
  coasters, 96–97

Index

commercialization of, 6, 8–9, 14, 41, 43, 44, 49, 52–53, 61, 72, 142–43
definition of, 2–3, 20
dietary staple, 14, 34, 77–78
diversity of, 1, 2–3, 19, 140–41, 155–56
engine, 65, 158–59
extreme, 150, 231–32
museums, 193–94, 230–31
non-alcoholic, 1
nutritional value of, 13–14, 133
shifting categories of, 106–7, 242–43
status of, 7–8, 39–40, 43, 49–50, 77–78, 91–92, 107, 108–9, 132, 178, 203–4, 206–7, 225, 235, 240–41, 246–47
see also festivals
beer gardens
Germany, 70–71, 82–83, 95, 96–97
global, 92, 117–18, 119, 122, 148, 191, 246–47
beer halls
Germany, 94, 189, 235–36
global, 95–96, 190–91
South Africa, 10, 133–35, 136–37, 138, 161–62
Beer Judge Certification Program, 221, 227
Beer Orders of 1989, 215
BeerAdvocate, 226
beer-bread debate, 19
beerstone, 22–23
Belgium
beer styles of, 100, 103–4, 142–46, 214, 240
brewing industry of, 1–2, 142–46, 149, 194, 200–1
consumer tastes, 141, 145, 146, 230
craft beers, 210, 212, 244–45
early breweries, 26, 146
exports, 112–13, 184, 201, 207
Bemba people, 2–3, 7–8, 132
Bengal, 109, 110–11
Benjamin, Walter, 14–15

Bennett, Judith, 32–33, 62
Berliner Weisse, 50, 103–4, 230–31
Best, Philip, 81–82, 83
biological control, 4, 67–68, 140–41, 162, 229–30, 242
Birmingham, 1–2, 86, 211–12
Birnhorn glacier, 78
Bismarck, Otto von, 1–2, 100–1
Black Death, 44, 51–52
Blancquaert-Merckx, Rose, 207, 210, 212–13, 240
Blatz, Valentin, 83
Bock, 1–2, 70, 97–98, 99, 100, 149
Bohemia
beer styles of, 70, 80, 81, 83, 100, 106
brewing industry, 3, 78, 80–81, 100–1, 147
bottom fermentation in, 67–69, 70
exports, 98, 99
see also Czech Republic; Czechoslovakia; hops: Saaz
Bohemia (Mexican beer), 149–50
Bolivia, 33, 122–23, 232–33, 235, 245–46
Bombay, 118–19, 160–61
Bomonti Brewery, 117–18, 119
Bond, Alan, 196
bottling, 66, 77, 83, 111–12, 115–17, 140–41, 150–52, 158–59, 247
bourgeoisie, 6, 16, 95, 142, 167–68
bouza, 21–22, 115
boycotts, 135, 147, 148, 156–57
brand
ambassadors, 189, 194
loyalty, 150–52, 195
personality, 188, 244
see also advertising
Brandenburg, 102–3
Braunschweig, 49–50, 72–73
Brazil, 114, 153–55, 163, 192–93, 196–97, 232, 233, 234
Bremen, 8–9, 10, 42, 44, 45–46, 112
Brewdog Brewery, 205, 231–32, 237

326 *Index*

brewers
associations, 87, 191, 213, 214, 218, 221, 234–35
common, 62–63
cottage, 211–12
publican, 62–63
see also gender: women brewers; migration: brewers
brewing
adjuncts, 13, 66–67, 83, 88, 89, 194, 227, 242, 245
architecture, 47, 91–92
collaborative, 233
contract, 140–41, 144, 153, 163, 173–74, 177, 178, 206, 214, 229, 230–31, 233, 244
flaws, 37–38, 66, 152–53
guilds, 9, 11–13, 48–49, 56–57, 58, 60, 62, 69, 72, 79, 247
ingredients, 18, 20, 25, 26, 50, 69, 74–75, 82, 88, 142–43, 232, 233, 235, 240, 242
institutes, 86–87, 125, 140, 148–49, 152, 166–67, 220–21
monastic, 8–9, 18, 30, 32, 42, 70–71, 72, 95, 146
professionals, 11–13, 87, 206, 221
schools, 9, 75, 85, 86, 87–88, 148–49, 157–58, 161, 211–12, 220–21, 247
scientists, 9, 10–11, 75, 85, 86–89, 125, 143–44, 152, 214
social context, 18, 242–43
Britain
brewing industry, 62–67, 158
changing tastes, 63, 66–67, 157–59
empire, 112, 113–16, 118–19, 120–21, 130–38
exports, 62–63, 66, 98, 108–9, 110, 111–13, 114–15, 128
festivals, 208–9, 210–11, 221
homebrewing, 92, 209–10
imports, 66, 177

innovation, 9, 61, 63–67, 77, 241
migrants, 159, 244–45
see also Campaign for Real Ale; England
British Commonwealth, 157–58, 163, 165, 177, 206–7, 211–12, 218, 232–33
Brito, Carlos Alves de, 196–97, 200–3, 248
Broihan, Cord, 49–50, 72–73, 229, 244
Brown, Horace T., 87–88, 90
Brueghel, Pieter the Elder, 6, 146
Brussels
breweries, 144–45, 149, 166–67
drinking cultures, 142–43, 144, 146
lambic, 1–2, 6, 140, 142–43, 146, 149
museums, 193–94, 230–31
Bud Light, 181–83, 184–85, 203–4, 245
Budapest, 80–81
Budejovicky Budvar Brewery, 197, 200
Budweis, 74–75, 83–85, 112–13, 147
Budweiser, 80, 83–85, 112–13, 174, 184–85, 195–96, 197, 200, 225–26, 227, 241
Bürgerliches Brauhaus (Citizen's Brewery, Pilsen), 3, 74, 79–80, 99, 105–6, 221–22
Burton-on-Trent, 61, 66, 67, 73, 86, 87, 96–97, 111, 193, 211–12
Busch, Adolphus, 83–85, 98
Busch, August Anheuser "Gussie" Jr., 156, 184–85
Busch, August III, 184–85, 201

Cabras, Ignazio, 233
Cairo, 112–13, 115, 119
Calagione, Sam, 228, 234–35
Calcutta, 112, 126, 128, 160
Calderón de la Barca, Fanny, 2–3, 54–55
Cameroon, 116–17, 161, 163
Campaign for Real Ale (CAMRA), 208–9, 210–13, 221, 232–33
Canadian Breweries Limited, 155
canning, 150–52, 230

Index

Cantillon Brewery, 144–45, 193–94, 231
capital
  access to, 47, 62–63
  accumulation, 42–43, 195
  demand for, 47–49, 56, 62
  markets, 11, 138, 183, 197
capitalism
  early modern, 8–9, 46–47
  global, 1–2, 55, 108, 109–10, 173
  history, 7–8, 13–14, 42–43, 195
  industrial, 5–6, 17–18, 40, 61, 107,
    241, 249
  modernity, 14–15, 27, 205
  twenty-first-century, 16, 248
  see also commodity
Capron, Horace, 125
Caribbean, 157–58, 159–60, 247–48
Carling Black Label, 155, 158, 159, 161–62
Carlsberg Brewery, 85–87, 88–89, 152,
  168, 177, 183, 194, 197, 198, 199, 200–
  1, 203, 236–37
Castel Group, 197, 203
Castle Lager, 120–21, 188–89
Castlemaine Brewery, 116, 196
Catholicism, 31–32
Ceccatti, John, 86–87
Celis, Pierre, 210, 214, 231
Central American Brewery, 153–55
Central Asia, 19–20, 29–30, 108–9, 183–
  84, 230
champagne, 6, 49–50, 66, 74, 96–97,
  103–4, 106, 142–43, 177
Chapman, Alfred C., 102
Charlemagne, 30, 32–33, 56
chemistry, 71, 75, 85, 86, 90, 92, 100,
  150
Chibuku, 162
Chicago, 86, 87–89, 97–98, 121–22, 152,
  231, 234–35
Chicago Lager Beer, 82–83
chicha, 2–3, 25–26, 33–34, 36, 39–40, 82,
  122–23, 235, 245–46

Chile, 34, 82–85, 86, 98, 104–5, 121–
  22, 153–55
China
  beer market, 112–13, 129
  brewing industry, 4–5, 166–67, 168–
    71, 198–99, 200
  brewing traditions, 7–8, 19–20, 24, 30,
    41, 166, 242
  craft beer, 235–36
  drinking cultures, 28–29, 167, 225–
    26, 240–41
  economic reforms, 195–96
  Maoist, 10–11, 165, 168–71
Chinese Communist Party, 168, 171
Cincinnati, 82, 83–85
Citizen's Brewery (Bürgerliches
  Brauhaus, Pilsen), 3, 74, 79–80, 99,
  105–6, 221–22
civil rights, 159–60, 165, 247–48
Civil War, US, 82–83, 87
civilization, 4–5, 29–30, 34, 40, 41, 92–
  94, 114, 117–18
climate crisis, 50–51, 52, 62–63, 67–
  68, 236–37
coffee, 50–51, 66–67, 146, 223–24, 235,
  236–37, 244
Cold War, 148–49, 168–69, 195
Cologne, 68–69, 102–3
colonialism, 51–55, 108–11, 114–15, 117–
  18, 128–29, 136, 138–39, 247–48
Columbian exchange, 51–52
commercialization, 6, 8–9, 14, 41, 43, 44,
  49, 58, 61, 72, 142–43
commodity
  agriculture, 6–7, 46–47
  attraction of, 6–7, 16, 240–41
  beer, 4, 15–16, 157, 171, 172, 173–74,
    195, 203, 205
  chains, 11–13, 55, 89, 92, 107, 110, 111–
    12, 138, 236–37
  definition, 6–7
  fetishism, 16

Index

commodity (*cont.*)
  global, 3–4
  markets, 58, 74–75, 89–90
  modern, 15–16, 75, 92
  trade, 13, 44, 46–47, 52–53
communal consumption, 11–13, 14, 23, 32, 38, 159, 204, 206–7, 235, 246–47
communal solidarity, 10, 28, 133, 135, 137–38, 142, 241–42
communism, 10–11, 148–49, 176–77, 207–8
Congo, 112–13
connoisseurship, 6–7, 11–13, 54–55, 58–59, 132, 222, 225–26, 229–30, 235, 242
consumer demand, 152–53, 172, 174, 210, 214–15, 229–30, 238–39, 242
consumerism, 11–13, 108, 126, 172, 173–74
contamination, 9, 18–19, 47, 63, 68–69, 141, 150, 229–30, 243
coolship, 230–31
Coors Brewery, 156–57, 184, 190, 193, 199, 200–2, 203, 214, 229
Copeland, William, 124–25
Copenhagen, 85–86, 88–89, 168, 194
Cornell, Martyn, 63
Corona
  advertising, 149–50, 181
  drinking culture, 153, 174, 180, 181–83
  success, 173, 179–81, 183, 192–93, 200
corporate raiders, 174, 195–96
Courage Brewery, 177, 196, 210
Covid-19, 237–38, 248–49
craft beer
  artisanal production, 5, 11–13, 218, 230–31, 235, 248–49
  dependence on big beer, 206, 213, 214, 220–21
  global craft, 218–20, 229, 230, 232–34, 235–37
  lookalikes, 214, 229
  mad scientists, 206, 211
  masculinity of, 227–28, 233–34, 237, 238–39, 244

  minority ownership, 231–32, 234–35, 238–39
  moral claims, 11–13, 214–15, 235–37
  status claims, 11–13, 221, 231–32, 235, 246–47
  supposed revolution, 9, 11–13, 205, 237, 243, 248
  tech industry links, 210–12, 226, 232–33, 235–36
  whiteness of, 227–28, 234–35, 247–48
  see also beer: extreme; brewing: contract; homebrewing; taste: vocabulary
Cuauhtémoc Brewery, 121–22, 149–50, 153, 181–83, 193
cultural imperialism, 4–5
Czech Republic, 23, 197, 218, 225–26
Czechoslovakia, 142, 147–49

Dai Nippon (Great Japan) Brewing Company, 124, 125, 126, 128–29
Danzig, 45–46, 49–50, 100–1
de Clerck, Jean, 152
De Splenter, Annick, 240, 241
Decolonization, 4–5, 157–58, 161, 165
Delbrück, Max, 86–87, 89, 101
Delhi, 114–15, 118–19
Denmark, 17–18, 177
Deregulation, 173–74, 195–96, 203
Dewolfs Freres et Soeurs Brewery, 144–45, 149
Diageo, 194, 199
Dichter, Ernest, 188
Disgust, 3, 25, 54–55, 117–18, 122
distilled liquors, 37, 50–51, 63–65, 98–99, 110–11, 117–18, 160–61, 179–80
distribution, 117, 155–56, 158–59, 160, 161–63, 173, 176–77, 179–80, 181, 183, 190, 211, 230, 237, 248–49
Dogfish Head Brewery, 228
Doppelbier, 70, 77–78, 100
Dortmund, 100–1, 112, 212

Index

Dos Equis, 122, 190–91, 243
Dreher, Anton Jr., 97–98, 99, 100
Dreher, Anton Sr., 75–76, 80–81, 106
drinking cultures
    Belgium, 142–43, 144
    Britain, 14, 95–96
    China, 31, 167
    Egypt, 115
    Germany, 70–71, 77–78, 94–95
    Mexico, 31, 38–39, 51–52, 53, 54–55,
        122, 173, 174, 180, 181–83, 235
    Japan, 58–59, 60–61, 125–26
    South Asia, 113–14, 160–61
    Southern Africa, 7–8, 133, 135, 137–38
    United States, 95–96
    see also vessels: drinking
drunkenness, 10, 27, 28–29, 31, 33, 61–62,
    94, 135, 137–39
dry beer, 178–79
Dublin, 66, 111–12, 163, 190–91, 192–
    93, 194
Dublin stout, 1–2, 103–4, 163
Dubský, Karl, 106, 107
dunkel, 76, 106, 241
Durban, 133–34, 135, 211–12, 246
Düsseldorf, 86–87, 102–3
Dutch East Indies Company, 110–11,
    118, 176

East African Breweries Limited, 161, 163,
    197, 237
East India Company, 110–11
economies of scale, 140–41, 150, 159–
    60, 172
Ecuador, 34, 196–97
Edinburgh, 75–76, 111–12, 157–58
Efes Brewery, 183–84, 246
Egypt
    ancient, 21–24, 28–31, 35, 36, 37–38,
        39–40, 41, 194, 240–41, 244
    brewing industry, 89, 119, 176
    drinking cultures, 115

Einbeck, 46, 49, 67–68, 70, 246–47
Elliott, John, 196
empire
    trade, 110, 112, 114
    tributary, 7–8, 13–14, 19, 33, 34, 40,
        41, 246–47
    see also Britain: empire; colonialism;
        England: empire; Germany:
        empire; imperialism; Japan:
        empire
England
    brewing industry, 32–33, 44, 47–
        48, 61–63
    empire, 62–63
    medieval, 13–14, 32, 36, 46–47
    migrants, 46, 61–62
    pubs, 9, 14, 159
    see also Britain
enzymes, 18, 20, 25, 37, 40, 63–65, 71,
    177–78, 242
Erlangen beer, 77, 83–85
Ethiopia, 119–20, 123–24, 197

Fahrendorf, Teri, 233–34, 237
Falstaff Brewery, 156
faro, 142–43, 144–45, 146, 149
Feith, Pieter, 176–77
fermentation
    bottom (lager), 1–2, 9, 68–69, 74–75,
        78, 81–82, 98, 100, 101, 102–3, 140,
        143–44, 244–45
    continuous, 150
    microbial, 19–20, 24–25, 30, 37, 40,
        56–57, 242
    secondary, 6, 66, 88–89
    spontaneous, 47, 103–4, 140, 142–43,
        193–94, 206–7, 229–30, 244–45
    top (ale), 1–2, 68–69, 100, 102–3,
        140, 143–44, 172, 220–21,
        229, 230–31
    see also vessels: fermentation
fertility symbols, 28, 115

festivals

Chinese, 167, 170, 192–93

Cinco de Mayo, 192–93, 204

craft, 206, 210–11, 212–13, 221, 232–33, 234–35

Great American Beer, 212–13, 229–30

Great British Beer, 208–9, 210–11

Oktoberfest, 76–77, 192–93, 194

St. Patrick's Day, 192–93

Xhosa, 131–32, 137–38

filtration, 10–11, 13, 21–22, 23, 24, 31–32, 38, 47, 59, 85–86, 102–3, 158–59, 178–79, 245

Five Star Brewery, 166–67, 168, 198–99, 221–22

Flanders, 47, 77, 118, 140, 142, 143–44

flavor profiles, 5, 89–90, 207–8, 214, 229

flavor wheel, 191–92, 214, 222–23

Flemish red ales, 1–2, 49–50, 230–31, 233

foam, 17, 28, 38, 101, 146, 152–53, 179, 227

forgery, 96–97, 116

founding father narrative, 205, 206, 207, 211, 225, 238–39, 244

Frederick Miller Brewery, *see* Miller Brewery

Fueger, Max, 81–82, 83

Gambrinus Brewery, 80, 197

Geller, Jeremy, 21–22

gender

domestic labor, 14, 17–18, 28

equality, 148–49

exclusion of women, 14

masculinity, 17–18, 206, 243

masculinization of brewing, 10, 14, 62

misogyny, 228, 234

sexuality, 30–31, 136–37

women brewers, 25, 30, 73, 133, 136–37, 233–34, 247

women brewery owners, 77, 78, 105, 156, 212–13, 233–34

women craft brewers, 212–13, 233–34, 240

women homebrewers, 30, 32–33, 137, 138–39

women in brewing industry, 148–49, 247

women in taverns, 30–31, 48–49, 94, 95–96

women's income, 18, 32–33, 130–31, 136–37, 138–39

gentrification, 173, 221, 235–36

geographical designations, 5–6, 35, 43, 74, 75, 83–85, 105–6, 147, 241

Germany

ancient, 26, 28

brewing industry, 49, 77–78, 79, 88, 102–3, 104–5, 147, 149, 158–59, 212

craft beer, 205, 230–31, 235–36, 241

East, 148–49

economic integration, 78, 98

empire, 109, 134, 165–66

exports, 83, 91–92, 98, 125, 177, 178, 190–91

imports, 3, 100–1, 143, 173–74

medieval, 13, 44, 46–47, 242

migrants, 82–83, 98–99, 108–9, 112, 125

nationalism, 89, 101, 147–48

political conflicts, 142, 147–48

travel to, 83, 87–88, 125

see also Bavaria; drinking cultures: Germany

Gilgamesh, 29–30, 41

Gilroy, John, 185, 194

Glass, Charles, 120–21

globalization, 3, 10–13, 89, 192–93, 195, 206, 214–15, 237–38, 240–41

Goddard, R. E., 116–17

Godin Tepe, 22–23

Goldman Sachs, 195, 196–97, 199–200

Goody, Jack, 40

Gose, 103–4, 107, 230–31, 232

Goslich, Christel, 91–92

Index

331

grain markets, 3–4, 89, 137

Grant, Bert, 215, 229, 248

gräwzzing, 69

Great Depression, 10–11, 155–56, 237–38

Great Leap Forward, 165, 168–71

Greece, 31–32, 119

Groll, Josef, 3, 74–75, 79–80, 106, 244, 245

Grossman, Ken, 205, 213, 214

gruit, 32–33, 36, 45–46, 69, 240, 241

gueuze, 142, 144–45, 193–94, 230–31

guilds

    decline of, 60, 72, 79, 86

    labor, 48–49

    limits on, 47

    male dominated, 14, 32–33, 247

    sake, 56–57, 58, 60

    symbols, 11–13

    training, 9

    women members, 48–49, 56–57, 62

Guinness

    advertising, 158–59, 185–86, 188, 189–90

    agents, 111–12

    Arthur, 66

    Diageo merger, 199

    expansion, 155–56, 163

    exports, 66, 114–15, 116–17, 163, 177

    foam, 115–16, 152–53

    global reach, 11, 115, 175–76, 189–91, 197

    health and, 113–14, 117, 185, 245–46

    niche markets, 9, 113–14

    quality control, 115–16, 164

    St. James Gate Brewery, 103–4, 163

    Storehouse, 194

    strength and, 109–10, 114–15, 185–86, 245–46

    trademark, 108–9, 114–15, 116

    world travelers, 110, 138

    see also Dublin stout; Harp Lager

Guo, Jackson, 36, 39–40

Haarlem, 50–51, 229

Hackel-Stehr, Karin, 3–4, 68–69

Haines, J. C., 111–12, 113–16, 118–19, 121

Hall, David, 119–20

Hallertau, 69

Hamburg, 8–9, 10, 44, 45–47, 49–50, 70, 100–1, 105–6, 112, 116, 246–47

Hammurabi, 28–29, 30–31

Hannover, 49–50, 72–73, 229

Hanseatic League, 8–9, 10, 43, 44, 50–51, 56, 110–11, 244

Hansen, Emil Christian, 4, 85–87, 88–89, 176, 194

Harbin, 165–66, 168–69, 170

Harp Lager, 157–58, 159

Harwood, Ralph, 63, 66–67, 72–73, 244

Hathor, 30–31

Hefeweisse, 70, 229, 232–33

Heileman, 156, 157, 196

Heineken

    acquisitions, 176, 177, 202, 237

    advertising, 176–77, 188, 189–91, 194

    Alfred "Freddy," 176–77, 244–45

    expansion, 161, 197, 198

    Experience, 194, 204

    exports, 11, 197, 225–26

    founding, 176

    market share, 179, 181, 184, 199–201, 202

    premium brand, 13, 177, 181–83, 203–4, 211

    private company, 199, 202

    refreshing powers of, 4, 11–13, 38–39, 188

helles lager, 106, 119–20, 241

Henius, Max, 86–87, 88–89, 121–22

Henrich, Friedrich, 81

Hertfordshire, 46–47, 63

Hertog Jan Brewery, 212, 214

Hierakonpolis, 21, 33

hipsters, 11–13, 235

Hodgson, George, 111, 244

332   *Index*

Hoegaarden Brewery, 200–1, 210, 214

Hofbräuhaus, 70–71, 72, 94

Hokkaido, 125, 212, 218–20

Holland, 43, 45–46, 47, 49–51, 61–62,
   68–69, 212, 242

homebrewing
   craft, 206–7, 209–11, 212–13, 218–20,
     225–26, 227–28, 231, 232–33
   decline of, 16, 42, 69, 115, 161–62
   premodern, 8, 28, 30, 32–33, 51–52,
     56–57, 62
   quality of, 39–40, 210–11, 247
   restrictions on, 128–29, 130–31, 135, 137
   see also gender: women homebrewers

hopped beer
   brewing efficiency, 44
   distaste for, 36, 42, 43, 240
   expansion, 13, 43, 46, 61–62, 67–68
   exports, 46, 50–51, 55, 62–63, 111
   origins, 13, 18, 44, 242
   replaced ale, 42–43, 69, 246–47
   status of, 49–50, 246–47

hops
   antibacterial properties, 44
   arms race, 228
   Bavarian, 69, 89–90, 92
   bitterness, 8–9, 36, 42, 215
   brewing with, 42, 44, 89–90
   cultivation, 69, 118–19, 125, 128–29,
     168
   eaten, 8–9
   Kent, 89–90
   markets, 47, 77, 87, 89–90, 125, 238
   medicinal, 42
   narcotic properties of, 8–9, 101
   Pacific Coast, 89–90, 92, 214, 215
   preservative, 8–9, 43, 63
   Saaz, 74, 79–80, 89–90, 101, 106
   sexual properties, 156–57
   Tasmanian, 121, 228
   wild, 61–62, 125

humoral beliefs, 167, 242–43

imperialism
   ideology, 14, 18, 33, 34, 138–39
   see also Britain: empire; colonialism;
     England: empire; Germany:
     empire; Japan: empire

importers, 173–74, 181–83, 190–91, 213,
   221–22, 229

India
   brewing industry, 118–19, 157–58, 160
   colonial markets, 10, 62–63, 66, 110–11,
     112, 113–16, 128, 160–61
   craft beer, 211–12, 232–33
   drinking cultures, 31, 161
   exports, 183–84, 185
   indigenous drinks, 25, 30, 31, 114
   Prohibition, 160

India Pale Ale (IPA)
   craft, 5, 15–16, 205, 206–7, 215, 218,
     226, 228, 229–30, 231–32, 241, 249
   New England, 228, 241
   origins, 66, 111, 127–28, 215
   West Coast, 228, 241
   see also international style pale ale

indigenous
   communities, 51, 52–53, 82, 108, 114,
     122–23, 128–29, 159–61
   revivals, 235, 245–46
   see also India: indigenous drinks;
     Mexico: indigenous drinks

industrial
   accidents, 47–48, 105, 106–7, 149
   bankruptcy, 4, 60, 104–5, 177–78
   concentration, 5, 11, 13, 50–51, 104–5,
     124, 140, 142, 149, 153–55, 157, 168–
     69, 172, 187–88, 196, 197, 208–9, 238
   espionage, 79
   food processing, 171–72, 243
   see also capitalism; quality control

infrastructure
   highways, 52, 140–41, 149–50
   railroads, 3, 4, 9, 13, 55, 66, 74–75, 78,
     80, 81, 98, 108, 111, 148, 150–52

Index 333

steamships, 74–75
transshipping, 181
see also vessels: storage
Inka Empire, 25, 34, 39–40, 122–23, 233
intellectual property, 195, 241
Interbrew, 193–94, 195–96, 198, 199–
201, 214
international style pale ale, 228
internationalization, 174, 195–96
invented traditions, 43, 72–73, 76–77, 142
investment bankers, 11, 155, 174–75, 195,
196–97, 199–200, 201, 202, 203, 248
Ireland, 1, 32, 77–78, 163, 164, 177
Istanbul, 4–5, 112–13, 117–18, 119,
148, 246

Jack-Op, 144, 149
Jackson, Michael
defining taste, 214, 215, 221, 222–25,
229, 243
followers, 208–9, 210–11, 212, 213,
221–22, 229
invention of styles, 5–6, 214
research, 207–8, 225
Jackson-Beckham, J., 11–13, 234–35
Japan
advertising, 190–91
brewing industry, 56–57, 58, 87, 109–
10, 124, 198, 203
craft beer, 212, 218–21, 233
encounter with beer, 124–25, 126–28,
189, 242
empire, 125–26, 128–29, 138–39, 166–
67, 168
innovation, 13, 150, 178–79, 245
nationalization of beer, 125, 129,
243, 246–47
see also drinking cultures: Japan; sake
Java, 25, 176, 185
Jesuits, 52–53, 55, 56–57, 58–59, 68–69, 71
Jewish entrepreneurs, 89–90, 148, 190,
207–8, 218

Jia Sixie, 24–25, 30
Johannesburg, 120–21, 130–31, 135,
194, 233–34
John, J., 76, 99, 100–1
joopenbier, 49–50
journals, professional, 85, 87, 91–94, 96–
97, 112, 125

Kalevala, 17–19, 22–23, 28, 41
Karachi, 114–15
Kenya, 137, 161, 185–86, 197, 237
kinship societies, 7–8, 14, 19, 27, 28, 34,
40, 41, 246–47
Kirin, 34, 35, 56, 124, 125, 126, 128, 178–
79, 198, 202, 203
Klein Schwechat Brewery, 80–81
Kobe, 58, 59–60, 124–25
Koch, Greg, 205, 215, 228, 234–35
Koch, Jim, 205, 206, 214, 244, 248
koji, 24–25, 50–51, 59
kölsch, 102–3
Korea, 10, 25, 128–29, 168, 232–33
koumiss, 19–20
Kräuterfrauen, 69, 247
kriek, 6, 142–43, 144–45, 207, 218–20
Kyoto, 56–57, 58, 59–60, 126

Labatt Brewery, 155, 163, 179, 199, 200–1
labels
advertising, 4, 9, 92, 96–97, 116–17,
124–25, 167
counterfeit, 124–25
craft beer, 207–8, 227–28, 234, 244
labor
domestic, 14, 17–18, 25, 26–27, 28, 40,
56–57, 72, 126
enslaved, 8–9, 23, 28–29, 52, 82, 116–
17, 247–48
migrant, 58–59, 60–61, 130–31, 137–
39, 173–74
mobilizing, 13–14, 18, 33, 41, 138–39,
241–42, 246

334   *Index*

labor (*cont.*)
  wage, 8–9, 11, 16, 42–43, 44, 47–48,
    53, 60, 75, 122, 133, 135, 137, 238–39
  see also gender
laboratories, 55, 77, 90, 152, 168, 176
Laboratory Club, 87
lager
  becoming lighter, 10–11, 16, 83–85, 98,
    100, 102, 159, 171–72, 177–79, 243
  cellars, 68–69, 71, 72, 77, 83, 95
  clean taste, 4–5, 15–16, 92, 106, 117–18,
    122, 123–24, 142, 178–79, 243
  civilization and, 4–5, 117–18, 123–24
  globalization of, 9, 13
  market growth, 102–3, 146, 155, 159–60
  see also Munich lager; Pilsner;
    Vienna lager
Lagunitas Brewery, 228, 237
lambic
  modernity of, 6, 103–4, 143, 144–
    45, 214
  nostalgia, 140, 142–43, 146, 149
  terroir of, 142, 231, 245–46
  see also faro; Jack-Op; kriek
Leipzig, 78, 90, 103–4, 105–6, 230–31
Lemann, Jorge Paulo, 196–97, 200–1, 202–3
Leuven, 86, 152, 200–1
Lewis, Michael, 220–21
Li Liu, 19, 21
Liefmans Brewery, 207, 210, 213, 223–24,
  231, 240
Lion Nathan, 196, 198–99, 202
localization, 10, 245–46
London porter, 1–2, 5–6, 9, 15–16, 61, 63–
  66, 76, 98, 106–7, 242
Lönnrot, Elias, 17–18
Louvain, 142, 144, 145
Low Countries, 43, 45–46, 47, 49–51,
  61–62, 68–69, 212, 242
Löwenbräu Brewery, 77, 94, 116–17, 177,
  178, 190–91
Lübeck, 45–46

Mackay, Graham, 195, 197, 200, 202
Magee, Tony, 228, 237
Magoshi Kyōhei, 124
maize
  beer, 2–3, 20, 25–26, 33, 34, 38, 40, 118
  brewing adjunct, 9, 88, 121–22, 245
  production, 51, 136
Mallya, Vittal, 157–58, 160
malt
  American, 89, 210–11
  archaeological record, 21–22, 24, 26
  barley, 36, 236–37
  beverages, 181–83, 203–4
  commodity chains, 46–47, 62, 121,
    183, 238
  enzymes, 20
  flavor, 63, 70, 226
  homebrew kits, 209–10
  mastication, 18, 40
  Munich, 76–77, 80
  origins, 21–22, 241–42
  pale ale, 80–81
  Patent, 66–67, 72
  Pilsner, 80, 86, 210
  pneumatic malting, 85–86
  production, 26–27, 38, 47–48, 63–65,
    74–75, 77, 120–21, 125
  quality, 66, 67, 74, 76, 88, 206
  sorghum, 153, 164, 236–37, 245
  see also fermentation: microbial; koji
Mao Zedong, 165
Marx, Karl, 11–13, 16, 42–43
Märzenbier, 68–69, 76–77, 80–81, 100
mascots, 184–86, 187–88, 189,
  205, 238–39
masculinity, *see* gender
mashing
  decoction, 71, 72
  definition, 20
  infusion, 71, 122
  origins, 24, 25, 26
  see also vessels: mashing

Index

Mathias, Peter, 63–65
Matilda Bay Brewery, 211–12, 214
Maximilian I, 70
Maytag, Fritz, 205, 211, 213, 214, 215, 244, 248
Mazumdar, Rasendra I., 157–58, 161
McAllister, Patrick , 131–32
McAuliffe, Jack, 205, 211, 213, 215, 244
McGovern, Patrick, 41
McKenzie, Bob and Doug, 179, 180
Mead, 19–20, 23–24, 26
Mechanization, 59, 61, 105
Meilgaard, Morton, 191–92, 214, 222–23
Mesopotamia, 8, 22–23, 28, 29–31, 41, 246–47
Mexico
    brewing industry, 4–5, 53, 55, 121–22, 149–50, 153, 183, 230
    craft beer, 232
    exports, 175–76, 179–83, 184, 203–4
    indigenous drinks, 2–3, 51–53, 122, 235
    innovation, 55, 153
    migrant brewers, 121–22
    modernity, 108, 122
    see also drinking cultures: Mexico; pulque
Michelob Brewery, 80–81
microscope, 21–22, 75, 85–86
migration
    brewers, 46, 61–62, 70, 78, 81–82, 83, 86–88, 98–99, 112, 120–22, 231, 244–45
    postcolonial, 159, 165, 247–48
    proletarian, 82–83, 247–48
    restrictions, 173–74, 180–81
    rural-urban, 44, 55, 60–61, 75, 130–31, 133, 135, 136, 137, 141, 171–72
    see also labor: migrant
Miller Brewery, 156, 178–79, 190, 195, 198, 200, 201, 202, 214, 229
Miller Lite, 177–78, 184–85
millet beer, 2–3, 24, 35, 39–40, 131–32, 136

Milwaukee, 81–82, 83, 95–96, 121–22, 156–57, 188
Mintz, Sidney, 16
Mitchell, Lex, 211–12, 248
mobility
    knowledge, 13, 74–75, 226–27, 231, 232–33, 244–45
    consumers, 75, 102, 158, 159, 230–31, 232–33
    social, 141, 171–72
    see also capital; infrastructure; labor: migrant, mobilizing; technology transfer; trade
Moctezuma Brewery, 121–22, 153
Modelo Brewery, 149–50, 153, 179–81, 183, 200–1, 202
modernity
    advertising, 191
    beer and, 4–5, 10–11, 107, 109–10, 122, 126, 171–72, 174
    capitalist, 92, 99, 106–7, 129
    consumerism and, 9, 107, 146
    middle-class, 138, 141, 161–62, 165
Moerlein, Christian, 81–82, 83
Molson Brewery, 155, 188–89, 200–1, 203
Molson Canadian, 4, 179, 190
Molson, John, 118
Moortgat Brewery, 210
moral panic, 66, 133–34
Morris, G. Harris, 88–89, 90
Mumme, 44, 50, 103–4, 244
Mumme, Christian, 44, 72–73
Munich lager, 1, 5–6, 9, 76–78, 83–85, 102, 106–7, 112
Murree Brewery, 118–19, 160–61, 183–84
Mussoorie Brewery, 118–19

Nagasaki, 59–60
Natal, 133–34, 136
Natal Liquor Act of 1928, 137
nation building, 140–41

Index

nationalization of beer, 4, 101, 140–41, 147–50, 161, 190

Native Beer Act of 1908, 133–34

Natufian beer hypothesis, 19, 21

Nazi racial ideologies, 147–48, 177

Nelson, Max, 26

Netherlands, 43, 45–46, 47, 49–51, 61–62, 68–69, 212, 242

New Albion Brewery, 211, 214

New Belgium Brewery, 231, 236–37

New Glarus Brewery, 231, 236–37

New York City, 86, 87–88, 95–96, 108, 112–13, 184–85, 235

New Zealand, 121, 196

Nigeria, 28, 116–17, 141, 161–62, 163–64, 175–76, 185, 188–90, 197, 225–26

Ninkasi, 22–23

nomadic pastoralists, 19–20, 28, 29–30, 247–48

nostalgia, 55, 92, 99, 111, 112, 146, 149, 160–61, 171–72, 174

Nuremberg, 46–47, 69, 70, 71, 77, 83–85, 89–90

O'Sullivan, Cornelius, 87–88

Oaxaca, 52–53, 108

Ogle, Maureen, 14–15

Ohlsson, Anders, 120–21

Oktoberfest, *see* festivals

Oliver, Garrett, 5–6, 231–32, 233, 234–35

Osaka, 58, 59, 60, 221

Osmotar, 17–19

Owades, Joseph, 177–78

Pabst Blue Ribbon, 96–98, 210–11

Pabst Brewing Company, 81–82, 83–85, 95–96, 104–5, 112–13, 155–56

Papazian, Charlie, 210–11, 212–13

Paris, 1, 78, 95–96, 97–99, 166–67

Pasteur, Louis, 85–86, 88–89

pasteurization, 59, 88–89, 98–99, 140–41, 158–59, 178–79, 222–23

Peru, 33, 82

Pfeffer, Josef, 119–20

Philadelphia, 83, 118–19, 237–38

Philip Morris, 184–85

Philippines, 10, 87–88, 112–13, 198

Pilsen, 3, 74–75, 79–80

Pilsner
commodified, 15–16, 225
de-localized, 3, 5–6, 74, 83–85, 99, 100, 105–6, 245–46
evolution, 100–1, 106, 245
global, 13, 83–85, 98–99, 122–23, 142, 157–58, 161–62, 225–26, 237–38
invention, 3, 74, 80, 106, 245
legal struggles, 74, 99, 105–6, 147–48
markets, 80, 99
modernity, 9, 106
political struggles, 101, 142, 148
popularity of, 14–15, 16, 83–85, 99, 100–1, 107, 140, 242–43
taste, 70, 81, 101, 106–7, 142
Urquell, 23, 105–6, 148, 197, 221–22
see also Bürgerliches Brauhaus

Powell, Hugo, 199–201

Power, Michael, 189–90

Prague, 71, 79–80, 83, 86–87, 105, 147

Princess Yi Di, 24–25, 41

prohibition
colonial, 14, 109–10, 130–31, 160, 246
United States, 14–15, 152, 155–57, 176–77, 190, 206, 210–11, 247–48

propaganda, 147–48, 168

prostitution, 28–31, 58–59, 165–66

Protz, Roger, 181–83, 208–9

Prussia, 83, 98, 100–1, 102–3

Pryor, Alan, 111

pubs
African, 194, 225–26
brewpubs, 32, 205, 206–7, 210, 212, 215, 218–20, 233–34, 238–39
English, 9, 14, 62–63, 158–59, 207–9, 211–12, 221, 246–47

Index

337

imperial, 110, 160–61
improved, 95–96
Irish, 190–91
revival of, 210, 235–36
tied, 65, 215
see also taverns
Pullman, Mellie, 212–13, 233–34, 237
pulque
consumption, 38–39, 51–53, 55, 118
curado, 42–43, 54–55, 235
dangers, 31, 38, 52
decline, 141, 235
production, 19–20, 25–26, 51–53, 55
regulated, 31, 53
revival, 235
taste, 2–3, 37–38, 54–55, 117–18, 122, 243

Qingdao, 129, 165–67, 168–69, 170, 192–93
Qode, 23, 35, 39–40, 41, 240–41, 244
quality control, 75, 126, 152–53, 164, 181, 184, 191–92, 214, 231, 247
quality designation (*Beschaffenheitsangabe*), 74
Quilmes, 181–83, 196–97

race
mixture, 52, 188–89
riots, 159
segregation, 14, 156–57, 159–60, 247–48
see also craft beer: whiteness of
Rach, Carl, 14–15, 100, 136–37
Radeberger Brewery, 105–6
Raqefet Cave, 21
Ratebeer, 226, 228
Rath, Eric C., 56–57
Ray, Rajat Kanta, 117
refrigeration, 4–5, 83, 85–86, 91–92, 95, 100, 102–3, 117–18, 138, 140–41, 150–52, 164, 176, 201–2

regulation
Assize of Bread and Ale, 32–33
Bavarian, 3–4, 14, 67–68
Bierzwang (sales rules), 70–71, 72
Reinheitsgebot (purity law), 3–4, 88, 191
Surrogatsverbot (ban on substitutes), 88
surveillance, 30–31, 47, 53, 130–31, 135, 136–37
research stations, 4, 9, 75, 85, 86–87, 88, 125
Rheingold Brewery, 155–56, 177–78
Rhineland, 46, 61–62, 68–69, 78, 102–3, 112
rice
beers, 114, 128–29
brewing adjunct, 83, 194, 227, 245
see also sake
Richards, Audrey, 2–3, 7–8
Richardson, John, 85–86
Rio de Janeiro, 114, 116
Rodenbach Brewery, 230–31
Rodrigues, João, 56–57, 58–59
romanticism, 18, 94
Rome, 26, 31–32, 246–47
Romero, Juana Catarina, 108, 109–10, 112–13, 138
Rooiyard, 130–31
Rostock, 44, 45–46
Rotterdam, 116, 176
Rüffer, Ernst, 77–78
Russia, 87–88, 89, 92–94, 98–99, 112–13, 129, 165–67, 168–69, 183–84, 197, 248–49
Rustomjee, H. J., 114–15
rye, 18, 36, 69, 191

saccharometer, 66–67, 75, 85–86
Sada, Luis G., 121–22
safe danger, 15–16
sahti, 18, 191

338 *Index*

sake, 3, 8–9, 56–61, 129, 212, 235, 245–46

Samuel Adams, 205, 213

Samuel Smith's Brewery, 207–8, 213, 229

Samuel, Delwen, 21–22, 37–38

San Francisco, 102–3, 115–16, 211

San Miguel Brewery, 198

sanitation, 13–14, 55, 77–78, 106–7, 122, 133, 146, 150, 248

Santo Domingo family, 153–55, 202

Sapporo Brewery, 124, 125, 184, 190–91, 218–20

Saqqara, 21, 28–29

Scandinavia, 43, 45–46, 87–88

Scharl, Benno, 68–69, 70, 71, 72, 101

Schivelbusch, Wolfgang, 9

Schleißheim, 72, 86

Schlitz Brewery, 83–85, 95–96, 155–56, 179, 201–2

Schwarz, Anton, 83–85, 86–87

Scotland, 75–76, 110

Scottish and Newcastle Brewery, 158, 200–1

Sedlmayr, Gabriel Jr., 75–77, 79–80, 86–87, 98, 106, 225, 238, 244

Sedlmayr, Gabriel Sr., 72

Sedlmayr, Josef, 77

Sexton, Phil, 211–12, 248

Shamhat, 29–30

Shand, Arthur T., 110, 111–12, 113–14, 115–16, 121–22

Siebel Institute, 152–53, 220–21, 233–34

Siebel, John, 83, 86–87

Sierra Leone, 116–17, 185

Sierra Nevada Brewery, 213, 214, 220–21, 228

Singapore, 128, 176, 193, 229, 235–36

Sleeman Brewery, 118

socialism, 16

socializing, 7–8, 94

soft drinks, 141, 181, 243

Sol Lager, 181–83

solidarity, 9, 10, 14, 28, 133, 135, 137–38, 142, 241–42, 246–47

sorghum

beer, 23–24, 130–32, 136, 141, 162, 194, 232, 235

malting, 153, 164, 236–37, 245

South Africa, *see* beer halls: South Africa; indigenous drinks: South Africa; South African Breweries

South African Breweries (SAB)

acquisitions, 197, 200

advertising, 187–88

anti-Apartheid, 161–62

buyout, 199–200, 202

expansion, 177, 197, 198–99, 201

Michael Jackson and, 207–8

museum, 194

origins, 120–21

sparging, 20, 47

Spaten Brewery, 72, 75–76, 77

Spring Valley Brewery, 124–25

St. Brigit, 32

St. Gall Monastery, 26–27, 39–40

St. George Brewery, 119–20, 123–24

St. Louis, 4–5, 82, 83, 108, 112–13, 121–22, 156, 188–89, 201–2

St. Pauli Brewery, 112

state formation, 28–29, 33

status

beer and, 7–8, 27, 50, 126, 235, 240–41

beer styles and, 39–40, 43, 77–78, 240–41, 246–47

craft beer and, 206–7, 235

imported beers and, 43, 107, 176–77, 178, 203–4

steam beer, 102–3, 211

Stella, 145, 184, 193–94, 199, 201

Stone Brewery, 205, 227–28, 232, 238–39

Stoudt, Carol, 212–13, 233–34

Stroh Brewery Company, 179, 189, 190, 191–92

style

capitalism and, 75, 107, 241

consistency, 75, 76, 85, 153, 241

Index 339

evolution of, 66–67, 81, 100–1, 106, 241, 245

invention of, 3, 6–7, 63, 66–67, 72–73, 74, 76–77, 80–81, 100, 106, 111, 142–43, 240–41, 244, 245

legal construct, 74, 99, 105–6

Suberbie, Philippe, 121–22

subsistence, 7–8, 13–14, 15–16, 27, 42, 73, 138–39

Sumeria, 22–23

Sumner, James, 66–67

supermarkets, 10–11, 158–59

surā, 25, 30, 31

sustainability, 11–13, 235, 236–37

Sweden, 26, 87–88, 134

Syria, 23, 35, 240–41, 244

Taiwan, 10, 129

Tassili n'Ajjer, 23–24, 28

taste

aroma, 39–40, 89–90, 101, 106–7, 152, 191–92, 224–25, 227, 240–41

bitterness, 8–9, 36, 42, 50–51, 70, 177–78, 215, 228

clean, 4–5, 15–16, 92, 106, 117–18, 122, 123–24, 142, 178–79, 243

communities, 126, 206–7, 225–28, 233, 242

fresh, 126

memory, 152, 243

mouthfeel, 38–39, 102–3, 106–7, 152–53, 177–78, 226, 227, 228

skunk, 153, 222–23, 227

smoky, 36, 63, 223–24

sourness, 37–38, 44, 50, 53, 77–78, 103–4, 110–11, 122, 144, 206–7, 223–24, 229–32, 243

sweetness, 18–19, 36, 43, 50–51, 121, 132, 206–7, 224–25

vocabulary, 214, 222–25

see also flavor profiles; flavor wheel; hopped beer: distaste for

tasting notes, 54–55, 222–25, 226, 227

tasting, blind, 126, 221

taverns

bars, 9

hotels, 159–60

izakaya, 58–59, 249

saloons, 95–97, 122, 150–52

shebeens, 130–31, 135, 136, 161–62, 233–34, 246, 249

Wirtshaus, 46–47, 94

Zäpfler (tapsters), 70–71

see also beer gardens; beer halls; pubs

tax, 32–33, 43, 45–46, 47, 58, 63–65, 66, 69, 70–71, 72, 87, 88, 92–94, 95, 100, 114–15, 155–56, 173–74, 207

Taylor, E. P. "Eddie," 155, 158, 161–62, 244–45

Taylor, William, 51–52

tea, 6–7, 50–51, 58–59, 60–61, 124–25, 126, 128, 160, 228, 232, 235–36

Tecate Brewery, 153, 179–80, 181–83

technology transfer, 61–62, 73, 76–77, 78–80, 87, 125, 163, 230–31, 244–45

temperance, 87, 106–7, 114, 125, 134, 246

Teotihuacán, 25–26

Terrell, Robert, 177

Tezcatlipoca, 31, 41

thermometers, 9, 63–65, 75

Thirty Year's War, 50–51, 70–71

Thomas, Keith, 220–21

tied houses, 70–71, 115–16, 120–21, 149, 194, *see also* pubs: tied

Tiger Beer, 176, 193

Tivoli Brewery, 95, 125

Tiwanaku Empire, 33, 34

Tokugawa Shogunate, 56, 57–58, 60–61

Toluca and Mexico Brewery, 122, 153

trade

Anglo-German rivalry, 112, 116–17, 128, 139

international, 98, 110, 173–74, 175–76, 183, 184, 244

340   *Index*

trade (*cont.*)
    long-distance, 8, 23, 48–49, 50–51, 244
    trickle, 46, 66, 98–99, 121–22, 123–
        24, 244–45
trademarks, 83–85, 87, 96–97, 105–6, 111–
    12, 114–15, 116, 124–25, 146, 185
Trappist ales, 142, 146, 230–31
tributary states, 7–8, 14, 18, 19, 28, 33, 34,
    40, 41, 246–47
Tsingtao Brewery, 1, 129, 165–66, 168–69,
    170, 190, 194, 198–99, 201, 202, 203

Unger, Richard, 13–14, 43, 47–48
Unilever, 161, 163
union activism, 94, 135, 156–57, 173–74,
    183, 185–86, 195–96, 237
United Breweries (India), 157–58,
    160, 161
United Brewing Company (Chile), 104–
    5, 153–55
urban brewers, 44, 62–63, 136–37
urbanization, 44, 57–58, 62–63, 73,
    133, 149–50

Valparaiso, 83, 104–5
Van Laer, Henri, 140, 142–44
Van Munching, Leo, 176–77, 181
Van Roy, Jean-Pierre, 193–94, 230–31
Verachtert, Hubert, 144
Versuchs und Lehranstalt für Brauerei
    (Research and Teaching Institute
    for Brewers, VLB), 86–88, 91–92,
    101, 102–4, 125, 148–49, 220–21
vessels
    drinking, 18–19, 23–24, 29–30, 33, 53,
        65, 94, 97–98, 103–4, 176–77, 227
    fermentation, 21, 24, 25, 33–34, 60,
        150, 218
    longnecks, 149–50, 153, 179–81
    mashing, 23, 26–27, 63–65, 71, 80, 89, 163
    storage, 22–23, 24, 26, 59, 60, 63, 66,
        71, 142–43, 206–7, 231
    see also bottling

Vienna lager, 1, 74–75, 80–81, 99, 100,
    106, 122, 218, 238
von Bingen, Hildegard, 42
von Justi, Johann, 50, 71
von Linde, Carl, 85–86, 176
von Sternburg, Maximilian Speck, 78, 79

Wagner, Therese, 77, 78, 105
Wahl, Robert, 86, 87, 88–89, 121–22
Wallerstein, Max, 107
water
    advertising, 187–88, 190–91
    brewing ingredient, 3–4, 18, 20, 26–27,
        69, 213
    chlorinated, 141
    hard, 59–60, 66
    purity, 13–14, 35, 37–38, 134, 164
    shortages, 44, 183, 236–37
    soft, 3, 59–60, 74
    terroir, 72–73
Watt, James, 63–65
Weihenstephan Brewery, 86–88, 91–92,
    100
Weinberg, Robert S., 214–15, 243
wheat, 3–4, 6–7, 20, 21–22, 24–25, 26–27,
    36, 69, 164, 166, 242–43
    see also Berliner Weisse; Hefeweisse;
    witbier
Wheeler, Daniel, 66–67, 72
Whitbread Brewery, 63, 158–59, 177, 199
William IV, 69, 70, 191
Willis, Justin, 161, 165
Windisch, Wilhelm, 101
wine, 30, 106, 108, 118, 174, 191–92, 207–
    8, 209–10, 218, 222–23, 246–47
witbier (wheat beer), 49–50, 200–1, 210
women, *see* gender
Women's Christian Temperance Union,
    134, 246
World War I, 121, 125
World War II, 126, 128–29, 148, 149, 158–59
world's fairs, 1, 83–85, 87, 97–98, 99, 118–
    19, 121–22, 176–77, 192–93

Index

wort, 1–2, 14–15, 20, 22–23, 26–27, 37–38, 44, 47, 48–49, 63–65, 76, 190–91

Worthington Brewery, 66, 87, 90

Württemberg, 82, 83, 112

Wyatt, Francis, 14–15, 86, 102

Xhosa, 131–32, 137–38

Yanjing Brewery, 198–99, 203

Yantai Brewery, 166–67, 168

yeast
    Brettanomyces, 127–28, 142–43, 229–30, 243
    natural pure, 88–89
    pure, 4, 37, 85–87, 88–89, 122, 170–71, 176, 194, 229–30

wild, 20, 21, 37, 68–69, 106–7, 141, 229–30, 231
    see also fermentation: bottom, top

Yebisu Brewery, 124, 125–26

Yokohama, 124–25

Younger's Lager, 112–13, 114–15

Yucatán, 10, 122, 153

Zambia, 7–8, 113–14, 162, 177, 197

Zappa, Frank, 1, 4

Žatec basin, 74

Zhu Mei, 166–67, 168–69, 170–71

Zimbabwe, 19–20

Zulus, 130–32, 138, 190

Zurich, 78, 86

Zymurgy, 210–11, 225–26, 227–28